SINGHA DURBAR

Sagar S.J.B. Rana was born in February 1938 in Baber Mahal palace, Kathmandu. He holds an MA in Jurisprudence from the University of Oxford. A descendant of the Rana family, he and his brothers were also actively involved in the Nepali Congress party, the principal democratic force that opposed the politically active monarchy. Sagar became a full-time activist in the mid-1970s. He was a Member of the Central Working Committee and the Head of Department of International Affairs of the Nepali Congress in the critical years, 2003–2006. Founder chairman of the Federation of Handicraft Association of Nepal, the author is involved with different institutions related to art, culture and heritage conservation. He is currently the Vice President of Nepal Art Council.

Praise for the Book

Sagar Rana takes us on a tour d'horizon of the century-long rule of the Rana dynasty, of his ancestors. Although much maligned by retroactive political correctness, we see in these pages an insider's perspective on this distinctive reign of hereditary prime ministers. *Singha Durbar* also covers the movement of national liberation in graphic detail. The most striking aspect of the book is how little regional geopolitics and domestic governance in Nepal has changed in the past century and half.

—*Kunda Dixit, Editor, Nepali Times*

Singha Durbar breathes life and colour into this exciting tale of the last fifty years of the Rana regime in Nepal, recounting deftly with memorable anecdote and panache the excesses of the Ranas that led to their revolutionary overthrow. A must read for anyone interested in modern Nepali history.

—*Gurcharan Das, Author of India Unbound and*
The Difficulty of Being Good

SINGHA DURBAR

Rise and Fall of the Rana Regime of Nepal

SAGAR S.J.B. RANA

RUPA

Published by
Rupa Publications India Pvt. Ltd 2017
7/16, Ansari Road, Daryaganj
New Delhi 110002

Sales centres:
Allahabad Bengaluru Chennai
Hyderabad Jaipur Kathmandu
Kolkata Mumbai

Photos and illustration courtesy: Author

The views and opinions expressed in this book are the author's own and the
facts are as reported by him which have been verified to the extent possible, and
the publishers are not in any way liable for the same.

ISBN: 978-81-291-4561-1

First impression 2017

10 9 8 7 6 5 4 3 2 1

The moral right of the author has been asserted.

Printed by Nutech Print Services, New Delhi

I dedicate this work to B.P. Koirala, the inspirational leader, whose memory has guided and helped me to write without fear, favour or bias

Contents

Foreword   ix
Preface   xiii

Part I: A Kingdom in the Clouds
The Land and Its People   3
The Valley of Kathmandu   6
King Prithvi Narayan Shah   10
Emergence of the Rana Dynasty:
Prime Minister Jung Bahadur Rana   26
Decline of the Jungs and Rise of the Shumshers   43
Maharaj Bir Shumsher (1885–1901)   48
Maharaj Dev Shumsher (March–June 1901)   53

Part II: High Tide of the Rana Regime
Maharaj Chandra Shumsher (1901–1929)   59
Maharaj Bhim Shumsher (1929–1932)   86
Maharaj Juddha Shumsher (1932–1945)   97

Part III: Quest for Freedom and Democracy (1940–1951)
Introduction   163
Palpa and Western Nepal   165
The Eastern Mountains, Terai and Biratnagar   184
The Nepalese and the Holy City   208
The Great Metropolis   225
Maharaj Padma Shumsher (1945–1948)   263
Maharaj Mohan Shumsher (1948–1951)   310

Notes   395
Acknowledgements   411
Index   413

Foreword

State formation in northern India during the eighteenth and nineteenth centuries despite colonial rule represented a major geopolitical process with profound implications right down to the present day. The founding of the Jammu and Kashmir state by my intrepid ancestor, Maharaja Gulab Singh in 1846, the political developments in the ancient nation of Nepal with successive dynasties, notably the Shahs and the Ranas; the founding of Bhutan and Sikkim; taken together, represent a remarkable story of conquest, assimilation and integration, which regretfully has not received the attention that it deserves either from western or Indian historiographers. The state structure in Nepal and Jammu and Kashmir has interesting parallels. Both are Himalayan states which combine disparate ethnic, linguistic and geographical entities beginning with the plains and going all the way up to Himalayan heights and beyond to trans-Himalaya. Knitting such diverse entities into a single state was indeed a remarkable achievement for a country, although with the rise of democratic politics, it was inevitable that ethnic and linguistic groups would reassert themselves to claim a fair share of the cake.

Shri Sagar S.J.B. Rana has, in this impressive volume, *Singha Durbar*, sought to explore the story of the rise and fall of the Rana regime in Nepal which began with Maharaj Jung Bahadur in the mid-nineteenth century and ended with the reassertion of Shah primacy supported by India in 1951. In his extensive research, Shri Rana has presented valuable detailed material regarding the pre-Rana history in Nepal and also the Rana regime founded by Jung Bahadur. He has specially dwelt on the regimes of three powerful twentieth century Rana rulers, Maharaj Chandra Shumsher (1901–1929), Maharaj Juddha Shumsher (1932–1945) and last Prime Minister, Maharaj Mohan Shumsher (1948–1951). These chapters give us a glimpse into the feudal aristocracy, their intrigues and internecine rivalries, as well as some concrete steps taken by them to improve the lot of the common people through encouraging industrial growth and rural development. The socio-economic transformation of Nepal, despite an oligarchic regime, had begun and would gather momentum.

Rana rule itself was a result of a curious and probably unique arrangement whereby the Shah kings remained titular heads of the state (Shree Paanch Sarkar), while the Ranas became hereditary prime ministers (Shree Teen Sarkar). Another curious historical legacy among the Ranas was that there was never a generational change because power devolved from brother to brother, thus ensuring a conservative gerontocracy. For a whole century, the Ranas ensured that Nepal remained isolated from the winds of change in India— represented by the freedom movement as well as successive social reform movements. There were no motorable roads even into the Kathmandu valley, and cars had to be dismantled at the Indian border, carried physically into Kathmandu and then reassembled there.

However, history cannot be sidelined artificially forever. Shri Sagar Rana has also studied in depth the anti-feudal movement which began in 1940 and resulted in the toppling the Rana regime in 1951. This saga reveals the multi-layered ethnic complexity of Nepal and its fallout down to the present day when the nation is still struggling to achieve a stable equilibrium after the democratic revolution. This section contains a detailed account of the various popular movements, many functioning underground in Nepal and in parts of India, specially Varanasi and Calcutta. People like B.P. Koirala, Ganesh Man Singh and Subarna Shumsher Rana all figure in the anti-Rana movement that ultimately led to regime change.

Let me add a personal note here. By a curious coincidence, the Dogra kingdom and the Rana regime were both established at almost exactly the same time, the former in 1846 by Maharaja Gulab Singh and the latter in 1847 by Maharaj Jung Bahadur. The regimes also came to an end more or less simultaneously; the Dogra regime after my father Maharaja Hari Singh left the state in 1950 and the Rana regime after the Shah reassertion in 1951. Even more extraordinary is the fact that in 1950, I, a direct descendant of Maharaja Gulab Singh, married Yasho Rajya Lakshmi, the granddaughter of last Rana ruler, Maharaj Mohan Shumsher. Additionally, it was I who delivered a message from Prime Minister Manmohan Singh to the last Shah, King Gyanendra, in April, 2006, advising him to hand over power to the seven party alliance to a leader of their choice. Having spearheaded the transition from feudalism to democracy in Jammu and Kashmir myself, I was thus also closely involved with the same transition in Nepal.

The Rana autocracy, like their Indian counterparts, delighted in building huge palaces. Unlike in India, however, where the palaces represent varied architectural styles incorporating many features of the regional traditions, the Rana ones were almost universally modelled on Buckingham Palace. Nepal has a glorious architectural heritage especially during the Malla period, which produced the most beautiful temples and courtyards, not to speak of their superb wooden sculpture, but these were not incorporated into the Rana palaces. The largest of the Rana palaces, Singha Durbar, which lends its name to this book, was built for and occupied by succeeding prime ministers even after 1951 or used as the central secretariat, the seat of governance.

I commend Shri Sagar Rana for his painstaking research over several years into this fascinating period of Nepal's history. I am sure this will be of great value to historians, students of modern Asia and all those interested in the beautiful but troubled land of Nepal. The narrative ends with the reassertion of power by King Tribhuwan in 1951, but that was many decades ago, and I hope Shri Rana will bring the narrative up to the present day in a companion volume.

Dr Karan Singh

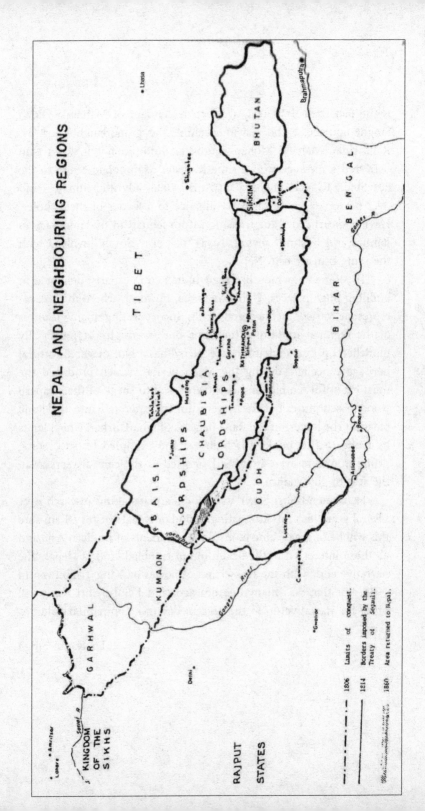

Preface

If there is a book that you want to read, but it hasn't been written yet, you must be the one to write it.

—*Toni Morrison*

There are no more than three members of the 'ruling' Rana family, those included in the Roll of Succession before 1951, and as such experienced the life in the palaces of ruling hierarchy and also got actively involved in the democratic politics post that date. All three are siblings. The eldest, Bharat, was a minister in the Rana government ousted by the revolution while still in his early twenties. Following the first general elections in 1958, he was elected to Parliament and leader of the opposition party (Rashtrabadi Gorkha Parishad). After King Mahendra staged his coup and usurped the power of governance in 1961, Gorkha Parishad voluntarily merged into the Nepali Congress, and Bharat was clubbed into the top rank of its leadership. Second brother, Jagadish, is recognized nationwide more for his literary work. As the youngest brother, born in 1938 and actively involved in Nepali Congress (NC) politics starting mid-1970s, I felt that at least one of us must write about the evolution of Nepali history—that will be more balanced than from those attached solely to one or the other side. The elder brothers left the task upon me and helped with their accounts. The challenge was daunting, as it was my first attempt at a book of any kind; it was tough work spread intermittently over a decade, but a rewarding experience.

As part of the Baber Mahal family, I was naturally privy to the accounts of the Rana family and life in the palaces. During my long innings in NC politics, in leadership of my district Lalitpur first, and later as member of the Central Working Committee and Head of the Department of International Relations, I have been privileged by my association with the top leaders of NC, including

B.P. Koirala, and down to the grassroot workers in remote villages, stricken with poverty. The experience has enabled me to obtain and collate valuable and some rare documents and reminiscences through personal accounts and one-to-one and often intimate interviews with scores of prominent leaders, not only of NC but of different political parties, key figures of history and the common man, still living at time of the interview, but sadly many gone now. I believe such critical input has instilled colour and life, and some new insight to the narration of the body of historical content in *Singha Durbar*.

The main focus of the book is concentrated in the last fifty years of the Rana regime; these are also the years when the voices, dissent and revolutionary activities against the excesses of the Rana rulers sprouted, spread and eventually uprooted the oligarchy in 1951. I have chosen four venues as centres of revolutionary activities, besides the obvious central space of Kathmandu valley. They are districts of western Nepal with Palpa as the centre point, of eastern Nepal with Biratnagar as the pivotal force, Banaras and Calcutta. Each is allotted a separate chapter. Attempt has been made to underscore the point that the revolution was led and headed by the Nepali Congress but triggered by a wide range of sporadic protests and uprisings throughout the country. The final twist of the saga, narrated in the last two chapters, reveal the devious role of regional geopolitics that has mired the political configuration of Nepal.

One hopes the book will be of interest to a widespread general readership but is especially targeted to the vast and growing number of the younger generations of Nepal or those with interest in Nepal— more comfortable with the English language. The writing is light hearted and backed by anecdotes relevant to the central theme. However, authenticity, to the best of my understanding, has been the guiding force throughout the narrative. In this single-minded attempt I may have offended some friends, relatives, leaders or sections of society, but I feel this is a necessary option rather than misguiding the far larger number of independent readers.

Part I

A Kingdom in the Clouds

Chapter One

The Land and Its People

Hundreds of miles of the Himalayas run across the Indian subcontinent and the Tibetan plateau, bisecting the terrain: five hundred miles of the middle part of this mountain range constitutes the northern boundary of Nepal. A flight along its southern flank unfolds arguably the most spectacular view on this planet. Unending lines of sheer and sparkling white peaks pierce the dark blue sky to the north. As the snow line ends, waves of undulating mountain ranges in different hues of green, blue and purple descend like waves of an ocean more than a hundred miles south, before giving way, abruptly, to the narrow belt of dark-green tropical forests and, finally, the flat Terai plains. Rivers carve their serpentine route through the deep gorges, hills and valleys, and then meander gently along the final ten-mile-wide densely forested strip of Nepalese territory, a journey of some 150 miles from the snow line as the crow flies, before flowing out into the grey-brown plains and scorching heat of Hindustan.

The earliest references to human settlements in the Himalayan foothills appear in the Vedas, which narrate the migration of the Aryans beyond the Indo-Gangetic plains, towards the Himalayas. Around 1500 BC[1], the Aryans from Asia Minor crossed the rugged passes of the northwest frontier and settled amidst the fertile Indo-Gangetic plains of Hindustan. Along the banks of the holy rivers, one can imagine rishis, the learned scholars of old, giving shape to the Vedas and scriptures, philosophical and literary works of scope and dimensions that overwhelm imagination. Meanwhile, those who wielded the weapons of battle and held the power of the state were named the Kshatriyas or Chhetriyas (Chhetri or Khas in Nepal). The farmers and traders formed the third category, the Vaishyas, while the artisans, the labour force and slaves were bracketed as the Shudras.

The Brahmins and the Kshatriyas placed themselves at the summit of the political and social ladder, looking down upon the Vaishyas as the 'working class' while the Shudras were cast aside from the society as the 'untouchables'. As the Aryans branched out in different directions independent 'states' emerged. During the formative stage of the Sanatana Dharma that forms the basis of the present-day Hindu religion, this four-tiered division was based on an individual's aptitude and profession but gradually these were bound within a rigid format and hierarchy based on the accident of birth[2].

Despite the mysteries of unfathomed antiquity, the linkage between the present-day Brahmins, and Chhetris—who live mainly in far western Nepal—with this ancient movement of people, is not without basis. In the east, the city of Janakpur is lyrically depicted in the Ramayana as the home of the virtuous Sita, and the fierce Kirat tribe from the mountains formed part of the Pandava army in the battle of Kurukshetra in the Mahabharata. If the Kirat legend is recorded, one can assume that other ethnic groups with similar 'Mongoloid' characteristics, the Gurungs and Magars, probably of Indo-Burman origin, and the Tamangs and Sherpas from Tibet, have lived in different parts of the mountain belt since ancient times. Similarly, the claim of the Tharus and Danuwars that their ancestors were the original inhabitants of the dense Terai forests who, through generations of persistence, gained immunity to malarial mosquitoes and bugs, and resisted the dreaded reptiles and beasts, is well substantiated.

By the turn of the sixth century BC, a few states in northern India; Vrijis, Magadha and the Sakya republic, occupied territories on both sides of the current Indo-Nepal boundary, in some places extending to the heart of the Indo-Gangetic plains. Prince Siddhartha was born in 566 BC in Lumbini near Kapilavastu, the capital of the Sakya rulers. Later, he left behind his family and home in search of a path that would reduce or eliminate the miseries and injustice inherent in his society. Eventually, he found enlightenment, nirvana, within the fold of Dhamma, the spiritual message that came to be known as Buddhism. As Buddhism spread through the subcontinent to coexist in harmony with the Hindu faith, some adventurous tribes, categorized now as Khas or Chhetris, entered the far west of present-day Nepal and settled in the Karnali basin at the foothills of the holy Muktinath[3]. Through the centuries the Khas state, backed by the priestly order of the Brahmins, grew in strength and reach. After the turn of the tenth century, more of their kith and kin joined them in the hills of Nepal, being unable to resist the Muslims's raids in northern India. By the thirteenth century, other than the Gandaki basin—where forty-six confederations of the Magars or Gurungs retained their supremacy[4]—the Khas Kingdom spread across the rest of west Nepal, including territories inside Kumaon and Garhwal, modern-day Uttaranchal and Himachal. Their political dominance declined in the centuries that followed, but their language, known then as Parbate Bhasa (language of the hill people), derived largely from Sanskrit and the Devanagri script, prospered, to be eventually recognized as the national language of the Kingdom of Nepal.

Chapter Two

The Valley of Kathmandu

Meanwhile, the people of the Kathmandu valley were weaving their own history. Legends and myths narrate that the valley was once a lake are substantiated by later archaeological findings. It is said that a celestial power (Vishnu in the Hindu and Manjushree in the Buddhist legends) cut asunder the mountain cliffs and let the pure blue water of the valley drain out. Sceptics, of course, discount this tale and stick to the mundane theory of gradual erosion of the mountains through centuries. Some decades or centuries after the fertile fields emerged, pastoral tribes often called Mahipalas or Gopalas entered this bowl-shaped valley of some 220 square miles. They lived here for several centuries before the Kirats moved in to establish their domination. Despite their being hunters and nomadic tribes, there is now credible evidence that the Kirats constructed some permanent dwellings and set up a rudimentary administrative order. In the early centuries of the Christian era, the Licchavis, a scion of the rulers of Vaishali in north India, moved in search of their own kingdom. Better armed and equipped for battle, they trekked and marched all the way into the famed valley to gradually drive the Kirats back to the eastern hills, and established a dynastic hegemony that lasted till about AD 900.

The Licchavis followed Hinduism and brought the religion to this land. They introduced a well-tested administrative apparatus and trading patterns that promoted and mobilized multiple opportunities the valley offered. The produce from the fertile fields was maximized by a sound system of water management and a farming community of rare skill. The idyllic location of the valley at a strategic point on the trade route between Tibet and Hindustan was fully exploited. A novel style of urban planning was introduced in the three main cities/city states of Kathmandu, Lalitpur and Bhaktapur that promoted closely knit communities—symmetric dwelling houses connected with each other and ample courtyards (bahals) for leisure and recreation. The benevolent mindset of the rulers is evident from the hospitality offered to Buddhist missionaries, whose inflow commenced during the reign of the Mauryan ruler, Ashoka, in the third century BC. Generous contribution from the state for promotion of all faiths and cultures, the architecture and the arts, helped build religious harmony at this early stage of history. Guthis, a home-grown institution based on community cooperation in socio-cultural milieu, sprung up in every locality and have lasted to this day. The prosperity and rich cultural heritage of the Kathmandu valley flowered during these early centuries of the Licchavi era.

A language (Newari) common to the Hindus or Buddhists, rulers, farmers, craftsmen or low-grade workers was taking shape, and in AD 879 a new era, 'the Nepal era', came into being. But, by this time, the Licchavi rulers had lost their former verve and vitality. A series of ineffectual kings, feuding nobility and ambitious courtiers weakened and eventually brought down the dynasty. During the centuries that followed, Kathmandu and the adjoining areas got fragmented into tiny fiefdoms with a confused and weak command structure. In the mid-thirteenth century, a devastating earthquake struck the valley and killed about one-third of the entire population. Before the end of the century, Khas warriors from the far west raided the hapless valley and carried away a rich haul of loot. In the middle of the fourteenth century, the residents endured an invasion by the marauding Muslim general, Illyas. The renowned Hindu shrine Pashupatinath and the Buddhist stupas of Swayambhunath and Boudhnath were among the monuments that were vandalized and looted.

Meanwhile, the Karnat rulers from south India had entered Nepal during the eleventh century. They established their domination over a large stretch of land in the foothills, some twenty miles south of Kathmandu. From their well-protected capital atop a lofty mountain, with its formidable fort, Simrangarh, they watched the chaotic conditions prevailing in Kathmandu. Jayasthiti Malla chose to enter the valley through a marriage alliance with a daughter of the ruler of Bhaktapur and, by 1382, emerged as the undisputed master of the entire valley. On assumption of full authority, he imposed some law and order in a society steeped in disorder by introducing a treatise based on the Brahmanic code of his native origin but giving due weight to the traditions and customs prevalent in Nepal. This Nepala Rashtra Sashtra, sacred treatise of the Nepalese nation[5], was the genesis of the Brahmanic order largely adhered to by the Shah rulers, and most of its provisions were incorporated in the Muluki Ain, the legal code of Jung Bahadur, the founder of the Rana regime 1847–1951.

The Malla rulers embraced the policy of religious tolerance and assimilated themselves in the Newari cultural milieu. The homogeneous environment allowed them to concentrate on the task of repairing the damage inflicted during the past two centuries. The trade route was once more given due protection and maintained in good condition. The ancient canals (raj kulo) that fetched water from the adjoining hills to feed the farmland and the wells were repaired. Inside each city, an ingenious network of deep underground aqueducts was built to emit ample and continuous flow of potable water into strategically located hittis, spaciously dug-in squares with stone spouts, shaped and crafted into exquisite works of art. Each of the three city-states competed to adorn their central squares with monuments and palaces that remain unmatched to this day. These complexes are now included in the UNESCO World Heritage list. These projects were funded through tax/duty levied on local produce and products, and exports of timber, medicinal herbs, musk and even copper, gold and semi-precious stones, according to some accounts. Duty on movement of goods along the trade routes contributed majorly to the state revenue. Kathmandu enjoyed an age of rare peace, harmony and prosperity, unmatched in other cities of the world.

But alas! Excessive wealth invited sloth, strife and misrule. Bitter infighting between the Malla kings of the three city-states erupted in the latter part of the seventeenth century. Ambitious and greedy ministers played one ruler against the other for their own profit.

The difficulties were compounded by the incessant attacks launched against the weakened and divided city-states by the neighbouring barons and chiefs from beyond the ring of mountains surrounding the valley. The lucrative trans-Himalayan trade suffered on account of the growing influence of the British East India Company, as it strengthened its colonial rule in Hindustan. The condition was ripe for external intervention. Prithvi Narayan Shah, the Raja of Gorkha, some fifty miles to the west of the valley, was waiting for just such an opportunity.

Chapter Three

King Prithvi Narayan Shah

Following the disintegration of the Khas kingdom in the fifteenth century, the entire area west of Kathmandu was fragmented into scores of small federations. Interstate rivalry and tussles for expansion of territory continued through successive generations. But by the middle of the sixteenth century, Dravya Shah, the Raja of Gorkha, was able to subjugate most of his neighbouring principalities/federations and carve out a powerful state. The renowned Gorkha Nepal Army traces its origin to these years. In 1743, upon his father's death, Prithvi Narayan Shah, the ninth descendant of Dravya, inherited the state. Ambitious beyond normal aspirations and possessor of courage and intelligence well above his peers, he visited India to learn about the science of modern warfare and 'procured the (superior) firelocks from the gunsmiths of Lucknow and Cawnpore'[6]. He held a grand vision of conquests, with the valley of Kathmandu as the ultimate prize. The Gorkha Army was battle-fit by now and led by capable commanders. Well-prepared and equipped, Prithvi began his journey of conquests. After each victory he used the gains to strengthen his army but at the same time divided the booty in shape of grants of land (later to be termed jagir) to his followers, and also those in the opposing ranks who acquiesced to the victors. Magnanimity, rather than revenge, won him many followers. Such an arrangement enabled him to consolidate his hold and move ahead to new pastures. However, the peasants and traders were left at the mercy of the jagirdars, in effect spreading the roots of a feudal order that was to last more than two centuries[7].

After twenty-five years of gruelling, often punishing campaign, Prithvi and his army, believed to be no more than 1,200 men at any time, captured the principality of Nuwakot. From its imposing heights he could gaze down upon the sprawling valley of Kathmandu. Yet it took him another eighteen months and two separate attempts to capture Kathmandu. During this time he was backed by his battle-hardened men. He also had to use deceit, moving in stealthily when the Newars were celebrating the annual festival of Indra Jatra, in September 1768. His campaign to capture the valley was marred by inhuman brutality that the residents of Kirtipur have not yet forgotten.

Prithvi's quest did not end here. He then sent a strong contingent of the army north to establish dominance right up to the high passes of Kuti and Kerung, atop the Himalayan watershed, gateway to the vast expanse of the Tibetan plateau. Prithvi then personally led his men eastwards to subdue the brave and proud Kirati people, once rulers of Kathmandu, and now holding sway over vast territories to the east and west of their heartland in mid-eastern Nepal. The Kirats put up a formidable resistance that exhausted the resilience of both sides. Ultimately, a deal was struck that in legal terms established sovereignty of the Gorkha state over Kirat but allowed the latter to retain semi-autonomy in local governance, and recognized the time-honoured rights, privileges, traditions and culture of their race. The raja of Gorkha was now the king of Nepal, with Kathmandu as its capital. His vision for the new nation reflected remarkable statesmanship and foresight, and a transformation that only great men can achieve with such finesse. They are expressed in short but telling snippets, known as *Divya Upadesh* (wise directives) that even the common people could understand. The salient features of his *Divya Upadesh* are set out below:

- I have a wish to establish law and order as did great rulers before us.
- This nation is not created by my little effort. It is a garden of all the people. Let all four castes, high and low and all thirty-six races be aware of this.
- The authority of the king should be sacrosanct.
- The king should always be just and never allow injustice.

Corrupt ones should be dealt with severely.

- The treasury of the ruler is the people of the country. If they are prosperous the state will be strong.
- This country is like a yam between two stones, keep good relations with the emperor of China. To our south, keep good relations with the emperor from across the seas, but he is very cunning. In the quest for establishing dominance over Hindustan they will one day come north. Build defences on their routes. Do not face them head-on. If we cannot defeat them in battle, make peace and treaties through a policy of appeasement, through every devious strategy.
- Do not abandon the customs of yore.
- Do not allow foreign traders into the country; they will impoverish the state.
- Forbid use of foreign cloth. Encourage local skills and weavers.
- Export local products such as medical herbs so that the state draws money from outside.

Prithvi set up a rudimentary framework of an administrative network and through it tried to govern the country in line with these directives. His death in 1775 came far too early, at the age of fifty-five. Yet during the barely four decades of his adult life, a new nation-state was born and set on a course and direction that remained largely constant until the end of the Rana regime in 1951.

Meltdown of the Monarchy and Expansion of the Kingdom

Between 1775 and 1816 when the Treaty of Sugauli was signed, the governance of Nepal was marred by a multifaceted tug-of-war between Prithvi's successors. This gave ample space for succeeding prime ministers, known as 'mukhtiyar', to vie for their own share in the pie. Pratap Shah succeeded his illustrious father and his first move was to banish his younger brother Bahadur Shah to Banaras, on suspicion of foul play. Pratap died just two years later in 1777, making way for his two-year-old son, Rana Bahadur, to be crowned. This was the beginning of six generations of infant or boy kings (of an average age of less than six) being placed on the throne of Nepal[8]. Bahadur Shah returned from Banaras to claim the position of the regent but Queen Mother Rajendra Laxmi got the 'intruder' arrested and thrown in jail. Aged twenty-six, she was young and adventurous. But within a year, she was charged with immoral liaison with Sarbajeet Magar, her chief minister, and jailed for it. However, she proved her innocence and mettle within ten months to regain her position as the regent. She drove her opponents out and ruled the country with rare verve, backing and encouraging the efforts of the army, often seated on horseback[9]. On her death in 1785, Bahadur Shah emerged again and, with support of the council of 'bhardars'—the nobility, comprising the five leading aristocratic families—seized power and held firm for another ten years before he was once more removed, this time by the twenty-year-old king, Rana Bahadur. However, even amidst the feud of the royals and confusion in governance, the expansion of the Nepali state continued unabated.

The aura of the Gorkhali Fauj (Gorkha Army) preceded their march. The districts adjoining Gorkha were captured under the leadership of the regent queen. The troops moved farther west under astute leadership of Bahadur Shah to gradually subdue the tiny principalities in the far west of Nepal. They then crossed River Mahakali that marks the boundary of present-day Nepal. One by one the rajas of the small hill states across the border and deep into Kumaon and Garhwal surrendered meekly or were subdued. The legendary hero Amar Singh Thapa, commanding the Nepal army in the western front, moved into the palace of one such state, of Arki, which served as the base for administration of the conquered territories. Another contingent of the army led by Damodar Pande had, in the meantime, moved north from Kathmandu, crossed the passes of Kuti and Kerung and marched unhindered to reach and capture the town of Tsigatze, halfway to Lhasa. The rich haul of booty, gold and precious stones looted from the Gumbas, Tibetan centres of learning and worship, far exceeded anything the Gorkhas had ever seen. At this point the Celestial Emperor of China, who always considered Tibet as its vassal, despatched a strong force to drive back all the invaders. Nepal was compelled to sue for peace. It was the first serious setback for the Gorkha Army[10].

Rise of the Prime Ministers and the Deadly Feud between the Thapas and the Pandes

King Rana Bahadur 1777–1798 was meanwhile coming of age, and turning out to be a reckless debauch. Popular legend has it that he was bewitched by a staggeringly beautiful Brahmin widow, Kantabati. He had her kidnapped, got her pregnant in his palace and a child, Girvanayuddha, was born out of the unholy union. The foolhardy act, an unacceptable sacrilege, antagonized the powerful priestly order. A curse was put on the couple that brought on the dreaded disease of smallpox on the girl. She killed herself, repulsed by her pock-marked face. The king became frenzied. There was a public uproar that forced him to abdicate in 1799 and he left for Banaras in garb of a *swami*, but after ensuring that the infant Girvanayuddha (1799–1816) was accepted as the king.

It was around this time that the bitter feud between two renowned families, the Pandes and the Thapas, burst into open hostility, in a deadly struggle to occupy the now powerful position of the prime minister.

Damodar Pande, the hero of Tibet war, first captured the coveted post and initiated a relentless persecution of the rival Thapa faction. But within three years, the swami king Rana Bahadur regained his worldly ambitions and assisted by Bhimsen Thapa, also languishing in exile after the persecution by Damodar, marched into Kathmandu. Regent Queen Rajeshwari, his wife, sent her troops under the command of Damodar Pande to intercept her husband's advance. But faced with the persona of the king and the formidable Bhimsen Thapa at the head of a strong contingent, exhorting them to take a bow to the 'real king', the soldiers obeyed dutifully, leaving Pande helpless. Rana Bahadur entered Kathmandu in triumph to seize power, as a regent of his son Girvanayuddha. Pande was executed, as Bhimsen Thapa, as an advisor to Rana Bahadur, controlled the reins of governance (1802).

In another bloody episode that followed, ninety-three members of the royal family and bhardars, the cream of non-Thapa nobility, were massacred by Bhimsen and his followers[11]. Rana Bahadur was then persuaded to take a new bride, a teenaged niece of Bhimsen, Lalit Tripura Sundari. In 1806, while the elder queens committed sati, she became the new queen regent. Bhimsen was proclaimed to be the prime minister. The duo retained the supreme and unchallenged authority of the state for three decades. The king meanwhile was kept in isolation inside the palace. The practice of enticing the youthful king into luxurious and amorous indulgence took root during these years.

Nepal now held sway over an approximately 700–800-mile stretch of the Himalayan belt from Sikkim to the borders of Punjab. However, Bhimsen, emboldened by his strong bond with the regent queen, wanted more. Experienced commanders advised him that it was time to halt the march and consolidate the territories conquered but the prime minister sent orders to press ahead and lay siege on the formidable fort of Kangra. The Raja of Kangra sought help from the Sikh ruler, Ranjit Singh of Punjab. The popular nomenclature of 'Lion of Punjab' fitted the latter's fierce looks and the ferocity of his army. The Sikhs arrived in force and in conjunction with the Dogra army of Kangra, drove out the Nepalese troops. Their retreat to the hilly regions of Himachal, Kumaon and Garhwal is viewed as the beginning of the end of the utopian ambitions of the 'Greater Himalayan Kingdom of Nepal'.

The Anglo-Nepal War and the Treaty of Sugauli

Bhimsen Thapa now targeted the fertile revenue-rich plains of the Terai, ceded to the East India Company by local rulers. The tactic of attack he chose was not an overt act of hostility but a gradual low-profile assimilation of fields and villages across the border into

Nepal. Such a move paid rich dividends for six years during which nearly 200 villages were annexed[12]. The East India Company was, no doubt, aware of the incursions but was engaged in more pressing challenges elsewhere. But by 1813–14, the challenge from the Sikhs, Marathas and the roving gangs of Pindaris had been contained by the East India Company. In Europe the French army under Napoleon tottered on the brink of final defeat. The rising power of the Kingdom of Nepal was now on the Company's radar. However, the British were aware of the treacherous mountain terrain, malarial forests and fierce fighting quality of the Gorkhas, a lesson learnt in 1766–67 when troops led by Captain Kilnox to contain the threat of disruption of advantageous trade by the army of the Raja of Gorkha had been mauled badly and had to head back crestfallen.

Therefore, diplomatic initiatives were mobilized to persuade Nepal to return the areas it had encroached upon. Bhimsen Thapa refused to budge despite a strong plea made by the military commanders for a conciliatory approach and a stern warning from Amar Singh Thapa, commander of the victorious Nepali campaign in the west all the way to the border of the Sikh Kingdom: 'we have hitherto but hunted deer, if we engage in this war we must prepare to fight the tigers.'

In the autumn of 1814, when the scorching heat and the monsoon rains had receded, the British forces attacked Nepal from four fronts along the nearly 700-mile border of that time. The Gorkha Army, outnumbered almost threefold, defended with uncommon valour and forced the invaders to retreat.

According to Sir Francis Tuker: 'This had been the hardest fought campaign of all those the Honourable Company had engaged in since the first arrival of the English merchants in India in the seventeenth century. It had come as a shock to the (British) Government whose very existence was now challenged.'[13] But valiantly as they fought, the Gorkha losses were crippling. And the British were not about to give up. They came back next year in larger numbers and with more powerful guns and cannons. The fort at Makwanpur, a couple of days' march south of Kathmandu, came under attack. The defence was stubborn as ever but the end was inevitable. The diary of a British lieutenant who fought in that battle mentioned: 'On going round the hill afterwards—it was scarcely possible to walk without stepping on their dead.'

Kathmandu had no option but to sue for peace. The British realized though that the Gorkhas had 'fought like heroes, proving themselves beyond a question, the best soldiers in the subcontinent, devoted to their country and resolutely united by the sacred bond'[14].

The Treaty of Sugauli was signed in December 1915 at a dusty little village by that name, now in north Bihar. Nepal's status as an independent country was confirmed. Each country agreed to accredit a minister to the court of the other though in practice, a British resident came to stay in Kathmandu, but not the other way around. Nepal was forced to pay a heavy price, more than one-third of its territory, won through years of battle, was ceded to the victors. Yet, the war had built a ground swell of national spirit amongst a broad range of the people. The Chhetris, Brahmins, the ethnic mountain communities, the Madhesis and the Tharus joined the national army to defend their territories stoutly[15].

The treaty opened the doors for the recruitment of Nepalese nationals into the British army, an arrangement that has lasted to this date. It has been termed as 'degrading' by some, and no doubt, thousands of brave men have perished in the course of service, but several times that number and their families back home have been elevated from the depth of abject poverty to a comfortable lifestyle and respect in society.

The Government of Nepal showed due respect to the British resident in Kathmandu but did not permit him to move freely even in the capital, beyond the compounds of his residence. The rest of the country was strictly out of bounds. The relationship could hardly be based on trust in these circumstances. Fortunately, for both sides, a new resident came to Kathmandu in 1929, who gradually got enamoured by the Himalayan Kingdom and its people. Brian Hodgson developed a congenial relationship with the prime minister and was permitted enough movement to allow him to explore, record and leave behind an invaluable collection of documents tracing diverse aspects of life in Nepal and the passage of its history in his time.

Despite the heavy loss and humiliation suffered in the Anglo-Nepal war, there was no challenge to the authority of Bhimsen Thapa inside the country. He ruled with an iron fist, cutting down his opponents ruthlessly at the first signs of opposition. While he wrestled with the political and military matters of the state, Regent Queen, Tripura Sundari, maintained a dignified stance even in times of political chaos and military debacle, and has left behind a splendid legacy in the fields of the art and literature. One of the first literary publications in the Nepali Language, the *Raj Dharma*, a translation of a section of the great epic Mahabharata, was commissioned by her. The first iron bridge over the River Bagmati, joining Kathmandu with Lalitpur, was constructed at her behest. A splendid urban-complex dominated by the two-hundred-feet-high minaret, Dharahara, a monument dedicated to the military exploits of the Nepal army and its prime minister that was commissioned by her, remained till the devastating earthquake of 2015. It was the most visible and attractive man-made landmark in the capital.

The unchallenged space Bhimsen Thapa occupied had much to do with the support of the Queen Regent and came under increasing stress after her death in 1832. King Rajendra Bikram Shah, three years old when he succeeded his father Girvanayuddha upon the latter's death in 1816, was nineteen by then and married, as was the practice, to two wives. The royals were not too fond of the domineering Prime Minister Thapa. Rana Jung Pande, son of Damodar, was waiting for just such a time. It was not difficult for him to persuade the royals that Bhimsen was disloyal. Gradually, men close to the prime minister were removed from office and finally the stalwart of many decades was arrested on a charge of sedition, shackled and dumped in a dungeon. Unable to bear the humiliation and inhuman cruelty, he committed suicide in 1839.

British Resident Brian Hodgson described how the royal family did not even spare Thapa's dead body: 'The corpse was dismembered—

the mangled remains thrown away on the riverside, where none but the dog and vulture dared further to heed.'[16] His relatives and followers were driven out of the country and seven generations of the Thapas were debarred from entering government service. The rampant acts of persecution that followed drove a major group of the bhardars to strong protests, and prompted Hodgson to forward an unusually stern letter from his government expressing 'extreme disgust and abhorrence'. Unable to withstand the double-edged threat, King Rajendra dismissed Rana Jung Pande. The scene was set for perhaps the most chaotic decade in the annals of Nepalese history.

King Rajendra was indecisive and weak. Senior Queen Samrajya Laxmi had died in 1841. Junior Queen Rajya Laxmi was stout of heart, ambitious, bold, capricious and, in the prime of her life, promiscuous. Crown Prince Surendra, son of Samrajya Laxmi, the most deranged royal in several generations, was now beginning to throw his weight around. The king was incapable of handling both the intrigue and infighting within his palace, and the affairs of the state outside. Never had the people of the valley suffered such chaotic misrule and uncertainty. In 1842, backed by the Bhardari Sabha and the army bigwigs, the now Senior Queen Rajya Laxmi was able to pressurize her husband to issue a royal proclamation that, in effect, gave her a decisive power in governance. But Rajya Laxmi could hardly control the chaotic situation on her own. While searching for a suitable prime ministerial candidate, she did not find anyone in the royal court to be the right fit. Her choice was Mathbar Singh Thapa, nephew of Bhimsen Thapa, who had been in prison with his uncle almost a decade back. He had been released in due course and now lived in Banaras, a city second only to Kathmandu in terms of the play of Nepali politics.

Mathbar bided his time, ensured that the principal supporters of the Pandes holding high administrative positions had been removed or eliminated and replaced by men of his choice, before he made his triumphant entry into Kathmandu. Well known for his capabilities in the past as governor of Palpa and close confidante of Bhimsen, he was greeted with hope and joy by the bhardars as he took up his office in Kathmandu. However, he now faced a thorny challenge. King Rajendra, though devoid of his legal authority, handed out orders to officers based on his whims. Crown Prince Surendra knew of no law that he should follow, harassing and punishing people at his fancy. In return for offering Thapa the premiership, the queen wanted her pound of flesh. She asked Mathbar Thapa to join in a plot to persuade the king to remove the unstable Crown Prince Surendra, to be replaced by her own son, a consuming ambition throughout her life. In the process, a few murders had to be committed; after all, Mathbar's wish for execution of *his* enemies had been met.

The prime minister started to look for an alternative power block in the palace. The queen may have got wind of this. She turned to her closest ally, suspected of being her paramour, Gagan Singh Bhandari, whom she had promoted to the rank of general. Between them, they came to the conclusion that Mathbar had to be removed by any means. They were able to persuade the vacillating king of a conspiracy being hatched by the prime minister against the royal family. The king consented to the murder of the prime minister. The man selected for this task was Jung Bahadur Kunwar, a rising star in the army, known for his uncommon feats of athleticism and bravado, and a trusted nephew of Mathbar Thapa. Summoned by the queen, the unsuspecting prime minister entered the chambers of the palace and Jung Bahadur shot dead his uncle in cold blood.

Jung Bahadur Kunwar Rana

The Kunwars belonged to one of the five leading aristocratic families who served the Rajas of Gorkha. They retained their premier position in the ruling hierarchy as the nation-state took shape. Apart from the Shahs and the Basnets, the Pandes, Thapas and Kunwars formed the bulk of the bhardars, and were joined by the high priests, the purohits, to form the Bhardari Sabha, the Council of Nobles, a powerful body that influenced crucial decisions of the state. Acts of exemplary service to the king and the country earned them hereditary titles, rich rewards and extensive properties, known as the jagir. Their clout in governance was further cemented by matrimonial alliances forged between them.

This may be the right place to outline the different layers of Nepalese society as generally viewed during the Rana regime. If in ancient Rome people were divided into Patricians and Plebeians, there were several layers of socio-political strata in Nepal during the Rana regime. Though devoid of political authority, the king and the royal family stood at the apex of the socio-religious hierarchy. The high priests, having through the ages attained the sole authority to interpret the scriptures and bestow divine blessings, occupied a pedestal above the rest of humanity. The all-powerful Ranas were unquestionable masters of all temporal matters. The prerogative of the prime minister in legislative, administrative and judicial matters was supreme and undisputable. Nevertheless, they did take counsel in state matters from the bhardars. Those in the military (Jangi) and civil (Nijamati) service enjoyed considerable respect and authority. The rest of the citizens were collectively termed as 'Duniyadars' or 'Raitis' (commoners, would be the closest translation).

Jung Bahadur Kunwar Rana was born in June 1817 at Thapathali Durbar, residence of Prime Minister Bhimsen Thapa. He spent his youth and teens in different climes and terrains, Dhankuta in the east and Dadeldhura and Jumla in the far west, where his father Bal Narsingh Kunwar was posted as a governor. He showed little interest in books but turned relentlessly to physically demanding activities like riding, swimming, hunting, fencing and martial arts. Under the tutelage of his elders, he learnt the art of governance as a natural inheritance of his race, and like them he too joined the army. At the age of twenty, Jung Bahadur learnt the vagaries of court life and the swift blow of foul murder the hard way. The once-powerful Bhimsen had perished and his relatives and followers, including the Kunwars, were suddenly thrown out of their appointments and their properties seized. However, the colourful adventurer was not one to drown in self-pity. Jung went to the thick forests of the Terai to earn his living by capturing wild elephants for sale. When that brought no profit, he turned to reckless gambling, with even greater misfortune.

Trying to find new avenues to make a living, he reached Banaras, and then Lahore, where his cousin Mathbar Basnet is said to have been in the employ of Maharaj Ranjit Singh. He did so, possibly, to follow Mathbar's path, or maybe for a more romantic adventure: the ghazals, mujras and dancing girls offering love and romance, a refined heritage of that renowned city.

However, it was in Kathmandu that he got married to a Basnet girl, Prasad Laxmi, and with the dowry, he paid off his debts. The Thapas came back to power once more and Mathbar, the new prime minister, took the young man under his wings. That was both his fortune and misfortune. The eccentric Crown Prince Surendra, who had heard about Jung's uncommon physical capabilities and growing popularity, was intent on finishing off the upstart. Two blatant attempts were made on his life.

One monsoon day Jung was ordered to jump into the raging River Trisuli from the high bridge, astride the horse he rode. On another occasion he was asked to jump into a deep well on threat of dire consequences if he refused the order of a prince. All those who witnessed the scene took him for dead but, incredulously, Jung came out of both ordeals, his reputation immeasurably enhanced. These feats may well have influenced Surendra, for he now tried to draw the indomitable man of action into his camp. The same logic drove King Rajendra and Queen Rajya Laxmi to entice Jung, or force him on threat of dire consequences, to commit the heinous crime of killing his own uncle and benefactor, Prime Minister Mathbar. Whatever the motivation or compulsions, Jung was now in the thick of intrigue, treachery and bloodshed, fully committed to the deadly power game of those days that led, as a Nepali saying goes, 'to the throne of Hastinapur[17]or life beneath the turf.'

The king, queen and the crown prince now pushed their respective candidates to the vacant post of the prime minister. An uneasy compromise was reached whereby four aspirants for the premiership were appointed 'Joint Commanders in Chief': Fateh Jung Shah, a royal relative backed by the king; Gagan Singh, the queen's confidant; Jung Bahadur; and Abhiman Singh Rana, an upright officer from the Magar clan. Fateh Jung was given the title of prime minister but Gagan, backed to the hilt by the queen, wielded the real authority. Such a prominent presence of the queen's paramour was intolerable for Rajendra and Surendra. The haughty behaviour of this 'upstart' also antagonized a whole set of the nobility. One cold evening in the month of September, while at his evening prayers, Gagan was shot dead. The identity of those who planned the murder or who fired the fatal bullet remains one of many unsolved mysteries of these times.

Queen Laxmi rushed to his house to be stunned by the still body covered in blood. Yet, her sadness was drowned by her uncontrollable fury and thirst for revenge. On her orders the bugle was sounded, a call for high-level officials of the state to assemble urgently at the Kot, a large-walled courtyard adjoining the palace complex. Jung was amongst the first to reach the Kot. His six brothers, trusted followers and army men under his command followed him, alert and armed to act swiftly on his orders. At the Kot, Jung first approached the queen to console her, but also to assure her that he and his men were there to protect her interests. There was no one else she could place greater trust on. The frenzied queen was on the hunt for the culprit amongst the high-ranking officers. She suspected one Bir Keshar Pande, who was known to have been inimical to Gagan, and wanted to execute him on the spot. When Fateh Jung Shah hesitated, she drew her sword in frenzy. Jung tried to calm her. However, each of the ministers too was suspicious of the other. Amidst the melee, confusion and heated exchanges, Abhiman Singh Rana was bayoneted by a guard and as he fell, wounded mortally, he pointed to Jung as the real murderer. Swords and khukuris were unsheathed, guns drawn and the killings began. A segment of Jung's armed men entered the courtyard and the annihilation was complete. King Rajendra had entered the Kot earlier but departed in a hurry. In the middle of the night he rode to the British Residency to seek some kind of assistance. He was stopped at the gate and told that this was not the hour for a meeting. He retired to his palace for the rest of the night. Crown Prince Surendra had not stirred outside his chambers, though fully aware of the mayhem. Jung stayed beside the queen, who had sobered down somewhat, as those she had suspected were amongst the slain, including the prime minister and Abhiram. She announced, amidst the horror around her, that as regent she had bestowed the title of prime minister and commander-in-chief on Jung Bahadur. She then returned to the palace. Next morning, Jung presented himself at the court as holder of those coveted titles. King Rajendra, Crown Prince Surendra and the bhardars did not object. In any case, all other claimants or aspirants were already dead.

The Kot episode has been dramatized as the 'black night of Nepali history when hundreds of brave men were butchered and their blood gushed out onto the street outside.' More recent research work including examination of the original letter written by Ranga Nath Pandit[18] to Brian Hodgson, available at the British Library in London, reveal a more concise data of no more than thirty men killed that night. Most of them belonged to the Chautaria family, including Prime Minister Fateh Jung Shah[19]. In comparison, ninety-three opponents of Bhimsen Thapa had been slain in a similar episode fifty years earlier. Both actions were precipitated by chronic anarchy that were preceded, and followed by several decades of relative stability.

Was there a better option for the betterment of the people open to Bhimsen or, later, Jung?

In the days and weeks that followed, scores of prominent nobles and members of their families escaped or were evicted from the valley or the country. The vacancy in key positions of governance was filled by Jung's brothers and trusted lieutenants. The royals were allowed to retain their respective titles and privileges. The queen, however, had not given up her obsession. She persistently pressurized Jung to promote her son as the crown prince. Rebuffed each time, she hired or gathered aggrieved elements inside the country or living in exile in India and roped in her husband, Rajendra, in plots to have Jung poisoned, assassinated or removed through an armed coup. Each time Jung was able to thwart her moves. Ultimately, the king was pressured to abrogate the authority conferred on the queen and for the first time in its history, the Council of Nobles headed by the prime minister, submitted a letter to 'Your Majesty', citing various criminal acts of the royal couple in the past, and expressed the 'unanimous will of the nobles and the people' to remove the king from office. Rajendra was forced to resign and Crown Prince Surendra succeeded his father in 1847. But the king, henceforth, was no more than a puppet that moved according to Jung's wishes.

Chapter Four

Emergence of the Rana Dynasty: Prime Minister Jung Bahadur Rana

Few would have placed a penny's bet on a boy born and bred in the rugged and remote highlands, who could barely write his own name. Yet, this boy waded through a labyrinth of ambitious nobles, vicious and eccentric royals, a path marked by treachery, bloodshed and murder, and emerged as the all-powerful leader of the kingdom. This day was merely the beginning of the test of his guiles, merit and mettle.

Jung's sense of history was impeccable. Nepal had once stood out in the subcontinent as a force that had challenged the rising presence and power of the East India Company. But times had changed. Lord Wellesley, the Governor General of India (1798–1805), had clearly sketched the new designs of Britain: 'India should be governed from a palace, not a counting house, with the ideas of a prince and not those of a dealer in muslins and indigo'[20]. Those designs were clearly visible in the Anglo-Nepal war. By the end of the second decade of the nineteenth century, the very fibre of British presence in India had been transformed. No more a dominion of the Company or indeed Britain, 'It was henceforth accurate to speak of Britain's Indian Empire'[21]. Jung Bahadur wanted to comprehend the measure of the strength of the Empire before charting a course for Nepal's foreign policy.

To England and France

Towards this end, Jung decided he would visit England and Europe. The mission was designed to meet other equally important objectives.

These included enhancement of the sovereign status of the nation, to interact directly with Queen Victoria and her ministers, and to learn about aspects of governance and strategies for growth that helped the little island's dominance over countries well beyond its geographic boundaries. The first objective, of attaining recognition for Nepal as a 'sovereign' country, was partially met when the British invitation addressed Jung as 'Plenipotentiary Ambassador of the Sovereign Monarch of Nepal'.

A fresh hurdle, from the priestly order, emanated before the trip could even commence. A 'divine' directive found in some ancient scriptures forbidding good Hindus to cross the seven seas had held all Hindus in bondage for centuries. Anyone who broke the law would lose his caste. No prince of India had dared face such an outcome! Jung cajoled and bullied the head priests to find a way to locate the rites to be performed in order to absolve his 'sins' on return. They obliged. Specific rites were prescribed to be performed at the holy city of Banaras before he re-entered Nepal. Thousands and then millions of Hindus now followed his lead to reach distant lands, never tread by their forefathers, and without facing the wrath of God.

The voyage that Jung undertook started off from Kathmandu in the winter of 1850. His entourage included about forty men: his two brothers, Dhir Shumsher and Jagat Shumsher; and alongside them, officers and professionals, each one selected for his proficiency in a given field or subject such as governance, law, military matters, industry, agriculture and the arts. The leisurely journey included a shikar in the Terai. In Calcutta a nineteen-gun salute greeted the entourage, followed by warm welcome and splendid receptions, a prelude to the hospitality and unceasing entertainments that were laid out in England. This English summer season belonged to Jung, 'thirty-two years of age, rather slight in figure but neatly formed, firm and agile, his features of the Tartar cast, he appears to have great courage', as noted by a London newspaper. Add to these attributes the colourful array of finery and precious lavish jewellery, and it was no wonder he excited the imagination of London society, particularly the young women, rarely exposed to such oriental style and splendour.

Queen Victoria and the Duke of Wellington met and entertained the 'ambassador' whose exploits and commanding position in his country had been briefed to the dignitaries earlier. His charm, though, was a revelation. After an opera show staged to honour him, Jung expressed his admiration and gratitude to his gracious host. In turn Queen Victoria queried, perhaps with some mirth, how he could have enjoyed the show without knowledge of the language.

'Does not Your Majesty enjoy the song of the cuckoo?' was Jung's reply.

Words to this effect, no doubt, charmed and impressed the dazzling audience. The social circle of London took Jung to heart and one lovely lady, Laura Montz, was reported to have had amorous exploits with the rugged prince from the east.

Of greater value to the visitors were the inspection tours of the arsenals, military and naval installations, the industries and farms, and the interaction with the legal fraternity and men who managed the famed civil service and military affairs in England and Scotland. At the end of summer the delegation left for France to be greeted and treated by their French hosts with similar warmth and understanding. One wonders whether this visit was undertaken to also show that Nepal had more than one friend in Europe. In the six weeks spent in France, Jung observed the similarities and disparities between the two countries, especially the legal system that gave him a choice for his own country. And, during his leisure time, he would be lost in sensual pleasures amidst the French Mademoiselles. 'If he could, he would have taken away two hundred young women with him,' reported *Le Opinion Publique*[22].

The team headed east to reach India when the weather had cooled down. As promised to the priests, the delegation visited Banaras and performed the prescribed rites. Before returning to Kathmandu, Jung managed to seek the hand of a Rajput princess from Kutch as well. A rousing welcome and public acclaim greeted Jung and his entourage as they entered the gates of Thapathali Durbar.

In his absence, the prime minister had assigned the task of managing the affairs of state to his brother, Bom Bahadur. Within a fortnight Bom Bahadur disclosed, hesitantly, that an assassination plot was afoot and Badri Narsing, another brother of Jung, headed the group of conspirators. The suspects were quickly rounded up. When confronted with irrefutable proof, Badri Narsing confessed his involvement. The incident, not uncommon in the volatile history of the Nepalese Court, is notable for what followed.

While the Council of State recommended the usual punishment of death, Jung opted for leniency. The prisoners were exiled to India, to be kept under British surveillance, a first for the Nepalese court.

It remains to be substantiated if the act of clemency was the outcome of Jung's exposure to the western world, but the overseas visit certainly opened up an entirely different vista for Jung, which in turn had a profound effect on the future course of the kingdom. Convinced of the utility of education, Jung started a school inside his palace and invited an English teacher to impart education exclusively to his relatives. He was blatantly partial to the interests of his own family and shrewd enough to understand that education would expose the commoners, the duniyadars, to 'dangerous' concepts such as freedom and democracy. However, he did set in motion the practice of importing from abroad varieties of seeds and plants, Jersey cows and bulls and Cotswold sheep, for upgrading agriculture, horticulture, floriculture and animal husbandry[23].Thoroughbred horses and pedigreed canines were also imported for entertainment purposes. The first tea garden was also set up during these years in Ilam, a place blessed with climate similar to the tea gardens of Darjeeling.

With King Surendra reduced to being a pliant follower of Jung, the 'court of Nepal' and the entire machinery of governance functioned under the latter's exclusive command. Thanks to established law and traditions, all the land now belonged to Jung. Not just him, all the Rana prime ministers who succeeded him assumed and exercised the prerogative to receive the entire revenue of the state and allocate such sum as they wished to the state treasury. The balance was to be dispensed at their will for personal use or as a reward (bakas) to their supporters and followers.

Within this framework, a basic administrative network was established to cover the whole country. Kathmandu valley remained the focal point of governance. The rest of the territory was divided into four geographic/administrative regions, each with a headquarter called 'gaunda', to which a trusted senior Rana officer was appointed as the governor. The entire Terai area, from east to west—it was easier to access and had major areas under forest cover—was clubbed into one. The mountain belt was divided into three regions. The eastern region, with its gaunda at Dhankuta, covered all the territories east of the valley to the Indian border. The areas of the central region started from west of the valley up to Doti, with Palpa as its gaunda. Doti became the gaunda of the west region and covered the remaining territory to its west, reaching River Mahakali, which bisects Nepal and India. Each region was further sub-divided into districts governed by badahakims, appointed by Kathmandu. This arrangement remained largely intact through the Rana period.

At the centre, under the overall command of the all-powerful prime minister, Rana generals ranked in order of seniority headed 'departments' that carried out the day-to-day functions. The principal departments comprised the Jangi Adda (defence), Muluki Adda (internal security), Munsi Khana (foreign office), Muluki Khana (finance and treasury), Kumari Chowk (office of the accountant general), Ain Kausal and Ain Khana (covering the judicial field), Sadar Dafdar Khana (land management and revenue collection) and the Hulak Khana (the postal service). The administrative structure was rudimentary but decisions of the government were carried out effectively and without delay. This listing of departments clearly shows the limited area of state concerns and indifference towards vital sectors of public welfare and economic development, such as education, health, transport, agriculture, commerce and industry.

The most far-reaching legacy of Jung is the Muluki Ain, a comprehensive and uniform legal code that covered the entire country. A 230-member council completed the mammoth task of framing this code after nearly three years of extensive travels throughout the country and discourse with all sections of society.

The document was presented to the prime minister and, with minor adjustments, stamped with the Lal Mohur (royal seal) of the king, in 1854.

The document states that it is 'based upon the moral principles and traditions of the shastras' which was indeed the case. But it also declares that since the provisions of the (ancient) shastras cannot be applied to all matters arising in the changing ages and times, and because conflicting verdicts appear (in the past) for similar cases or offences: 'henceforth, on breach of law the punishment to all people high or low, shall be uniform in accordance with the nature of the crime and the caste of the person'.

On several counts the Muluki Ain is a landmark document. Starting with the 'Dharma Shastra' introduced during the Malla period, the law of Nepal was based on a legal treatise subject to change or interpretation by those holding legislative and/or judicial authority of the state, and not by the high priests. The Muluki Ain 'rationalized the judicial structure and codified legal principles of a common law throughout the nation that further substantiated the status of a sovereign state'[24].By defining the powers inherent in, and assigning definitive responsibilities to, institutions of governance, including that of the monarch and the prime minister, it ensured that specific provisions of law replaced arbitrary verdicts and thereby recognized the concept of 'rule of law', a vital element of the modern-day 'democratic' constitutions.

The Muluki Ain gave sanction to most of the extant bodies of religious practices, customs and social tradition of different regions and communities. In the process it did incorporate certain customs and practices, including those that propagated caste- and ethnicity-based discrimination. This provision has been quoted to condemn Jung Bahadur as the offender who gave sanction to the unequal caste divide. However, as narrated earlier, the offending interpretation of the caste divide based on accident of birth rather than the individual's mental temperament has prevailed in the Indian subcontinent for more than 2,500 years. It was given quasi-judicial sanction in Nepal by the Dharma Shastra, and the Shahs continued to uphold the practices.

Jung Bahadur could hardly have revamped the entire structure of the social order prevailing throughout the Hindu world, even if he wanted to.

However, some attempt was made by him to introduce reforms: savage forms of punishment were replaced by less severe alternatives; welfare measures for the marginalized sectors of society were incorporated; relationship between the state and the citizen, the landlord and the tiller was defined; and measures were initiated to alleviate the extremities attached to practices such as slavery and sati. The stranglehold of the feudal order and most of its ills remained intact, but a legal framework to quantify their limits was set by the Muluki Ain and the door was opened for future generations to initiate appropriate reforms.

The Muluki Ain covered practically every facet of governance, as well as public and private law. It left little room for discretionary interpretation, which often leads to abuse of power. It remained the basic legal treatise of the country until the 1960s and even thereafter with some essential changes and alterations from time to time. Many of its legal tenets continue to be operative to this day.

✖

Jung wrote a series of letters from Europe to his brother Ranodip Singh Kunwar, the caretaker premier. The precepts given therein should be viewed as his guidelines for good governance.

- The man who aims to earn a good name must abandon greed and adopt kindness.
- Give up wealth and control anger in order to please the majority.
- Convince your subjects that your decisions are fair, and all are equal in your eyes.
- Work done without compliance of the people will soon face problems.
- If you penalize ironmongers, cobblers and such (low-caste) workers, industry will suffer.[25]

Foreign Policy

The tour of Europe had confirmed Jung Bahadur's belief that England was the most powerful nation in the world with a dominant presence in India. Therefore, he felt that he needed to appease the British Empire to secure Nepal's southern border. The north was different. If need be, Nepal could confront Tibet to protect its interests, as China was not in a position to assist Tibet at the time even if it wanted to. And from the news reaching him from Tibet, Jung sensed that a need to face Tibet could arise soon.

The last time the two countries had gone to war was in 1772. At the time Nepal had been compelled to retreat and give up its claim to the strategic posts of Kuti and of Kerung, nestled atop the Himalayan watershed to the north of Kathmandu. However, the kingdom had retained the rights of trading in Tibet and of posting its envoy, the vakil, on a permanent basis in Lhasa. Relative peace had lasted near eighty years but by the mid-nineteenth century, Nepalese traders in Tibet were being harassed, their trading rights denied, and duty and fees extracted where none were due. Failing to redress the situation through negotiation, Jung decided 'we will now fight them'. It is evident that the prime minister was personally involved in every detail of the 'hit' on Tibet[26].

A detailed 'Military Code' was penned for the operation. Starting with the religious merits and glories attached to a war for the motherland, the handwritten 176-page document contained directions related to the code of conduct and pattern of behaviour required of the soldiers and officers; details of arms and ammunition, diet and uniform; minute notations of the route; the lay of the land; the distance to be covered each day; and places for night halts on each of the thirty-eight days' march from Kathmandu to Lhasa, across the high passes, including Kuti, Kerung and the flat Tibetan plateau thereafter. It assessed the strengths and weaknesses of the enemy, Tibet, and their possible supporter, China, and strategy of battles expected.

Consider the detailing of trek of one such day. The eighth night's halt from Kathmandu was at Tato Pani, still inside Nepalese territory. On the ninth morning, the soldiers had to set out for an eight-mile trek to Khas.

The first mile is a steep climb over stone steps—you cannot take the pony here. From the top of these steps there is a trek of one kos where you find an iron bridge, some fifty hand-measure in length: on this side is our territory and across the bridge, the Bhotiyas' (Tibet). After about another kos inside the Bhotiya territory, you will find another such bridge some twelve-hand-measure long. Further north from this bridge a narrow track of a mile along the gorge takes you to the small village of Khas: there are about twenty huts of the Bhotiyas in Khas; in addition ten soldiers, one Havaldar and one clerk, Khardar are posted there by the Tibet government. They will search the travellers before issuing passports needed to proceed further. You cannot get any provisions here. The route thereafter, a mile to the Kuti pass, is closed during three winter months when there is heavy snowfall; but if you have a guide to clear the snow and proper shoes, you can always cross over.

Three other 'major' trails were similarly mapped, constructed or repaired. One connected the capital with Ilam at the eastern border. The third and fourth ran westwards, one ending at the western border. The fourth, running some twenty miles apart, touched the celebrated holy Hindu pilgrimage sites, Badrinath and Kedarnath, 356 kos (one kos is equal to about two miles) or seven hundred miles and sixty-seven night halts away from Kathmandu. It was a remarkable achievement for those times.

As in past wars, teams of gaines or gandharvas, wandering minstrels with their one-stringed sarangi instruments and stirring battle songs, moved from village to village exhorting men to join the army. Contributions were sought, in cash, kind or in the form of labour, from each household, and the funds raised were used for production or procurement of weapons, tents, uniforms, animals and foodstuff, and to train and feed not just the soldiers but engineers, guides, porters, cooks and a whole range of helpers, carefully listed in the military code.

Prepared mentally and physically, the Gorkhali Army moved to 'hit' Bhot (Tibet) from five-high passes across the Himalayan watershed, under the overall direction of Jung Bahadur and the leadership of his brothers, including the indomitable Dhir Shumsher. As in the war some sixty years earlier, the first phase brought victories, forcing the enemy to sue for peace. However, the negotiations dragged on, possibly a clever move by the Tibetans, till the winter set in again. The next year, in 1856, the enemy regrouped and came back in greater numbers. The bare, jagged crags of the high Himalayan passes are dark and forbidding at any time of the year but in the winter, the bone-chilling cold, rarefied air and howling winds render the key outposts atop the cliffs in Kuti and Kerung a most sinister look—an ideal retreat for dracula! Dhir Shumsher was able to hang on to the key position of Kuti. But the battles were bitter, exhausting, and drained human and financial resources on both sides. Both agreed to meet at the negotiating table. Nepal agreed to withdraw its troops and forsake its claims on the mountain passes of Kuti and Kerung, Tibet to respect the rights of Nepalese traders to set up business in Lhasa, allow duty-free access for the import of Nepalese goods and make a token but symbolic payment of 10,000 rupees per annum. The Nepalese Vakil stationed in Lhasa was to monitor the terms of the treaty. Though challenged periodically, this arrangement remained largely intact until the end of the Rana regime.

Before the year ended, Jung suddenly resigned and handed over premiership to his brother Bom Bahadur. The reason remains unknown, but his future actions show that he moved swiftly to further consolidate his own authority and that of his family. The monarchy, in the form of the reigning King Surendra, soon surrendered what little powers remained with it. Through a Lal Mohur, dated 6 August 1856, Jung Bahadur Rana was granted the title of Shree Teen Maharaj of two districts of Kaski and Lamjung, and practically unlimited powers of governance over the entire kingdom, sole prerogative over a whole range of legislative, judicial and executive authority, and the position of an 'advisor' to the prime minister. The king ordered, 'my chiefs, nobles and army to abide by your orders even if I offer any resistance'. The new maharaj was granted these powers in perpetuity for himself and, upon his death, to his 'offspring and their offspring'[27].

Despite having the title, Bom Bahadur was bereft of all the authority of a normal prime minister. Furthermore, Jung was the senior member of the family and possessed a powerful personality, while Bom Bahadur suffered from tuberculosis. Yet, the British chose to deal with him, the prime minister, and ignore Jung. Perhaps, it was a matter of protocol or—more likely—they found the weaker man more amenable to the interests of the East India Company. The dilemma of duality of authority ended when Bom Bahadur died within a year of his assuming the office. For a few months Jung allowed another brother, Krishna, next in line, to rule as acting premier. But soon enough, the 'Sepoy Mutiny' or 'the First War of Independence' in India was at hand. Jung was not going to play second fiddle to anybody during such a critical phase in history. He persuaded King Surendra to issue a fresh Lal Mohur that restored the premiership to him. From 1857 to 1877 he ruled Nepal as Shree Teen Maharaj and prime minister, and did so with a combination of astute mind and iron hand that no other prime minister has been able to match.

The Indian Uprising of 1857–58 and 'The Lucknow Loot'

The maharaj was faced with a crucial decision as news of Governor General Canning seeking to quell the Indian Mutiny filtered in. If the British were discreetly seeking Nepal's support, Jung was also receiving messages from some Indian princes and nawabs beseeching him to join their valiant war against the colonial imperialists.

What should Nepal's stand be?

Besides the strength of the national army, there were two battalions of the British Gorkhas—the Sirmaur and Kumaon Battalions—operating in India. Their role in the Mutiny could not be taken for granted; Jung understood his position of strength.

Furthermore, he was in close touch with Brian Hodgson. In the 1830s the British resident had reluctantly left Nepal, following a disagreement with the governor in Calcutta. However, his profound interest in Nepal and the Himalayas was to remain his lifelong preoccupation. Not in a position to return, he continued to operate as an independent researcher and observer of Nepalese affairs from Darjeeling. His advice advocating closer friendship with Nepal was now being taken seriously by Calcutta and indeed London. Similarly, his counsel to Jung to help the British in their hour of need and seek adequate rewards in return made sound sense and was taken up with alacrity. Jung sought the help of the British scholar to do a little homework: what would be the yearly revenue from the areas lost by Nepal through the Treaty of Sugauli in 1923?

Hodgson came back with the figure of 500,000 rupees. Jung made his own simple calculations: multiply this figure by the forty-three years that the territories remained with the East India Company. He then offered to send his troops to suppress the rebellion but sought compensation for the revenue lost by his people and country. Preposterous as the logic and figures seemed, it was a good starting point for negotiations. Before the Nepalese troops were committed to the battle front, the British agreed to compensate the war efforts with rich returns.

The Sirmaur and Kumaon battalions marched to provide reinforcements to Delhi in the searing heat of midsummer. Two months later, the first Nepal army contingent under the command of General Dhir Shumsher left Kathmandu to relieve Lucknow. A few months later still, on the special request of Lord Canning, Jung himself led a force of 9,000 men to join the combined Indian and Gorkha forces in Awadh, enroute to Lucknow. In both the theatres of war, despite having to face the superior numbers of a determined and valiant opposition—the more organized and experienced fighting force under The East India Company—the supporting Nepali contingent ultimately prevailed.

'The defence of the main piquet in Delhi ranks with the defence of Lucknow among the epics of the centuries,' writes Sir Francis Tucker.[28]

Nine months had elapsed since the garrison in Meerut in North India had risen in mutiny to trigger off a widespread uprising. Staunch Indian nationalists and even some Nepalese point a finger at Jung for supporting foreign occupation in the subcontinent. In essence, the war of 1857 started as a mutiny in Meerut grew and spread rapidly to take the form of an uprising. Heroic battles were fought in many parts of Hindustan but in several regions the local rulers and the people sided with the British. As for Nepal, it was an independent nation with treaty obligations with a friendly and powerful Britain. Jung had looked where Nepal's interest lay and doggedly worked towards that end. At the end of the war Nepal was able to retrieve its costs involved in the war, an additional sum of 200,000 rupees and, crucially, some 2,000 square kilometres of fertile land in the western Terai plains[29]. This was not a magnanimous a reward as has been generally depicted; it was the outcome of Jung's shrewd and reasoned bargaining that preceded the involvement of the Nepal army.

For his family, his men in arms and himself, Jung was able to amass riches well beyond their imagination. In acts of vandalism and rape that generally follow such victories, the palaces and havelis of the nawabs were looted at will. As per unverified accounts, 400 bullock carts were hired to squeak their way slowly to Nepal, laden with what came to be known popularly as the 'Lucknow loot'. If the estimation of volume seems exaggerated, the value certainly is not. The nawabs of Lucknow possessed a collection of exquisite precious stones, jewellery and antiquities that matched or surpassed those of any other ruling chiefs. The treasures of the cultured nawabs of Awadh now belonged to the families of the rough and tough mountain warriors of Nepal.

Consolidation of the Rana Oligarchy

The tumultuous events of the twelve years following the elevation of Jung as prime minister in 1847 had helped take the power and prestige of the country and of the Rana oligarchy to a new level. In

1858, Britain decided to take full and direct control of governance over its territories in India and the Company passed into the pages of history. At the same time the Kingdom of Nepal was beginning to be viewed by some rulers of Hindustan as the one remaining free state and kingdom in the subcontinent where they could seek asylum from the vengeful colonial overlords. Many of the nobles and rulers in India and their family and followers, both Hindu and Muslim, who had sided with the rebels or indeed led the forces against the 'firangees', including the well-known Nana Sahib Peshwa, Rani Chand Kaur of Punjab and Begum Hazrat Mahal, wife of Nawab Wajid Ali Shah of Awadh, escaped, entered the southern territories of Nepal with a fairly large number of their followers and then sought asylum.

Jung first ensured that their fighting force was disarmed and then accepted their plea halfway. Nana sahib was told that Nepal was an ally of the British and so could not accept the men who had fought against them. Jung did offer asylum, though, to the womenfolk, the ranis and begums, and their children and dependants. They were escorted safely to Kathmandu and housed in comfort and with the respect due to guests of royal lineage. This gracious act was not driven by chivalry alone. The families of the nawabs and the princes had brought with them precious stones and jewellery, some of which matched the best in the world.[30] A 'naulakha haar', a necklace of multiple strings of the finest pearls, was and remains the proudest possession, last reported to be with the Darbhanga royal family. A three-inch long clear emerald, once used as a royal seal by the Peshwa, now became the centrepiece on the glittering Sripetch[31] of the prime ministers[32]. Passing through many hands, a brilliant single stone diamond ring, reported to weigh forty carats, was, decades later, presented by Richard Burton to Elizabeth Taylor on her fortieth birthday. The weight may be an exaggeration, but it does reflect the impression the treasures created.

Along with the power and the riches, Jung had moved to upgrade the social status of the family. Soon after he assumed the premiership, relying on[33], inscriptions carved on a large stone plaque in the Udaipur palace he was able to link the genealogy of the Kunwars to the House of Mewar, the Sisodias, said to be descendants of the Sun God, no less. In 1848 Jung obtained a Lal Mohur from King Surendra confirming the Sisodia lineage and the privilege to adopt the name of Rana. It opened the route for the Ranas to strike marriage alliances with the Rajput princes from India. Inside Nepal, too, Jung started the tradition of matrimonial alliances with the royals, he married Hiranya Garva Devi, a sister of Fateh Jung Shah, the former prime minister. His son Jagat Jung wedded a daughter of King Surendra, and his six-year-old daughter was given in marriage to Crown Prince Trailokya, just three years older. Hiranya Garva Devi was Jung's fourth wife, but given the highest honour and title of Bada Maharani. She played an important role in Jung's life. However, the nearest to his heart was Putali Nani, a comely maid-in-waiting, attached to Queen Rajya Laxmi, who used to bring all the news of the palace to Jung before he became prime minister. She then moved to the Thapathali Durbar and the warm embrace of Jung.

As Greta Rana wrote, 'Marriage alliances were generally axes of power 'not affairs of heart'[34].

Around these decades, the court of Kathmandu gradually moved away from the rustic ways and manners of the mountain people. One notices a distinct attempt to adopt the western style. Elaborate attire, rich in texture and in line with European fashions, new styles to suit the long hair (tradition forbade women to trim their hair) and facial makeup adorned the ladies of the court. Italian marble, ornate mirrors and crystal chandeliers from Europe enriched the ambience of the palaces. In other matters, Jung preferred the traditions and tastes of the princely states of India. Urdu words, as were in vogue in Hindustan, entered the vocabulary of the court and law courts, in particular. Chefs from the maharaja or the nawab households were brought in and the rich flavours of Mughlai cooking wafted out from the palace kitchens. Several wings were added and attached to the Thapathali Durbar to accommodate the scores of married maharanis and ranis Jung acquired, as well as the hundreds of nani sahibs (concubines), talimes (maids selected for their musical talent and beauty) and maidservants he chose to 'honour' for short amorous forays or more permanent cohabitation.[35] Some of his young brothers and sons, too, at times, sneaked into the Zenana (ladies') quarters to enjoy one or two comely maids from their father's vast collection[36]. These indulgences produced a large number of daughters and sons.

Perhaps to consolidate his personal powers or prune the disloyal or incapable, Jung Bahadur introduced and imposed the convention of the Roll of Succession through a Lal Mohur issued by King Surendra. It listed, in hierarchical order, the names of his brothers entitled to succeed him, on the basis of seniority, and then those of the following generation. He omitted some of them at his sole discretion. He altered this order once more in 1868. Furthermore, he chose to induct his 'illegitimate'[37] male offspring into the Roll as well. This practice is not adopted by the Shah rulers or the Rajput rulers of India from where the Ranas claim their lineage, or by the rulers of Europe or Great Britain. However, Jung was not inclined to follow others and compiled the list as he found fit. Citing this convention, arbitrary decisions, often disregarding the criteria of seniority or legitimacy, but designed to suit the interests of the individual prime minister, were made by prime ministers who succeeded Jung. The strain and bitterness, such a practice generated, ultimately tore apart the ruling family in 1934.

The country, however, moved through a rare period of stability. In stark contrast to his earlier life of stress and tumult, Jung spent his last twenty years (till his death in 1877) in leisure attending functions to honour him, riding, picnicking, and hunting each winter in the Terai; the evenings were spent with the women in his life and the lull of opium. There were a few hiccups, no doubt. In the summer of 1860, a cholera epidemic devastated the capital, killing and driving out thousands of its residents and three years later a famine raged in Kathmandu and several hill districts. The smooth relationship with Tibet, that had prevailed since the treaty of 1848, was rudely shaken fifteen years later on account of a thrashing meted out to a Nepali Vakil by the courtiers in Lhasa, following heated discussions related, once more, to the rights of Nepalese traders. Mercifully, before the incident could explode into another war, peace and harmony was restored following an apology from Lhasa and formal assurance that such behaviour would not be repeated in future.

Jung had to deal with a curious incident during the last phase of his reign. A Magar in mid-west Nepal was seized by a premonition that he was an incarnation of Ram Lakhan Thapa, a renowned leader of his race in ethnic lore, and that their traditional goddess Manakamana had ordered him to restore the rule of the Magar people. His spirited call to the simple people of that race to take up arms met with a spontaneous response from more than 1,500 men. However, Jung sent a sufficiently strong contingent to subdue the rebellion. Those engaged or suspected of involvement in a plot to assassinate the maharaj, including Ram Lakhan, were executed.

In 1877 Jung left Kathmandu for his annual hunting expedition. Some say he knew it would be his last. The year before, he had already distributed most of his personal wealth and property to his ranis, children and other close relatives and followers. He was taken seriously ill and died before he could be taken back to Kathmandu. Hiranya Devi and Putali, out of several of his ranis and nani sahebs, chose to commit 'sati', even though Jung was known to have expressed his wish for them to avoid the ordeal.

Chapter Five

Decline of the Jungs and Rise of the Shumshers

Jung's death plunged the country into another phase of battle for power. As decreed by the Lal Mohur of June 1857, King Surendra appointed Ranodip Singh, Jung's eldest surviving brother, as the prime minister[38]. However, another edict dated 6 August 1856, as mentioned earlier, had bestowed the title of 'Maharaj' on Jung, and with it the right to exercise full authority of governance over the kingdom. The powers attached to this title were to pass to Jung's eldest son, Jagat Jung.

Neither of the two protagonists possessed the gumption to act decisively. The powerful intervention of Dhir Shumsher, the youngest brother, a fearless leader respected by the bhardars and the army alike, tilted the balance. It was but natural for Dhir to back Ranodip, for his own claim on the Roll of Succession could only be derived through and after his brother. King Surendra was persuaded to confer the additional title of maharaj and the prerogatives attached with it upon Prime Minister Ranodip Singh. As 'Shree Teen Maharaj and Prime Minister of Nepal', Ranodip now inherited full authority of governance and Sripetch that projected the rising power of the Rana oligarchy. Hereafter, the agnatic system was adopted and followed in all cases of succession to these titles and the position. However, Ranodip was not fated to wield his authority in full measure or enjoy its fruits for long. Suspected to be weakened by consumption, he was content to let Dhir, patriarch of the Shumsher clan, to take charge of most of the affairs of the state.

Jagat Jung was well aware that his rightful claim was being usurped. He was determined to fight back. Crown Prince Trailokya (son of King Surendra and grandson of Rajendra, still alive then in captivity) backed his campaign to repossess his title and powers of maharaj. But Trailokya died shortly after, as did Surendra, a few years later in 1881. Thus, Prithvi Bir Bikram Shah, the five-year-old son of the late crown prince Trailokya, was placed on the throne. Jagat Jung, realizing he had lost his support base, decided to find a safe exit to India. Then the Ranas had to contend with another serious threat within a year, a united front of the old aristocracy, the Thapas, Pandes and Basnets. These families had been victims of persecution and purge that had removed them from the centre stage of power, and were now planning a comeback. However, Dhir got wind of a plot to assassinate leading members of the Ranas, especially the Shumshers. In his role as acting prime minister while the maharaj was in the Terai on shikar, he moved swiftly to dispatch a contingent of armed force where the leading conspirators were gathered. Taken by surprise, they were arrested without resistance, kept in chains, tortured and made to confess their crime. Upon return of Ranodip all those convicted and suspected of involvement either faced death sentence, imprisonment or expulsion from the valley of Kathmandu. The Shumshers and their trusted men moved into key positions in the reorganized state structure.

The sweeping coverage of the victims, severity of punishment and strict vigilance that followed ensured that members of these aristocratic families never again raised a rebellion and were gradually assimilated within the favoured fold of the Rana administration. Although Jagat Jung was in India at the time, he was held guilty and debarred from entering Nepal.

The smooth course of life in the capital was once again disrupted by the death of Dhir Shumsher in 1884. Jagat Jung saw an opening and moved to the battlefield of Kathmandu court politics. He had contacted and found potent allies in the Thapathali Durbar, the senior Maharani of Ranodip, and Hari Priya, a burly bully whose voice was often decisive in state matters. The power equation between the Jungs and Shumshers now fluctuated fitfully, each side aware that defeat would lead to annihilation. At a crucial stage of the tug of war, destiny placed the trump card in the hands of the Shumshers. Bir Shumsher, eldest of Dhir's seventeen sons, had been assigned the task of leading a contingent of the Nepal army to participate in a military exercise in Delhi on invitation of the British. The brothers, sons of Dhir, decided to strike while the iron was hot at the very heart of the power structure. One cold November evening, five of the seventeen brothers moved into the Narayan Hiti Palace where the prime minister resided[39]. Some of them stood guard at the entry points and the rest entered the private quarters of the prime minister, their uncle who had been trusting and kind to them. The old man was reclining in his private chamber, leisurely getting his feet massaged. He was shot several times and died instantly. In the meantime, the palace guards stationed outside had been either intimidated or taken into confidence by a group led by Chandra Shumsher. The Shumshers had also managed to garner the support of the junior Queen Mother, Lalita Kumari, who now helped them get the Lal Mohur appended and signed by her ten-year-old son, King Prithvi Bir Bikram, appointing Bir Shumsher as the new prime minister and maharaj of Nepal.

The ruthless coup was executed with remarkable speed and precision. It was a quick and cruel act, undertaken to counter the threat to their lives. That same night, groups of armed squads loyal to the Shumshers moved to eliminate leaders in the opposing group, including Jagat Jung. Some others from the Jung camp managed to flee and took refuge in the British residency. They were later moved to India. Property of those who fled or were exiled was seized.

The death of Jung Bahadur, the succession of his younger brother Ranodip rather than Jung's son, and the assassination of Ranodip eight years later by the Shumsher brothers are historical milestones. In the valley of Kathmandu, including the rented rooms of Nandikeshwar Koirala[40], such news was a topic of discussion, but the remarks of his wife Rajya Laxmi in Dumja (a two-day trek, east of Kathmandu), an intelligent woman whose husband was a government officer, speaks for all those who lived beyond the valley.

'What does it matter to us whether it is Surendra or Prithvi as King, or Jung, Ranodip or Bir Shumsher as the prime minister? We merely have to accept and follow the order of the ruler. Still, at least the Ranas are not cowards. The country cannot prosper under spineless kings.'[41]

Many who lived in remote parts of the country got the news months later.

The policy of keeping the country isolated from outside influence, adopted by Prithvi Narayan Shah and followed by the Ranas, had multiple dimensions. It helped safeguard the sovereignty of the country and at the same time preserved the feudal order by blocking 'dangerous' concepts such as freedom and liberty. The prime minister exercised his absolute authority and held a tight rein on the governance of the country, despite its arduous terrain and difficult access. The Jagirdars and Birtawals, the pillars of the despotic oligarchy, owed their total allegiance to the prime minister. They relied on the favours 'nigah' of the Maharaj to govern the huge tracts of 'Birta' land bestowed as a grant, to levy and collect tax from the peasants, or mete out punishments for any real or perceived misdemeanour or felonious act. The governors appointed by the Prime Minister and empowered with wide ranging authority were often more indiscriminate than the rulers in far off Kathmandu; but each and every one of them and the officials under them were subject to dismissal or worse during the yearly reviews, under the dreaded Pazani system. The peasants were saddled with several layers of masters and burdened with payment of tax or levy, in cash, kind or in the form of free labour, leaving them to scratch out a subsistent existence at best.

Despite these constraints, the situation of the peasants and labour force was better than that of their counterparts in India, where the British colonialists or Indian princes extracted even greater toll from the subjects, the *ryots*. Shiploads of agro products, acquired at the lowest rates, left the seaports regularly to feed English mills, whereas both the state and the traders in Nepal ensured that export of food grains, herbs, purified butter, musk and opium, amongst other products, fetched the highest available price across the southern or northern border. Conversely, where the Indian market was flooded with machine-made goods from England, causing great distress to weavers and local producers in general, the policy of restricting imports helped households or cottage industries in Nepal keep the wheels of production turning and meet the demand for practically every need of a simple lifestyle. As a result, the balance of trade of the country, whether with India or Tibet, remained in favour of Nepal throughout the Rana period. And so, communities, even those suffering the humiliation of an inferior social status and forced into the confines of menial jobs, learnt or were resigned to live within the limits of a hard, unequal but homogeneous lifestyle. This internal stability and self-reliance provided a cushion for the national economy withstand the crippling blow of an alternative, much shorter trade route built by the British in the 1880s to connect Tibet with Calcutta. With this route, Kathmandu lost its pre-eminence as the pivotal centre of the Indo-Tibet trade route[42].

Chapter Six

Maharaj Bir Shumsher (1885–1901)

The new maharaj, Bir Shumsher, moved quickly to alter the Roll of Succession, removing all other Rana brothers and cousins including the Jungs, Bikrams, Prataps and Narsings. The new Roll consisted of seventeen Shumshers exclusively, headed by Bir. Six of them were to rule Nepal in turn as maharaj and prime minister until the fall of the regime.

The cold-blooded murder of Ranodip was viewed by the British authorities as a barbaric act and the viceroy was reluctant to recognize the new prime minister. Even the moderate British resident, Colonel Wylie, wrote in a letter that ultimately recommended recognition of Bir, 'the present Minister and his family are as bad as they can be—even Jung Bahadur was steeped in blood' but then went on to add 'and it seems to me that it does not matter to us which set of cut throats has the upper hand' as long as they 'render services to us'. Two months later the British governor general reluctantly confirmed his government's official recognition of Bir Shumsher as maharaj and prime minister.[43]

A bright and hardworking student at the school in Thapathali Durbar, Bir had been selected from among dozens of Rana boys to go to Calcutta for 'higher' studies and later as a 'Vakil'. He lived up to the expectations of his elders and attained proficiency in Sanskrit, Nepali, Urdu, Farsi and English. By the time he took up the reins of prime ministerhood, he had gained wide experience in governance, including as Governor of Palpa.

On assumption of the Rajya (state power), immense wealth fell into the hands of Bir Shumsher. The Muluki Ain conferred upon the prime minister the right and authority to possess and disburse state funds at his sole discretion. From the single-crowded dwelling they shared earlier, each of the seventeen brothers could and did move into mansions of their rival cousins or nobles who had been killed or exiled. In due course, they were also granted additional Birta lands, measuring thousands of hectares. However, Bir's most valuable acquisition was the bounty of precious jewellery—sparkling diamonds, emeralds, rubies and pearls that came from the treasuries of the fleeing Indian royalty. A major portion of that priceless collection, either from the Lucknow loot or from royal refugees who had sought shelter in Kathmandu, had been passed on to Prime Minister Ranodip, the eldest son Jagat Jung, and possibly some of the other brothers. Bir now got hold of the whole lot and retained the major portion for himself.

The Jungs, however, had not yet given up. With assistance of some Rajput princes, Jit Jang, the eldest surviving son of Jung Bahadur who had escaped to India, were able to assemble a sizable armed force and launch a series of skirmishes across the border. But contrary to their expectations they found little support inside the country and were driven back each time, often with heavy losses. Attempts to assassinate the Shumsher rulers too were nipped in the bud. The Shumshers had a firm hold over the army and created an effective intelligence network. Gradually, Bir was able to build a healthy working relationship and develop personal rapport with the British in India that commenced with his visit to Calcutta and meeting with Viceroy Lord Dufferin in 1888. Concessions in recruitment of the Gorkha troops was reason enough for the firm footing on which the British–Nepali cooperation and friendship flourished. Restraining anti-Nepal activities by the Jungs or any other element in India was a natural act of quid-pro-quo. The Jungs were facilitated to acquire ample landed property in the vicinity of Allahabad, where the family founded their permanent base.

A plot to assassinate the prime minister emanated from within the country. His brother Khadga, next in line of succession, was the prime suspect while being actively involved with one of the queen mothers and two daughters of Jung Bahadur. Either the able and energetic brother was not satisfied with the distribution of riches after the coup or that the maharaj pulled him up for exceeding his authority. As soon as the allegation was brought forward, he was arrested and expelled from Kathmandu. He was later appointed governor of Palpa, a convenient place of banishment from Kathmandu but also one of importance.

As time passed, Bir expanded the family alliance between the royal family and his own children, the Shumshers. He also initiated measures for the welfare of the people. A piped drinking-water system was installed for the first time in the valley, to supplement the traditional sources through the Raj Kulos (royal canal system). Underground drainage and sewerage lines were laid in the inner cities, 'large enough for ponies to run along the interior'. Indeed, they still constitute the main drainage system for the vastly increased waste of the cities. A well-equipped, modern (Bir) hospital and the city clock tower are two prominent landmarks constructed by Bir that continue to serve the people of the valley. A few bridges and health centres were created outside the valley, a feeble gesture no doubt, but the first hints of intent. As with most Rana prime ministers, Bir made little effort to spread education amongst the duniyadars, but did build a splendid edifice to house the Durbar High School, attached with a well-stocked library. For the first time students other than those belonging to the Rana families, could attend high school.

Bir's most spectacular and lasting contribution to the country, however, was as an avid 'builder' of grand and splendid palaces. Within months of his accession he started planning the construction of three large palaces. The Seto Durbar (white palace), Rato Durbar (red palace) and Phohra Durbar (fountain palace) were built in one spectacular line, flanking and overshadowing the royal Narayan Hiti palace. They were constructed under the supervision of a Nepali architect, using local building material, but the style was western, reflecting Calcutta's grandiose colonial architecture and what Bir had seen in photographs of the neo-classical palaces of Europe. The interior, too, was wholly international. Snow-white Italian marble flooring, fountains, sparkling chandeliers and mirrors framed with colourful glass work, exotic rugs and carpets from the Middle

East, priceless Baroque French furniture and Ming vases, rendered these palaces a fairy-tale grandeur. The accusation that the Ranas neglected the traditional Licchavi and Malla styles is valid but practical considerations influenced the decision. The neo-classical structures form a distinct wing, a tangent perhaps, of the Kathmandu skyscape. Spread across the country, albeit sparsely outside the valley, they now find their rightful place as important heritage sites on the architectural map of the country.

More perceptive observers may, however, admire the prime minister as an avid propagator of classical music, an uncommon trait amongst the rulers of Nepal. It was perhaps in Calcutta that Bir picked up his taste and ever-consuming interest in Hindustani classical music, Shashtriya Sangeet. When he learnt that two extraordinary music masters, Wastaj Taj Khan and Dhundi Khan, who were attached to the court of Nawab Wajid Ali Shah, were compelled to spend their days as wandering fakirs, after the nawab was kept under house arrest in Calcutta by the British government, he is said to have visited Lucknow personally and persuaded them to join his court in Kathmandu. There they imparted their skills to keen students. Amongst a galaxy of ranis, nani sahibs, maids and the talimes, maids carefully selected for training in dance or music, housed in the opulent palaces Bir had built, they found a readymade school of music and dance.

The two Wastaj from Lucknow volunteered to take the most skilled and talented under their wing. As was the practice in case of maids in the palaces, the talimes were given fascinating new names, *Ishk Pari* (angel of love), *Husn Pari* (angel of beauty), *Angoor Pari* (angel of grapes) and *Hari Maya* (God's love).

More lasting gift of Bir to the growth of classical music was his personal and the state's patronage of several informal schools that sprung up in Kathmandu. They have blossomed into modern-day institutions of classical music and flourish under the wings of colleges and universities.

In the final years of Bir's reign, a memorable festival of classical music was held in Nepal. The venue chosen was a little-known village,

Bagari near Birgunj. Camps were erected to accommodate more than a hundred performers from India, each a maestro in their own disciplines. After several days of rousing performances, the winner was rewarded with coins to cover his whole body and the gift of a pearl necklace presented by the maharaj[44]. Nothing like this festival has ever been staged in Nepal before or since and the grandeur of the Bagari Music Festival is talked about by generations of musicians in the subcontinent to this day.

Bir died in 1901 to be succeeded through a smooth transition of power, by Dev Shumsher.

Chapter Seven

Maharaj Dev Shumsher
(March–June 1901)

Maharaj Dev Shumsher was the first Rana prime minister whose disposition was genuinely liberal. Within weeks of taking charge of his office, he called a 'Grand Council' of the nobility, religious leaders, high-ranking civil and military officers, businessmen and also some farmers and common people. The aim was to involve the people in the decision-making process. A day-long assembly held in the Thapathali Durbar was the first of its kind in Nepal and threw up several suggestions. He followed up on this initiative by installing a number of 'suggestion boxes' at key junctions in the valley. The launch of the first newspaper of the country, the *Gorkha Patra,* was his outstanding and lasting contribution. It has since occupied a premium position in the Nepalese media world.

Dev was keen to end the age-old practice of slavery and issued a proclamation to liberate all female slaves in Kathmandu and the two districts of Kaski and Lamjung. His most ambitious project called for the introduction of 'universal primary education' in the country. He appointed an exceptionally talented young man, Jaya Prithvi Bahadur Singh, the Raja of Bajhang, to launch the programme[45]. As a follow-up, around fifty elementary schools were launched in different parts of the country. Well-meaning and liberal as these measures were, they lacked necessary planning and preparation. The prime minister had not consulted, or at least failed to involve, his brothers, senior and powerful members of his government, in his overambitious enterprises. Second in the Roll of Succession, Mukhtiyar Chandra Shumsher believed that the goals set by Dev were impractical and the schemes and measures detrimental to the longevity and interests of the Rana regime. The powerful majority of the Bhai bhardars and dominant components of both civil and military administration were of the same view.

Furthermore, the good intentions of the maharaj were in stark contrast to his indulgent and indolent lifestyle. It was customary for a new prime minister to celebrate the occasion of his accession by a Sindure Jatra, where the maharaj along with a grand procession drove down the streets of Kathmandu, mounted on an elephant, in a splendid carriage drawn by eight horses. Dev repeated this costly function at least three (some say six) times in less than four months that he managed to hold on to his office. His passion for women, too, carried him well beyond the line of discretion. The maharaj made a habit of visiting the royal Narayan Hiti Palace, at times spending nights there, to indulge in amorous play with the nanis, a slight to the dignity of the royal household. In one of his inebriated bouts he asked his hazuria general, Gehendra Shumsher, son of Bir, to deliver a young woman, the latter's favourite, to the Thapathali palace for Dev's pleasure. Through these and similar excesses, Dev soon lost the trust and support of key members of his family, the bhardars and the civil and military officers. The indulgent activities allowed the prime minister little time for effective governance or to detect the ambitious intentions of his brother Chandra. Had he been more alert, perhaps he would not have chosen Chandra to lead the team to manage the Shikar Camp in Morang, eastern Nepal, where the chief guest was Lord Curzon, the dynamic new governor general of India. On the pretext of a hunting trip, Curzon had come to learn about the state of politics in Nepal, first hand. Some authors have suggested that Chandra briefed the governor general about his brother's extravagance, his unrealistic plans for reforms, and got tacit approval for unseating the prime minister. These claims are unsubstantiated, but the dramatic events that followed clearly suggest that Chandra made a good impression upon Curzon. It was to stand him in good stead during the decades that followed.

Capable, shrewd and ambitious, Chandra moved stealthily to

unite and galvanize the forces of dissent into a telling weapon to remove his brother, and elevate himself to the top-most tier of political power. It was not difficult to convince the royal palace or members of the Rana family, victims of Dev's condescending behaviour and lascivious designs on their women.

Senior officers of Bijuli Garat, the special force posted to guard the prime minister, were also drawn into the plot. Dev was isolated from the very forces he trusted to guard his interests. On a hot and humid afternoon in late June, Dev was lured by Bir's sons, including his trusted hazuria general, to visit Seto Durbar to mediate on a family dispute. Chandra was also invited. On entering one of the inner chambers of the palace the prime minister was overpowered by his brothers and cousins, tied up and told by Chandra that he was being deposed as he had lost the confidence of the court. While the stunned and helpless Dev was kept under surveillance, Chandra proceeded to another room where King Prithvi Bir Bikram Shah, then twenty-six years old, had already been brought in from the Narayan Hiti Palace across the road. Willingly or otherwise, the king put his seal on a letter ordering Dev's banishment and issued the Lal Mohur that conferred the title of maharaj and prime minister on Chandra Shumsher.

Armed by the official sanction of the monarch, Chandra now emerged from Seto Durbar with the king at his side to proclaim his new position. No one stood up to oppose him.

Dev Shumsher and his rani were sent to Dhankuta, the headquarters of eastern Nepal, the same evening, with an adequate but not generous pension. After some years, Dev proceeded to Mussoorie with his family and followers. There he built a mansion, raised his family and lived in comfort till the end of his days.

A trusted advisor of Chandra has recorded verbatim the thoughts of the new maharaj, 'Circumstances forced me to do what I never wanted to. On the basis of a unanimous view and for the good of the country and of the Rana family I had to undertake this action'[46]. The claim is supported by the fact that he had marshalled a wide range of crucial power centres of the state to achieve the meticulously planned coup without Dev, the prime minister, ever sensing the emerging plot. Chandra always took this stand and pointed out that not a drop of blood was shed in the takeover. Yet, the fact remains that it was a devious coup.

PART II

High Tide of the Rana Regime

Chapter One

Maharaj Chandra Shumsher (1901–1929)

The decades either side of 1900–01, as Chanda Shumsher became Prime Minister, are replete with dramatic breakthrough in science and technology in the western world, and of unprecedented industrial growth. In Asia, to the north of Nepal, the peasants' revolt in China—where more than 100,000 rioting men reportedly looted and killed about 1,500 foreign residents and missionaries—was eventually quelled by American and European troops; a strong contingent stayed back in Peking to quell future uprisings. Across Nepal's southern border, the yearning for Indian nationhood was rising rapidly. By the year 1900, the Indian National Congress openly threw a challenge to the British Raj. 'Swaraj (freedom) is my birthright and I will have it,' Bal Gangadhar Tilak roared and his words raced across India, inciting an unquenchable hunger for freedom and human dignity.

In Nepal, however, the Rana oligarchy was able till then to keep the people away from the news of the stirring upheavals elsewhere, and thereby, postpone the quest for freedom from oppression.

It was in this scenario that Chandra Shumsher took command of the state of Nepal. The responsibility of bringing some order and progress to this land of rugged terrain and racial diversity fell on the slender shoulders of 'this maharaj with a tiny and thin neck, miniscule waistline and a chest the size of a bird, who they say, looked exactly like a sparrow plucked of its feathers when he shed his clothes!'[47]

Chandra took pains to wrap his upper body in a thick cummerbund before donning the official regal attire, so that he carried himself as a maharaj, the centre of supreme power and authority of the kingdom. He more than made up for his fragile physical shape through his sterling qualities.

In his twenty-nine years as the prime minister, Chandra proved that he was as adept at statecraft as he had been at political cunning and manoeuvre earlier. Lord Morley, the Secretary of State for India during that period, described him as 'certainly much more than an ordinary man'. Sir Francis Tuker[48] thought of him as 'the best fitted of all the prime ministers of Nepal to exercise the powers of that office'. Adrian Sever[49] sums him up aptly, 'a benevolent dictator who would brook no opposition to his rule...no detail of business was too small for his attention and little escaped his notice'.

Chandra was ruthless when achieving his purpose, astute in the handling of state affairs and 'scheming' or a 'tyrant' in the eyes of his critics. He selected wise and competent counsellors and possessed an inborn talent for 'man management' that served him well. B.P. Koirala, whose family suffered greater hardships than anyone else on account of Chandra, concedes that 'once one meets him, nobody can forget him.'

After his early years in Nepal, Chandra Shumsher was sent to Calcutta for higher studies. The only one among the seventeen male siblings of Dhir Shumsher who completed his matriculation, Chandra received high praise from the English Vice-Chancellor, 'a young student who holds a high military command in the army of Nepal and has shown on this occasion that he can handle the pen no less efficiently than the sword'. He excelled in English language. Those days, very few in Nepal, if any, possessed this proficiency, and it gave him an added edge in the course of his eventful reign. An even more distinct trait separated him from all other Rana rulers—he was a workaholic. From six in the morning till his bedtime, he devoted his energies to affairs of the state. Though he did take out some time for his daily prayers, he had little interest and lesser time for outdoor activities or sports. His habits were spartan. He ate sparingly, did not indulge in alcoholic drinks or drugs, had one wife who he loved dearly and married a second one, reluctantly, upon the early demise of the first[50]. His household and personal expenses were carefully budgeted to provide for a simple but comfortable lifestyle. Many of these qualities were passed on to his children, and further to the generations after them.

Consolidation of Authority

Having gone through a series of plots and counter-plots along his route to the premiership, Chandra's first priority was to try and ensure his safety and tenure of office. On this front he was fortunate in many ways. The second in line of succession, Bhim Shumsher spent a great part of his day in elaborate religious rituals. He was not an ambitious man and not inclined to take any risks to upstage the prime minister. He remained loyal and always extended his sincere and valuable support to his senior brother. Next in line was Juddha, a powerful character, but twelve years younger and wise enough to wait for his inevitable turn. Fourth in line was Rudra, with whom Chandra shared a genuine feeling of mutual goodwill and affection. Padma, a weak and solitary man, was fifth and thereafter came a formidable trio of Chandra's three capable sons, Mohan, Baber and Keshar. Mohan, appointed to be hazuria general, justified the trust placed on him as an astute and able administrator. Baber was a natural athlete, born to be an exceptional military leader. The third brother, Keshar, equipped with an eidetic memory, was a veritable encyclopaedia. A degree of competitive edge might have coloured the three brothers, but in matters of common interest they combined their respective strengths and maintained a powerful influence in state affairs.

Chandra did not feel the need to make any change in the roll as it stood. Nevertheless, following similar actions of his predecessors, he assembled at the sanctum of the 'kul devata' (family deity), twenty-eight senior members of the Roll and persuaded them to sign the Dharma Patra, a document swearing allegiance and support to him and to a revised Roll of Succession he might choose to establish at a future date. Those who signed the document were mostly the legitimate 'A'-class Ranas but also included some 'C'-class nephews[51]. It was only during the final years of his reign that the issue of A, B and C classification created a friction within the Rana family.

Again, following the trend set by his predecessors, indeed the age-old strategy of consolidation of power through matrimonial alliance, the new maharaj negotiated weddings for three of his sons with the royal princesses. Nevertheless, a strict vigil was kept on the affairs of the palace. Such alliances continued through the generations but did not fulfil the aim and hope of a strong political bond between the two families. Neither ever trusted the other. The royal hand, eventually, was a critical propellant in bringing down the Rana oligarchy.

The British Connection

Chandra was determined to cement his position and that of the Rana regime on a broader front. He was convinced that good relations with the British Empire would be the cornerstone on which the Rana regime could build a sturdy base; a policy guideline set by Jung Bahadur. The measures he adapted to this end also fitted his goal of making his country a sovereign nation, free from the bondage of colonial rule that prevailed over the rest of the subcontinent. He worked tirelessly and astutely to meet these two primary goals. Even as a young student in Calcutta, he had noted the significance of the British Raj in India. On return to Kathmandu, with a good knowledge of the English language, he was an automatic choice to assist Prime Minister Bir as a modern-day foreign minister. He accompanied the maharaj on his visits to Calcutta and learnt the norms of diplomatic etiquette and, indeed, the character and motives of the British rulers of India. By the time he assumed supreme powers of the state, Chandra was well aware of the strength of the British Empire in global politics, and so cultivated their friendship and managed to gain their confidence and respect. The British resident in Kathmandu, Colonel Wylie, reported to the viceroy in Calcutta that Chandra Shumsher was 'clever, sharp and ready to be loyal' to the British interests[52]. These were some of the reasons why the British were not unduly perturbed by the manner in which Chandra engineered the eviction of his predecessor Dev through a devious coup, and recognized him as the new prime minister without delay[53].

As prime minister, Chandra duly reciprocated. One of his first moves on assumption of office was dispatch of a letter expressing his 'sacred duty and valued privilege to cultivate and continue unimpaired, the friendly relations subsisting between the Governments of India and Nepal'[54]. The gesture of friendship was sincere, but so was the hint of claim of the status of two independent nation-states. Chandra welcomed the opportunity to visit Delhi in 1903 on the invitation of the viceroy. He took a firm stand to be recognized as an ambassador of a different country. They exchanged notes about the threat posed to both Britain and Nepal by Russia's intervention in the ongoing conflict between China and Tibet. It is reported that during a meeting with the viceroy, the latter sought and received the commitment from Chandra that Nepal would assist Britain in the event of British invasion in Tibet. Within a year the viceroy was to make that decision. British forces in India, under Colonel Francis Young Husband, were sent across the border, with Nepal's consent. Overriding the obligations of the Nepal–Tibet Treaty of 1856, Chandra obliged the invading army, giving access to mules, yaks and porters to transport the large stock of equipment and materials across Nepalese territory. Once the Tibetan resistance was broken and British troops entered Lhasa, Chandra helped broker the treaty. The British presence in Tibet was also in Nepal's interests: it prevented Russian dominance and balanced the Chinese presence in the global power game, thus preserving the position of Nepal as a convenient 'buffer state'.

Chandra combined finesse in international diplomacy with his personal touch of friendship and hospitality. The same year he invited Lord Kitchener, the commander-in-chief of India, to visit Kathmandu. The maharaj was bestowed with the honorary rank of general in the British army, a much sought-after 'honour' by Indian princes. The grand shikar expedition of King George V in 1911 inside the dense forests and diverse topography of the southern plains, the Terai region, was one of the high points of the Emperor's trip to the subcontinent[55]. The rare adventure of the shikar and sumptuous hospitality of the state attracted the son of the emperor, Edward, Prince of Wales, on a similar expedition ten years later, in 1921. These gestures did strain the resources of the state but they also laid the groundwork for Chandra's ultimate aim and achievement in gaining the status of a sovereign nation-state for the mountain kingdom in 1923.

Chandra also wished to visit England. He wanted to meet the British monarch in person and gain direct, first-hand knowledge of various aspects and wings of governance of the most powerful empire in human history. He also wanted to learn about the social and cultural life of Europe, so very different from Asia, as well as go for a medical examination and possible treatment of suspected tuberculosis. However, his ultimate goal was to obtain Nepal's recognition as a sovereign nation-state. In May 1907 he sent his emissary, the eminent Sardar Marich Man Singh with a letter to Viceroy Lord Minto expressing his wish to visit England to 'pay homage to the King Emperor', to make it clear that he would be honoured if he was treated as distinct from 'all the native Princes of India'. He cited the precedence of his visit to attend the Delhi Durbar in 1903 to press his case. After the exchange of a series of letters and dialogues between emissaries, a via media was sought that did not diminish the status of Nepal. Chandra would be given the honour of a nineteen-gun salute[56] and due recognition as the maharaj and prime minister of Nepal and emissary of the maharajdhiraj, king of Nepal. Imperial Britain was not yet prepared to recognize a sovereign status for Nepal, equal to that of England. But by the end of his trip, Chandra's unrelenting pursuit of such a position was duly understood by the British as a signal that he would not give up easily on this issue and that the 'loyalty' of Chandra and the support of Nepal was not to be taken for granted. The effort to this end got a powerful boost after the changed scenario wrought by the First World War.

Administrative Reforms and Infrastructural Development

The new prime minister also moved adroitly on the home front. There had been little change brought about by his predecessors in the structure of governance created by Jung Bahadur some fifty years back. Chandra moved to restructure, reorganize and streamline various wings of governance. The tradition of the supreme and unhindered authority reposing squarely on the maharaj continued unchanged but was institutionalized under the framework of Khadga Nishana Adda, an apex body of the entire administrative apparatus that functioned under direct control of the prime minister. The prime minister headed the highest court of appeal and the Foreign Office. The commander-in-chief (an incongruous title), also known as mukhtiyar, headed the civil service and the Jangi Laath security services. The 'lesser' departments were headed by 'directors' appointed on the basis of seniority in the Roll of Succession. A number of divisions or branch offices were set up in and outside the capital city. A new Department of Education was established. The 'hazuria general' was a new post, appointed by the prime minister at his discretion, irrespective of his rank in the Roll of Succession, who reported directly to the prime minister on all matters of state. This arrangement helped in coordination, maintained a degree of check and balance and allowed the prime minister to concentrate on matters of high priority. The prime minister's eldest son, Mohan, was the first to be assigned this job.

The administrative chain-of-command structured by Jung Bahadur, moving down from the prime minister to the four regional governors and then to the district governors, was streamlined. The prime minister's office acted as a link to coordinate the activities of the district administration with the central departments.

The structure and pattern of administration shaped by Chandra remained largely intact until the end of the Rana regime and was, according to Adrian Sever[57], 'the genesis of far reaching social, economic and administrative change that would consolidate and institutionalize the power of the regime to an extent that its founder, Jung Bahadur could only have dreamed of'. Supported by this well-structured machinery of governance, Chandra was able to accomplish some notable works of public benefit and development. A narrow- gauge rail line joined the Indian town of Raxaul with Amlekhganj, from where the mountain ranges rose northward. A ropeway line over the hills to Kathmandu connecting the Terai plains facilitated the swift transport of considerable bulk of goods. A hydroelectric plant brought the electricity in the capital. New sources of water were located and developed by homegrown engineers to substantially increase the flow of potable water in the settlements of the valley and some other towns of the Terai region, in particular. Granaries were built, both in Kathmandu and at carefully selected locations, especially along the long stretch of the Terai plains that produced surplus food grains. Comprehensive repair work of the principal trekking routes along the mountain belt of the country from east to west, popularly known as the Mool Bato or Postal Route, was carried out and subsidiary routes connecting the north and south followed. The greatest constraint in internal transit, transport and connectivity in Nepal is the large number of rivers and rivulets that descend from the mountain heights. Chandra is still remembered in the rural and even urban areas, thanks to the network of bridges, steel girders, wire ropes or suspension bridges and foot crossings throughout the country that he built. More than sixty such 'important' bridges are identified and credited to him. They minimized the utter isolation of the people and reduced the hardships they had to face[58].

Chandra commissioned a massive palace, Singha Durbar, a residence for successive prime ministers, their families, a large number of personal staff and to house the offices of most of the departments of the government. It contained more than 1,400 rooms and several halls for state functions or private entertainment. It still stands steadfast in mute testimony to the grandeur of those decades of the Rana regime. There were no toilets, though, in most parts of the palaces. When once taunted about the lack of toilets by a royal guest from India, the host is reported to have answered, 'No, we do not go to the toilet, *they* come to us', referring to the chamber pots that were invariably brought in the bed rooms at night time.

Each palace maintained beautifully landscaped gardens, with stately trees of diverse shapes and sizes, shrubs and plants, fountains, fish ponds and aviaries; they were integral parts of, and indeed more appealing, than the palaces themselves. Several smaller bungalows and outhouses dotted the vast grounds and were used for recreation, for housing the clerical staff or the military guards, stables for the horses and as cattle sheds.

As opposed to other palaces, which were owned by individual Rana families, Singha Durbar was owned by the state and occupied by succeeding prime ministers. As the years passed by, Singha Durbar earned the distinction of being viewed as the pivotal centre of power and symbolized state authority in the same way as the White House, the Kremlin or the Westminster.

Some thirty-six similar but smaller palaces came up thereafter in different parts of the valley, as residence-cum-offices for the high-ranking Rana rulers. They still house the bulk of the government offices in the capital city.

Construction of these roads, bridges, palaces and similar properties was done with proper planning and preparation. Chandra, and Bir Shumsher before him, had the foresight to send a number of talented young professionals for training overseas. They returned well equipped with skills and know-how in new technology, architecture, engineering and faculties such as farming, horticulture, forestry, fine arts, cottage industries and manufacturing.

Commitment to Social Reforms

The treatment of slaves in America seemed a lot harsher as compared to those in Nepal. Rarely did one hear of cases of lashings, whippings or such inhuman treatment. Often, the trusted ones were treated as members of the family. The Muluki Ain stipulated, amongst other reforms, that a free person could not be bought or sold. Nearly fifty years later, in 1901, Dev Shumsher initiated the process of emancipation but implementation had proved ineffective, even in the limited areas it was tried out.

Chandra possessed the will and commitment and devised effective strategies for implementation. He approached institutions and leaders of society, friends and foes alike, seeking their goodwill and support for this humane undertaking. Adequate funds were set aside for compensation to be paid to the owners and suitable land acquired for rehabilitation of those emancipated in Amlekhganj. He called a public meeting at Tundikhel and addressed the gathering, explaining the moral basis for abolition of this 'cruel practice', and appealed for public support. Within two years the task was effectively completed. The public announcement of the successful culmination of the momentous enterprise, at a massive gathering in Tundikhel, was greeted with collective acclaim of 'Shree Teen Maharaj ko Jaya' that vibrated through the cool afternoon air of November 1924.

The ancient Hindu practice of sati, rooted in the belief that a widow who immolates herself on the funeral pyre of her husband will join him in the afterlife, was originally a voluntary act. It gradually turned into an odious ritual forced upon widows, often to usurp her property. In the nineteenth century the reformist movement of Raja Ram Mohun Roy in India against the archaic and cruel practice led to the legal abolition of sati, enacted by Governor General Lord Bentinck in 1828. In the 1850s, the powerful hard-line priestly order in Nepal bitterly opposed the proposal of Jung Bahadur for legal abolition of sati and the prime minister conceded insofar as to permit only free and willing performance of sati, that too by those widows free from the responsibility and duty of raising and supporting their families. Bir Shumsher took the reforms a step further and Chandra finally abolished the practice altogether through a legal edict in 1920. He ordered stringent actions to punish those guilty of coercing women into this practice. Nevertheless, it took a long time before the deep-rooted custom was fully eliminated. Indeed, one still hears of stray and rare incidents of sati in some tradition-bound villages south of the Nepal border.

Another episode demonstrates how difficult it was even for a shrewd and powerful prime minister like Chandra Shumsher to break the stranglehold of conventional practices. In the spring of 1923, a large conference of Pandits and Brahmins from India and Nepal was called to debate the issue of animal sacrifice for the worship of Goddess Shakti. The maharaj asked his grandson Mrigendra to attend and report on the proceedings. Mrigendra writes[59],

'I knew Grandfather was for giving up the cruel practice: (some months earlier) a goat being led to the sacrificial alter had escaped. It came running and fell straight between his feet. His eyes were full of tears. Against all protests he ordered release of the goat and a substitute was sacrificed. Since that date he had tried to wriggle out of this practice.'

'The Nepalese pandits, led by a much-respected and learned patriarch, Hem Raj Pandey, were staunch defenders of the faith and practice of animal sacrifice. To counter them, Chandra had invited a renowned scholar from Banaras to lead the debate for the pacifist group. The proponent[s] for non-sacrifice (Banaras Pandits) spoke slowly and quietly. The Nepalese side was loud and vociferous. They created pandemonium, shouted down the opposing voices and felt triumphant.'

The debate lasted a whole week. The final evening, Mrigendra reported to his grandfather that the case for retaining the status quo was made out very strongly: the majority from the home front were in favour of it. But the Banaras Pandits clearly quoted the provision in the scriptures that offered substitution of vegetables or fruits as an alternative for animal sacrifice. Chandra was both happy and relieved by the outcome and rewarded Mrigendra for listening to the debate attentively, with a handsome gift of ₹5000, a huge sum those days.

'The following day, the verdict was announced amidst a large gathering of pandits, government officials, special invitees and servants. Chandra said slowly and deliberately amidst hushed silence that the Nepali pandits had made out a strong case for retaining the practice and offered high praise for Pandit Hemraj Pandey. "Those who have faith in it are all free to carry on animal sacrifice; I have no objection." There was vociferous acclamation from the (Nepalese) Pandits before the prime minister continued, "But for myself, since the scriptures allow a substitute, I resolve to give up animal sacrifice in my private life from today." There was absolute silence. The Banaras Pandits stood with folded hands, eyes brimming with tears. Grandfather slowly walked back.'

From that day on, the prescribed variety from the vegetable kingdom substituted animal sacrifice in the Chandra household, as opposed to the official functions of the state. The predictions that Chandra would succumb to the wrath of the Shakti and perish within a year proved baseless.

The effect of the debate was not limited to the Chandra family. Balakrishna Sama, a literary genius, was also one of the invitees at the function. He confirmed that the head pandit from Banaras was Swami Sacchitanand, a renowned theologian. Sama's narration of the debate does not differ in essence from that of Mrigendra. In conclusion he writes, 'I was truly impressed by the Swami's lucid exposition and the prime minister was happy. My brother who was with me and I, gave up meat and fish from that date. It was an unforgettable day for me.'[60]

However, this episode was an exception. The powerful priests were able to impose orthodox Hindu fundamentalism to effectively undermine the non-Dhagadhari Hindus[61] and other religious faiths alike.

Tight Control of Education

Chandra felt that the scheme for 'universal primary education' as advocated by his predecessor was not practical, and detrimental to the interest of the Rana regime. A policy to restrict operation of schools and literary activities 'to a manageable limit' was adopted and personally monitored by him. It was the principal deterrent for the growth of the nation and remained unchanged until Padma Shumsher became prime minister in 1948.

Such retrograde thoughts and policies of the regime have perhaps done greater harm to the growth of the nation than anything else. It was also one of the the most hated aspect of the Rana regime and a critical cause for fuelling the rebellion that eventually brought down the oligarchy.

However, Chandra did establish the Tri Chandra College in Kathmandu in 1920 It was the first college in Nepal. On return to the palace after the inauguration, the Rana Prime Minister asked Batuk Babu, a bearded veteran and principal-designate brought from Bengal, 'What have I done today?'

'Oh Your Highness, you have done a great thing. It will preserve your fame and of your sons and grandsons throughout the ages,' Batuk Babu replied.

'No, Batuk Babu, I have done a deed which will shorten and cut down the ruling life of my family. But it was something that had to be done it is for my progeny to adjust themselves.'[62]

Chandra may have been conscious of the values of liberal reforms, but his decisions and actions were more often guided by the interests of the Rana dynasty. During his reign of twenty-eight years, no more than eighty-four schools or reading rooms were sponsored or permitted to operate in different parts of the country[63]: the state was determined to limit the spread of education and learning to an 'acceptable level'.

World War I and the Anglo-Nepal Treaty of Friendship 1923

The Great War erupted in Europe in August 1914. A shrewd observer of international events, Chandra had foreseen the outbreak of war earlier than most, and with it the likelihood of expansion of Anglo-Nepal cooperation well beyond the framework of goodwill and courteous interaction. Within its fold he visualized an opening for his cherished goal of a sovereign nation-state. With these thoughts in mind, he offered to place 'the whole military resources of Nepal at the disposal of His Majesty'.

During the difficult four years of the Great War 'Nepal made a contribution out of all proportion to its size and resources' to the Allied cause. The first contingent of the Nepalese army marched into India under Commander-in-Chief Padma Shumsher. Within months the war started going badly for the Allies and on request of the British resident, reinforcement of six regiments with some 7,500 trained men under the command of General Baber Shumsher, the second son of the prime minister, joined their colleagues in India.

Baber would be defined in current parlance as a 'fitness freak'. He took a robust ride on a jet-black stallion every morning, and in the afternoons undertook vigorous bouts of physical exercise. He took great care to groom himself elegantly. His voice was rich and commanding, despite a hint of stutter. As a son of the ruling prime minister, Baber joined the service at the age of fifteen, and was promoted to lieutenant general at eighteen. As inspector general of police[64] he helped the prime minister set up a highly efficient intelligence network that operated throughout the country and even managed to get inside information from the British residency. The role of the intelligence network was crucial later in quickly detecting political activities and plots against the oligarchy.

Baber was a member of the Nepalese delegation during Chandra's tour of Great Britain and Europe in 1908 and at the Delhi Coronation Durbar in 1913. When Nepal sent its troops to join the Allied forces in the First World War, he was selected to go to India. There 'he held the important and responsible assignment and post of Inspector General of the Nepalese contingent in India—and was attached to the Army Headquarters, representing the views of the Government of Nepal and in order to exercise overall supervisory functions.'[65] He remained in India for the duration of the World War and the Anglo-Afghan war. Baber was eminently suited to these rigorous assignments. This might not have been the only reason for his being sent out of the country—palace whispers strongly suggested that the father and son shared a common passion for a comely maid named Mausam who served Chandra, a dangerous liaison no doubt for the young man. This amorous attachment was perhaps one of the factors for a rather cool personal relationship between the father and son.

In India Baber gained a reputation for personal valour and able leadership. Sir Beuchamp Duff, the commander-in-chief of India, wrote in his letter to Maharaj Chandra, 'the Nepalese troops were stationed in Abbotabad and Dehradun...and the General soon began to devote himself whole-heartedly to his duties…He visited Dehradun while the cholera epidemic was attacking the Nepalese troops, and set a splendid example to all ranks by the fearless way he visited the patients…I find the advice of so capable an officer of your government most valuable at all times.'

The war in Europe was intensifying, and the theatres of battle spreading to new areas, including the Middle East and Africa, inflicting heavy casualties on both sides. The Allies were in urgent need of more troops. At this juncture, the British faced a new challenge within the subcontinent. The Mashuds in Waziristan started relentless hostilities against the British, as the winter receded and the spring of 1817 approached. Britain turned to Nepal once more and Chandra sent about 8,000 additional troops. And on especial request of Sir Beauchamp Duff, he appointed General Baber to lead a contingent of the Nepalese troops to the troubled area. The General was happy to oblige. In June 1917 Baber left Shimla for Waziristan. The Mashud resistance was stubborn but was subdued within a few months. The exploits of the Nepalese contingent has been written up in poetic praise in the Nepal. Baber joined the soldiers in the common mess and shared the frugal rations during the field operations; he 'shared with his men all the dangers of a campaign and was several times under fire…a rifleman having been once hit by the enemy's bullet a few paces from where the General was standing'.

Once this difficult front was secured, the Allied troops, including the Gorkha soldiers, could move to the main venues of war. By the beginning of 1918 the war was turning in favour of the Allies and victory was attained in November 1918.

'When added to the 26,000 Gorkhas already serving in the regular Indian army at the outbreak of war, the steady supply of men trained and sent to replace the heavy losses at the front … the total number of men who left the country (Nepal) for military purposes exceeded 2,00,000 from a total country population of five million'[66] Besides soldiers, mechanics, arms and ammunitions, tea, cardamom, a large number of railway sleepers and cash funds exceeding the expectations of the British government as grants or loans were made available by the prime minister of Nepal.

The 'sacrifice of so many brave men' has met with severe criticism, and not without reason. In some parts of Nepal, mid-west in particular, the strong bodied men had all gone to war leaving the countryside to waste. But, it is important to note that the gesture was an extension of a diplomatic courtship, leading to the cherished goal of a fully sovereign nation. Left to their free will, Britain might have wished to continue with the semi-dependent status for Nepal as imposed by the Treaty of Sugauli of 1816. However, the contributions of Nepal to the imperial war efforts and the acts of valour of the Gorkha soldiers drew global attention. Britain was sincerely grateful to and obliged by the 'whole-hearted support it received'[67]. At the same time, the war had taken a high toll on the resources of Britain and emboldened the freedom movement in India. The dynamics had changed. The Empire needed friends and allies more than ever. All through the four years that the war had lasted, with victory and defeat often hanging in balance, Chandra had never raised, even obliquely, the subject of Nepal's interest. The astute strategist waited for the right time to claim the dividend of his investment in the war effort. Now the time was ripe and he moved swiftly but carefully. Negotiations were taken up for a new treaty that was to be a landmark in the history of Nepal.

The Anglo-Nepal Treaty of Friendship was signed in Kathmandu on 21 December 1923. It was signed by His Highness Chandra Shumsher and by the British 'envoy' as opposed to 'resident' and ratified not by the Viceroy as in case of the princely states of India but by King George V himself. Thus a clear line was drawn between the Indian princely states that were 'dependent' on the British crown and the legal status of full sovereignty for Nepal. The status of state sovereignty as opposed to dependency was a matter of paramount concern to the Nepalese during those decades, and is still a matter of heated political debate these days.

There were two unforeseen outcomes from the war and the treaty that had long-term impact on the economy and politics of

Nepal. The Shah and the Rana rulers had doggedly adhered to the policy of keeping foreign-made products out of the country, resisting the constant attempt to open up the Nepal market for entry of British goods. The result was the growth of a resilient self-reliant economy, based largely on a network of vibrant cottage industries. However, the soldiers who had ventured into foreign grounds had been exposed to, and had the money to buy, colourful mill-made fabrics and garments, tea and cigarettes, soap and toothpaste, and other such 'goodies', in the Indian market. At the same time the treaty opened the gates for trading. The Government of Nepal, too, was happy to mobilize this lucrative source for revenue and set up tax offices at different entry points. The policy of restriction on imports was effectively punctured.

The army men could also see the infinitely greater opportunities available in India for gainful employment, for facile livelihood for the womenfolk in particular, as compared to the back-breaking hardships in Nepal, and for the education of their children. Thus, many of them settled in India at the end of the war. There they were directly exposed to the revolution against colonial dictatorship that was bubbling in India and could not but fail to comprehend the inequities and injustices inherent in the Rana oligarchy. The 'Pravasi' Nepali community had much to do with the stirrings of anti-Rana movement in India.

Winds of Change and the Beginning of Dissent

The winds of change that were sweeping India had begun drifting into Nepal. Until the dawn of the twentieth century few had dared to talk, far less raise their voices, against the Rana regime. Acts of dissent against the existing order were infrequent, detected quickly and the 'culprits' dealt with in a severe fashion. The first acts of open socio-political defiance and a call for reforms took root in the first quarter of the twentieth century, emerging from the wombs of the Buddhist faith or the Arya Samaj sect.

Buddhism is a vital part of the Nepalese society. Lord Buddha was born in Lumbini. His teachings, however, reached the valley of Kathmandu later. The entry of his followers into Nepal is authenticated by the stupas built atop raised hilltops in Patan (Lalitpur) around 250 BC and visit and preaching of the missionaries. A pillar of Emperor Asoka has been found in Lumbini and his daughter, Charumati, did visit and stay in Kathmandu before proceeding to Tibet with her followers. Lamaist Buddhism, deriving its doctrines from the Mahayana sect, spread widely amongst the hill tribes of Nepal. Two types of priests/monks emerged to teach or preach the Buddhist Dhamma—'household monks' who devoted themselves to learning and practice in the monasteries or within the privacy of family residence, and 'celibate monks', who spent time spreading the teachings of the Buddha amidst the populace[68]. The Hindu rulers and their followers were, of course, in majority and comprised the dominant force, but were not oppressive. During the almost fifteen centuries of the Licchavi and Malla rule, Hindu and Buddhist faiths grew side by side, and the devotees of one often visited the shrines of the other. Religious practices, rites, customs and festivals of each faith flourished in tandem, particularly in the valley.

The state of harmonious coexistence gradually gave way to intolerance under the Shahs and the Ranas. By the beginning of twentieth century, the Buddhists and liberal Hindus started to feel suffocated by the suppressive measures adopted by the rulers under the influence of the priestly order. In 1920 a group of young Newar Buddhists, the Sakyas, established a religious organization, the Buddha Dhamma Uddharak Sangh. Primarily dedicated to practice of the Dhamma, they gave shelter to the oppressed sections of the society. The issues discussed and debated in hushed tones covered the socio-political inequities and exclusions that prevailed in the country. The close-knit community-living style of the Newars was well-suited to such clandestine activities and went undetected for a while. Around the same time, some young 'celibate' Buddhists travelled all the way to Tibet and attained the status of Lamahood. On return to Kathmandu these bhikshus roamed the streets, seeking alms from the faithful, as ordained by their faith. This practice was viewed as an attempt at conversion and thus transgressed of the law of the land. Furthermore, the administration got an intelligence report that one or more of the bhikshus had been planted by a 'foreign power', not an improbable method of espionage, in the course of the 'Great Game' being played those days[69]. To counter such moves the orthodox priestly order of the Hindus took on the role of protectors of the faith, as they had done for centuries past. Backed by vocal urgings of the high priests, Chandra decided to nip the potential danger in the bud. Many of those under suspicion were apprehended, condemned for breaking the law, physically assaulted at times and forced to leave the country. While the threat of any imminent danger was averted, the actions antagonized the entire Buddhist community.

The Arya Samaj movement proved to be an even greater threat. A religious (as opposed to secular) reform movement that emerged in India during the first half of the nineteenth century, it was spearheaded by Raja Ram Mohun Roy. He claimed 'reason and the rights of the individual' to be the fundamental basis of the Hindu holy texts, the Upanishads. With 'copious scriptural quotations, he attacked the practice of sati and the abuses of caste, advocated raising the status of women and the abolition of idolatry'[70] and the archaic rites and rituals attached to it.

Despite the opposition of the orthodox Hindus, the Arya Samajis opened the doors for non-Hindus to enter its portals and reached out to most communities of the subcontinent. The liberal Hindus from Nepal were gradually attracted by the movement. Madhav Raj Joshi was one such. He visited India and was initiated into the new sect under the tutelage of Swami Dayanand Saraswati, who headed the movement in northern India[71]. On his return to Nepal in the last decade of the nineteenth century, he started to preach the reformist tenets of the Arya Samaj. In the beginning, Chandra gave the movement free play and even overlooked the establishment of an Arya Samaj Centre in Patan. Encouraged, perhaps, by this initial soft stance, Madhav Raj crossed the line and questioned the very divinity of idols including the sacred Pashupatinath. He disputed the authenticity of archaic rituals and tantric practices. The high priests were bitterly opposed; their monopoly on interpretation of the scriptures was challenged and their source of earning affected. Prime Minister Chandra received a spate of complaints and bitter protests from the trusted and powerful raj purohits of his court. At an officially sponsored religious function to discuss and debate the issue, the reformists were vastly outnumbered, isolated and accused of blasphemy against the deities and established religious practices. Joshi and some of his followers were arrested and sentenced to jail. The rest were assaulted, harassed or hounded out of the country, as was Joshi in 1907, after two years of incarceration. The teaching and practice of Arya Samaj rituals was banned.

However, the liberal and reformist awakening of society could not be halted. A social organization named Satyacharan Malami Guthi emerged to carry forward the reformist movement. Perhaps reading the liberal mindset of Maharaj Chandra on such issues, the first call of the Guthi was against the outdated customs, rites and rituals following deaths in one's family. The high priests voiced their objections again. The Bada Gurujyu (senior high priest) pressured the prime minister for action: the activists were chained and brought to the trial court or the Ijlas. The accused confessed that they sought reforms, but for the good of the ancient faith. The prime ministers had always accepted the High Priest as the final arbiter in matters of religion and the latter demanded punishment as laid down by law, in this case either at least twelve years of imprisonment or exile. The maharaj turned to the prisoners and asked what would be their preference. Tulsi Mehr, one of the leaders of the Guthi, pleaded that he wished to go to India and to the ashram of Mahatma Gandhi to learn the practice of charkha spinning and the weaving of khadi cloth. Impressed by the purpose of the young man, Chandra consented to his request and arranged for the state to bear the expenses for his travels and a stipend of twenty rupees per month as long as he remained in the ashram[72].

Tulsi managed to reach the ashram in Gujarat after many days of journeying through unfamiliar country. The Mahatma liked the simplicity and industry of the young man and took him in as his personal assistant. Tulsi nursed his mentor and teacher like a son and became his ardent disciple. He also mastered the skills of spinning and weaving. After five years, Tulsi returned to Kathmandu to teach his countrymen what he had learnt at the ashram. Carrying a charkha and five bales of cotton-wool, he commenced his journey in 1925. Back home, the officials blocked his move to teach or promote khadi-weaving. He had to resort to a one-man peaceful struggle, sitting down each day with the spinning wheel at a vantage point regularly traversed by the maharaj, before Chandra noticed and summoned him to Singha Durbar. Patiently, Tulsi explained the utility of the khadi industry in generating income for the poor and unemployed and of khadi as a home-grown product to substitute imported cloth. Chandra was convinced and Tulsi received the support of the state as well as a suitable venue for a training centre. But he had to struggle against the state's perception of khadi as an instrument of rebellion, as was the case in India, for many decades.

Under four Prime Ministers who succeeded Chandra before the fall of the Rana regime, Tulsi and his eager followers were backed by the warmth of public support. They found protection and sympathy under some Prime Ministers but suffered persecution and incarceration under others, but carried on, undaunted till the triumph of democracy in 1951.

How was it that Tulsi Mehr was tolerated or treated well by the Rana rulers, whereas others who practised and advocated the Arya Samaj tenets were persecuted? Was not Madhav Raj Joshi jailed and then hounded out of the country during Chandra's reign? Was not his son Shukra Raj actually hanged on Juddha's orders?

'We remained confined to social work, promotion of Khadi. We avoided idol worship and the outdated rites, advised our followers to discard discriminatory customs, but did not involve ourselves in political activities,' Mulmi answered, an ardent follower of Tulsi, in interview with the author.

The prime minister was, however, confronted by more aggressive opposition, clearly coloured by political moorings. A bundle of 'torn and patched, lice-laced, bug-infested, dirt-covered swatches that passed for human apparel' arrived in Singha Durbar one day, sent by Krishna Prasad Koirala from his hometown in Biratnagar. This was the soiled and tattered clothing of some jobless porters, along with a note that pointed out the injustice of the vast divide that separated the handful of ruling elite living in luxurious comfort from the rest of the populace, the impoverished duniyadars of the same country. The bundle was unfolded and the message read out in open court. Expressions varying from incredulous shock to outright indignation followed. Chandra was silent, his reactions inscrutable. A week later, an order was sent to arrest Koirala as well as several of his relatives and associates. Krishna Prasad escaped to India and then Banaras with some of his extended family members and followers, including his three-year-old son, B.P. Koirala. The small bundle of worn-out clothes and the flight of the Koirala family to India ignited the conscience of civil society inside the country, established Banaras as a prime venue for the burgeoning revolt against the Ranas and ultimately led to the demise of the Rana regime.

Stray acts of clandestine defiance in different forms were beginning to show up now even in some towns outside the valley. Though sporadic and uncoordinated, young men expressed or displayed resentment against the regime at social gatherings. In 1920, one Krishna Lall Adhikary, a government official, wrote a book, *Makaiko Kheti* (Corn Farming). Revolutionary ideas such as equal redistribution of land were obliquely inserted between the lines. At one place he wrote that 'the rising moon, Chandra' did not benefit the young (plants); at another, in a rather crude analogy, he condemned imported technology as 'the foreign dogs sleeping on their couches'. The state came down upon him heavily. Not merely the author but a number of other suspects were rounded up. The prisoners were paraded around the city, often bound in chains, with a view to create a general sense of fear. The principal actors were then jailed for long years, and even those suspected of dissent or possessing the book were handed lesser terms, or fined. The Nepalese activists in India expressed their empathy for their comrades in Nepal. A spate of newspapers that came out from Banaras, Dehradun or Darjeeling condemned the acts of suppression and injustice of the Rana oligarchy and called for its termination. They were effective in spreading the message of discontent in their respective areas and a few copies were smuggled into Nepal. But Chandra ensured, through his connections with the British rulers, that the publications lasted no more than a few years, even in India. All through Chandra's reign his government remained in full control of the state.

While political dissidence and activism were viewed as crimes against the state and its proponents treated ruthlessly, Chandra did at times debate whether or not some liberal political reforms should be introduced. In this context, one more episode covered in Mrigendra's unpublished work portrays a rarely revealed side of his grandfather's character.

One morning (sometime in 1926–27) he told me that he had called a meeting of the top Rollwallahs. I was not entitled to attend the meeting but could carry a satchel and come as his grandson. After a few preliminaries he posed the question, 'Is it time to introduce some constitutional change in Nepal?' There was a chilling silence. One or two voices, my father (Baber) amongst them, murmured something about giving the question a thought. The rest were glum. 'Consider the matter and I shall talk to you all again,' grandfather suggested before he left abruptly. There was a chorus of protest. 'We are too poor. The time is not yet ripe.' The meeting dispersed. The next morning grandfather asked me what I saw and felt. 'Everybody, including my uncles, is against it.'

'What was the reason?' he queried.

'Perhaps they would have accepted it if they had been given some money/incentive before.'

Grandfather was sullen. 'Yes, I should have anticipated this earlier. It is too late now.' He never brought up this matter again. That evening my father (Baber) spoke to me, 'the word "constitution" has a strange connotation in Nepal. Everybody thinks change in constitution means making the country a Republic.'

The Chasm Within

Acts of socio-political defiance and opposition by the duniyadars did require some attention from the prime minister. However, the more compelling and perhaps painful dilemma Chandra faced during the last phase of his reign was because of the bitter rifts within the Rana family. There were twenty-five to thirty names on the Roll of Succession, all of whom constantly jostled for their turns for plum posts. Uncertainty, tension and fear gripped the aspirants, especially at the time of the inevitable new list each succeeding prime minister drew up.

During the final years of Chandra's long reign the infighting reached chronic proportions. The distinction between legitimate and illegitimate had been diffused by long years of practice of equal status and treatment. So far, all prime ministers had emerged from the rank of legitimate issues. However, Rudra Shumsher was the fourth in line on the Roll. He was a popular and an able man from the illegitimate branch. The division between the two groups now took the shape of a class tussle to overshadow the personal rivalry. At times the legitimate issues had to salute the illegitimate ones placed in the higher order of the Roll, and in consequence wielding greater authority and power. Removal of all illegitimate members from the Roll at this stage would result in expulsion of cousins holding critical positions in governance, which could generate serious reprisal. Chandra was reluctant to follow this course at this late stage of his reign, when his health was failing. Remaining inert and not responding to the rising urge of the powerful body of legitimate issues, including his own sons who stoutly stood behind him and rendered crucial assistance in governance, was no longer a tenable option. A way out had to be found.

Chandra devised a scheme that formally recognized and

categorized the distinction between, A, B and C classes. 'A' class were the legitimate children born from a married high-caste Chhetri wife, 'B'-class children were from the Chhetri caste but born out of wedlock, and 'C'-class children were born out of wedlock and from lower-caste mothers. Children of such 'C'-class sons remained in the same class even if their mothers were Chhetri women duly married to the father. This clearly defined division was introduced in a book, *History of Nepal*. Chandra had invited Perceval Landon, an English professor, and commissioned him to produce this first comprehensive historic record of Nepal in the English language. Crucially, although the book clearly spelt out the distinction between the three categories, the prime minister did not alter the Roll of Succession and continued to retain those 'C'-class members who were already included in the extant Roll. The repercussions of the expulsion of B and C classes from the Roll of Succession were left for his successors to face. Nevertheless, Chandra is viewed by some historians as the one who initiated the process of internal division within the family and by many B- and C-class Ranas as the 'author and tyrant who planted the seed of hatred among the Ranas'[73].

Indeed, the classification was a clear enough pointer to the option of wholesale expulsion as carried out by Maharaj Juddha some five years later. The fallout in the long term was serious. Many observers, writers and stakeholders in the turbulent years that followed claim that the Rana regime would not have been terminated so early or easily had Chandra not spelt out this distinction or Juddha not wiped out the claim of *all* the 'C'-class Ranas. Yet, there is little likelihood that the Ranas would indeed have remained united if the issue had been allowed to remain fluid with the sword of Damocles dangling above the claimants and aspirants, and the sense of insult and resentment caused by the demotion in rank, each time the 'Roll was changed'.

The Move from Singha Durbar

Chandra died in 1929 after a short illness, within two years of publication of the *History of Nepal*. Next in line was Bhim. The formal distinction of A, B and C, limited as it was in the pages of the book, did not deter the new prime minister from using his prerogative established by long-standing precedence. As in previous cases of transfer of authority, Mohan, Baber and others in the higher ranks in the Roll of Succession knew very well that on their father's death, the unbridled power and authority would devolve on Bhim. Bhim himself was seen as a well-meaning and considerate person before he became prime minister, but he had fathered many 'C'-class sons and their attitude towards Chandra's sons could hardly be benevolent. They were convinced that the three older sons of Chandra were, in fact, the chief instigators in persuading their father to formalize the class division. Chandra had instructed his sons to try and remain on good terms with Bhim and *his* favourite sons, most of whom were of the 'C' category, and they had followed the sound advice. Upon the death of Chandra, there was great mourning but even greater fear. Revenge for commissions or omissions of earlier years, or political considerations, could result in retribution. All senior female members of the family were told to wrap themselves inside the folds of their long cummerbunds and twelve-yard-long saris (which was the normal attire of high-ranking ladies those days), all items of high value that could be readily concealed were hidden away as a precaution against the need for hurried departure. Nannies were told to keep the children's essential belongings packed and ready. Fortunately for the family, no drastic situation arose. Immediately after the death of Chandra was reported to Bhim, he sent an emissary to Singha Durbar to convey his condolences to the family. In the process Bhim was opening the door for a compromise with Chandra's sons, powerful within the Rana hierarchy, in the new equation of the power game that would follow. In return, Bhim sought their goodwill for promoting some of his sons, including those in the 'C' class, into the Roll of Succession.

'Everybody had expected this,' writes Mrigendra, 'but not in such unholy haste. The body of Maharaj Chandra was not yet cold.' The sons in mourning agreed to 'abide by the decision'.

In 1931 the Chandra household moved from the prime minister's official residence, Singha Durbar, to spacious palaces already built for the sons at different locations in the valley. Baber moved to Baber Mahal. There was no loss in the comfort levels they had enjoyed earlier. But 'it was a cruel wrench, leaving our birthplace and seat of our boyhood and youthful days. More than fifty members of the family had lived and hobnobbed here together. More than 500 servants' lives were involved'[74].

Chapter Two

Maharaj Bhim Shumsher (1929–1932)

Bhim Shumsher had served his elder brother Chandra for twenty-eight years as mukhtiyar and commander–in-chief (C-in-C) patiently awaiting his turn at Premiership. The nomenclature of C-in-C is confusing, as the mukhtiyar in fact headed the civil administration directly, while the Laath Saheb, the next in the line of succession, handled all matters related to the armed forces. Bhim carried out his duties 'with plenty of ability, but content with his present position'[75]. A pious devotee of Lord Rama, Bhim had modelled himself in the role of Rama's devoted brother Bharat. Even after he succeeded Chandra at the ripe age of sixty-four he continued to spend long hours each day in worship.

The internal rivalry between the 'A-class' and 'C-class' Ranas took centre stage during the three years of Bhim's premiership. If Chandra's elder sons strived to gain confidence of the new prime minister, Bhim sought their loyalty and support. Baber moved to befriend the ambitious and capable Ram Shumsher, a C-class cousin, now viewed as the prime minister's right hand.

In the 1970s, Ram's son Mana Shumsher confided to me, 'Your grandfather, Baber, was very close to my father. In fact, a fortnight after Maharaj Chandra passed away, he came to our palace and offered to hand over the keys of his private treasury as a token of trust. My father Ram was moved and requested Baber to retain the bunch of keys and be confident of his continuing goodwill.'

Bhim in turn rewarded them with important positions in governance as he had promised Chandra during the latter's last days. Yet Mohan, Baber, Keshar and the other A-class Ranas had to remain ever-alert to retain their diminished hold in the power equation.

Humanitarian Measures Mixed with Unworthy Acts of Revenge

Bhim initiated several humanitarian measures and reforms, in line with the reign of the mythological Rama. He had hospitals built in a few parts of the country outside of Kathmandu, extended the existing piped drinking-water services in Kathmandu and Morang District to eastern Nepal, enacted legislations to protect the rights of land tillers and tenants, reduced or removed tax on several items of daily consumption or needs of the poor people including salt and cotton and removed the levy on cattle-grazing at common pasture lands. More than anything else, he will be remembered for formally abolishing the death sentence, an act that eludes many of the 'developed' and democratic countries and most authoritarian regimes till date[76].

However, there was another streak in the man that was contrary to the compassion, balance and wisdom of the legendary hero of the Ramayana. Bhim was vindictive towards a whole group of honest and able officials of the state who had rendered valuable service to Chandra and the Rana regime for many decades. Some officers were dismissed; others were forced out of the country on trumped-up charges or flimsy pretexts. A wiser ruler would have channelled their experience and talent to serve his and the country's interests. Several generations of the Acharya Dixit family had held important positions in administration and served the Rana rulers and the country well. They were close to Chandra and may had at times failed to display the kind of respect or courtesy expected by Bhim. The bulk of the members of the family were now harassed, hounded and thrown out of service or the valley of Kathmandu. One of them, Kashi Nath, had diligently penned ten handwritten volumes of accurate records of day-to-day events. He had passed them on to his son Narendra to get printed when the time was right; but 'it was impossible to get them published during the whole Rana period' writes Narendra, as it would amount to high treason. Even when Narendra did venture to get the work published in 1972, twenty years after the fall of the

Rana regime, he decided to censor several portions. These portions were marked by dotted lines for the readers to understand that the observations were considered too dangerous to bring out in print. The parts that did get printed reflect the deep-rooted hatred against Bhim's excesses and the Rana regime in general. After one such lengthy dotted line Kasi Nath writes,

After such unworthy acts are committed by a Rajput ruler he must suffer their negative impact. The people can only get squeezed dry, never prosper under such a prime ministerial reign. The money derived by the state from the sweat of the people is stacked in the prime minister's treasury, or vanishes in their entertainment, songs, music and wrestling. Even if it was deposited in the state treasury it could be used for the benefit of people who suffer due to some natural calamity. People are denied justice. The prime minister is a kind of dacoit. After such acts of robbery they carry a constant fear of losing state authority, their efforts are centred all the time on strengthening themselves and there is no time to think about justice and injustice. That is the reason people live in such misery. The common people, the bhardars, administrators, businessmen— none of them are in a position to trust the government and as a result none keeps their earnings inside the country. No one invests in productive trade or industry, skill or the arts. Instead they prefer the safety of 4 or 5 per cent interest through deposits out of the country. For, if someone loses favour of the prime minister he will ruin his enterprise and take away his assets, even as Bhim has taken vengeful actions against us in retaliation of Maharaj Chandra's demoralizing domination over him during the latter's reign. This man does not care what people will think of him. What a cruel and villainous nature! Chandra had treated him and his followers kindly. These stupid actions have thrown out those working sincerely for the prime minister and rewarded those that work against his interests. We too observed, listened to, served and came to know well five maharajas, Jung, Ranodip, Bir, Deb and Chandra; never have we seen, known or heard one such as this! It seems it is the will of Lord Pashupatinath to degrade the position of the prime ministerial system in this state as well—not merely the Shumsher family but the entire Rana clan will be doomed, to the benefit of the bhardars, civil and security forces, officers and all the people of this country![77]

Another vindictive act was directed against Janak Lall Dhungel, a high-ranking officer who had worked for many years without any blemish on his record in the state treasury. During the time of the Waziristan War, he had headed the accounts section of the contingent of Nepalese forces in India, obviously a position of great trust and responsibility. But when Bhim became prime minister, Dhungel was accused on thirty-two counts of wrongdoing and asked to pay fines on each. To add to his humiliation, on many occasions his wife or a son was ordered to personally appear in office to pay the fines! Janak Lall left the country in utter disgust. He returned when Juddha took office and appealed for review of the cases. Found to be not guilty on any of the counts, an order was passed to refund all the fines he had paid and for his reinstatement to his original post.[78]

Many officers of the state and courtesans and the bhardars, suffered similar humiliation or reprisal, well beyond the norm of reshuffle, following the change of the prime minister. One can then guess the extent of fear and uncertainty, the injustice and oppressions the less fortunate duniyadars endured.

An episode related to Basanta, Bhim's lone grandson from his married maharani, is perhaps the most bizarre. During those years there was a lot of talk amongst the young generation of Ranas that gold could be produced by mixing mercury with some other compounds. Basanta, often an eccentric, was trying out this experiment one day, aided by a couple of his like-minded friends, when they were caught in the act by one of the detectives of Ram Shumsher, Bhim's half-brother, now the chief of police. Ram promptly reported the matter to Bhim with a wicked twist that the culprits were trying to produce lethal explosives aimed against the maharaj. The three young men were summoned to court. Not inclined to listen to long-winded explanations, Bhim ordered an instant whipping. When the young men, his grandson in particular, remained obstinate, denying any wrongdoing, the pious devotee of Rama 'went berserk, unmindful of his own painful legs (he was suffering from an attack of gout at the time), rushed across the room and with the thick walking-stick he carried lashed out at Basanta, kicking and flaying at the same time. Juddha had to intervene and calm down his elder cousin.'[79]

A New Twist in the Roll of Succession

Despite the displacement of many of their father's followers from important positions in the court and the government, Chandra's sons continued to wield considerable influence in affairs of the state. Bhim meanwhile was intent—as all his predecessors had been—on promoting his close associates to key positions of governance in order to secure *his* hold on governance. He had fathered several C-class sons, who had been raised and treated on equal footing with Padma (later maharaj), his eldest and only son from his married maharani. The maharaj always felt closer affinity to and placed greater trust on his C-class sons. He, therefore, restructured the Roll of Succession in 1930, elevating six of his nephews and sons born out of wedlock, a move that automatically reduced the rankings of several A-class cousins. Hiranya Shumsher and Ram Shumsher were given key positions in governance. Ram Shumsher, the more dynamic of the two, headed the Home portfolio, the most powerful position in the administrative setup. Subarna, the son of Hiranya Shumsher, was promoted to major general. An attempt was made to balance this altered juxtaposition by appointing Mohan as the additional commanding general and by promoting the senior grandsons of Chandra to the rank of major-general; Mrigendra, the elder son of Baber, was made director of education. The British resident noted that 'this system is likely to be severely tested in the near future.'[80]

The stakes were raised higher as time elapsed. After spreading his roots and influence in the administrative structure, Ram Shumsher gradually initiated a move to induct *all* C-class Ranas into the Roll of Succession. Such a course would have tilted the entire balance of power in their favour. However, Bhim died before the plan could gather momentum[81]. The A-class Ranas held on to their power and positions in governance, shaken and enfeebled perhaps, but not uprooted, and were ready to bounce back once Juddha succeeded Bhim.

Glimpses of Impending Change

At times Bhim's erratic decisions led to positive outcomes. Balakrishna Shumsher (later Sama) was a young captain in the army but a genius scholar in the fields of literature and the arts. Confident that the maharaj would be pleased by his latest publication, a nationally acclaimed play, *Dhruba,* he had it encased in a finely carved box before making a humble presentation. Bhim was displeased and castigated the author: 'What is the use of such useless tales and stories? We need writings on the science of Tantric practice and other sciences.'

Balakrishna was transferred to the post of teacher in Tri Chandra College. 'But this was no punishment for me; it placed me in a profession of my choice, and I worked under your father quite happily for many years.'[82] Mrigendra too, who had been recently appointed Director General of Education, was more than pleased. The gifted cousin was an invaluable addition to the team he was trying to build in the new department. He started teaching at the Tri Chandra College. 'Once more I felt the thrill of my boyhood. I managed to rid myself of the timidity in my nature and the slight stutter in my delivery. Gaining in confidence, I began to lecture standing, which no one did in Nepal earlier. In addition I started to complement delivery of parts in my plays with acting. Some in the teaching fraternity were critical. But students were enthused; many from other classes were now crowding outside my classroom to look inside. General Mrigendra complimented me.'

Mrigendra, Chandra's eldest grandson, had returned from Calcutta with high academic honours. Considered a 'lesser' department at that time, Mrigendra saw great potential and challenge in his new job. He had observed as a student in Calcutta the emerging struggle for an independent India; Mahatma Gandhi and his Satyagraha movement, Nehru and his stirring oratory, the dramatic burning of British goods in a bonfire and the Dandi Salt March. Chandra's favourite grandson sensed that the tide would soon reach the Himalayan kingdom, and the department he headed would have to play its part in handling it.

The first of these 'incidents' occurred within a few months of his appointment. Some fifty young educated men approached the government, seeking permission to establish a library in Kathmandu. The prime minister received a report that the library was intended to be used as a meeting place for anti-Rana activities. Without proper investigation, the young men were accused of political dissent and all of them arrested. Mrigendra was far too junior to influence the decision. A case was filed but in absence of evidence of criminal intent they were let off lightly with a fine of ₹100 each; the permission for operating the library was summarily rejected. 'Bhim Shumsher proved to be no less of an oppressor than Chandra in matters related to liberal reforms.'[83]

Prachanda Gorkha

A more direct blow against the Rana oligarchy was planned in the 1930s by a group of ambitious men. It was a plot to assassinate the top order of the hierarchy. The young men involved were exposed to the currents of political unrest sweeping India and carried the 'seeds of revolt'. On their return to Kathmandu, however, these feelings had to remain bottled-up, for even the 'walls had ears in Nepal', a phrase often repeated those days. One such young man, Maina Bahadur, happened to meet another, Khadga Man Singh, both in their early twenties, at a playing field. They became firm friends and gradually they shared their deepest thoughts with each other. Their common desire to strike against the Rana regime bonded their friendship. They had to wait for two more years before they could find a third man with the same purpose. In addition, he was more mature and possessed greater experience. Captain Khadga Man Singh was some twenty years older and had resigned his commission from the Nepal army, unable to bear the insults he had to suffer under the haughty Ranas. On account of his maturity and wider range of contacts the Captain was accepted as the leader. A fourth man, Ranga Nath Sharma, from a priestly family, was soon inducted. Someone else was needed now who could offer some financial support. Umesh Bikram Shah, a nephew of Captain Khadga Man, was a scion of the Shah rulers. He had grown up in India where his parents were settled and so the young Shah, too, was enthused by the freedom struggle. Inside Nepal, he was deeply resentful of the maltreatment the women of his family or of his relatives and friends had to endure after their marriage into a Rana household.

The ruling Ranas competed with each other on the number, variety and looks of their wives and concubines, treating women like decorative chattel. The first wife invariably came from a high-caste family such as the Thakuris, Shahs or Thapas, who took pride in their lineage. Uneducated and married off when barely pubescent, few could blossom into a life of happy contentment, as a constant flow of new wives or concubines shared their husband's bed. Physical and mental abuse was not unusual. Neither law nor social norms offered recourse or protection. Most of them, even those closely related to the king, were compelled to make a desperate peace with the situation. A select few did fight back. A sister of King Tribhuwan, Laxmi Rajya, reported to her brother, the king and to Prime Minister Juddha, the mental torture and physical violence she suffered at the hands of her husband Keshar (in the 1940s) and was allowed to live in a separate palace built for her. Others objected in extraordinary ways.

Baber was married to a petite and pretty girl, Bedabhakta, who belonged to a proud family of Thakuris from Bajhang, a remote district in the western hills. The couple lived in blissful harmony for about fifteen years and she bore him five children, but after the death of the eldest son aged thirteen, their relations soured. A few years later, ignoring the pleadings of his wife and the heated arguments that followed, Baber brought a concubine, a Tamang maid-servant, into his bedchamber. Bedabhakta refused to share her husband with another woman. She moved out of her husband's chambers and demanded accommodation in a separate wing of the palace. No amount of threat or pleadings from Baber would persuade the steadfast and courageous lady. She was prepared for verbal abuse or physical ill-treatment but would not consent to return to his chambers. It was Baber who blinked first in the confrontation and she was allotted a separate well-appointed wing in the palace adjacent to her husband's. Bedabhakta then ordered an iron grill to be installed at the entry point of her room, which she chained at night, making it perfectly clear to her husband that he was not welcome. As years passed, relations between the two thawed gradually to a point of live and let live. Not many estranged wives could gain such a position.

Umesh Bikram Shah was one of the many relatives who resented the humiliation and atrocities suffered by their dear ones married to the Ranas. He was bold enough to act against it. He was warned by Khadga, his maternal uncle, of the dangers involved in the course they were embarking upon, but the newly married young man was determined to join the battle. As the monsoon rains were still drenching the valley of Kathmandu these five men met in secret hideouts in different parts of the city. In August 1931 they agreed to form a 'political party'. Its stated objective was to capture power, and establish a rule of the people under the constitutional leadership of Shree Paanch, the King of Nepal[84]. The party was named Prachanda Gorkha. The consent and support of the king was essential for activating the plan and a link to the palace a prerequisite. Laxman Bikram Shah, a relative of Juddha who had occasional access to the palace and was known to harbour bitter feelings against the Rana regime, was persuaded to join the team. The action plan was revealed to Laxman, which included assassination of Bhim, Juddha and other senior members of the Rana rulers, on the occasion of Thamouti, the annual function in which each civil or military employee of the state was reappointed, promoted, demoted or dismissed. In a well-designed rapid follow-up, King Tribhuwan would proclaim revocation of all powers conferred upon the Rana family since 1846 and resumption of powers of the state by the king, followed by introduction of a 'constitutional monarchy'. But before the appointed date, the prime minister received an intelligence report of the plot and all six were promptly arrested. Laxman was suspected of being the informer. Four of the six accused were beaten savagely, first by the guards at an open public hearing and then by the prime minister himself. They were questioned separately and their involvement established. High treason, known as 'aiming at Gaanth Gaddi' (the throne and person of the ruler), was punishable by the severest sentence prescribed by law. But the maharaj had abolished the death penalty only a few months previously and so the four commoners were sentenced to life imprisonment. Laxman Raja was set free on intervention of Juddha. Sahebju Umesh Bikram Shah, a descendant of the royal family, was banished to Palpa and carried there inside a bamboo cage, a practice that was aimed at and did deter to a large extent 'such foolish bravado' in the future.

The reference of the incident as the first act of political rebellion against the Rana oligarchy and the claim of Prachanda Gorkha of being the first political party may be disputed on account of the involvement of just six persons. It may have been viewed merely as a 'failed assassination attempt'. However, the inhuman treatment of the prisoners ignited flames of hatred against the Rana rulers that still flickers to this date, more than eighty years later. The prisoners were not allowed to go out of their tiny dark dungeons that allowed little movement; they were compelled to urinate and excrete in baskets placed inside. The sweepers came in the morning to clean the muck but could never do a good job, as the water was not sufficient to do so. The floor remained constantly covered with human waste. Heavy balls of iron were tied to each of their feet and manacles hung over the chests of both Khadga Man and Naina Bahadur[85]. The rations were not sufficient to maintain normal health. Many prisoners jailed inside these 'black holes' died of malnutrition and the resultant diseases.

Captain Khadga Man, over fifty by now, could hardly move his body with all that weight tied to his legs; he was taken ill and met his death bravely, unbroken in spirit, pleading with the others to carry on the struggle. Naina Bahadur used to receive a few rupees from his family, most of which he gave away to those weaker than him. Whenever possible, Naina cooked some halwa (semolina porridge) and forced Khadga Man to eat, saying that at least one of them should live to tell the tale and continue the fight against the Ranas. After a couple of years Naina contacted tuberculosis and met a slow death, faintly calling for his mother every so often. The prisoners carried the body around the prison premises, chanting 'Jaya Naina Dai', and only then allowed the guards to take custody of his body.

Khadga Man Singh did live to tell the tale of inhuman brutality and to carry forward the battle. The tortuous life in those cells is perhaps poignantly related in one short sentence in the book, 'in Ramayana, Tulsi Das writes, "may God ordain one a life in hell rather than the company of the evil." But we were saddled with both'[86].

Bhim did not live much longer after his furious outburst during the trials. He was destined to rule for less than three years in all. He became addicted to drugs and took increasing doses of marijuana as he got older. He had very odd eating habits and is said to have suffered from a binge-purge cycle and 'on one fateful evening he took a heavy meal as usual and later tried to extract it out. But it got obstructed...later he collapsed and died'[87].

Chapter Three

Maharaj Juddha Shumsher (1932–1945)

The reign of Juddha from 1932 to 1945 was the most eventful. The most dramatic after Jung Bahadur, he is often compared to King Henry VIII of England. He was forceful, direct and bold in all he did, ruthless in his treatment of opposition at times, a creative nation-builder at others, and a womanizer. Juddha held a commanding posture and presence that never deserted him. But 'sudden bursts of anger' led him to unpardonable recklessness during the final phase of his reign.

Balakrishna Sama, the rebel in the family, praised him at first, saying, 'Juddha was not educated but well experienced and well versed in the essence of power play and national politics. If he was given to sudden bursts of anger he was also kind. He was brave, resolute and impressive'[88].

The Great Earthquake and Sweeping Purge of 1933

Juddha continued with relish, the practice of Daudaha Sawari, a royal tour of the Terai region, with the purpose of field inspection and monitoring the state of affairs in the southern plains bordering India, as well as the pleasures of big-game hunting in the thick forests and marshy landscape. These were the natural habitat of the one-horned rhinoceros, wild elephants, massive gaurs and Bengal tigers, besides a wide variety of flora, fauna and avian life. In the winter of 1934, too, Juddha made this annual trip, accompanied by his ranis and nanis, and a large entourage of relatives, courtiers, and servants. Baber and Mrigendra were also favoured with this privilege that year, and inevitably the hazuria general, the eldest son of Juddha Shumsher, Bahadur, accompanied his father. The young poet Balakrishna, an accomplished photographer, besides his genius in the field of literature, was included as well.

After the official work and big game hunting of the day was done the long evening hours before and after the inevitable gourmet meals was the time to relax around bonfires and relate the adventures of the day. Unlike in India, alcoholic drinks were forbidden to the Chhetris in Nepal by sanctimonious high priests. But most of the youngsters wriggled in the forbidden wine and liquor into their private tents, and the evenings were merry. A surreptitious swig or two atop the Haudas while spotting big game was by no means unheard of.

Even amidst the pleasant surroundings of camp life, the pressing issue of the Roll of Succession occupied the minds of, and led to hushed discussions among, the senior A-class members of the entourage[89]. The division of 'A', 'B' and 'C' underscored by Chandra some five years back, and left for his 'progeny' to complete, could no longer be dodged or delayed. The second in line of succession was Rudra, now holding the important post of mukhtiyar, a friend of Juddha since boyhood and confidant in later years, but a C-class nephew. Padma, a rather forlorn figure, considered a weak man by those who knew him, stood next, third in line. He was followed by the three sons of Chandra, and then by the powerful bully, Bahadur. As matters stood, Rudra would succeed Juddha and could bring about drastic change in the Roll, perhaps oust the A-class Ranas en-masse. Padma and the formidable foursome backed by most members of their class pressed Juddha to act first, boldly and swiftly.

On the afternoon of 15th January the shikar party, led by the maharaj, were out hunting. Seated on the Haudas astride elephant's back, they barely felt the earth move. Those in the camp did feel some tremor, but they were minor in the far west region of Mahakali, the venue of the Daudaha that year. It was only four days later that news of the devastation wrought by the great earthquake reached the camp. Kathmandu was in ruins and so were the roads and bridges en route. It took Juddha almost three weeks to reach Kathmandu, making detours around the damaged parts. No doubt the prime minister's mind was heavy with the news of the tragedy and the challenges of reconstruction work he must face. Yet, the problem of the Roll of Succession continued to nag him. A couple of days short of reaching Kathmandu the party rested for a day at Amlekhgunj. During the morning meal, when only the A-class Ranas were present, Juddha shared his thoughts. Mrigendra, then in his mid-twenties, remembers the scene, and the gist of words spoken, heavy with concern.

> I have to reach a decision now. It cannot be delayed any longer. I know we are facing difficult times in our country; and they (the 'C'-class Ranas) are also suffering. But if I delay the decision until the palaces and buildings damaged are rebuilt, their loss will be even greater. They would then have to abandon their newly constructed houses and bear the additional loss of sums spent in reconstruction. So I have made up my mind. You will no doubt keep this secret. I will inform you of the steps to be taken when we return to Kathmandu. Remain prepared and alert.[90]

The immediate task was to assure the people of relief work and prompt implementation of rehabilitation and reconstruction. The measures were swiftly announced at a public function upon the prime minister's arrival at the capital. The task was handled with rare competence. The work is seen as one of the finest examples of good planning, dexterity, efficiency and of cooperative efforts between the citizens and the state apparatus. All expenses were met by the state or raised from donations primarily amongst the Rana family, except for some construction material received from Japan. The New Road and Juddha Sadak, flanking the old city, were planned and constructed during this period. The plots flanking these streets, broad for that time, were offered free to Kathmandu residents whose houses were badly damaged. At that time few wanted to be away from their ancestral places of residence but those who did were wise, these strips form the main shopping and business centre of modern Kathmandu, commanding near the highest land price in the country. The impressive life-sized statue of Juddha still stands steadfast, rising impressively at the crossroad of these two streets. Loans extended to those badly affected were later remitted[91].

Simultaneously, Juddha was preparing the groundwork for the momentous declaration of the purge, described by the British resident as a coup de main. The strength and financial clout of the C-class Ranas, now in total unity, was not to be underestimated. Rudra was a popular C-in-C, with a large flock of the C-class Ranas backing him. The sons of Bhim promoted to the Roll only a few years back had built their own contacts. Bir Shumsher and indeed Juddha himself had fathered a large number of C-class children, many grown to full maturity by the time their father became maharaj. Juddha needed to keep his plans close to his chest but at the same time mobilize his trusted aides into key positions, both in the army and the civil services. He also needed to plan out the fate of those who were being cruelly driven out of their homes and hearths to distant destinations and an uncertain future. More than a hundred kith and kin would be affected and traumatized.

Rumours of the intended purge had nevertheless reached Rudra and the C-class Ranas. They met to examine the options. Some of the younger members wanted to 'strike first' but it was eventually agreed that they had already been outmaneuvered and resistance would be futile. Soon, the order came from the prime minister for all senior members to assemble in Singha Durbar for some important state business, which they guessed was a pretext. As happened during such times of imminent danger, the women of the household were told to wrap up valuables in the folds of their long cummerbunds and heavy saris before the men took leave. Unusually heavy security arrangements, including body searches at entry points to Singha Durbar, were ample warnings of the actions to follow. The members assembled in the first-floor hall, the common meeting place for such gatherings. After a long and tense wait, they saw King Tribhuwan descending the stairway after his meeting with the prime minster. He sat down with the C-class Ranas in silence. He lit a cigarette and inhaled deeply, in obvious mental pain. After a few minutes he stood up, moved slowly, close to each of those he now knew were being driven out of the valley, looked into their eyes as if to bid a fond farewell, and left the scene quietly without a word. Minutes later Juddha emerged from the top of a flight of steps, armed with a revolver in each hand. His A-class sons and guards were similarly armed. Others were lined on two sides of the hall.

Without much ado he told Rudra, in a halting voice choked with emotion, 'We have waited patiently and tried to unite the two factions of our family but you are unable to work and live in harmony. I have no option left except to remove you now from the Roll, along with those who are not present here today. You will be given important positions in governance outside Kathmandu, and will be looked after well.'

After this short and terse declaration Juddha left abruptly. The stunned silence lasted some time, before the guards entered and led Rudra out of the palace. The rest followed[92]. Rudra was escorted to a vehicle parked outside, and driven straight to Thankot and from there the following days along and over the hills on horseback southwards, to his final destination, Palpa. The rest were given forty-eight hours to collect their respective family members, assistants and servants, pack their belongings and cross the mountain passes out of Kathmandu. Each family would be informed of their respective destinations before departure.

This en masse expulsion of the C-class from the Roll and its banishment from Kathmandu is one of the most audacious and controversial acts of the regime. It is intricately linked with the fall of the Rana regime and the dawn of democracy in Nepal.

The New Setup

Of the twenty top positions in the extant Roll, four had been held by the 'C' class. All of them were struck out. The top order now was Padma, Mohan, Baber, Keshar and Bahadur, in that order. Chandra's sons were experienced in all areas of governance, well informed of the internal currents and undercurrents, and well connected with the British establishment. Bahadur, eldest son of Juddha, may have seemed to be 'overbearing and brusque' to one British observer[93] or worse still, 'hot-headed and unbalanced, with scant brain power or political ability' to another[94], but as a forceful and blunt bully, he became a perfect foil to the subtle ways of the three elder cousins. They did have one weakness, common to most autocrats—they failed to assess, gauge or pay due heed to the urge of the people for freedom and democracy, and the winds of change moving ever closer to the Himalayan kingdom via the plains of Hindustan.

As with other Ranas at the top end of the Roll, Juddha had risen gradually in the ranks and received ample salaries, benefits and Birta land from the nigah, the good grace of successive maharajas. While such an income was adequate for a comfortable lifestyle for most high-ranking generals, Juddha was different. He had outpaced his competitors by many lengths in the matter of the large number of women he had, wedded or otherwise, and the children they had produced.

Like all Rana Prime Ministers, once in that seat, the entire revenue of the country was at his disposal. He built palaces for his numerous sons and lived in 'great style and luxury'[95]. Early mornings in Singha Durbar began with a 'light' breakfast of rich mutton broth for 'strength and virility'. Most Rana households lunched by ten, but Maharaj Buba ate around noon, after completing much of his routine work. The sumptuous mid-morning meals were Nepali but laced with Muslim influences. Silver platters brimmed with several varieties of fowl, meat, game, and sometimes fresh fish from the river, relished with rice, lentils, a potato dish, and delicious fresh chutneys. Sweetened yogurt, cut fruit and a sweet dish would follow. The afternoon 'high tea' would consist of savoury treats like beaten rice, flatbreads or puffed swari breads served invariably with a potato-vegetable dish, eggs or meat, followed by sweetmeats. Dinner was a fanciful replica of lunch or often European-style with a five-course gourmet menu. The chefs of Indian nawabs and maharajas had been lured to Nepal. Not permitted to enter the kitchen or touch the food, they instructed the Brahmin 'bajai' cooks in Nepalese palaces from afar, spearheading a gastronomic tradition that rendered splendid results.

In the afternoons, the maharaj would preside over the Bhardari Sabha in Singha Durbar where Rana stalwarts, purohits and bhardars all assembled. The four senior generals and departmental directors would present their weekly reports and received instructions. The head priest, Mahila Gurujyu and Bada Kaji[96] Marich Man Singh would be at hand to offer their sagacious comments—if asked. In a tradition initiated by the music-loving Maharaj Bir, a live band would play soothing classical tunes as the rest of the assemblage took their seats in order of seniority, of course. On special occasions, His Majesty graced the meeting and was greeted with due respect by the prime minister and assemblage, as was customary at public spaces, and was seated on a larger throne than the prime minister's. But in a display of his own grandeur, the maharaj sought permission to smoke his hookah, which, needless to say, was granted. His Majesty would stay for a few minutes, converse softly with the prime minister and be respectfully escorted out from Singha Durbar by the maharaj. After the king left, the meeting was set in motion. An informative, orderly interaction on most days, emotions would spill out and voices be raised in times of crises.

External Relations

Juddha had inherited a firm base of understanding and friendship with Imperial Britain. The new prime minister continued to nurture it. He also strived to ensure that the status of a sovereign state, as distinct from the princely states of India, was upheld and reinforced. Now he took steps to enhance bilateral links with other nations of the world. The Italian Consul General based in Calcutta visited Kathmandu to bestow a prestigious medal on behalf of King Victor Emmanuel, in recognition of cooperation and assistance given by Nepal to the renowned scholar and explorer Professor Tucci. The French Consul General followed suit and awarded Juddha the Grand Cross of the Legion of Honour on behalf of the French President, in appreciation of the assistance provided to the French scholar Sylvian Levy. Both these learned men have left behind valuable documentation related to the host country. The Consul General of China on behalf of President Chang Kai-shek, the Belgian delegation on behalf of King Leopold III and finally a German mission representing Chancellor Adolf Hitler visited Kathmandu to exchange greetings and honours.

These exchanges took place within a remarkably short period, the first few years of Juddha's reign, during an age when it took many weeks for a letter to reach Calcutta, and a month or more for European destinations. The grand public receptions staged during these occasions were highlighted by splendid pomp and fanfare, military drills and colourful processions that infused a sense of national pride and stamped an international seal of recognition to the hard won sovereignty of the kingdom.

More substantive test of statesmanship followed. Hitler was beginning to flex the military muscles of the well-drilled battle machine he had assembled. The vibrations of Nazi activities and preparations for war were discernible to shrewd observers across the globe. Juddha may have foreseen the inevitable approach of another great war even before the British Prime Minister Neville Chamberlain. A full year before Britain declared war against Nazi Germany, Juddha had 'offered to provide a Gorkha contingent to support the allied cause'[97]. The offer was politely declined. The decision to offer support to Britain had been hotly debated in Singha Durbar. Mukhtiyar Padma Shumsher, second in command, had led the group who argued that the Nazis were better prepared to emerge victorious and Nepal should back the winning horse or else remain neutral. However, Juddha took the stand that Nepal should stick to its long-time friend Britain, anyway likely to come out on top in the long run.

Hitler's German army started invading countries in eastern Europe, 'On 4th September 1939, the very day Britain declared war on Germany'[98]. Prime Minister Juddha repeated his offer which was gratefully accepted this time. The 'Johnny Gorkha' was marching out to war once more.

'The total number of men who went forth from the hills of Nepal to fight for the cause of the Empire reached 160,000'.

The tales of Gorkha soldiers fighting in the dense tropical forests and humid heat of Burma or Malaya, the hot and dry deserts of Africa or mud and slush of severe winter in western Europe are legendary. They were dogged in defence, stealthy in camouflage; deadly in surprise strikes at night, and particularly feared by the enemy as they charged headlong in close combat, khukuris raised aloft.

When the war eventually ended the 'Gorkhas returned to their bases modest, cheerful and careless, unaware that their name as a fighting race was now a household word in the western world and that they had placed Britain, the United States and the rest of the Allied nations deeply in debt to Nepal and indeed the Rana family. With them the Gorkhas brought ten Victoria Crosses. Behind them they left a prodigious sum total of valour and achievement'[99].

The wholehearted assistance of Nepal to the British war effort stood in stark contrast to the confused and indeed divided allegiance the Indian leadership presented. A larger proportion of the population of Nepal was killed or wounded than any other country involved in the war'[100].

The population of Nepal at that time was around two million; if one excludes the women, children and the aged, and remembers that a large percentage of those recruited belonged to the ethnic hill community, one can imagine the devastated state of the affected areas[101].

The Raktapat Mandali

Plots were brewing at home, too, against the Rana regime. The first involvement of King Tribhuwan against the ruling Ranas that has come to light is dated around the same time that underground activities of the Nepal Praja Parishad commenced—in the mid-1930s. The plan drawn to assassinate leading members of the ruling Ranas in one quick stroke was naturally enshrouded in great secrecy. Besides Tribhuwan's sons, the three princes, Mahendra, Himalaya and Basundhara, only a small number of 'outsiders' were involved, each carefully tested for their loyalty.

Bhuwan Lal Pradhan[102] lists just five persons. 'Compounder'[103] (physician) Chandra Man, three employees in the palace, and surprisingly Agni Shumsher, a son of Juddha who was sent by the Ranas to serve as ADC to the king, but was said to be 'disenchanted with his father'. Perhaps there were others who were involved. Some believe that Basanta Shumsher, son of Padma was one such. Mahavir is another possible contact.

Without such links how could they procure the hardware required?

The plan was for the king to invite Juddha and other senior Ranas to a reception or film show in the palace and set alight the explosives in the hall after the king came out on some pretext. The attempt was scheduled for more than one occasion but each time some mishap intervened. This plot may never have come to light, but it was divulged by one of the activists arrested and interrogated following the Praja Parishad episode of 1940. Since that date the secret group came to be known as Raktapat Mandali or the bloodshed group.

The plot was kept totally hidden from the king's secret contact with the Praja Parishad leaders, the latter never guessed or suspected that the king had an alternative plan for terminating Rana rule. Almost fifty years later, after the death of Tribhuwan and Mahendra, Ganesh Man Singh, during one of the memorable evenings that I spent with the affable leader, recalled the past, 'I can say now that Tribhuwan had no intention other than transfer of power from the Ranas to the Shahs. Had we correctly analysed and taken into account this intent of his and that of his son Mahendra later, we might have acted differently. The history of Nepal would have taken a different route.'

The aims and objectives of the Praja Parishad were quite different. Brave men were prepared to and did sacrifice their lives for that goal, of freedom and democracy. That action of 1940 marks the pivotal tipping point of open and active public rebellion against the Rana oligarchy.

A Strategy for National Growth

'His Majesty, the King, has given me the responsibility to manage the administration of this country. Yet the country belongs to all of us. The country can prosper and progress only if the people support me in my endeavour. I seek the opinion, recommendations and freely expressed advice of each of you in determining the course to be taken for progress of the country. This is my appeal to you.' [104]

Juddha had made this ardent plea at the beginning of his reign during a public meeting. A man of vision and honest purpose, he must have reflected upon the existing impoverished state of Nepal and sought the support of the people in his endeavour for its growth and progress. His postures had struck a positive note and he proved true to these words.

Once the C-class Ranas were dispatched to different districts, Juddha could concentrate on the issues of economic progress and a strategy for growth, backed as he now was by his homogeneous team and a tested administrative network he inherited. The presence of the state and its apparatus of governance had also reached, or at least been felt, in most parts of the Kingdom through the governors and under them the thalus or mukhiyas (local chieftains). They were vested with extensive administrative and quasi-judicial powers and authority, and to raise taxes on behalf of the government. In return they signed a bond to raise and deposit a minimum pre-determined sum, failing which the defaulter had to pay the balance through his private resources (Ghar-gharana). Land tax (Malpot) formed the major part of the state revenue, collected through the land revenue officers. It was an effective and efficient system of governance but rooted around the age-old feudal format and limited in scope. With nothing other than the narrow foot trails and hill tracts connecting the mountainous terrain, the countryside and the people remained isolated, devoid of basic services, but self-reliant for subsistence existence on strength of local produce and products. Despite the 'crippling loss' caused by diversion of trade via the shorter trade route connecting Calcutta with Tibet, the national economy of the country was robust. In 1902–03 exports stood at more than 26 million rupees and imports at less than 17 million. In 1919 exports rose to near 33 million and imports less than 23 million[105].

The advent of the First World War had a mixed impact on the balance of trade. The entry of mill-made produce adversely affected the prospering cottage industries of Nepal. But there were many positives. The dense forests that cover the Terai belt have always been a rich natural resource of the country. The increasing demand for sleepers, for the nation-wide railway link the British extended throughout India, enhanced this trade in no small measure. Gradually, braving the malaria prone hot and humid landscape, adventurous settlers and tradesmen were beginning to clear the forest fringes and grow food grain and cash crops like jute, sugarcane, tobacco and the lucrative poppy seed along the fertile plains. The Rana rulers encouraged such initiatives, often bestowing free land as an incentive for entrepreneurs to clear the forest and cultivate the land. The Indian railway network touched several towns in India bordering Nepal, which gave a significant boost to the connectivity and growth of the entire region. The total trade figures rose appreciably in the decades of the 1930s and '40s while the balance of trade continued to remain in favour of Nepal till the very end of the Rana regime.

When Juddha took command at the helm, he looked for a major leap forward for the growth and progress of the country. He looked beyond Nepal's borders for inspiration. The Industrial Revolution had catapulted Europe to entirely new heights, and placed the continent in a commanding position of power and prosperity. The prime minister could hardly think of such a growth for Nepal. Thus he looked to the Indian subcontinent. The East India Company and Imperial Britain had paid a pittance to the labour to extract minerals from the mines or to the farm hands for the produce of the lush fields of India, to feed its mills back home for their phenomenal wealth, but at the same time India had gained some residual rewards: national network of railway lines, bridges and roads to connect disparate parts of the vast country, canals to irrigate arid fields, and a communication system that reached the far corners of the subcontinent. Indian entrepreneurs saw new avenues for growth, and moved ahead from running small and medium manufacturing units to venturing into large-scale industries in products such as jute, sugar, cigarettes, textile, steel or cement. The Birlas and Tatas are some of the well-known families who started to grow and prosper under conditions of stability in governance and policies, law and order, and opportunity for a decent education, for the middle and upper class.

The situation in the balance more than 40 per cent of the land mass, some 560 princely states ruled by the Indian princes under British paramouncy was startlingly different. The rulers of most states were masters of the resources and revenue of their territories. 'The rule of law under the Muluki Ain that gave protection and security of life and property to every subject of the Kingdom of Nepal was completely lacking in most of the Indian princely states'[106]. Ganesh Man Singh who suffered perhaps the most brutal treatment, lashings and beatings in Rana custody than any other human being, concedes, 'One of the special features of the Rana regime was that they did not use any such force without verified evidence.'[107]

'The introduction of public amenities and institutions in Nepal, though lagging far behind British India, compared favourably with the princely states. For example, famine-relief measures undertaken in Hyderabad[108] in 1876 were no more comprehensive than the measures that the Government of Nepal had implemented during the great famine of 1863–66. Not many of the state capitals had piped drinking water when Bir Shumsher provided this utility to Kathmandu in 1891, nor electricity when it was installed in the Valley in 1911.'[109] In 1909, the Resident Lt Col Macdonald wrote, 'The people of Nepal are happy, content and uncommonly well off'. By contrast a British official travelling in Cutch State in Gujarat in 1932 lamented, 'If any European has been here before, he has not left any trace!', and a Political Agent in 1937 'would not have imagined that things could have been so primitive and backward in a place we have ruled for over a 100 years'.[110]

However, there were a few Princely States, large and small, that infused remarkable level of representative participation in governance and achieved a high level of all-round growth. Mysore (29,445 square miles), Baroda (8,182 square miles) and Gondal in Gujarat (1,024 square miles) were categorized as 'model states'.[111] Each invested prudently in river irrigation schemes or lake water usage; electricity was generated under some of these enterprises. Promotion of improved methods of cultivation and high value crops substantially raised production. Revolutionary land reform programme was introduced. Cooperative movement was extensively promoted. Handlooms and small- to medium-scale industries, based on agro-based raw material, sprouted in several parts of each state. Bank of Baroda and Bank of Mysore were founded in 1908 and 1913. Construction and operation of railway lines and expansion of motor roads on a priority basis served the twin purpose, of facile movement of men and material, and substantial contribution to state revenue. Healthcare, a pet project of Bhagatsinhjee, Maharaja of Gondal, was taken to the rural villages, and hospitals founded in key townships. In Baroda 'almost the entire school going strength nearly 230,000 students' received some sort of instruction in 1913–14. These figures were 'compared favourably with Bengal, the most advanced of the Indian provinces'. Colleges in Arts and Sciences, in Engineering and Medicine preceded the opening of the renowned Mysore University, in 1916. Rulers of the states around the year 1900 introduced reforms to allow representative participation in the decision making process. Constitutional bodies such as legislative, executive councils and judiciary were empowered to carry out important functions of the state independently, and subject to assent of the maharaja only on the most critical issues.

These Princely States were exceptions to the general trend. A vast majority of the others were not so fortunate; British Governor Generals had to intervene repeatedly in several states that failed to maintain the minimum standards in state management, growth and progress. In the first quarter of the twentieth century, even prosperous and historically renowned States such as Udaipur, Bikaner, Bharatpur and Alwar in Rajasthan, Nabha in Punjab, Dewas and Indore in Madhya Pradesh amongst others, were administered so negligently or the finances so grossly mishandled that the 'paramount power had to resort to taking drastic steps, such as curtailing the ruler's powers, enforcing the appointment of a special British administrator or in some cases, adopting the extreme measure of having him forcibly deposed'.

Industrial Policy and Social Reforms

Juddha saw the backwardness in his own country and was determined to lead it forward on the path of progress, at least in the economic sector. He was a good listener, good judge of men, and chose capable and astute counsellors, such as Ananda Bhakta Rajbhandary, Bhim Bahadur Pandey, Chandra Jung Thapa, Juddha Bahadur Shreshta and Ram Lall Golcha. The first step was enactment of Industrial Act designed to launch a programme for broad-based industrial growth.

The concept and institution of Public Limited Companies was introduced. At that time Nepal did not have a single commercial bank. Private money lenders thrived and petty traders set shop to carry out the business of money exchange. In 1937–38, Nepal Bank Ltd, with its head office in Kathmandu, was inaugurated amidst great fanfare. Gradually, branches were established at key centres. Similarly, so far only small-scale manufacturing units and cottage industries operated within their limited localized market space. Now, based on a 'master plan' and economic survey, a number of industries were set up to produce jute goods, cotton fabric, sugar, vegetable oil, paper, cigarette, matches and chemicals. The industries were located in principal townships all along the southern plains, particularly in the eastern Terai the most suitable terrain for procurement of raw materials and sale/export of manufactured products, via the port city of Calcutta.

The Ranas were not permitted so far to participate in trade or invest in industries. The rule was based on the rationale that those holding powers of governance and privileges attached to it, should concentrate and limit themselves to the field of governance so that 'a level playing field' was created for those who wanted to take up business as their field of engagement. Yet, the ruling Ranas were by far the wealthiest families, followed by the rajgurus and bhardars. So the restrictive rule was waived in case of Public Limited Companies and it was the Rana families who were encouraged to invest the capital required to set up these companies. These companies operated under state supervision and professional management, akin to public-private partnership of these days. The concept of 'limited liability' was new to Nepal and the investments were not without a considerable element of risk. Not all the Rana families were keen to contribute their share without some arm twisting. Incidentally, the restriction imposed on the Ranas, not to engage in private business continued throughout the regime,

Juddha was well aware of the benefits of industrialization in the national context. He was also aware that industrial activities would open up space for social and political dissent and activism. To his credit, he pursued the plan vigorously and as was his nature, did so boldly, without doubt or remorse. Within a short period of ten years an industrial base had been laid for future generations to build upon.

At the state level separate Departments of Commerce, Industry and Agriculture were instituted. Watershed management programme in the mountain belt and a scheme for linking the Himalayan river system for the benefit of the Terai in particular were initiated. Import and distribution of high-quality seeds, construction of granaries, a program to upgrade animal husbandry and forest management formed part of the comprehensive package. Reclamation of unused or marshy lands in the Terai area was targeted in particular for the settlement of retired army personnel. Nepal Bureau of Mines was assigned the task of a nation-wide survey of mineral deposits and their commercial viability. Introduction of banknotes facilitated commercial transactions, so far limited to the cumbersome use of coins, which often had to be transported on elephants or other animal backs, bullock carts or pushcarts. A Department of Roads was instituted and a company of the Nepal army headed by Samar Jung was assigned the task of repair, maintenance and construction of roads and bridges. The Bureau of Statistics was set up.

Cottage industries and in particular the Khadi spinning, promoted some thirty years back by Chandra through Tulsi Mehr Shreshta but heedlessly derailed by his successor Bhim was revived once more. A separate Department of Cottage industries, the Gharelu Adda was established. General Brahma Shumsher headed the Department. He personally visited key areas including those of difficult access and terrain, to identify and promote local skills and crafts. Cotton wool was imported and distributed in carefully selected areas based on a survey conducted to identify existing skills and capabilities. Interest-free loans were extended and a marketing network set up. The farming community in particular, could now engage themselves in this gainful work during the slack seasons. Concentrated inside Kathmandu valley and adjoining districts in the beginning, the industry gradually spread to cover a few other parts of the country. The men and mostly women, who spun the cotton and wove Khadi in the 1940s and 50s, have passed on these skills to succeeding generations. Today, this 'skill heritage' forms the backbone of the woollen carpet, pashmina and other woven fabrics/products that provide employment to a workforce of more than a million. The handloom and handicraft sector makes a major contribution in the export trade of modern Nepal[112].

Brahma had a non-conformist streak in his makeup, rare in those feudal times. He took a self-imposed vow that he would only don garments made from khadi woven in Nepal. He was aware that this would be akin to the 'swadeshi movement' of Mahatma Gandhi, a symbol of revolt, but he was willing to take the risk. His father Baber's disapproval and the wrath of the intimidating Prime Minister Juddha were inevitable, but he was let off with a severe reprimand that a Rana should not indulge in such antics.

Juddha, like Chandra, was genuine in his desire for social reforms. Permissible age for marriage was increased and expenditure on weddings and dowries restricted. Army personnel engaged in warfare were exempted from the strict restrictions on diet and loss of caste status after overseas travel. Similarly, he bulldozed the priests to shorten the compulsory mourning period upon death in the family, drastically, from one year to just thirteen days, for all those employed in government service, and that included all members of the Rana family. One may safely assume that the souls of all Ranas and their ancestors do not go to hell on *this* account.

Law and Order

The Law Commission established by Jung continued to monitor the legal and judicial activities set by the Muluki Ain. There were no more than two dozen adalats (courts) in the country in the early stages following promulgation of the Muluki Ain and the lone court of appeal, the Chaar Khal Adda, was located in Kathmandu. Chandra expanded the reach of law to cover remote parts of the country including, for example, Humla, Darchula or Dadeldhura in the far west, and Ilam in the eastern-most part of the country. Law courts for the Nepalese were established even in Tibet, Lhasa, Kuti and Kerung. By the end of the Rana regime in 1951 about sixty district courts and thirteen courts of appeal were in service.

Successive prime ministers initiated reforms to restructure the courts of appeal, and demarcated areas of their jurisdiction, but the authority of final decision remained firmly with the prime minister throughout the Rana regime. The prime minister was also empowered by law to pass judgement on all political cases, exclusively, through direct intervention if he so wished. He, and he alone, had the authority to alter the provisions of law, but neither he nor even the king possessed the prerogative to override provisions of the law as it existed. Thus the nomenclature of 'Hukumi Sashan' or Rule by Diktat, that is tagged on the Rana regime is justified at the highest level but the Rule of Law, unjust as the laws may be, was an integral part of the regime. In practice the prime minister invariably consulted his immediate successor, the mukhtiyar, who headed the legal department, and at times of the Bhai bhardars in cases related to common law, and the head priest in ethical or religious matters. Strict vigilance was maintained, through the official intelligence network and private sources, to detect corrupt practice at the lower levels of the judicial or administrative ladder and punish the offender. But, once a case was decided at the first court of hearing, the physical distance all the way to Kathmandu and expenses required to register an appeal, made the exercise almost redundant. From here the Bhardari Sabha, a kind of House of Lords in England, headed by the mukhtiyar was, barring exceptional cases, the final court of appeal. Rarely, generally on pleadings of senior members of the family, the Prime Minister would ask for the case to be brought to him for final dispensation. The District Governors and officers under them were empowered with wide discretionary powers that could be and were at times used indiscriminately, unjustly and with a great deal of contempt and disdain for human dignity. Dictatorships, wherever they thrive, in whatever form or in any age, breed feudal order down the line that misuses authority more readily than the rulers through whom they derive their authority.

Whatever its merits or shortcomings, the Muluki Ain of Jung Bahadur retained its central position in the legal framework of the country for some two hundred years. (Many of its tenets remain intact or are still reflected in the current legal treatise or usage.)

Mechanism of the Top Tier Ijlas

There was a saying in the country those days, 'if you want justice go to the 'Khari ko Bot', the massive tree surrounded by a round platform erected in the middle of Tundikhel in Kathmandu. That is where the high ranking rulers including the mukhtiyar, assembled most mornings. The mukhtiyar was the ultimate arbiter in every appeal and all cases, barring intervention by the prime minister. But the decisions were made strictly according to existing provisions of law and carefully preserved precedence.

The 'appeal', to the level of the mukhtiyar was routed through the channel of the officials assigned for the purpose. But it was also possible to petition the mukhtiyar directly through a Binti Patra, a simple handwritten entreaty seeking justice. Baber Shumsher, when he was mukhtiyar liked to be in public view. Splendidly attired, astride his tall dark stallion, he would move along a route protected by the guards between hundreds of the duniyadars that lined the road. The onlookers, too, liked to be well dressed, but most could afford no more than the soiled worn-out clothes they had not changed for days, perhaps weeks. The reasonably well-off city dwellers, the farmers or artisans of the valley, those visiting Kathmandu from the Madhes, and the diverse ethnic mix from the mountains, mostly men but also a sprinkling of women, the young and the old, each in their own traditional attire, presented 'a thrilling spectacle'.[113] Most of them came to offer their salutations, Chakari or watch the spectacle, some to present their grievances. Baber would direct his attendants to collect the written petitions, others struggled through the crowd to personally reach out to present their Binti Patra, to be scrutinized later and briefed to him by the judicial officer.

The procedure for pleading, and delivering a verdict were uncomplicated, though some may see it as primitive. There were no lawyers. The Jhagadias (contestants) presented their respective cases verbally, backed by supporting documents. If needed relatives or friends were allowed to speak on behalf of the Jhagadia, or appear as witnesses. The most accomplished judicial assistants/clerks Ditthas and Bicharis, assigned to the mukhtiyar would have briefed the facts of the case before he, Baber, sat down to conduct the proceedings. Baber listened intently from a high ground floor balcony, occasionally asking searching questions, or seeking clarifications from the pleader or the witness, or consulting the judicial assistants, seated next to him. The verdict would be announced within a couple of days. A meticulous record of each case would be maintained for future reference and precedence.

Baber strived to ensure he was impartial and to be seen as such. I once happened to be present, when he was speaking about his deep concern about a particular verdict that day. Relaxing on his couch in the evening he turned to his senior lady-in-waiting, seated comfortably on the carpeted flooring. Baber confided in her, a noble-hearted Tamang, with whom he shared his bedchamber and his deepest thoughts, and asked in a sombre tone, 'Pansy (that was the name given her in the palace), did I give the correct verdict this afternoon? It was not a straightforward matter and the stakes were high.' I was ten years old but sensed that he was talking to his own conscience as much as to his trusted confidante, and seeking redemption, as it were, in case wrong had been done.

Baber was a powerful advocate of the 'hard line' who strived for longevity of the Rana regime; however, he was sincerely committed to the principle of Rule of Law, which one should understand, is not necessarily synonymous with the concept of natural justice or liberal values. Natural justice is a universal concept; laws are enacted by rulers or legislators who are, at times, opposed to the concepts of natural justice. And yes, a question may well be posed as has been done by Nepal's own genius Balakrishna Sama, 'who art thou to restrict freedom with rules and regulations?'[114]

A little flashback to the previous generation to Maharaj Chandra, who once confided in his grandson Mrigendra, expressing similar doubts and remorse about his earlier action, as Baber did to his Pansy, will be of interest here.

'Amir (this was his pet name for Mrigendra), your grandfather is getting old. It is time he should retire.'

'But why grandfather, what has happened?'

'Last week I punished a man. I dismissed him. Yesterday, I found he was innocent. He was wronged. If I was younger I would have firmer control of events and such mistakes would not have occurred.'

'It is not a serious matter, now that you have my uncles who are mature, and you have me, also grown up'.

'Yes, thank you. The matter is small but not trifle. God has given us untold powers. That must not be misused. The blot with which a prime minister smears someone cannot easily be wiped out. He was an army man. I shall try to give him a civil job. But, he is from a family with (proud) traditions. He may not accept a civil job!'[115]

These introspections by two powerful men, Prime Minister Chandra, and a couple of decades later his son, Mukhtiyar and Commander-in-Chief Baber, reveal the inner turmoil that at times nudged the conscience, and troubled the minds of the Rana rulers, underneath the indestructible exterior they stoutly maintained. 'At times' is an apt term here, for such scrutiny or considerations were rare and far between in the general course of Rana administration.

The Pazani System

The yearly *Pazani* was the most dreaded event for every government servant, civil or military. Unless 'reinstated' the employee simply lost his job. 'For those who had to face it, the *pazani* was a nagging fear and agonising distress.'[116]

The prime minister, as in most other areas of governance, was empowered by law to be the final and unquestionable arbiter, in this case for dismissal or reinstatement, promotion, demotion, reward or punishment. The unrestrained authority gave room for misuse of the powers that was seen in 1931. Understandably, it was perceived and projected as one of the most Draconian instruments through which the Rana prime ministers subdued and subjugated the entire administration, and through it, the people of the country. Nevertheless there was another side of the coin.

The mukhtiyar, as the head of civil administration, was primarily responsible for evaluating performance and for presenting a report to the maharaj for his final decision. A grand function called Thamouti (retention) to display the pomp and grandeur of the regime was held each year to reappoint the mukhtiyar/commander-in-chief, by placing the glittering Sripetch[117], headgear, on his head. The other members of the ruling family were also reappointed through the same procedure. However, the responsibility of correctly evaluating every single employee of the government was squarely placed on the mukhtiyar. When Baber attained that position he delegated some of his responsibilities to his twenty-five-year-old son Colonel Mrigendra, the newly appointed Director of Education. Mrigendra's memoirs are revealing:

> I was shocked by the massacre of 1931, when an unsecure new Prime Minister Bhim Shumsher targeted a whole group

of honest officials whose personal loyalty he suspected. Twenty-eight senior officers and many more in lower ranks were summarily dismissed and junior ones promoted.[118] It was only when I began helping my father in the mukhtiyar's office that I realized that 1931 was an exception. I began to unravel the complexities of the process. Within thirty-five days of year ending (mid-March) every officer had to send a report regarding the men under him. I had submitted many reports from the different posts I held but never knew the inner working earlier. Travelling over hill and dale along dirt tracks, reports from five hundred offices from across Nepal and around 10,000 office bearers poured into the Muluki Adda, office of the mukhtiyar.

The details were comprehensive, astounding. The number of days absent, files/cases dealt with, pending or delayed, competence/ deficiencies at work, everything. Assessment of departmental chiefs and a report of the performance of the office itself had to be submitted. Father was meticulously conscientious about this work, putting in long extra hours each day. The task took the better part of three months before a comprehensive report was presented to the maharaj. The latter included his changes before the list was finalized. The decisions were rarely arbitrary or whimsical. Those marked for dismissal were usually warned earlier. Hardly anyone was dismissed on the spot. Some officers pleaded their case for promotion at the time of the pazani: some of them were reviewed. Unfortunately, lack of transparency gave rise to unwarranted distrust, spreading widespread fear. Only years later, when this system was abolished, did the old adage ring true: 'Do not destroy an old edifice before you build a new and better one.

Some eminent scholars echo this view, 'The pazani system was abolished in the administrative reforms of 1951 in the interests of providing civil servants with a broader degree of job security. Actually however, the results were not those intended. Under the old system,

government servants were assured at least limited security of tenure...
of one year. Post 1951, Nepal on the other hand, government servants
have often been dismissed without notice.'[119] One must add, however,
that the right of appeal to the courts of law as exists post 1951 was
missing in the Rana regime. The separation and balance of legislative,
executive and judicial power is a powerful deterrent to its misuse.

Education

General Mrigendra presided over education in Nepal as Director
General[120] of Public Instruction for nearly twenty years, starting 1930.
The manner in which he helped raise the standard and quality of
education during this period stands in stark contrast to the negative
attitude of the rulers towards education and strict restrictions
placed on promotion and spread of institutions of learning. Yet the
resentment and opposition against the regime took root and spread
from the very acts of denial or permission to open and operate the
schools, colleges and libraries. Parts of his handwritten memoirs
shed light on these developments.

Like the vast majority of the Nepalese including the Ranas, early
education of Mrigendra was in Nepal. On his 17th birthday, in 1920,
his grandfather asked him to name any gift he wanted. Mrigendra
wanted to continue with his education'. The old man was elated. But
permission from Baber, who was in the Waziristan campaign at that
time, was required. An urgent telegram was sent. Some weeks later
Chandra gave the good news. 'Your father no longer objects. You
have my blessings' Mrigendra completed his term at Durbar High
School, joined the prestigious Calcutta University as an Honours
student and earned a Masters' degree in the Liberal Arts—the first
Rana and third Nepali national to do so. On his return to Nepal,
he continued to be groomed lovingly by Chandra until his death,
sadly that very year.

Though considered a 'minor' Department, Mrigendra coveted
the new position of director general. He was not unduly surprised
but nevertheless disappointed to find that the rulers had little interest

in promoting education. The 'Department' was allotted just one part-time clerical staff. There were no files to be handed over. Throughout his tenure of this office from 1930 to 1951, excluding few years in the late forties, he had to carefully balance his natural inclination for promotion of education, literary works and free expression, with the negative attitude of the regime he was a part of. However, on account of the strength of the Chandra family, and his superior academic background, he was confident of retaining his office and improve the quality of education.

He commenced the task in earnest, but then after Bhim's death, he had to learn to work under a new maharaj, who proved to be very different. Juddha achieved much during his Premiership, but his priorities lay elsewhere, in particular in the 'industrial revolution' he initiated. To his credit the 'affable despot' was happy to allow his grand-nephew a free hand in the literary field as long as the young man's enthusiasm did not cross the line of discretion, to the detriment of the Rana regime.

Much before a state-sponsored school system was introduced the upper caste and in particular the Brahmin children were taught basic Sanskrit and arithmetic, and to read and write simple sentences in the Nepali language by their father, elders in the neighbourhood or from the local priest. The Khas language, using the Devnagari script, was the mother tongue of the Chhetris and Brahmins settled in the mountainous ranges, termed jointly as Parbates (people living in Parbat i.e. mountains). It was also in usage, as a second language amongst most other native ethnic groups and the Madhesis. Its use by the ruling elite in Kathmandu and in the Muluki Ain gave it an official status but the major impetus in spreading its roots as a national language came from a Brahmin boy born in the mid-west district of Tanahu, without any connection with the ruling class. Like most other Brahmin boys in the country, he learnt Sanskrit and Nepali from his father, tended cattle and helped his family with their daily chores. Unknown to anyone outside of his family and village folk, young Bhanu Bhakta Acharya, 1814–1868 took upon himself the enormous task of translating the Hindu epic Ramayana from the original Sanskrit into his mother tongue. Its popularity was phenomenal but it was only after his death that it was published, in Varanasi in 1887. Thereafter its readership spread far and wide throughout the country and to parts of India where the language was in use. Those who were illiterate, young and old, men and women, including communities who spoke their own dialects, liked to memorize the lilting verses, listen to and relate the fascinating tales to avid audiences. The Khas language took the status and shape of a national language—Nepali. Cruelly, the Dalits were excluded and women discouraged from all forms of learning. Overall though, Bhanu Bhakta's 'Ramayana' gave a tremendous boost to the tradition of teaching within the household and in close-knit communities. In the absence of a 'census' it is anybody's guess as to what percentage of the children became literate in this manner, before state-sponsored schools started to appear. But a large portion of the male population of Brahmins, Chhetris and some amongst the women and the ethnic communities, became literate in this sense.[121] It is a pity that this tradition of informal learning within the family or community met a slow decline following the introduction of a formal schooling system which was anyway severely restricted during the Rana regime.

The comment of Daniel Wright, a surgeon in the British Embassy during the 1870s, that the subject of education in the country 'may be treated as briefly as that of snakes in Ireland' is not far off the mark. Indeed formal education in Nepal until the time of Prime Minister Dev Shumsher (1901) was all but non-existent. Dev's attempt to promote formal schooling was cut short by his successor Chandra, as narrated earlier. Maharaj Chandra's reign of twenty-eight years has been hailed for noted achievements on many fronts. But despite his educational background of a matriculation from Calcutta, and exposure to the outside world, his long reign had little to offer in this field. Some middle-level schools were established in Patan, Bhaktapur and some of the Gaundas and townships outside the valley. Tri Chandra College was a noteworthy contribution being the first college in Nepal but oddly, not a single high school was added to the solitary presence of the Durbar High School, and the number of students enrolled remained low.

> Until 1901 there were only seventeen students in the class studying in Durbar School and in 1918 one hundred and forty two ... there were just five students when Tri Chandra was established and some twenty five or thirty in the mid-thirties. The students merely tried to mug up and memorise the lessons and recite it in class the next day, there was not much meaningful learning imparted. There were no extra-curricular activities at all and outdoor sport was limited to occasional and unorganized games of volleyball or football on special occasions.[122]

On the other hand, in many palaces of the Ranas and mansions of the bhardars, teachers came to the respective residences and the students did not necessarily go to school. As has been described in other chapters, the vast spaces of the palace compounds provided ample scope for exercise and entertainment. But they were open to and used exclusively by members of the family and the *chakariwals*. *Chakri* was an institutionalized form of relationship, between those who attended the courts and/or visited the royal or a particular Rana palace to proffer allegiance to a benevolent patron of choice, in return for protection and patronage. A chakariwal was one who indulged in this practice which in some cases bordered on sycophancy. But at a higher level, they acted as retainers whose advice in personal or state matters was greatly valued, and in return were amply rewarded.

The manner in which Mrigendra took charge of the education sector in 1932 as the Director General (D.G.) has been narrated earlier. His observations are as disparaging as those of Pandey. 'There were no records or files in the office of the Department, no policy or program either for establishing new institutions or for raising the level of excellence in the existing ones'.

Mrigendra visited different schools and colleges and found their teaching methods to be 'antiquated'. He personally examined answer papers of higher classes and found them 'substandard beyond belief—

one boy got five out of 100 in Mathematics; some boys could not write a single sentence correctly in English'. Asked in annoyance whether they would pass the SLC examination, the teachers replied: 'that is impossible': every year they fail in at least one subject but it was 'customary to let them pass'.

Mrigendra told the teaching fraternity that such negative practices should be stopped. Those who failed in one or more subjects more than once will henceforth not be promoted. The teachers agreed readily. The news travelled rapidly. Mrigendra was deeply embarrassed and worried to find that some of the students affected were his younger cousins or nephews. A couple of the parents thought this was some sort of victimization. Patiently, Mrigendra explained the rationale of the decision; it was for the good of the boys and their career. 'If allowed to carry on as before, they will not pass the SLC exams. Besides, it is imperative that all students be judged with the same yardstick.' At long last, they were convinced and indeed grateful for the action taken in good time.

Mrigendra was able to persuade all four ruling prime ministers he served under (Bhim, Juddha, Padma and Mohan) to allow him a free hand in the task and in deciding measures to improve the standard of education in schools and the one solitary college, Tri Chandra. However, Juddha was careful to ensure that their number remained restricted. He was unwilling to allow state funds to be used for sustaining a spate of new schools or colleges, which he knew would function as 'breeding grounds for revolution against the Rana oligarchy'. Furthermore, any attempt by local communities to run a school, library or informal centres of literary interaction was viewed with suspicion, often discouraged and forced to close down. Mrigendra had to move cautiously within these parameters and constraints. Some months after Juddha became prime minister, Mrigendra was summoned to appear before him. A dour and angry-looking prime minister asked his nephew, in charge of the department, 'I hear you have appointed all your own people in the key positions of your department. Is it true?' Mrigendra pondered a bit and then answered, 'Your Highness, your observations are well founded. But who else could I appoint, except people I knew and trusted to carry out the duties I have been assigned by you? If anybody knows of others who have better credentials for a specific position, I am always open to consider them and make necessary adjustments. I will always follow the guidance of Your Highness'. Juddha was stumped by the answer! After this dialogue the issue of appointments was left to Mrigendra's discretion.

A few experienced and dedicated teachers from India were also brought in to join the team of capable local teachers. Gradually, the quality of education improved to touch a high standard. A veteran political leader of Praja Parishad, Ramhari Sharma, who suffered many years in jail, remembers his schooldays with nostalgia, and a tinge of regret for the new education system, 'I passed my SLC exams from Durbar High School. There was strict discipline and the teachers were dedicated and so good that none of us required any coaching outside These days one can rarely find a teacher of that calibre.'[123]

Juddha was keen, however, to impress upon the people that he had a positive attitude towards education. On request of Mrigendra and the Principal of Durbar High School, Rudra Raj Pandey, the prime minister attended a function at the college and distributed books and presents to the students. Juddhodaya High School was inaugurated by the Prime Minister amidst great fanfare. A Council of Education, 'Vidya Parishad', was established in 1934. A gathering of prominent educationists of the time met on the premises of Tri Chandra College under the leadership of the D.G. The meeting resolved that the Council would establish centres for promotion of different skills, arts and crafts in Nepal and help publish literature related to the specific subject in the language (mother tongue) of the respective community. *A Short History of Development of Education in Nepal* was published in 1937; it traced the evolution of education in Nepal and outlined a policy paper for the future.

A few schools were established by the state and permission granted to a limited number of private applicants, vetted and screened to ensure no 'undesirable elements' were involved. One such school was the Mahavir Institute. It was the very first school in Kathmandu that was allowed to function without formal permission from the government. The Institute which also housed a library was founded and governed by respected scholars of the time and attracted many learned teachers and academics. They worked without fees or remuneration in the faith that such a platform would allow them to infuse socio-political awareness in the minds of the young generation in particular and society at large. The Rana hierarchy perhaps allowed the school to function freely, with a view to demonstrate a 'liberal face' of the regime. But they were unable to fathom the depth of the resentment against them. It was only in 1940 when the episode of anti-Rana leaflets led by Praja Parishad shocked the Rana rulers, and indeed the citizens of Kathmandu, that the truth finally emerged that many of the promoters, teachers and students of Mahavir School were directly involved in or supported the action. They emerged from the 'middle-class' families that energized the democratic movement, and led it to its ultimate success.

Juddha conceded certain openings in some other areas of the literary and cultural field. Chandra had established the 'Gorkha Language Publication Committee' to promote, monitor, regulate and censor all literary works before publication. Gradually its office and space turned into a forum for intellectual inter action, in quiet tones. The appointment of Balakrishna Sama to head the Committee was greeted well and the D.G. oversaw the gradual growth of some open discourse. The prime minister did not intervene. Encouraged, a group led by Balakrishna sought permission for publication of a literary monthly. They approached Mrigendra and he presented the proposal to the prime minster, with his positive recommendation. Despite negative mindset of the Bhai bhardars and the British resident, whose opinion was sought, Juddha approved the idea: *The Sharada* was born in 1938, and has provided sterling services in the promotion of Nepalese literature. Another monthly, 'Udyog', covering the industrial sector followed. Now Sama approached the maharaj humbly, and with some trepidation, for permission (nigah) to stage a play he had scripted, *Mukunda Indira*: he clearly remembered the abuse of Bhim in respect of 'Dhruba'. Ten years later, Juddha was happy to oblige and was pleased to attend the opening show at the ornate theatre in the Singha Durbar compounds. Some days later it was enacted at the large open courtyard in Baber Mahal, a perfect venue for the tragic love tale. That enchanting evening is etched in my memory, a boy of perhaps seven or eight at that time.

During near three decades of his leadership in the field of education Mrigendra had to walk a tight rope, the primary objective of the department he headed was to promote and improve the standard of education in the country but the directives he received were to monitor, censor and restrict the spread of education or publication of literary matters within 'manageable limits' which meant that they should not devalue or discredit the Rana regime. He knew very well that 'knowledge' could not be separated from 'awareness', that freedom of expression was essential for broadening the mental and intellectual horizons. His exposure to life at Calcutta University, the hotbed of the revolutionary movement in India, and his interaction with the body of teachers and friends, had infused certain values that he could not possibly abandon. Nor could he disregard the urgency of voices for reforms with in Nepal now. He needed a team of wise and talented men to manage the delicate and arduous task. Fortunately, such men of substance were available even amongst the limited number of educated men in Nepal those days. Some of the noted scholars, thinkers and educationists he engaged such as Balakrishna Sama, Rudra Raj Pandey, Rishikesh Shah, Yadu Nath Khanal, Ram Prasad Joshi, Kul Nath Lohini, Bishnu Prasad Dhital, will always be remembered for their valuable contribution to the field of literature and education in Nepal. They helped him in improving the quality of teaching and raising the standard of education to a level comparable to the rest of the subcontinent; but in terms of widening the base of education and of promoting new institutions of learning, they had no option except to accept the strict diktat of the State. Only Padma in his short term of office as prime minister (1945–48), was willing to accept and able to implement a policy of widespread expansion of literacy and education.

Rise, Rise, Awake and Rise

While Juddha did provide a major push to modernize commerce and industry he continued to follow the policy of the Rana oligarchy to restrict spread of education, and isolate the people from external contact. Permission of the government was required for travels even with in the kingdom. It was only in July 1946 that common citizens were 'graciously granted' permission to possess radio sets. (*Gorkha Patra Daily:* 8 Sravan 2003 = 24 July 1946). Under these conditions there was no way people could make a comparative assessment of the conditions they were living in, vis-à-vis the rest of the world, or to be aware of the rising tide of rebellion against the colonial or authoritarian regimes. But the signs of dawn to come emerged without much warning.

> 'Rise, rise, awake and rise.
> Move on the road of progress,
> Now at least abandon your deep sleep.
> You have slept long enough, now arise.'

Dharanidhar Koirala (*Naibedya,* 1917) did write these and other moving lines, but then moved out of the country to join others in exile.

Siddhicharan Shreshta dared to include a fiery line, *'Kranti bina shanti maru'*—*'There can be no peace without revolution'* in his Newari language and was promptly arrested and imprisoned for long years in the dark cells of Kathmandu jail. Other leading literary figures including Lekhnath Paudyal, Laxmi Prasad Devkota and Balkrishna Sama wrote a few lines to highlight the injustice and oppressions in society. However, the bulk of their voluminous work skirted away from socio-political issues until the last few years of the Rana regime. The ire against the Rana rulers was, however, spreading its reach, wider and deeper. The growing circle of the middle class was restive as they watched the luxurious and decadent lifestyles of the ruling elite, in stark contrast to the impoverished conditions of the common masses. All the high ranks of the civil and military administration were exclusively reserved for the Rana hierarchy. The rest were obliged to seek 'nigah', the favours, of rulers through the humiliating sycophantic practice of *Chakari*. Outwardly, they displayed allegiance, bowed in reverence, but with little sincerity.

'If this was the state of mind of the bhardars and their kin and of those who were under the employ of the state, or 'close' to the Ranas, what could one expect from the duniyadars?'[124]

Amongst the duniyadars too, the barriers of isolation were breaking down in the years that followed the First World War. The institutions of learning and education that had sprung up, though limited in number and scope, nevertheless produced youthful groups alive to the struggle for democracy swirling across the border. Increasing numbers of the young generation crossed over and joined colleges and universities in Indian cities like Patna and Calcutta in the east, and Banaras and Allahabad in the north, the hotbeds of the Indian freedom struggle. They were thrilled by literature that talked of concepts such as democracy, rule of law or civil rights, or narrated the drama of the Bill of Rights, the gradual supremacy of the Parliament over the monarchy in England, the French revolution or the Constitution promulgated by 'we the people' of USA. Novels like *A Tale of Two Cities* and *War and Peace* were widely read. Political writings of Karl Marx and Engel were passed on in strict secret amongst political activists and other Nepalese who had found employment in the orchards and tea gardens or in the cities of India, or the retired Gorkhas who settled down there. The 'Pravasi' Nepali, and in particular the political exiles, the like the Koiralas, Bhattarais and Bhandaris, in Banaras, or and leaders of the ethnic communities in north India formed an integral part of the movement that eventually toppled the Rana oligarchy. The urge for freedom invaded the minds of its educated citizens, and slowly but surely the desire for liberty and dignity trickled down to cover ever wider sections of society.

Within Nepal, covert and subtle ways had to be adopted to express opposition to the repressive state. The socio-religious sector

provided openings for expressing dissent, reformists raised their voice
in different ways, and many were prepared to suffer or perish as much
as the political activists. One generation earlier Madhav Raj Joshi and
other followers of the Arya Samaj movement had been manhandled,
imprisoned and/or forced to leave the country. Nevertheless the
doctrines of the Arya Samaj continued to gain momentum and spread
to different parts of India and Nepal. The Terai belt was always
receptive to the progressive ideas floating across the border. In the
1930s one Raja Lal Kalwar from Birgunj offered his residence as its
office. In the meantime, Shukra Raj Shastri, following the footsteps of
his father Madhav, had quietly rebuilt the organization in the valley.
Similarly, a new generation of politically conscious young activists
had mushroomed, driven by the urge to establish a forum to seek
peoples' right to civil liberties. The two groups mingled freely as
did their ideas, dreams and goals. In 1937–38 an organization by
the name of *Nagarik Adhikar Samiti*, Civil Rights Committee, was
set up in Kathmandu. Young Shastri was chosen as Chairman and
Kedar Man Byathit as the Secretary, unanimously. Kalwar and Ganga
Lal Shreshta (later to attain martyrdom with Shastri), were amongst
the audacious young men to join the committee.

Watched closely by the vigilant intelligence network of the
Rana regime, the formation of the committee was easier than the
implementation of its programs. Radio sets were strictly banned
those days. As the great war was going badly for the allies in
Europe even the few Bhardar families who were permitted their
use were ordered to return them Juddha did not want the people
to know about it. However, such restrictions only whipped the
appetite for news and exchange of views. Amongst the small stalls
and stores that now flanked the streets of central Kathmandu, a
clutch of book stores had come up near the Durbar High School.
Owned by the enterprising Newars who also formed the bulk of the
socio-political activists these shops turned into venues for dialogue
that stimulated the mind to rebellion[125]. Students, teachers and
activists from the neighbouring schools and college, members of
the Civil Rights Committee, or those working in utmost secrecy to

form a political party, later to emerge as the Nepal Praja Parishad, converged here in small groups. They spoke in hushed tones about the ongoing freedom movement in India, the changing fortunes of battles being fought in Europe and the Middle East, or the now rampant Japanese in East Asia, and of course about the socio-political malaise inside their own country.

Members of the Civil Rights Committee were seeking ways and means to propagate their doctrine, in public spaces. Providence led them to Pandit Muralidhar Bhattarai, a popular preacher of the day, with thorough knowledge of the scriptures and the political undercurrents within and outside of the Kingdom. He was a reformist with in the Hindu faith that matched with the doctrine of the Committee. A full four months of the *Chaturmaas* were approaching when religious discourses or *prabachans*, from the *Puranas* are staged throughout the country. There could be no better occasion for Murlidhar to display his talent of subtle and telling delivery. The venue chosen was an open public square in Asan, at midtown Kathmandu. The verses of the *Purana* are common but the interpretation and the commentary is left to the inspiration and elucidation of the preacher. The discourses that followed in the four autumn months of 1939 were different from anything that such an assemblage had ever heard before. Though the bulk of the subject matter from the numerous speakers was purely religious Murlidhar selected verses and tales in the Hindu scriptures that condemn injustice and tyranny, and delivered a measured but effective criticism of the ongoing suppressive governance and politics in Nepal. Mahatma Gandhi figured prominently and the call for Satyagraha and agitations raging in India, calling for an end of autocratic colonial rule, were narrated with telling effect.

The news of the exciting discourses travelled fast and far, and people poured into Asan, the numbers growing each passing day. The political undertones of the speakers were not difficult to discern and were reported to the prime minister and the Rana hierarchy. They became the focal point of discussions each evening in the palaces as much as in the tiny rooms of the common citizen. On any other occasion, the order for a clamp down would have been issued without delay. But this was a discourse, *Satsang*, ordained by the holy scriptures. Many speakers confined their deliveries to purely religious sermons. Disruption of such a function was considered a cardinal sin. Juddha was not a strict follower of archaic rituals and had initiated many reforms in the socio-religious practices that the high priests did not appreciate. However, he too believed in the powers of God, worshipped the deities and indeed had some of the Hindu epics translated into the Nepali language, for free distribution. Besides, some counsellors warned that forcible disruption of such proceeding would antagonize the populace. Juddha decided to refrain from a potentially sinful and politically risky act. The four exciting months came to a close in joyous prayers.

The Committee reviewed the outcome of the four months' celebrations and came to a conclusion that such exuberance of the people should not be allowed to cool down. They decided to commence weekly public sermons. The details of date, time and venue, a larger open public courtyard at the very heart of town in Indra Chowk, were discreetly disseminated in advance. Huge crowds started gathering, well before the appointed hour. The chief speaker was Shukra Raj. He quoted verses from the Bhagavad Gita once more and then moved on to castigate the acts of repressions by the State. In concluding, he called for social, religious and political reforms. Byathit, the conductor of the proceedings, then turned to the audience and invited anyone who dared, to come up to the platform, take the *paan* he offered to redden the mouth, and speak fearlessly. Young Ganga Lal, still in high school, could resist no more. 'Like an injured tiger he bounded atop the platform', munched the *paan* and delivered a stunning speech. After depicting the sorry state of the poor people of the country, he exposed the acts of tyranny of the Rana regime and extolled the citizens to fight and extract the rights and liberties due to human beings. 'Everyone has to die. I am a brave son of the soil and am prepared to offer my life for the country.' Thunderous applause greeted the brave heart[126].

This was not a regular religious discourse and the speakers had crossed the threshold of discretion. The administration moved in swiftly. Shukra Raj was arrested from his residence the next morning, soon tried on charge of sedition, found guilty and jailed. Ganga managed to escape. But his mother had died recently and his father was in government service. If he absconded, his father would have lost his job, perhaps face sterner punishment. Friends and relatives pressured and eventually persuaded the young man to give himself up and seek Juddha's pardon. The prime minister obliged.

The Civil Rights Committee could no longer sustain its programmes. However, during the past months its activities had stimulated the mind and spirit of a greater number of the citizens than ever before. As expected, the news travelled from Kathmandu beyond its ring of hills and reached the far corners of the kingdom and the eager ears of the Nepalese living in India. Never had such a sustained and pointed condemnation of the regime been exposed from an open public platform, and in Kathmandu! Right under the noses of the haughty Ranas! The urge for rebellion and change that swelled was firmly imprinted into the hearts of the citizens of the valley—it would never diminish. It would remain passive at times, but erupt time and again, at critical junctures. Not only the members and followers of the Committee or the Arya Samaj group, but many in the audience during these discourses and public meetings were to soon enter the battlefield of revolution. Ganesh Man Singh was one such man.

'I was in that crowd and felt that these people, Shukra Raj, Pandit Muralidhar and Ganga Lal have upstaged me. I was jealous of them. But I could not do anything then, for even if I had the opportunity to address a gathering like that, the police would quickly arrest me, which would defeat the purpose.'[127] Thus, Ganesh Man went back to Calcutta to complete his studies. However, his mind was made up; and there were many like him in that crowd who were prepared to take the plunge when the right time was at hand. That time was to arrive soon. The Praja Parishad episode exploded in less than two years' time.

It is unlikely that the leaders and protagonists of the exercise, or indeed the Rana rulers, smug in their resplendent palaces, nor the spectators who watched the long drama play out, comprehended the full measure of the impact that the incidence had created or the ripples it was to generate. Books on Nepal's history have not given due space or cognition to the actions of the Civil Rights Committee. However, on deeper introspection, one can arrive at a conclusion that the future agitations on the streets of Kathmandu emanated from here. The ripples gradually turned into the wave that eventually swept away all before it. The high tide of the Rana regime started to ebb from this point, and the Praja Parishad episode followed.

Genesis of Discontent and Rebellion in the 'Last Shangri-La'

'You do not have to close your eyes and imagine how the city was 400 years ago, for nothing has changed,' Michel Peissel, a French visitor, writes about Kathmandu in the 1950s[128].

The grandeur of the central palaces, the Durbar Squares, one in each city, remained largely the same till the 1970s, with temples and stupas rising in harmony with the urban dwellings. The rulers lived in the Durbars[129] while the nobles, courtiers, and priests, built their houses around them. Then came the houses of the tradesmen, artisans and farmers, and finally, in the outer fringes of the city, lived the smiths, cobblers, butchers and similar castes, whose occupation and trade needed open spaces for waste disposal. Cobbled streets were flanked by rows of small houses connected in harmonious embrace and surrounding open square courtyards (bahals) in between. Patees[130], wells or shrines dotted the square where the young and old gathered to play, relax or for rousing devotional singing in the mornings and evenings. Womenfolk met around the Hitis built at strategic locations throughout the city: fresh and clean water channelled through canals from far-off foothills filled the ponds and wells. Deities and motifs of superb craftsmanship in metal, terracotta, wood or stone around monuments, on doors, windows and eaves at every niche and corner highlighted the traditions of the valley. Beyond its surrounding walls, each city opened out into a huge open ground, the Tundikhel, with a large pond on one side, another dimension of the city plan.

◆

Siddhi Lal Singh[131] was born in one of the quaint little houses. He belonged to the farming community called Jyapus, one of the earliest inhabitants of the valley. From a young age he carried a kharpan[132] each morning and with his elders walked to their farm located outside the city wall, as did hundreds of other men, women and children. They would carry farm implements, some beaten rice and salty chutney for the afternoon snacks, and an earthen container full of thick rice beer. During harvest time they would carry back huge loads of seasonal produce, bulging out of the baskets, dangling and dancing in tune with the rhythm of the happy masters. Siddhi Lal declares:

> Even when I was elected to the House of Representatives in the nineties, I carried out this chore at times. The Jyapus are renowned as the best farmers in the country; but the name Jyapu is used as a derogatory term even by the traders, the Shrestas, within our own community (Newars) . This is unfortunate. For the word Jyapu is a mix of 'Jya' meaning work and 'Phuku' meaning skilful, my proud heritage.

Archaic caste barriers prevented their entry into the more lucrative and prestigious professions and services. Most Jyapus lived in a state of acute poverty and squalour, as did the Dalits. Siddhi's family was one of the lucky few that owned a good piece of farmland. Siddhi's father was employed as a peon in the Patan High School and remembers how the pay scale rose from ₹30 to ₹90 per month in late 1940s. Regular festivals added spice to life. Siddhi was a diligent student, at the school his father worked. In the spare time the city offered plenty of space for play and frolic. The Bagmati River was nearby and the boys could paddle happily, swim in its currents or roam around the splendours of the city. The weather was pleasant, the air clean and fresh. One fine day when he was ten, Siddhi joined a procession.

...more for fun than any other reason. It was led by Tulsi Mehr Shreshta chanting praises of the almighty. Suddenly, policemen surrounded us. I remember clearly how and at which spot the leaders were arrested, but I was let off being too young. Later that evening I realized that he was a Gandhian reformer. As I grew older I began to comprehend the gravity of injustice and atrocities we suffered. I joined the farmers' wing of the Communist Party, drawn by the call for freedom from the despotic Ranas. I was in and out of jail but we communists generally worked underground during and even after the revolution of 1951.

Siddhi slowly climbed up the ranks and was one of the two top communist leaders, with Man Mohan Adhikary, in the People's Revolution of 1990.

Outside of the city walls the landscape of the valley changed after the Gorkha conquest. Unlike the city-bred Newars, the hill people prefer to live in individual houses built on a separate plot of land, so the newcomers occupied farm or fallow land outside of the old cities and built their houses on separate plots, using local bricks and tiles for the sloping roofs. The bhardars acquired or were granted freehold land in these areas by succeeding prime ministers.

◆

Dimon Shumsher Rana[133] was one of these beneficiaries. The turn and twists in his life mingle with history. Neither revenge, as in the case of one group of Ranas, nor poverty nor any sense of socio-political injustice drove him to the ranks of the revolutionaries. He was not included in the Roll of Succession; neither were his father or grandfather. His family was content in the comfortable lifestyle of the second rung of 'bahirya' or 'C' Ranas. Maharaj Dev Shumsher had granted their family property and a large plot of Birta land in the Terai to his grandfather. Ample stock of food grain arrived regularly from the land regularly. Each adult male in the family was enlisted in the army with a rank of an officer and the pay and privileges attached. They enjoyed a life of comfort and leisure. As was the practice, Dimon needed to choose someone from the top echelons of the ruling Ranas as his patron/mentor to whom he was then obliged to pay homage, chakari, an institutionalized system of linkage similar to one that prevailed in medieval Europe between kings, lords or noblemen and their 'retainers'. Dimon chose Mohan Shumsher well before he was the prime minister, a wise choice, no doubt. He attended to the army duties in the mornings and rode his bicycle each afternoon to Maharaj Ganj Palace, a good hour each way from his home in Patan. Once inside, he was treated well by Mohan and the family. Like most members of the aristocracy Dimon took little interest in studies, but unlike the others, he was not fond of sports either. He became friendly with Avnesh Chandra Roy, a Bengali teacher brought to Kathmandu for tutoring students, particularly of the ruling family. He too was not the sporty type and there was not much else to do in Kathmandu after work hours. Roy was impressed by young Dimon's quick intelligence and offered to introduce him to English literature. 'In that "Eureka!" moment, I found my abiding passion in life,' says Dimon. He devoured the prose and poems of English authors and poets, and gradually turned to Nepali literature. He started writing, and in a few years' time had completed his first historical novel *Basanti*, an enthralling tale of love, life and intrigue within the Rana palaces. However, permission from the Department of Education was required for its publication in Nepal.

Mrigendra Shumsher was the Director of Education. Dimon's request for a darshan, an audience, was granted readily. At a drawing room of Baber Mahal he presented Mrigendra with the manuscript of *Basanti*. 'I seek your honour's kind permission for getting it published,' he pleaded humbly, as was the customary manner of approach. Mrigendra flipped through it, looked piercingly at the expectant author, asked him to wait and went out of the room. On return he handed over another manuscript to Dimon. 'Go read this and come back to me after a week. I will consider your request in the meantime.' Dimon went home and eagerly read the contents. It turned out to be a romantic novel, entitled *Ek Paap ko Katha*[134] about a 'noble family' living in Kathmandu. At one point he stopped, moved by a vivid narration of a passionate love scene between the young nobleman and a country girl. He turned the pages to look for the name of the writer; it was missing. He completed his reading of the gripping saga and on the appointed time and date returned to Baber Mahal. Mrigendra was expecting him.

Without much ado he asked Dimon, 'Tell me, can that be published in Nepal?'

Dimon hesitated, 'It may be a bit too bold, Sir.' he stammered back.

'That is why I refused its publication,' Mrigendra shot back. 'You are a Rana and you think I can give you permission to publish *your Basanti?*'

Acknowledging the stark reality, Dimon went home, deeply disheartened. Some years later when Mohan became prime minister, the persistent novelist made up his mind to visit Banaras and get his opus printed, come what may. It was a popular novel and sold well. Once he returned to Kathmandu, he had to bear the full brunt of the resentment and anger of his kinsmen and his mentor, now the Prime Minister. He was ostracized by those he had considered his friends and even by his relatives, and he did not dare to continue going for chakari to Mohan's palace. His chances of a promotion in the army had vanished overnight. He watched the ongoing movement against the Rana regime from the sidelines, holding on to his job but unable to offer sincere support. The course of his life was destined to take a dramatic turn, very soon[135] that will be related later.

After the overthrow of the Rana regime, *Basanti* became a big hit and Dimon went on to pen some more bestsellers. To his astonishment, he also saw the novel *Ek Paap ko Katha* finally getting published. The writer's name was Randage Rimi. A strange name, but reverse and roll it around, you will get Mrigendra.

◆

Indra Bahadur Rai, who guesses he was '…about seventy-seven years old,[136] lives near Dumja, a two-day trek or three-hour drive east of

Kathmandu. It is the ancestral village of the Koiralas from where they migrated to Biratnagar a 100 years ago. Some distance away from Dumja, I spotted an old man lounging beside a mountain slope overlooking the lovely river Sunkosi, and stopped to chat, on a hunch. Traces of the old Postal Route can be seen running along the steep mountain across the river, in obvious state of disuse. On our side we could see, far off, a tar-topped road being built with Japanese aid. It was named B.P. Koirala Road.

The old man was wrinkled and wearing a soiled and tattered bhoto-suruwal[137], the usual dress in villages across the mountain belt. A good opportunity, I thought, to hear a first-hand account of what life was like in these hills in the 1940s. He was friendly and happy to talk about old times.

'What was it like living in these mountains in your youth, while the Ranas still ruled? Was life good?' I asked.

'How can it be good on these hard unforgiving slopes without any water? The meagre produce fed the family for barely half a year. For the rest we lived off the roots and nettles from the forests. We eked out a living by working in the fields of the more affluent, but the pay back in kind was a pittance. The women walked hours to fetch water. We did have a couple of buffalos and goats and so some milk products for most of the year. Now we have tap water in the village, and the road has brought some money, we can send and sell the milk in Kathmandu.'

'The Ranas never wanted us to learn. There were no schools; so I have never gone to school and my sons are also not educated... but now they do some wage labour in Kathmandu and earn a few rupees when they are hired.'

'Why did they not join the army, as your caste is Chhetri and so suited for that line?' I queried.

'They should have, when young; but now they are past thirty and so their lot is set. They do not want to come here and work in the fields either.'

I asked when the first school was built nearby. By this time two young boys, his grandsons, had joined us and intervened. 'It was built in 1952; this was one of the first gifts that the village got after the Ranas were gone, since we are near the ancestral home of the Koiralas.' I looked down at the young boys, bemused, and was rewarded by two bright and happy faces smiling back at me; they had just returned from school. Life was still hard for the family members; but they looked healthy and clean. And school life had given a ray of hope for the future.

I turned to the old man again, 'I want to know more about that old Postal Route there across the river.'

'Oh that! It is not used now; we have motor roads. But during the olden times it was our lifeline. It was narrow, steep and dangerous in some parts. I once helped carry a criminal, a murderer along this route to Kathmandu. A large cane cage with bamboo poles at each end was built, and four strong men carried it with the culprit tied inside. It took us four full days, instead of two. This kind of punishment warned all the people along the route. Crime of any kind was very rare those days.'

'What about now?' I asked.

'You know more than me,' an answer born of hidden fear and threat. 'But they do not bother us.' He was not naming the Maoists. 'We have nothing and so there is nothing they can take from us. But yes, many bad things have been done and although they are in the government now, they still demand money from anybody who has an income.'

The Nepal Praja Parishad and the Martyrs

Ramhari Sharma was born in 1916 in a Brahmin household. By now the cityscape of Kathmandu valley outside of the old cities had changed. The use of mortar and cement to replace the brick exterior had commenced with the Dharara minaret, before the Treaty of Sugauli (1815–16). Schools and hospitals, and the colossal white neo-classical Rana palaces dominated several vantage points in Kathmandu.

Ramhari lived in a pretty double storeyed house built amidst a fertile farm land at Godavari village on the outskirts of Lalitpur. The elders in the family were either professional purohits performing religious rites or joined the civil service. Yet others were 'writers' who helped clients prepare legal documents in the Law Courts or Land Office. Ramhari was two when his father died and his grandparents looked after him as their own, taught him Sanskrit and shlokas from the scriptures. His uncle often visited a family of the Acharyas. They held higher positions in the government, owned more than hundred Bighas of fertile land near Janakpur and a spacious twenty-room house in Kathmandu. Cattle and horses were kept in the sheds and stables of the compound. Bada Hakim, Tika Prasad Acharya, had two wives, three concubines, numerous children. Tanka Prasad was the brightest, five years older than Ramhari and was already well-versed in English. Ramhari started learning English and he was delighted. My life started moving in a new direction, a path that few thought existed those days, but one that brought me exhilaration and yes… overwhelming fear at times and untold suffering at others.' The friendship between the two boys later grew into a political bond of critical significance.

Tanka Prasad liked to be regarded as a member of a middle-class family not willing to admit the 'semi-feudal' surroundings he grew up in. Tutors came to their residence, a luxury that few could afford. Tanka Prasad buried himself in books, Nepali, English and Hindi. Short, plump and with odd features in a round face, he often ended up at the wrong end of the pranks. But there was a glint in his eyes that reflected the steel in his makeup, he was born with a natural talent to lead men and uncommon commitment and valour. One of the finest compliments comes from Ganesh Man Singh, no less, when both faced a charge of sedition and possible verdict of capital punishment, 'during the course of his interrogation, I saw the difference between a coward like me, shaking with fear, and he— sitting unflinchingly cross-legged and facing the terrible personality of Nara Shumsher, without a hint of fear. I told myself, this is how I will face my interrogation when my turn comes. I will surprise the Ranas by the strength of my response. But when I faced the interrogators, I was like a frightened dog once more'.

That spirit of rebellion in Tanka Prasad was ignited when his father Tika became a victim of the wrath of the rulers. Tika had risen gradually in the ranks to be appointed governor of Biratnagar, a position of supreme authority in the district and good salary. The three years of Tanka Prasad's life in Biratnagar in his early teens were 'free of worry, full of comfort and entertainment'. That life was shattered when his father was held guilty of misappropriation of a large sum of state funds, dismissed and directed to pay the unaccounted sum. The Acharyas had to sell parts of their ancestral family home and their land near Janakpur to pay off the penalty. 'This act of gross injustice sowed the seed of hatred against the Ranas in my mind although there were other issues that influenced me'[138].

Tika was jobless. When working as Chief Officer in the Land office in Kalaiya in Bara District he used to visit the Barewa Durbar, a splendid palace of a branch of the Shah rulers. The Acharya family headed there. The Shahs were connected by marital alliance with the ruling Ranas. Mohan Bikram Shah, popularly acclaimed as Ram Raja of Ram Nagar[139], had looked upon Tika with favour and kindness. Gradually, Ram Raja was to invest jointly in a business with him, to operate two inns at each end of the trekking route joining the plains (Bhimphedi) with Kathmandu.

Tanka immersed himself in his studies. Newspapers from India, more readily available in the Terai, were filled with the exciting news of the freedom movement that had gripped the Indian imagination and was now playing games with his mind. His hatred of the Rana rulers moved now to a desire for revenge and rebellion. He was looking for ways to meet like-minded men when providence seemed to lead him to that horizon. A handsome young man, Dashrath Chand riding on an elephant with huge tusks caught his eyes, one bright and hot day. He was close to Ram Raja and helped him manage the estate. The Chands are descendants of the Khas, who had established their hegemony and dynastic rule in the far west many centuries back, they take immense pride in their lineage. Dashrath had inherited the handsome features, athletic build, love of sports and pleasing manners of his kinsmen, but not the arrogance or haughty disposition. Like many students from well to do families of western Nepal, he was sent to Banaras for his education and at times visited Calcutta. Later he joined the Durbar High School in Kathmandu. An eligible bachelor much sought after by the Ranas and the Shahs, he finally married a daughter of Rudra Shumsher, Governor of Palpa. The young man was sympathetic to the freedom movement in India and admired the leaders as much as he surely abhorred the ruling Ranas who had thrown out his father-in-law from Kathmandu. In their background and looks, Tanka and Dashrath were poles apart; but it did not take them long to discover their shared ardent desire to dislodge the Rana oligarchy.

The inns of Tika Prasad were doing well now and he supplemented the business with a bunch of ponies for convenience of the travellers to cross the mountains. Tanka preferred to return to Kathmandu, to continue his studies, and with revenge against the rulers in mind. He met Chand frequently. One fine day while the two colleagues were strolling along a road outside the Narayan Hiti Palace, Dharma Bhakta Mathema also happened to be walking along the same road. Dashrath knew Mathema belonged to one of the distinguished Newar families. For many generations they had occupied the highest posts allowed to non-Ranas in the civil service. His father Adi Bhakta was given the title of 'Subba' at his birth, a rare honour at any age! He joined active service at an early age and also helped the family business of precious metals and jewellery. But, following a deep misunderstanding with Maharaj Chandra, Adi Bhakta fled with his family to Calcutta carrying all his valuables. They were able to start a flourishing business in Calcutta too and lived in great style. Dharma Bhakta, on the other hand was stimulated by the freedom movement that was in full swing in India and on occasions joined the *Satyagraha* call of the INC[140]. He excelled in all aspects of the martial arts. On return to Kathmandu he started a wrestling school and was soon hired to teach these disciplines to the members of the Royal family at Narayan Hiti. Tanka Prasad had for a long time thought that a link in the palace would be a crucial factor in any plan or strategy to unseat the Ranas and was now convinced that the impressive figure he saw across the street was such a man. Dashrath remained cautious; it would be too risky to disclose their intent to one who belonged to a family traditionally loyal to the Ranas. Indeed several top ranking Rana rulers including Baber Shumsher patronized the Mathemas and their business in Calcutta. Tanka decided to follow his hunch. Some weeks later while Tanka was at the inn of his father in Bhimphedi he got the news that Mathema wanted to hire ponies for his return journey to Kathmandu. At the break of dawn the next morning he reached the lodge where Mathema had halted, with the best ponies of the stable, and offered to ride together up to the check point for entry into Kathmandu. As the mountain ponies lumbered up the steep and stony ascent the two men talked about their country, the people and the rulers. Tanka gauged the mindset of his fellow rider and decided to take the gamble. Carefully he asked the aristocratic Newar from Kathmandu to help the noble cause of democracy; a pledge was made as the riders reached the check point at Chisa Pani Gadhi. Dharma Bhakta Mathema laid down his life for the cause within four years from that fateful day.

A team of like-minded young men were united now and they started to meet secretly, often at the house of Mathema in mid-town Kathmandu where he ran the school. In the summer of 1936 Tanka Prasad, Dashrath Chand, Mathema, Ramhari and a fellow student in Tri Chandra College Jeev Raj Sharma gave shape to a political party and named it Nepal Praja Parishad (NPP), with Tanka Prasad as its founding President. Every move of the party needed strict secrecy, the sleuths of the regime were everywhere and had so far quickly detected and quashed every such move. Thus no written document was maintained to define the structure, objectives or other details. But a Commemorative Issue published on the occasion of the Golden Jubilee, edited by Ramhari Sharma in 1986 sets out the principal objectives: 'To end the dictatorial rule of the Ranas and establish a democratic regime under the constitutional leadership of the King'. All members took a solemn oath placing the Gita on the temple, expressing readiness to make any sacrifice required for achieving the goals set.'

'We started the party but our strategy was unclear'[141]. Dashrath Chand was assigned the task of going to India to arouse popular opinion against the Ranas. He contributed articles in his pen name in Gorkhali and Janmabhoomi published by Koiralas in Banaras but soon the British, on pressure of the Ranas, closed down the press. The task of approaching King Tribhuwan and seeking his support was assigned to Mathema. On his recommendation and assurance of sincerity, the royal medical practitioner by the name of Chandra Man 'Compounder', was inducted into the party as its sixth member. This was the same compouder involved in the aborted Raktapat Mandali plot. Both visited the Narayan Hiti palace regularly and the royals may well have offered financial support. However, the nature of action still eluded the leaders. The usual mode of assassination of the Rana rulers was discarded on pressure of Tanka Prasad who wanted to involve the people. Somewhere along the line, an idea was mooted that pamphlets with a direct message to the people to rise against the injustice and atrocities of the Ranas should be scattered in all three cities of the valley. Almost two years after the party was born a definite strategy had emerged that for the first time in Nepali history, aimed at mobilization of the people at large. The idea was simple but the task monumental.

Tanka Prasad volunteered to raise the funds and undertook the task of smuggling a duplicating machine to Kathmandu. Ram Raja provided the funds, the machine was purchased in Calcutta, carried across the open border and kept hidden in a farmhouse in the Terai[142]. Transporting the bulky machine to Kathmandu without detection appeared an impossible task. Here, the business run by Tika Prasad proved to be the redeemer! Practically every day his men crossed the check point of Chisa Pani Gadhi with the travellers who hired the ponies. Tanka too had taken that route very often and he was well known to the guards. In Kathmandu, weeks before the final journey Ramhari Sharma had identified and inducted in the party a trusted volunteer who was also a competent mechanic. On the fateful day the machine was placed at the bottom of a crate and camouflaged with innocuous material.

Thirty odd years later in the 1970s, Tanka Prasad related the tale at his sparsely furnished drawing room in Kathmandu: 'At the check point, I sweated heavily under my collar, although the weather at the hilltop was chilly! I shared a cigarette or two with the guards. This day, I was particularly pleasant and jovial. After a cursory look inside the crate the head guard declared that we could proceed. I did not allow my face to reflect the great relief I felt'. 'Did you not offer anything more than cigarettes to the guards?' I asked mischievously. His guttural laughter marked his unshakable sense of humour.

The arrival of the duplicating machine was greeted with relief and joy in Kathmandu. In the meantime two new men were inducted into the party after a thorough vetting. Both of them were keen trainees in the wrestling school of Mathema. The teacher warned them constantly that they should concentrate wholly on the training and avoid any insidious act. But the two friends had heard whispered rumours about the party called the Praja Parishad and wanted to join in. They spent days on end trying to find the leaders, constantly walking the streets of Kathmandu. After observing the duo for perhaps weeks, Mathema decided they were indeed committed to the cause. He took them for a stroll along the lonely road to the hillock where the Swayambhu Stupa rises in all its glory. When alone, to the utter astonishment of his industrious trainees, Mathema disclosed the guarded secret 'I am one of the founding members of the Nepal Praja Parishad'. The two trainees were incredulous until Mathema took out a pamphlet from his pocket and showed it to them. They joined the party then and there, through a solemn oath of secrecy and commitment to the cause, at a nearby temple of Bhagawati. 'When will the pamphlets be strewn?' they queried. 'In two days' time, they were told[143].

By the summer of 1940 about twenty members had been inducted into the party. 4,000 pamphlets were copied out in the duplicating machine. The contents narrated the atrocities committed by the Ranas, how they had sucked the blood of the people to enrich themselves and how the people were treated worse than dogs. They urged the people be prepared to sacrifice their lives if need be and join the struggle for freedom. As darkness descended on the date of the *Indra Jatra* festival, when the night curfew is lifted to allow gambling for twenty-four hours, the volunteers moved silently along the dark streets sticking the pamphlets on walls and tree trunks and strewing them at the crossroads and vantage points.

At break of dawn 'Kathmandu was stirred as never before,' recalls one old timer. 'I could hardly believe what I saw. The haughty Ranas were abused in a most derogatory way, condemned openly! It was unheard of! I quickly hid a few pamphlets inside my shirt and rushed home. I read them repeatedly. My neighbours had also surreptitiously collected the pamphlets. At last the pent-up rage of the people was expressed openly'.

The State mounted a widespread search, keeping tags on hundreds of social workers, teachers, poets, writers and suspected activists. Lucrative cash prizes were announced for information related to the 'criminals' involved; but no one was traced.

Encouraged and emboldened, similar operations were carried out during the next couple of months, now ever closer to the palaces and army or police offices. A shock wave ran through the Rana palaces. 'For the first time I was clueless about the operation and even about the existence of the party,' admits Nara Shumsher, the trusted grandson of Juddha, in charge of Home Affairs, and a dreaded bully. 'They had contacted even His Majesty and garnered support from him.'[144]. After some weeks one insider divulged vital information, possibly during intensive interrogations and torture: the secret documents and papers were hidden inside the house of Mathema. Nara personally headed the search operation. The informer suspected to be a brother of Shukra Raj Shashtri, had provided minute details. Secret papers concealed under the floor and behind the thick walls were pried out. A list of the members of the party and their supporters was also discovered. Every bit and piece, including cash and valuables were taken away. Within a few days, all the members of the party, plus some hundred others were arrested and locked up inside the outhouses of Singha Durbar[145].

Prime Minister Juddha was rattled by the sudden crisis, and the bulk of evidence emerging from the interrogations that established beyond any doubt that the king and members of the royal family were intricately linked with the 'nefarious act', not merely in this incidence but also in the Raktapat Mandali. The very schools and education institutions he had permitted to operate or promoted had produced men who plotted his downfall. Where ever he had tried to improve the life of his people, whether through social reforms and public utility works or bold initiatives in the economic/industrial sector, he sensed no gratitude. He never imagined that Tribhuwan, whom he had raised fondly, would join his enemies and support a conspiracy to terminate his rule, or even assassinate him and others of the family, notwithstanding the marriage alliances between the two families. He felt betrayed. Yet, Juddha did not dare retaliate or place himself in open confrontation with the king, believed to be an incarnation of Lord Vishnu by most of his subjects. Another compelling reason for restraint was the inclination of the British to retain the monarchy, a policy that remained constant throughout the Rana regime. About the same time the war in Europe was turning horribly wrong—the Germans were threatening to annihilate the whole continent.

The combination of these pressures and frustrations changed the very mindset of the man. Many noticed that Maharaj Juddha was now 'more haughty, irrational and even desperate.'[146] He turned to the prisoners in Singha Durbar to vent his fury and soothe his frustrations.

The prisoners were heavily chained, shackled and made to parade around the town and the Tundikhel grounds, and led to Singha Durbar. The people watched in fear and in silence, their anger locked in their hearts. 'They passed along the street outside the army headquarters, dragging the heavy chains, twisting and jangling. The Ranas, their relatives, junior officers and petty officials watched, basking in the warmth of the winter sun on the lawns. Their derisive twitter and humiliating remarks added fuel to the rage burning within the citizens as they watched the wretched prisoners walk past.'[147]

More than 200 prisoners were detained as the trials proceeded. Besides some forty members of the Praja Parishad they were students, teachers, poets or those engaged in similar professions. Tied up across bamboo poles they were lashed or beaten up mercilessly to extract more information or at times merely on a whim to vent anger if the prisoner dared to talk back. Dashrath Chand, Ganga Lal, Dharma Bhakta and the compounder Chandra Man Saiju were the worst sufferers, 'face and body smeared with blood, often unable to walk and able merely to crawl along the ground' is how Ganesh Man Singh remembers the scene. The high-caste Brahmins were tied up for long hours but not physically assaulted. Both the Manu Smriti and the Muluki Ain forbid the death sentence to a Brahmin criminal or physical assault other than by another member of his caste. It is possible no other Brahmin could be persuaded to undertake such an act. All was revealed: involvement of the royals even those who had financed the operation such as Ram Raja.

After three months of gruelling interrogation the prisoners were lined up for announcement of the verdict, at the football ground of Singha Durbar. Sometime later, the lone but defiant figure of Shukra Raj Shashtri chained and bound, was brought to the ground, straight out of prison where he had been languishing for more than two years, convicted for 'making a public speech without the permission of the government and for preaching the Gita despite being a Newar'. He had no connection with the Praja Parishad or its activities. The Rana rulers, high priests and bhardars were seated under a large tent facing the prisoners. Then King Tribhuwan and his sons walked in. Revolver uncased, Nara Shumsher escorted them to the chairs assigned to them. Finally, Maharaj Juddha made his entry, offered a cursory salutation to King Tribhuwan and took his seat. 'Father had made sure that the king and the royal family would be summoned and made to watch the trials of men he had supported.'[148]

Juddha was like a man possessed; he raved, ranted, howled at the prisoners calling them criminals and murderers. When Shukra Raj tried to put in a word of defense he screamed back 'You should be hung first!' After the vicious tirade he asked the large assemblage what punishment should be meted out to the criminals. The message was clear. Some cried out for 'death' and the veteran and the learned Pandit Hem Raj Pandey, Mahila Gurujyu, quoted from the scriptures to justify capital punishment in such cases, even to Brahmins. King Tribhuwan recommended in his soft, cultured voice and in English 'punishment should be moderate'. Asked angrily what that meant, Mohan Shumsher intervened and explained in Nepali that His Majesty meant leniency. There were some stray voices advising restraint, expressed obliquely. The bellow for harsh punishment was loud and vehement. 'Hand me a sword maharaj and I will behead them right here!' screamed one sycophant[149].

The dramatic hearing was little more than a staged charade. The issue had already been discussed amongst the high-ranking Ranas and a decision on most cases reached earlier. Even amongst the Ranas, opinion was divided. While Juddha and his son Bahadur were intent on dealing severely with the criminals who had confessed to the act of treason, Baber made out a case for a more balanced approach. He pointed out that capital punishment had been abolished by former Prime Minister Dev Shumsher; a retrograde move now would arouse greater indignation against the Rana regime. Then he pleaded for a more even hand of justice. The decision to let off Ram Raja, who had avoided arrest, with a fine of a mere ₹500, and a verdict of capital punishment or lengthy jail terms to others involved in the same crime/operation, would be indefensible. A small number backed Baber's view but the majority followed the line of the prime minister[150].

The verdict was announced that very afternoon—capital punishment for Dashrath Chand, Mathema, Ganga Lal and Shashtri; confiscation of all properties and lifetime imprisonment to ten persons including Tanka Prasad, Ramhari Sharma, and Ganesh Man Singh: Prasad and Sharma escaped capital punishment as they were Brahmins; but hair shaved and forced to carry a dead pig, a terrible mental torture for a Brahmin, they were paraded round the town as a spectacle of ridicule. Ganesh Man may have escaped on the plea of his grandfather, a senior counselor in Singha Durbar. Prison term of between three months to eighteen years was announced for another twenty two. The rest were fined ₹500 or less, or released earlier after interrogation[151].

The group of four was locked up in different cells. Within a few days each faced death in his own way. Shukra Raj asked for a dip in the holy River Bagmati and then read a few shlokas from the Gita. Finally, he expressed his wish to take the rope dangling from a branch of a tree in his own hands and made his way to the next world. Mathema was also hanged but on the third attempt, as the branch of the tree was not strong enough earlier. Nara Shumsher personally supervised the brutal killings of all four martyrs; Dashrath Chand and Ganga Lal preferred to be shot. Juddha gave orders to comply with this last wish of the prisoners. Details of how several shots were fired in different parts of the body in case of Dashrath and who fired the lethal bullets differ, but all the raconteurs agree on the cruelty, and gruesome outcome of that dark night.

In its aftermath, Mohan Shumsher has been quoted as declaring that 'now, the rebellion will not be able to rise again for a hundred years,' in line of the thinking of the rulers. Himalaya Shumsher, grandson of Prime Minister Dev Shumsher, as a teenaged lad was taken by his father Laxman to observe the corpse of Shukra Raj left dangling from the tree with the intent of intimidating the onlookers. 'These men were foolish to think they would succeed,' he remembers his father comment, and a few seconds later 'but you may one day, see before you at a major public place…a statue of this tree with the body of Shukra Raj dangling from it'[152].

The latter view was to prove prophetic. The Praja Parishad as a political organization never again made a telling impact in the struggle for democracy but the indomitable spirit of the martyrs who faced death with rare dignity and defiance had inspired the minds of the citizens. The dangling body of Shukra Raj inflamed hatred against the rulers. From early morning people trickled in and out, crowding the tragic venue many in tears. Madav Raj Joshi, now eighty-two years of age and in the orange robes of a sanyasi, came up to his son's body and paid respectful obeisance; 'you have enhanced the dignity of your father and the nation, my son', he spoke proudly. Then there was Ganga Lal's brother, Pushpa Lall, the founding President of the Communist Party of Nepal a decade later. For now they grieved and worked in silence against the Ranas in secret conclaves.

The Final Phase of Juddha's Reign

The ugly episode may have haunted Juddha for the rest of his life, despite his outward bravado. The series of religious rites of absolution he performed thereafter are proof enough of his overriding sense of guilt. Whatever the state of Juddha's mind, or the divided opinion amongst the rulers and the advisors regarding the harsh punishment meted out, the incident firmly closed the door on the possibility for better empathy and cooperation between the Rana rulers and the people of Nepal.

Juddha turned into a confused man, beset by suspicions even about those loyal to him. He kept a watchful eye on his grand-nephew Mrigendra, conscious of his educational background and formidable record in nurturing academic and intellectual excellence. And on Balakrishna Shumsher, the genius teacher, poet and dramatist, was chosen to be the second man in the department of education. Fate now played a sinister hand. Going through the SLC exam papers in Tri Chandra College, (1940–41) Balakrishna, the chief examiner, found that a student by the name of Chalise had used a derogatory word, 'napunsak', in reference to the Rana regime. It appears Mrigendra and Balakrishna, keeping the youthful fervour of the student in mind, decided to detain him in the same class for a year but not refer the matter to the prime minister. The matter was laid to rest. But someone leaked the information to Juddha. Mrigendra was summoned to Singha Durbar and sternly reprimanded. Chalise's case was taken over directly by the prime minister. Chalise was arrested and jailed. The youth died there, a few years later. The call for the removal of Mrigendra as Director of Education, by the hardliners, germinated from here. Eventually he was relieved of his position. His gentle, affable cousin Sharada, the eldest son of Mohan, was brought in as the new Director General. He followed Juddha's directions obediently and remained in that position until the Prime Minister's voluntary retirement. As for Balakrishna, his every act now came under scrutiny and his critics sent in negative reports. Quick-tempered and self-righteous about being decisive, Juddha demoted and punished Balakrishna on some minor charge. Balakrishna was driven closer to the dissidents and eventually joined the ranks of the revolutionary forces. Balakrishna Shumsher Jung Bahadur Rana decided to take a new name, 'Balakrishna Sama' and that is how he is hailed and celebrated[153].

The Dividend of World War II

There were limited occasions for Juddha to celebrate during the final years of his reign. Victory in World War II was one. As the allies started to claim victories in important theatres of war, Juddha celebrated each great victory from Alamein in 1942 to the Victory Day in 1945, by declaring public holidays and gambling festivals. The critics who had opposed Nepal siding with the allies were silenced. The radios sets confiscated during the early years of the war, even from the few bhardars who held licence for use were returned now. The state now encouraged their use in public places.

The overall effect of the two Great Wars on Nepal, however, is a disputed issue. At times the recruitment of Nepali soldiers into the British and later the Indian army has been vocally condemned as undermining the dignity of a sovereign nation. These outbursts, part of political rhetoric, refuse to recognize that the recruits are happy to join. They remit part of their pay to help out their families back home, living in acute poverty. The remittances form a major source of support for both the local and national economy. The negative aspects include the exodus and loss of able-bodied men from the villages and downturn in productivity. Yet the level of progress at the centres of recruitment, are far ahead of the rest of the mountain region in every facet of human development.

It is true that the sufferings of the wounded and bereaved, and the loss of life cannot be compensated by the glory of victory or medals for bravery. However, in the Hindu scriptures death in a righteous battle is considered the noblest, a certain path to heaven. Lyrics penned in praise of their valour were popular ballads the nation sang and danced to. The red handkerchief dangling from a Lahure's pocket and the khukuri pinned across his lithe body, or the rail ride in the winding rail car to Nainital or Nautanawa were cast in romantic lyrics accompanied with the vibrant beat of the madal drums and the dancing feet of the Sorathi dance troupes. Their status and earnings were and are way above those of the thousands of labour force that now leave the country each year often to unknown destinations in the middle east or the far east, or India

Juddha had viewed Nepal's participation in the war as a means for consolidation of the bonds between the two countries and between the British rulers and the Rana oligarchy. In both these ends he was to be sorely disappointed. On the economic front the industries he helped set up at the beginning of his reign, received a positive boost. But the flow of mill-made merchandise into the country that started in the twenties now gained strength, at a severe cost to the local cottage industries that had sustained the livelihood of the bulk of the people living in far-flung villages. In another front a large section of the 'retired Gorkhas' bolstered the strength of the revolution against the Rana regime in due course of time

The British rulers in England were genuinely impressed by the bravery displayed by the 'Gorkhas' and grateful to the rulers of Nepal for their wholehearted contribution to the war effort. But the conservative party led by Churchill, the domineering figure of British victory, was defeated in the general elections that followed. The new Prime Minister Clement Atlee and his Labour Party had made a public commitment to disengage Britain from colonial rule, a process that had necessarily to begin with India, where the call for self-rule was most ardent. And the leaders of socialist Britain were infinitely closer in thought and style to the leaders of Indian National Congress, the social democrats, and their Nepali colleagues, than the pompous and haughty rulers of Singha Durbar. The dividends of victory did not come Juddha's way.

Hanuman Nagar and the Indian Connection

Juddha though, had little time to dwell on his misfortunes—the winds of change were blowing across neighbouring India and speeding towards the Terai foothills. The Quit India Movement had sparked wide spread protests throughout India. The socialist wing within the Congress commenced disruptive and violent activities especially at their strong hold provinces of Uttar Pradesh and Bihar, rimming the southern edge of the Nepal border. Revolutionaries led by Jai Prakash Narayan and Ram Manohar Lohia were pursued by the British security forces and cornered near the Bihar border. They crossed over into Nepal. The Madhesi people in the Terai area have relatives and close links south of the border and were well tuned with the freedom fighters in India. Krishna Prasad Koirala, now in Biratnagar, was at the forefront of arranging shelter for Indian activists escaping into Nepal. The residents of Hanuman Nagar, a small township in the district of Sarlahi welcomed and offered warm hospitality to the two leaders and their group of activists. Their presence could hardly be kept a secret in the sparsely populated township. A small contingent of the Nepal police force was also stationed there and they quickly learnt about the whereabouts of the Indians. They were arrested and confined in police custody. A few days later armed freedom fighters from Bihar entered and overpowered the small Nepali police force, set free their colleagues and doubled back. The Nepal government immediately sent a strong army contingent to Hanuman Nagar to arrest those who had helped the Indian leaders and took them back to Kathmandu. Baber was in charge of the trial. Based on irrefutable evidence of involvement they were convicted and imprisoned for six months.

This episode led to a bond of comradeship between the social democrats in India and the Nepali Congress that transcended national boundaries and matured with the passage of time. Unfortunately, the social democratic movement in India was weakened and fragmented as times passed; but whatever the political alignment or position of the individual socialist leaders of that or future generations, they were at the forefront of activities in support of democracy in Nepal at the hour of need. In the successive revolutionary movements of 1950–51 against the Ranas, the people's movement of 1990 and the latest one in 2004 against the Shah rulers, their active involvement has been a critical factor in molding public opinion, in influencing the decision of New Delhi's South Block, and at the highest echelons of leadership in India.

After the Hanuman Nagar incident the Indian media increased its coverage on Nepal Patna gradually became the hot spot for anti-Rana activities.

Political, Social and Religious Resistance Groups

In Kathmandu valley the peoples' wrath against the Rana oligarchy had not faltered. The martyrs did not perish in vain. Within days secretive groups of young men and women worked in silence to broaden the reach of rebellion. The lifestyle of the Newari people, living in close-knit circles, and their quiet nature were particularly suited to this kind of maneuver. The groups worked in isolation and independent of each other so that if one group was exposed, the cover of the rest remained intact. Their single goal was to overthrow the Rana regime. Leaders, who later chose either the democratic or communist blocks, including Prem Bahadur Kansakar, Pushpa Lall Shreshta, Surya Bahadur Bharadwaj, Raja Ram Karmacharya or the Pradhan sisters Sahana and Sadhana, were one in their purpose[154]. Amongst a group of student volunteers Nutan Thapalia was one of the youngest and most active. 'I was of small stature, as I still am, but thin and wiry. We were not allowed to possess radios before Padma Shumsher became Prime Minister. I could walk fast and for long distances and so was able to carry messages between the three cities. At that time, this was the only means of communication'[155]. As long as Juddha was in command they worked in this manner, waiting for the right opportunity to emerge.

The resurgence of the Buddhist monks was again an irritant for the Rana administration. Lines of monks in flowing yellow robes, their cleanly shaven heads shining, and bowls for alms in hand walked the streets of Kathmandu, calm, composed and fearless. Their preaching attracted much public interest, especially amongst those marginalized by the upper class Hindus and the orthodox Brahmins. Simultaneously, the Newars were demanding recognition of the *Newari* language, as the second national language of the country. In effect both these movements disturbed the tenets of the Rana regime. Juddha ordered preaching in public places to be halted and banished the monks out of the country. Such actions further antagonized the minority communities.

Ganesh Man Singh's Dramatic Escape from Jail

Ever since he was brought to jail after the dramatic trial in Singha Durbar, Ganesh Man was looking for an opportunity to escape. In the beginning many of his colleagues were willing to be part of the team but most backed out when they realized the risk involved and the consequence of certain death if the attempt failed. But Ganesh Man persisted. He persuaded two prisoners who swept the floors and were familiar with the grounds to gradually loosen the bricks from a weak part of the outer wall. But one of them was addicted to opium and in his stupor gave away the plan. But though tortured, they did not divulge the secret plan. After another year he was given a new suggestion by a handyman: use the discarded jute sacks lying about to make a rope, beat and bend an iron rod to shape it into a hook to be tied at the end of the rope, somehow lock in atop the outer wall. A young convicted thief volunteered to whisk away the iron rod lying inside the guards' quarters in secrecy. The arduous and risky task of heating and bending the iron rod into a hook took weeks.

The stray chance of the hook hurled from ground level sticking fast atop the wall was tried repeatedly on dark nights and during the short intervals when the guards rested. What seemed to be a suicidal task frustrated all until only the irrepressible compounder was willing to continue with Ganesh Man. Finally, one night in late June, the hook held firm. Ganesh Man, athletic and in his late twenties, had no difficulty pulling himself up. The compounder, heavier and older failed repeatedly, time ran out and he had to return tearfully to his cell. Ganesh Man landed on the open grounds outside. Avoiding the curfew guards on the main routes he reached members of the underground network that was formed during the four years he was in prison. But Ganesh Man decided it would be safer to travel alone. He dressed as a dealer in live buffaloes who took the animals into Kathmandu for sale from India and also took a longer route westward, to Gorkha and then Butwal. There, a close childhood friend had set up a trading business. Only when Ganesh Man introduced himself as Hira Kaji (his pet name) and spoke in the Newari language did his long-lost friend recognize and warmly embraced the friend on the run. After a couple of days of rest and some wholesome meals, at last, he escorted his friend across the border to Nautanawa and then he took a train to Calcutta. The legend of Ganesh Man was born. Conversely, the escape was a huge embarrassment for Juddha and a massive boost to the morale of the freedom fighters.

The Grand Exit

Some say that Juddha had considered retirement to a life of spiritual pursuit much earlier, and that he continued on account of World War II and urgings of his family. After the war his resolve was firm. One may never know whether the decision was based on his natural inclinations or his sense of disappointment at the lack of appreciation from his people or the shock of royal treachery or on account of advice of an astrologer as has been reported by some but, 'not due to lack of confidence in his own abilities. You only have to look at his posture to know that father kept his head high until the very end of his life.'[156]

In late November 1945, the maharaj summoned all important functionaries of the state to Singha Durbar, and invited religious leaders (Santa, Mahanta) and leaders of the now growing community of trade and industry (Sahu Mahajan).

According to Satya Mohan Joshi, a junior officer at the time:

> We appeared in our finest official attire and plumed headgear, with medals and decorations dangling and waited in anticipation, high-ranking members of the Rana family and the high priests inside the palace in the large hall, the rest of us in three different tents pitched outside, graded according to our respective ranks. Each of us, even a junior officer like me, was presented with a silver box, *Paan Batta,* with fine etchings all over, and Juddha's monogram carved at the centre. After some time Juddha walked in, tall, broad shouldered and erect as ever, a regal presence that had always been his hall mark. He still donned the majestic Sripetch (crown) of the Shree Teen. We were more or less aware why we were summoned. In a moving speech, he asked Padma to take up the responsibility of the high office of Shree Teen Maharaj of Nepal that he, Juddha, had served to the best of his abilities, and implored the good citizens of the kingdom to assist his successor fully in the task and challenges that lay ahead. Symbolically and in a regal gesture, he placed the Sripetch on the head of Padma, the latter visibly in tears, and then donned a saffron turban himself, that signifies entry into *Sanyas,* the spiritual life. He drove out seated on a state carriage drawn by four horses. The route was crowded by a cheering line of people, many in tears. *'Maharaj ko Jaya, Maharaj ko Jaya'* they called as they stooped in respectful salutation.[157]

PART III

Quest for Freedom and Democracy

(1940–1951)

Introduction

The year 1940 can be viewed as the tipping point for the Rana oligarchy. Their supreme and unchallenged authority was irreversibly shaken by the Praja Parishad episode that year. While plots or protests against the Rana rulers had erupted earlier and are historically relevant, involving brave men and women, none of them created any lasting impact. The Praja Parishad episode, on the other hand, reached out to and galvanized a wider circle of the people and the waves it generated refused to ebb till the Rana regime was eventually toppled in 1951.

The chapters that follow move out of Kathmandu to areas where clandestine activities or more open protests gathered momentum. To western Nepal and Palpa that will provide a general view of the first mumblings of dissent in the mountainous regions; to Biratnagar in the southeast that traces the struggle of the Koiralas in the hot plains of the Terai and the Kirat race in the mid-eastern mountains; to Banaras, that also sheltered and nurtured the socialists of India and Nepal; and to Calcutta, where one section of the Ranas, forcibly evicted from Kathmandu, sought refuge and set their hearts upon seeking retribution from their cousins ruling the roost back home. All such activities were tributaries that entered the mainstream of revolution led by the Nepali Congress to topple the Rana oligarchy.

The revolution of 1951 was an inevitable outcome of both a national awakening and international convulsions ushered in by the march of time. It was the pivotal movement that brought together the scattered forces of dissent and uprisings in the country into a combined and decisive force.

Kathmandu, however, remained the nerve centre of the nation. In the final five years under Prime Ministers Padma and Mohan, the flames of revolution surrounded and ultimately consumed the century-

old Rana oligarchy. The crucial role of the royal family and the devious hand of India provide a final twist to the outcome of the revolution, as narrated in the last chapters.

Chapter One

Palpa and Western Nepal

The township of Tansen, the capital of Palpa District, is located some twenty miles north of the Indian border and a 100 miles west of Kathmandu. Some of the most picturesque hills and valleys and the mighty rivers that gush out of the Himalayas are located in the mid-western mountains of Nepal along the Mahabharata range. 'Whenever my memory turns back to my birthplace, somehow my heart aches a little,' ruminates Keshar Jung Raymajhi, a prominent leader of the communist party born and raised near Palpa.[158]

It was on account of its geopolitical location, however, that Palpa was chosen to be the headquarters or Gaunda of the 'central' (now the mid-west) region. Not too near the Indian border and shielded by the Shivalik range, it was protected from easy incursion from the south. Conversely, the Terai plains lay a couple of hours trek downhill and so facilitated early response to any disturbance along the southern border, which was volatile at times.

Governorship of the Palpa Gaunda was the most important posting outside of the Kathmandu Valley. The Palpa governor was appointed by the prime minister from amongst his trusted and ablest Rana generals. During extraordinary circumstances, those cousins exiled from Kathmandu were assigned governorship as a consolation posting. Even in such cases the senior most of those exiled was given charge of Palpa. Normally, the Gaunda governors would wield extensive judicial and administrative authority including that of recruitment, promotion or demotion of military or civil servants in the lower ranks. For the common folk of these remote districts, the governor was the highest authority of the land, for they could hardly ever reach or approach anyone higher. Over and above the supreme position he held in his district, the Palpa Gaunda governor also supervised the work of the governor of Doti Gaunda that extended to the farthest western borders of the country. A strong contingent of the state army was posted in Tansen to help the governor maintain law and order over the vast territories under his jurisdiction.

Jung Bahadur chose his trusted brother Badri Narsingh Rana as Governor of Palpa Gaunda. In the last decade of the nineteenth century Khadga Shumsher was deposed as prime minister, expelled from Kathmandu and posted to Palpa as governor. He was one of the ablest of the seventeen sons of Dhir Shumsher. Under him the township expanded and prospered around an impressive palace he built on the lap of the steep mountain side. The Rani Mahal located a few miles away was his masterpiece. The edifice perches like a large white pearl atop a hillock that rises from the blue waters of the Gandaki River. In the excellence of its design and architecture, the perfection of its location amidst and in union with the pristine greenery, it surpasses all the larger and grander palaces built in Nepal. Khadga's most lasting and benevolent gift to the people of Tansen is the ingeniously constructed drinking water supply system that fetches spring water from a long distance across the mountains. The sturdy six-inch-radius metal pipes that pierce their way through the hills are still intact and remain the most reliable source of potable water for the residents.

Many Newar families moved out of Kathmandu valley to practise their skills or establish their business here. Palpa grew to become the main centre for trade between the Madhes plains to its south and the rugged mountain terrain to the north reaching across the Tibet border. The beautiful brass-bronze and copper utensils of Palpa are popular inside and outside the country. The pre-eminent status of Palpa in the western region continued till the 1970s when the lake town of Pokhara in Kaski district, connected to Kathmandu by air and a highway, found greater favour with an increasing number of tourists.

The Administrative Setup in the Hill Districts

The number of 'regions', along the mountain belt remained unchanged throughout the Rana era. Each region was subdivided into a number of districts, and headed by a district governor who reported to the regional chief governor. Their primary tasks involved tax collection and maintenance of law and order. Land tax was the main source of state revenue, collected either directly or through various village-level mukhtiyar or jimmuwals, most of them traditional village headmen now co-opted by the state. They were entitled to a share, generally 5 per cent of the total collection, but their role as representatives of the state carried the real prestige and weight. Their words of rebuke could prove costly to the offending individual, and a nod of appreciation could fetch rich bounty. They were the 'mouth, ears and eyes of the governor'[159] who in turn had linkages at high places all the way up in Kathmandu. Periodic tours or daudahas by monitoring teams from Kathmandu ensured an effective check on performance of the district administration. Any act of negligence or corruption was dealt with swiftly and severely. 'There was no possibility of misappropriation of a single paisa, and none dared such an act.'[160] With the passing years, the range and volume of work covered new activities such as the collection of duty on import and export of goods or levy from local mining of iron ore or copper, and produce such as cotton, wool, cane and bamboo. With the rising demand for railway 'sleepers' in India, duty collected from export of logs and timber formed another major source of revenue. Movement of people and goods between the two countries and import of products such as mill-made textiles, soaps or cigarettes multiplied after the First World War. Each traveller needed a permit for crossing the border or for entering Kathmandu.

The Rana rulers were able to keep effective control on the situation of law and order over remote regions that took days or weeks of hard trek to reach. Army units were posted only in the Gaundas and some districts along the borders, and there was no regular police force. However, 'the Militia was the cornerstone of district administration in the hill Districts'[161]. Village lads or retired soldiers were recruited and given short-term training before their enlistment as militia. Dressed in the official attire with a white cummerbund and a flat black turban with a silver medallion, and black shoes, they stood out clearly amidst the common hill folk in patched, torn clothing and bare soiled feet. Their numbers were limited and the pay scale minimal. However, their 'linkage' with the state apparatus created an aura of power and authority quite disproportionate to their physical prowess. Their collective presence instilled a sense of awe, and of security, at the same time. Perhaps a more effective deterrent against wrong doing amongst the rural population in particular was generated by the age-old code of conduct regulated by the teachings of the scriptures or laid down by law. Anyone declared immoral by the priests or guilty by the state was invariably treated with contempt and disdain by society. The entire village community considered itself protector of the faith and custodian of the law. The dictum of constant reference, 'There is no medicine for call of death or answer to the hukum (order) of the state' was deeply ingrained into the psyche of the people. Physical force was rarely needed to enforce law and order.

Divisions of Caste and Occupation

While society was bound by a sense of unity and harmony, the social order was far removed from the principles of justice and equality. The exclusion and discrimination stemming from the division of caste hierarchy and the evil of 'untouchability'[162] suggest that the apparent 'unity and harmony' was a cosmetic surface that covered up the injustice and indignity heaped upon the 'lower caste'.

It was not easy to get hold of a reason for the absence of the Dalit community in the anti-Rana movement of 1951. Most people evaded an answer; others were short or curt. It was in the idyllic ambience of a lonely mount in Palpa that a local community/political leader[163] finally offered an insight. Tika Ram Gahat Raj was born in 1940 in a Sunwar family that commands a 'higher' standing and more lucrative profession of the goldsmith, as compared for example to the 'Chamars' sweepers who lived in squalid and miserable conditions.

Every male in the village, a five-hour trek from Tansen, was trained
in the profession, 'as were our forefathers as far back as we remember.
As everybody in Nepal owned some gold ornament, there was no
dearth of work'.

'Yet there was exploitation by the Brahmins and Chhetris. They
owned the best land, with access to water, forests for cattle fodder.
Dalits were hired at a pittance for the hardest and dirtiest jobs that
no one else did. Then there were avid moneylenders who exploited
us: once into their net, life was drowned.'

'In such conditions why did your community remain aloof from
the revolution against the Rana regime; they made Muluki Ain that
cast you as untouchables,' I interrupted.

After drawing a deep breath, Tika responded patiently, his eyes
far away, 'We know about the Muluki Ain. However, we have suffered
indignity, poverty and exclusion for more than a thousand years and
not only in Nepal.' A mix of deep anguish and anger now distorted
his countenance.

Our women, even underage girls and married ones, were often
raped. The entire society was against us. When we walked along
a path and a Brahmin, Chhetri or even the Magars and Gurungs
came from the opposite direction, they did not even wish to
be touched by our shadows, so we scampered sideways off
the track, there is no such provision in the Muluki Ain! We
always behaved respectfully, more often out of habit or fear, and
invariably saluted them as required by custom. There were some
kind ones but surprisingly, the wealthier people treated us better.

I will tell you a story which will explain why we did not, in
fact could not, join the revolution. This incident happened in the
1970s. My son had joined a school in the village. Most of the
upper-caste boys still avoided touching him. Then a school party
was arranged to visit other parts and schools in the country.
The boys naturally ate together in a common mess. My boy
entered the dining area. He was beaten up, nearly killed! When
they returned to the school it was my boy who was rusticated!

I pleaded with the headmaster to take him back, but in vain. Then I went to Kathmandu, though I could hardly afford the cost. With great difficulty I was able to present a letter to the minister of education through his secretary, but I could see that no action would follow: we people, have developed an 'instinct'. I then tried to meet another minister: he was not a Dalit but I think a Tharu or Yadav from the Terai. He called me into his office, read my letter carefully. His face was grave, even sad. I knew help was coming. He telephoned someone … I will never know who. After replacing the receiver he turned to me and assured, 'You go back to your village; your son will be reinstated'. And he was.

Can you now understand what our position was in society, even as late as the 1970s when the offending provision in the Muluki Ain had already been removed? Can you now contemplate and imagine the social environment in 1950–51 even amongst the freedom fighters, consisting as you know mostly of the upper castes? Why we could not 'join' the movement against your forefathers? Can you now understand why most of the Dalits have now sided with the Maoists?

The ethnic Mongoloid hill communities stood one rung higher than the Dalits in the caste hierarchy. The earliest-known settlers in the mountainous regions of the country, and consisting mainly of the Magars and Gurungs, in the mid-western region, they too were non-Dhagadharis[164] but could mix freely with the upper castes and engage in farming or trading. Bakhat Bahadur Gurung guesses that he was born 'eighty years ago'[165].

When I was six or seven, I began helping my elders with the daily chores. In between, I was taught a little bit of Nepali by my father and at times the village elders. We owned a small piece of land and just one buffalo; we could never find money for another. Some months of the year we survived on roots and sprouts foraged from the forest, and boiled nettles. The womenfolk trekked many hours daily to fetch water and we had to walk three days to Butwal for salt. The women in the house were skilled weavers, a traditional asset of our race. When I was a little older, I learned that we had borrowed money from the moneylender and had to work hard to pay back. The burden was like a nightmare. We worked, worked and worked but earned just the interest amount and never came near the capital.

He drew a long, sad sigh before he smiled brightly, the natural good humour of his race quickly in evidence. 'At last a lucky break in my life! A relative living in Pokhara sent a message that the Indian army had started recruitment. On my father's bidding I went quickly to try my luck and was selected from nearly a 100 who had turned up. It was a different life in India, a happy one. I got two square meals a day and I could save some money to send back home. Our days of poverty were over. I had reached the rank of Subedar when I retired, with some pension.'

The strength and valour of the hill ethnics was an ideal mix for the armed profession and a boon for the community. Rtd Colonel Tirtha Bahadur Gurung joined the Gorkha Army at the age of eighteen and gradually rose in the ranks. At retirement he bought 1,100 ropanis of fertile land near Pokhara, built a nice house, and raised herds of cattle, sheep, goats, chicken and ducks. He belonged to the growing community of newly affluent retired army men that matched the upper-caste men in wealth and power. The hill ethnics formed a strong component of the armed revolution of 1951. Some like Bakhan Singh Gurung were fielded as candidates by the Nepali Congress in the first Parliamentary elections in 1958. He was elected by a comfortable margin and occupied a key position in the cabinet of Prime Minister B.P. Koirala.

The Newar community, traders par excellence, had moved out of Kathmandu to settle in the mid-western hills in significant numbers, at different times in history and for different reasons. They set up their business in the heart of practically every district headquarters and even small towns and villages in the mountains and the Terai area alike, and extended the strong trading link of the Newars.

The Nepali Congress and the revolution against the Rana regime invariably found support from the bulk of the Newar population throughout the country.

Sarbhagya Man Pradhananga, head of one such prosperous Newar family, resides in Pokhara Bazaar.

> Many generations back when we Mallas were defeated by the Gorkhali King my ancestor left Bhaktapur with twenty five others and built this home at this very market place. We learnt the Gurung language, a must in the trade. Meen Bahadur Gurung, a right-hand man of B.P. Koirala inducted me into the Nepali Congress around 1947. This house became like an office of the party: we hosted B.P., Ganesh Man and other leaders when they visited Pokhara.

Another wave of Newars fleeing from the smallpox epidemic of the 1850s settled down at a beautiful hilltop called Bandipur, midway between Kathmandu and Pokhara[166]. Maheshwar Lal Shreshta, a respected father figure of the Nepali Congress, is a fifth-generation descendant of the original settlers; he joined the Tansen Padma High School in Palpa.

> Many of the teachers in the school were aligned to the NC. Once a large number of us donned white Gandhi caps that cost ₹1.50 that time, and paraded the Bazaar of Tansen … it was a novel way to demonstrate solidarity to the cause of freedom. Later when the call for an armed revolution was made in 1951 we joined the demonstrations led by Kamal Raj Regmi in Tansen, and Palpa Gaunda fell into our hands.[167]

'Kamal Raj Regmi, born in 1928 in Palpa, is one out of the four elected members from the Communist Party of Nepal (CPN) in the 108-member House of Representatives of 1959. Still fully alert, he recounts:

> Way back before the unification of Nepal, the Raja of Palpa had gifted our ancestors Birta land that spread from the high

mountains to the Terai plains. We were priests attached to the Raja and each generation continued in the same vocation, a well-respected profession that also generated ample cash income, over and above the produce from the Birta. At the higher ranges, the Lekh, our forefathers had built several comfortable houses for the extended family, each with cowsheds for the herds of livestock. The Magars who worked for us also stayed nearby in separate huts built for them. They were made to dig, turn, till and plough the fallow land and when well prepared for cultivation, moved to another site. Although slavery had been abolished, the manner in which the lower caste workers were exploited, maltreated and forced into bonded labour was not very different. It was an exploitative feudal society (the Marxist phrase slipped out with practised ease).

We grew up in the same Vedic tradition, of learning everything verbatim from the local elder, basic Nepali, Sanskrit, arithmetic and astronomy. At fourteen, I was taken to Kathmandu. Across the border I was exposed to the outer world—bicycles, motor vehicles, shops brimming with exciting merchandise and then the serpentine length of the thunderous whistling train! In Kathmandu I was admitted to the Sanskrit Durbar High School. Nineteen learned teachers and a wide choice of subjects were like a huge jump from a deep well to the high seas!

'The 1940s,' continued Regmi, now in full flow, 'can be called a decade of awakening. The exposure was euphoric. The trumpet of revolution was already sounded, in diverse ways. The Jayatu Sanskritam movement in Kathmandu (2004) was the outcome of these early political stirring.'[168]

Life in Isolation and Community Collaboration

Despite the state of social discrimination and economic exploitation, the rural populace in the isolated mountain villages learnt to live in peace, resigned to their fate perhaps or knowing no other way of life than the iron-bound pattern society had ordained. Such an order was bolstered by the national policy of isolation from the outside world. A ban on the import of foreign goods barring the essentials, strict restrictions on travels within and outside the country, insignificant developmental assistance from the state and the denial of even the most basic means of communication like a radio set or telephone—'the Iron Curtain' aptly describes the isolated state of the countryside. However, its impact was not all negative. It taught the people to survive within their respective areas of habitation on the strength of their individual and collective efforts, enterprise, wit and wisdom. And the communities in most parts of the mountain kingdom, with some tragic exceptions, did build for themselves a simple life of hard work but relative harmony derided by the modern day economists as 'the subsistence economy'. Land and livestock were the principal forms of wealth in those days. The upper caste owned the prime land and the best herds, followed by the hill ethnic communities while the Dalits were denied both. However, the collaborative effort of all communities was essential to build a robust self-sufficient economy.

Community work was mandatory for each household, as much on the direction of the authorities as by common consent. They assembled to clean and repair irrigation channels and waterways regularly so that the common ponds remained replenished. All able-bodied men worked freely to repair and maintain the mountain tracks, wells, public rest houses or temple complexes. The womenfolk happily helped in works of public welfare and religious merit. There were some areas of work/labour or odd jobs that the state authorities imposed upon the villagers, such as carrying goods to the offices or to officers, with little or no pay.

The upkeep of the postal route, the single most important link in the country's middle mountain belt, was a vital necessity till the end of the twentieth century. Meticulously mapped during the premiership of Jung Bahadur, the major trails of the country were widened, improved or foot bridges built to traverse the gorges during the reign of his successors. But state assistance was granted only when major repair work was undertaken; regular maintenance was undertaken by the local community. The sites marked for 'night halts' in Jung's map gradually took the shape of charming and shady resting complexes where the weary traveller could pause or spend a night free of charge, and the locals gather and gossip. Collectively and individually they were and are a unique feature of the country's heritage.

Hindu scriptures ordained preservation of nature as the obligatory duty of each individual. Plantation and conservation of trees was viewed as an act of religious merit, the destruction of forests or mature trees, as an act of 'sin'. Some species, like the peepal, the banyan, the sami and the barr, were venerated and worshipped. . As a consequence, the villages and mountain slopes were covered with plentiful trees and greenery. The rich vegetation attracted rainfall: natural springs sprouted in many parts of the hills and mountains. The forest provided ample dry firewood for cooking and fodder for the livestock. Men and women toiled in the fields: they took pride in raising the best crop, strongest pair of bullocks or the finest variety of cows and buffaloes that produced plentiful milk or the most robust goats or sheep, the fattest pigs.

Stones and slates were available nearby to construct the simple dwelling houses. Locally grown cotton and the wool from mountain sheep were transported to villages where skilled hands, especially of the industrious Gurung and Magar women, worked to spin the yarn and weave it into sturdy fabric. Different sub-castes, especially of the Dalits, were skilled artisans, masons, iron mongers, carpenters or tailors worked with leather, copper, brass, silver or gold to fill every need of the community.

Life in rural Nepal was hard but marked by festive occasions galore. Each was dedicated to one or the other deities, or marked to herald the planting, sowing or harvesting of seasonal crops, and were celebrated with feasting, singing and dancing, when romance could sprout and blossom into fruition. Village life moved on in blissful isolation.

While Nepal stuck to a 'closed-door policy' to protect its local production, the East India Company made strenuous efforts to 'encourage trade and remove the impediments that obstructed its progress...for mutual benefit of the people of each'[169]. The correspondence omits to mention that the movement into the Nepalese territories was largely of 'manufactured goods' and entry into the Indian territories was of raw material and farm produce. The mistrust of 'foreigners' was giving way to a greater understanding and closer contacts with British India after World War I. Expanding Indian Railway network reached the border towns adjacent to the Nepalese villages such as Biratnagar, Janakpur, Birgunj, Butwal and Nepalgunj, from east to west. Sleepy hamlets earlier, they were transformed gradually into prosperous centres of cross-border trade. Subsidiary trekking routes sprouted to connect the Postal Route with the Indian border towns and the new motor road from Raxaul to Amlekhganj combined with the ropeway line crossing over the Mahabharat range to Kathmandu signalled the new mood of the ruler, Maharaj Chandra. The more open-trade policy endorsed by 1923 Treaty was driven by the view that it was now beneficial to the interests of the Kingdom as well. Ever-increasing demand for railway slippers and multiple requirements of a punishing war upgraded the balance of trade in favour of Nepal. 'During World War II my kothi[170] alone exported 100,000 Maunds[171] of surplus rice to India each year. The hill people converged in Nepalgunj Bazaar in large numbers carrying ghee, other milk products, herbs and musk,' says Krishna Gopal Tandon, a Marwari businessman. With a sad sigh he laments, 'These days, forget about exports, people go hungry in the interior.'[172]

After World War II, tens of thousands of soldiers and officers returned home within a few weeks or months. They carried back with them their earnings, which some estimates suggest was a whopping 1.3 billion rupees—more than thirteen times the annual state revenue of that time![173] They walked in their polished boots, sported smart jackets, tilted their caps, flashed their colourful handkerchiefs or smoked cigarettes, and gave a new twist to the slumbering society. Young men wanted to copy them and young women pined for their attention. They spent their money visiting the local drinking and eating joints and spent freely on fancy clothes, finer-looking yet less expensive than the rugged homespun fabric, and on imported gadgets and cosmetics. The 'lahures' as they came to be known, or the Johnny Gorkhas as the British preferred, made their impact wherever they lived. It seemed to be a win-win situation for all sides. However, the demand for local products dwindled, unable to face the competition of mill-made fabrics or machine-made products from India and faraway England. The skilled weavers and crafts people found their livelihoods in peril. Steep inflation was an inevitable outcome of the free-spending lahures. The local population suffered, heralding a beginning of the end of a 'self-sufficient', internally reliant country.

From Isolation to Awareness

As in the rest of the country the only means of formal learning/ education for a young man in west Nepal was from his village elders or the purohits. A more 'public' space was available at the open spaces of the Patees generally found at the temple complex located in each village. 'Education' was limited to the same narrow confines as narrated by Kamal Raj Regmi. The purohit did not take fees from the students and the students readily helped with the chores in the teacher's household or offered gifts, respect and obedience. This opening, too, was denied to the women and the Dalits and although the ethnic groups, Magars, Gurungs etc. were allowed to join, few participated or ventured to mingle with the 'elite' caste of Brahmins and Chhetris.

There were all too limited sources that brought news from 'Nepal' as Kathmandu was called. However, these opportunities were open to all, without social or caste barrier. A tiny number of men or women from practically every village found employment in Kathmandu, in the army, civil service or the 'Durbars'. A few ventured beyond to India for pilgrimage to Banaras or in search of employment. Their return was an event of great expectation and excitement. They related countless tales of Kathmandu to the awestruck audience of the 'Durbar', about the splendid attire, sparkling jewellery, rooms and halls each bigger than any house in the village decorated with glittering lights, chandeliers, mirrors and furniture imported from across the seven seas, chefs sent by Maharajas of India or groomed in Kathmandu preparing exotic dishes beyond imagination, the silver, and at times, golden platters, how the 'Maliks' (masters) enjoyed the warm company of beautiful maidens from all parts of the country, how all who had the privilege to serve in the Durbars, a hundred or more in the larger palaces, enjoyed two good meals each day, clean and warm beds to sleep in, how nice some members of the family were and how nasty the others. And the intrigues within the Rana family or the occasional voices of protest and call for change heard in the streets of Kathmandu, were relayed within close circles and in hushed tones.

Those in the military or civil service would relate vivid accounts of the marvels of the valley. The great temples and stupas, bewildering varieties of devotees and yogis, some even stark naked, the great green stretch of Tundikhel where the pride of Nepal the splendid army men marched and paraded each day, the tallest tower named after Bhimsen Thapa, the Dubar High School and the great water tank Rani Pokhari. Those perchance returning from Calcutta, Banaras or the tea gardens of Assam or Darjeeling had their own tales to tell…as magical as any…of the "Bada Sahibs", the white Mem Sahibs, rulers of the seven seas, and with a hint of gravity and awe, they talked about the rising tide of revolution in India led by a frail old man in a loin cloth, who they revered as Mahatma Gandhi. And at times the wandering minstrels, the Gaines, passed through the village bringing news from far and near couched in their rustic songs. These tales were rare gifts for communities living in medieval isolation. 'The credit of keeping alive the national spirit and historic heritage of Nepal alive those days, goes to none other than these poor outcasts.'

Shakespeare in Palpa

If the capital city was a focal point for revolutionary dialogue and activities, mid-western Nepal did not lag much behind. Proximity with townships such as Nautanawa or Gorakhpur, Banaras and

Allahabad, vibrant cities of learning were not too far and some young men crossed the border for their education. Some members of the administrative staff, too, were of liberal bent of mind or of academic background. Palpa Gaunda, and its neighbouring districts became the hub of cultural activities, dance, music and plays. Few would readily believe now that Shakespearean plays were enacted here in 1910–11. *Romeo and Juliet* or *Hamlet* was staged and 'fluent English' was spoken, one well-researched report suggests[174]. The play it seems was directed by a visiting Muslim artist, Mohammad Sultan, who worked in the famous Corinthian Theatre in Calcutta and the cast was entirely Nepalese.

Festivals and cultural programmes based on local myths and customs offered space for entertainment. Invariably, they were linked with folk songs and mythology, but on occasions undertones of socio-political dissent errupted from the young and the bold. A more open challenge to the Rana regime appeared during the second decade of the 20th century. A growing number of the restless youth force was seeking release from the bondage of arbitrary restrictions imposed on literary activities, even if sponsored on local initiative and without any financial burden to the State. The first reading room outside of Kathmandu, the Shri Ram Library, was established in 1915–16 at Taulihawa, a few miles north of the Indian border where a majority of the residents conversed in Hindi under guidance of Mathura Prasad Gupta, a learned scholar. Although permission for starting a school was not officially obtained, the Governor Kishore Narsingh Rana was invited and inaugurated the 'library'. It kept primarily religious books and documents but also with newspapers and other media publications from across the border where the freedom movement was in full swing. Maharaj Chandra allowed such an undertaking, when he had ordered the closure of libraries in other venues such as Palpa some years later and his successor Bhim came down heavily upon a similar group that planned to set up a library in Kathmandu in 1930. Whatever the motive or rationale for allowing similar activities in some cases or places, and not in others the actions and reactions they generated sent emotional ripples right across an otherwise static society. On account of financial constraints, this particular reading room could survive no more than eight years. Yet it had aroused and stimulated the quest for knowledge and education an urge that intensified with every passing year.

A few years later a family named Lakout and a group dedicated to learning decided to establish a library, this time in Palpa. In order to avoid interference from the authorities, they called it 'Pustak Padhne Dalan', a hall for reading books, and avoided the red-rag word library. Pratap Shumsher was the governor of Palpa at that time. Although sympathetic to the promoters, he could not but report the matter to the maharaj, that besides the readings, issues related to education, and social concerns, at times coloured with political undercurrents, were also discussed. This time, the order came from Maharaj Chandra for immediate closure of the library and action against the organizers. It took another ten years before another group of Palpa residents took up a similar cause: the Dhawal Pustakalaya was inaugurated in the mid 1940s. By then times had changed. The new Prime Minister Juddha allowed it to continue and one year later the Department of Education, functioning effectively by now, issued an official permission. Located at the very centre of the charming Tansen Bazaar, the public library was a landmark destination for the locals and many visitors until the first few years of the twenty-first century.

In 1940 a primary school, Vidya Mandir, was established in Baglung and a library was set up within its premises. In the mid-1940s, the Palpa Sahayak Mandal was formed, led by a group of active young Newars. They started agitations against the big time traders for malpractices in the supply and sale of salt and other basic commodities. This was another first 'movement' of this nature. As expected, the nexus of privileged traders and the administration joined hands to halt such a move. A warrant was issued for the arrest of the leader, who quickly escaped to Banaras. But the Mandal and its activities remained popular with the common folk: a football club was formed, under its auspices followed by a health centre named Palpa Swastha Mandal in Tansen. Similarly, Seva Samiti in

Taulihawa, district, near the Indian border, engaged in activities to help the sick and disabled. Enthused by the news of a new constitution announced in 1947 by Prime Minister Padma Shumsher, young men in Taulihawa formed a Nava Yuvak Sangathan that spelt out its objectives explicitly 'to conduct social and educational activities and develop good character of the youth force'. Whether the stated objectives education, social reforms, community service, medical assistance, or sports, they were engaged to a lesser or greater degree to raise voices of dissent against oppressive actions and biased decisions of the local authorities or the central government.

The incidents and activities narrated here are a selection from a larger number documented and backed by ample evidence[175]; and there may be others in different parts of the country that never found the light of exposure.

The challenge to the feudal order emerged in different forms. The Halo Andolan movement started from the districts of Tanahu, Lamjung and Kaski. The priestly order had ordained centuries ago, that the Brahmins should refrain from ploughing the fields and apply themselves instead, to spiritual pursuits. A section of the Dalit community called Halis, were consigned to carry out the back-breaking task of ploughing. In the late forties, a group of liberal minded Brahmin youths decided to break this archaic taboo, as a symbol of protest against discriminative practices, demeaning to a section of the human race. They appealed to others in the community to join this 'revolution'. Despite a lukewarm response and the open hostility of the conservative elements these brave few took up the challenge and plunged into the unaccustomed task. Large numbers of onlookers gathered to watch the 'spectacle' some in derision, others in appreciation. The Halo Andolan was not a planned or guided movement, but the activists had been inspired by the call for revolution raised by the Nepali Congress and most of them later joined the party.

Kamal Raj Regmi has every right to claim 'the trumpet of revolution was already sounded'. When the call for armed action was raised by the Nepali Congress in 1950 and the political activists, and the Jana Mukti Sena entered Nepal, the people of the mid-west responded readily.

The presence of Rudra Shumsher as governor of Palpa Gaunda added another dimension to the anti establishment moves in west Nepal. When he was one final step away from that ultimate prize of being maharaj and prime minister, he had been expelled from Kathmandu. In March 1940, more than a hundred members of the family, women, children and their followers had trudged across the mountains and hills to a new and an unknown destination. The governorship of distant Palpa was a poor substitute.

The family was provided with generous allowance to live a life of comfort, indeed of luxury. Rudra retained a galaxy of wives and concubines, a passion he shared with Prime Minister Juddha. Both took pride in the variety of women they slept with and the number of children they produced through their long lives. The Rudra house hold matched the prime minister in the variety and richness of gourmet meals. Rudra was served a whole partridge every day. The rivers and thick forests in Palpa were full of a wide variety of fish and fowl. Still at times Rudra wrote to the prime minister seeking a raise in his allowance. When such a letter reached Maharaj Mohan in the late forties, he asked Baber, second in the Roll of Succession now, to enquire into the reason for such a large expenditure. The response letter arrived a month later:

> Your Highness is in the know of the large family that accompanied me to Palpa. Since then, by God's grace and the goodwill of your Highness, my family has grown in number. Now, ninety boys and girls, their mothers, (a subtle reference to the unmarried women, the nani sahebs) share the meal each day in my kitchen. That is why your brother is troubling you with this humble request'[176].

His brother obliged.

However, in the political configuration they, as with other families expelled from the Roll of Succession in 1934, were viewed and treated as political pariahs. 'The extent of our isolation and helplessness dawned on me as I grew. Our uncles, and even grandfather, though holding the title of governor, were not given any say in the administrative work. We were debarred from visiting Kathmandu and not even permitted to move out of the district without the permission of the maharaj. Permission sought for me to join a school in Nepalgunj or Gorakhpur was granted only after four years.'[177]

Rudra did not turn against the establishment for many years. But his sons secretively veered to the side of the NC. One of them, Gopal Shumsher worked for the party and regularly shared news and views with Subarna Shumsher in Calcutta. Such moves emanating from the household of the Governor of Palpa, in command of a strong contingent of the Nepal army did not go unnoticed by the erudite leaders of society, and energized the activists working against the Rana oligarchy.

Chapter Two

The Eastern Mountains, Terai and Biratnagar

The Tharu community, original inhabitants of the Terai belt, form approximately seven per cent the population of Nepal.[178] The dense forests and hot, humid jungle environment of the Terai was the perfect habitat for the big game mammals, reptiles, and swarms of deadly mosquitoes and bugs. Only the indigenous tribes built immunity to the deadly disease through generations of habitation, and lived along the river banks or inside the forests, happy, content and in tune with nature. Their ancestry is diverse and disputed. Animists in the beginning, they gradually adapted some of the Hindu beliefs and culture, though some of them claim ancestry from the Rajputs of India and Gautama Buddha himself.

'We belong to this soil,' Surendra Choudhury, elected to the House of Representatives on three occasions, asserts.

> Yes, in prehistoric times our people lived off the forest; they were tribal and aboriginal. Very few owned any land and the rest worked as farm labour even later. There is still much illiteracy and poverty, but there is no conceit or duplicity like we see outside. We did not mix much…even with the Madhesi people who had migrated from India, mainly because they, too, looked down upon and maltreated us and took advantage of our simplicity.

Surendra's family was 'like the rulers' in their area. Their forefathers fought against the British in the Anglo-Nepal War as bravely as any other. 'We owned near 15,000 bighas of land, several elephants, hundreds of farm animals, servants and what goes with all this.' His father Ram Dayal was a rare exception who 'taught himself through the local pandit, made himself proficient in Nepali and Sanskrit, besides our mother tongue, and even played classical music'. The teachings and life of Mahatma Gandhi inspired him and he always wore homespun khaddar, and never used leather shoes. Some of the Hindi newspapers trickled through to Birgunj even during the Rana regime and he used to read them avidly. 'During one of his visits to India he met B.P. Koirala. Like for many of us, there was no turning back from there. He had no hesitation whatsoever in joining the armed revolution that raged near and around us.' The Tharu community and the Madhesi people fully backed the Nepali Congress until the 1990s.

Depicted in the Mahabharata as valiant and fierce warriors, the Kiratis had ruled a great part of Nepal including Kathmandu at one time. They managed to hold back the Gorkha invasion of Prithvi Narayan Shah in 1768 and retain some sort of semi autonomy in their core area of habitation primarily the districts of Okhaldhunga, Khotang and Bhojpur located strategically at the central point in eastern Nepal. The Rana rulers respected these arrangements and the Kiratis, more popularly termed Rais and Limbus, joined the mainstream of Nepali nationhood and served the country with utmost valour during the two great wars.

The chief governor of the eastern zone was stationed in Dhankuta and all districts in the zone came under his jurisdiction. Yet in the Kirati heartland; the authority and powers of the traditional headman, the Thalu, were left largely undisturbed. Late Bal Bahadur Rai is a grandson of one such Thalu from Okhaldhunga, and renowned for the splendour of its landscape. Okhaldhunga was also prosperous, with several streams and rivulets running through the region. The Dudh Kosi River was teeming with diverse sizes and variety of fish, the Goond 'as large as water buffalos at times'. The soil was fertile.

'An area almost as large as Kathmandu valley came under my grandfather's domain, Rai recalls[179]. 'We entertained a lot of people in our house. The same food was served to everyone—other than the Dalits who remained a little distance away according to time-honoured traditions. But the hookah was separate for each caste. The farmers were very poor, especially those with little or no land: they laboured all day but in the end received just one meal and four pounds of rice per day, barely enough for a family's needs. However, there was no animosity between the races and castes in those days; this is a recent tragic trend'.

The Thalus of the Kirati heart land held wide ranging executive and judicial powers. Management of state owned land, transfer of private properties, revenue collection 'of which we retained a small cut' and maintenance of 'harmony between castes' fell under his jurisdiction. He could levy fines on miscreants and in cases of more serious offences 'punish the culprit by placing his legs between two bamboo poles, squeezing hard and hammering the poles from the outside' but there was a thorough investigation before any case was decided and punishment meted out.

There was no corruption, 'not a single paisa', claims Bal Bahadur with emphasis. 'How is it then you joined the Congress Party, as did many others from you community?' I asked. There was a deep and telling response, one that spoke volumes about the inner sense of outrage of the people at large against the Rana oligarchy.

'I could not be a general, which was my aim! We the Rais, Limbus and Gurungs were in the third rung of caste hierarchy and could not rise beyond the rank of a Subedar, the Tamangs could only join as porters. The Chhetris could rise up to the rank of a Colonel but only a Rana could be a general... some as soon as they were born! Imagine that. Even in the civil services we could not rise beyond a Subba'.

Bal Bahadur[180] went to Dhankuta for schooling. Simultaneously, he enrolled into the Rana army as a foot soldier and later joined the civil service as a clerk. He learnt about their freedom movement in India, and how our Nepali leaders had challenged the Rana regime. Inspired by these stories, 'a feeling of rebellion grew inside me and I began to work quietly against the Rana rulers. I heard Nepali Congress was formed but I was not sure about things. When at last I learnt that King Tribhuwan had escaped and taken refuge in Delhi (November 1950), I quit my job and returned home to join in the revolution. Under the command of Narayan Mani Thulung of the NC, I was soon marching with the Mukti Sena, a gun in hand.'

Pillars of the Rana Oligarchy

In the process of his conquest and unification of the country, Prithvi Narayan Shah had inherited and adopted a deeply entrenched feudal order: all the land belonged to the Crown that could then parcel out parts of it to different stakeholders, usually those who sided with the conqueror. The Rana rulers readily adopted the structural and legal precedence. Under the Rana regime the Crown, Shree Paanch Maharajdhiraj translated into Shree Teen Maharaj, the prime minister. Succeeding prime ministers gifted huge chunks of state land as Jagirs to the Jagirdars in return of their allegiance and services, usually military or political. Similarly, Birta land, termed Mauja, was gifted as a personal favour, nigah[181], mainly to the Ranas, and smaller pieces to the 'nobles and the gentry'. Under the paramount authority of the 'crown', a few rajas in western Nepal such as Raja Prithvi Bahadur Singh of Bajang and the Jagirdars, Birtawalas and Thalus, like the ancestors of Bal Bahadur Rai, retained some part of their hereditary rights and authority in governance in return for their allegiance to the Rana regime.

The greatest beneficiaries of the system were the Ranas. More than sufficient food grain arrived at the residence of even those holding minor ranks, to support the family and dependants. The richest and biggest largesse was granted by Bir Shumsher to his three sons, Rudra, Pratap and Tej. Their estate or Mauja stretched south from the base of the Mahabharata Range all the way down to the present day east-west highway, estimated to be a staggering 120,000 bighas, much larger than the valley of Kathmandu. They were entitled to the land revenue of the cultivated area in cash or kind, plus a variety of levies and taxes from the tillers, raitis. They could collect and use dry fodder and dead wood from the forests within the Mauja, and to fell mature trees with a girth of three feet or more, for their personal use, provided new saplings were planted.

The rules were strictly enforced. They could bring under cultivation or use for residential purposes any piece of land that they chose to. Unlike the Rajas and Thalus, most zamindars or birtawalas were absentee landlords who appointed managers or clerks to collect the dues and manage the property. Their contact and interaction with the tillers was minimal.

Jagirs or Birtas dotted the entire country. In coordination with the district administration these feudal lords served and stood firm to sustain the Rana oligarchy, at least till its end appeared imminent, their presence in distances several days or weeks away from Kathmandu acting as citadels of the regime.

Another citadel of the Rana oligarchy in the eastern hills were the 'Mugali Thapas' of Dhankuta. The special privileges and rights conceded by Prithvi Narayan Shah to the Kirat chieftains needed to be interlinked with the powers of the governors. Ram Chandra Thapa from a village near Pokhara was assigned this delicate task. He befriended the Kiratis and tackled the issue of smooth integration so well that the chieftains willingly granted a whole hillside near Dhankuta for him to settle down, with his family and assistants. That colourful hillside with its inviting red clay covering the gentle slopes, named Muga, has remained the permanent domain of the 'Mugali Thapas' for eight generations. They had wielded wide-ranging executive and quasi-judicial authority and worked closely with succeeding district governors for steady progress of the region. Muga remained the stronghold of the State in the eastern hills until the very end of the Rana regime.[182]

Influx of Madhesis in the Terai

It was under the aggressive expansion policy of the East India Company that new human settlements, moved to clear the forests and inhabit some parts of the Terai plains. Common ethnicity, language, and culture transcended the national boundaries. Whether living to the south or north of the Indo-Nepal border, whatever their caste or creed, they came to be known as Madhesis, as opposed to the Parbates, the hill people or indigenous tribes such as the Tharus.

One of the earliest groups to move into the Nepal Terai from the south was the Karnas, from as far away as Karnataka in south India.

There is no record of when we first settled here. Many centuries back we moved north, perhaps along the rivers and, settling for some decades en route before finally entering and spreading our roots in the Nepal Terai. Thereafter, migrants came in groups or at times waves from the south. We are Kayasthas and our occupation was farming and trading[183]. However, the Kayasthas knew the value of good education and many of them were engaged in the teaching profession or helped illiterate people prepare their pleas for the courts or government offices.'

C.K. Lal[184] an erudite media person, speaks of the relationship between the Madhesis and Tharus.

There were only the Tharus and other indigenous tribes, hardly any hill people before the 1960s when malaria was controlled. Deep mistrust kept us apart. They rarely owned property and they preferred to work for others, and remain content with what little they earned. They enjoyed the present, did not save anything for the future, and their sexual mores were liberal, quite different. They did not want to change their lifestyle and outsiders to enter the seclusion of their huts or habitation: they feared for some trickery, or the safety of their womenfolk, not an entirely baseless suspicion. Conversely, our community looked down on them as uncivilized and unclean, and often treated them as inferior beings. There was an apprehension that they had magical powers and could cast a spell that could change us into different animals, render us crazed.

My grandfather learnt English during the first decade of the twentieth century. He joined government service and gradually rose to be chief officer of the forest department, position of great prestige, power and responsibility, rarely given to Madhesis by the rulers. He lived and travelled in great style on horseback to distant places to collect revenue surrounded by sixteen guards, each with a rifle. Bank notes had not yet been introduced, so heavy loads of coins were carried on mules, horses, bullock carts or even elephants. Thus our family had a good income and we were sent to school. Grandfather wanted to build a brick house for the family, a rarity for the common people: most houses in the Terai region were made of wood and thatch, and built on stilts, in view of the wet ground and occasional floods. Construction of a dwelling near a Rana residence was forbidden, so we started the foundation work more than a mile away from the mansion of Ram Shumsher, the governor. But he would not have it: ordered suspension of work and the bricks were taken away. This was the first incidence that made me aware of the excesses of the Ranas, their snobbery and injustice. Grandfather continued in his duties. One day he was at the elegant mansion of Ram Shumsher. He addressed grandfather in English. But when he responded politely in that language it was taken as an affront. The governor was furious and dismissed the errant officer on the spot. Those days such dismissals caused the loss not only of job and source of income but prestige in society. The family was ostracized by the community. Grandfather took to the bottle. I developed a rebellious trait. We have been 'proletarians' ever since, and were gladly and secretly involved in activities against the Ranas.

Chitralekha Yadav and her husband Dr Sriram Yadav too can trace their ancestry to Janakpur and to the early twentieth century, but not beyond. Sriram's grandfather, one of the first to move to this part of Siraha district, cleared the forests built the very first house in that area. Now, nearly 25 per cent of the population in Siraha district are Yadavs. Chitralekha prepared lunch for us with help from a young assistant and personally served the delicacies. Few would guess that she was the Deputy Speaker in the House of Representatives (2002) With a master's degree in English from Tribhuwan University, she has a passion for learning. She is multilingual and as comfortable conversing with the poorest in her village as in representing her country confidently and ably at national or international forums.

She was born in the mid-1960s into a well-to-do middle class family at a tiny village in Siraha district. I wanted to learn about the life of a Yadav girl-child in her mother's time. The warm, dusky countenance turns grave.

Why talk of those times—even when I was young the girl child was an unwanted burden. There was no question of schooling for most girls. They were not permitted to talk, sit and chat, far less mix with any male except those of the household. She worked from dawn to dusk and ate the remnants after all others were done. The only concern of the parents and the men folk was how to get her married off, which was usually done and dusted between nine to twelve years. The house of the in-laws was no better, and husbands showed little concern. The daughter-in-law worked even harder and was despised if she could not beget a child, a male one, of course. Really, we were no more than chattels as far as the men folk were concerned. The only relaxation was working in the fields when women in groups of similar age could chat freely. There were festivals of course, but then the housewife had to do double the work.

I was lucky. Our family was above average financially. My father had a good job in the city. So it was grandmother who looked after and put me in a school nearby, a luxury not available in earlier years. And I always topped in class. I refused to marry early, but when I reached fifteen I had no option. Fortunately, my husband is a learned, liberal man and I have reached this position.

One of the better known quotes from Karl Marx—*proletarians have no country*—applies to all those stimulated by trade, commerce and industry'. This is how the late Hulas Chand Golcha, the head of a leading business house in the country, viewed his own race, the Marwaris. Most members of that community left their hot and dusty villages of Rajasthan and branched out to different parts of India and beyond, to set up business empires quite disproportionate to their numbers. Ram Lall Golcha, father of Hulas, was one such roving adventurer who tested the grounds of several locations in Bangladesh and India before he entered district Morang of Nepal in 1925 and found his Karma Bhoomi, a base for him and his future generations.

The searing heat and the dust did not deter him, nor did the untold dangers of the new frontier. Just a few thatched hutments had been erected in the past ten years not far from the dense forest, where Biratnagar stretches out today. A bullock cart track passing through dense jungle on both sides, and brooks that rose high during the rainy seasons was the only means that led to the rail head of Farbesganj across the border line. 'Four of his children were killed by snake bite, malaria or small pox'[185]. Such hazards daunted the strongest and fittest of men; but did not dampen Golcha's zeal. This, after all, was the area most suited for cultivation and collection of raw jute and Ram Lall decided to make it his home. For some years he toiled and laboured, extending his contacts with farmers and local leaders, and gaining their confidence. He also nourished his relations with Marwari brethren across the border, the mill owners and experienced business men and financiers, including Seth Chamadia. Golcha stood as a trusted bridge between the suppliers and buyers. Gradually he was able to buy land for a home and office in the name of Hulas his newborn son, entitled to Nepalese citizenship. Farmers attracted by the higher income from the jute crop and the reliability of the hardworking Marwari, started to deliver jute at his doorsteps. The house of Golcha was taking its first steps on its way to reaching the very pinnacle of Nepal's business world.

However, the transport of raw jute through the tortuous route to the nearest mill at Katihar in Bihar was a hazardous and costly exercise. Ram Lall started dreaming, planning and talking about a jute mill in Biratnagar. The exciting prospect was discussed amongst the 'Young Turks' now moving in to Biratnagar, attracted and stimulated by its commercial potential. The Koiralas, Thapas, Rijals, Lohinis, other Marwari brethrens from the south and the forward looking Governor, Shiv Pratap Thapa, met regularly. Through the grape vines they had learnt that the new Maharaj Juddha was a forward looking man of action with a genuine interest in the progress of the country. As *kismet* would have it, the Maharaj scheduled his Daudaha visit to Morang in the winter of 1935–36.

The shikar camp was erected at a soothing setting of a river bank. Through the good offices of the governor, time was granted for a group audience to the young entrepreneurs. Ram Lall was determined to create an impression. He found how fond the maharaj was of the 'good things of life' and so ordered a wide array of the choicest dry fruits to be brought from Calcutta. Not just a few trays, but three cartloads of the most exotic varieties. In more practical terms he requested select members of the Koirala and Lohani family to accompany him, in order to fully brief the prime minister about the project in proper court language which he had not yet mastered. The eldest of the new generation of Koiralas, Matrika Prasad was chosen for this purpose. Chamadia came from India to demonstrate his commitment for investment and technology and the governor was of course on duty. After listening to them intently the maharaj assured them of his full cooperation. With in three years Biratnagar Jute Mill was to emerge as the first Public Limited Company to be registered in the country. It was also the largest, well planned and laid out jute mills in the subcontinent, amongst several such companies that came up in the late 1930s and 1940s in the Indian subcontinent. Around this time, Adolf Hitler was beginning to make his military moves in Europe and sharp observers could sense that war was at hand. Golcha and his associates in India were amongst the first to do so. They started buying jute and silver at bargain prices. When war did break out, prices zoomed. Ram Lall reaped a rich harvest; the business house of Golcha never looked back. Simultaneously, propelled by demands of war time, the industries set up in the Terai region grew rapidly to provide welcome source of employment to the jobless and a significant boost to the national economy, Biratnagar was destined to rise and take its place as the leading industrial city of the country.

Influx from the Hills

For a majority of the hill folk, life in the rugged mountain terrain was tough as tough can be. Most families, sometime or the other, toyed with the idea of moving south where water was plentiful and the earth more responsive, where education for the young or healthcare for the sick was not impossibly far. The more adventurous families ventured forth. Few regretted the move and those who settled in the greener pastures invited friends and relatives back home to join them. Although there was no overt animosity between the hill people, the Parbates and the Madhesis, there was always a comforting feeling of intimacy and ease when 'one's own kind' were around to mix with. Koirala and Thapa families were the early settlers.

As descendants of Bhimsen Thapa, the Padma Jung Thapa family was one of the elites amongst the bhardars in Kathmandu. With this high rank the Subba Saheb was entitled to don the 'Chand Toda'. 'Somehow after many years in service, the Chand Toda was lost. Father learnt that the Maharaj Chandra received confidential report from his sources that Subba Saheb had sold his Chand Toda, an unacceptable affront. Before any action could be initiated he slipped away across the border to live with my maternal uncle in Tadi. That is how our family moved south to the Terai.'[186]

Tadi proved to be a blissful haven. They could be out of reach from the clutches of the law yet remained not far from the homeland. The Thapa family settled down in peace and comfort, amidst the fertile fields, adapting to the new lifestyle, local customs and the Maithili language. Bishwa Bandhu was born there. 'Around this time the Koirala family, living in exile in Banaras, were looking for land in this area and father helped them locate a suitable place. That is when the long association between our families started,' recollects Bishwa Bandhu some six decades later, with a tinge of nostalgia. 'Then there was news that Maharaj Chandra had died and Bhim Shumsher had taken over'. The change of guard opened the doors for those in the bad books of the previous Prime Minister. Krishna Prasad Koirala and Padma Thapa now headed back to the capital to seek pardon, for both had fled Nepal accused of similar charges. Thapa, a member of the bhardar family, presented himself before the Prime Minister with due pride, dressed in the traditional attire, whereas Koirala was dressed simply and talked in his usual soft voice. Bhim looked down upon the contrasting figures and manners of the two. He turned to the Brahmin and told him he could now return to Nepal. Thapa was stunned when the Maharaj announced twenty years of jail term for him. "Bhim Shumsher thought that my father was too pompous to deserve his pardon. Father was taken to prison, our family was devastated. The Koiralas returned to Biratnagar. 'Fortunately, Bhim died in less than three years and Juddha became Prime Minister. Father was granted pardon straightaway.'

Juddha Shumsher now made an earnest attempt to develop Biratnagar in a planned way. He opened Jhora; certain forested areas, near the urban centre were set aside for conversion into farmland and entrepreneurs were encouraged to clear the forest at their cost and get the land registered in their respective names. The Thapas seized upon this opportunity. It was during these years that the two families knotted a bond of friendship that still remains intact, with its usual highs and lows. Bishwa Bandhu narrates an incidence of much public interest.

'Pitajee had bought a bicycle for the family when we were all in Biratnagar, but Girija monopolized it. When pressed to share it with others also, he took it to an isolated place and damaged it. He never liked to accept any rules but wanted everybody to accept his. That was his nature. But he was a bold man.'

Bishwa Bandhu joined Banaras Hindu University after his schooling in Biratnagar and became Secretary of the Nepali Students Union. He was actively involved in and got arrested during the labour movement in Biratnagar. On release after four months of incarceration, he rejoined BHU. When B.P. Koirala gave a nationwide call to join the armed revolution, he returned and was part of the attack on Biratnagar.

Biratnagar and the Koiralas

The ancestry of the Koiralas is traced to Lamjung in western Nepal. They were Upadhyaya Brahmins but adopted the middle name of Koirala around and after the 1920s on account of the grove of Koirala trees[187] near their home and non-conformist trait in the family. One branch of the family moved to Dumja, in Sindhuli district. While the Upadhyayas almost invariably relied on the traditional profession of a *purohit*, the Koiralas preferred to seek service in the government. Nandikeshwar Koirala managed to find a job of a middle-level clerk in the civil service in Kathmandu, a three-day trek from Dumja. This was during the final years of the reign of Jung Bahadur.

Nandikeshwar was a compassionate man. Once he brought home a leper and despite understandable objections from the family and neighbours gave him shelter. 'One must be charitable in life' he explained. His grandson B.P. relates this tale with pride[188]. B.P.'s father, Krishna Prasad was the youngest of the four sons of Nandikeshwar. The eldest, Kalidas, made a decent earning as a high-ranking officer in the civil service, enough to purchase some good land in Janakpur. The food grain from the farmland supplemented the cash income from salary. Nandikeshwar and his wife readily took up the responsibility of looking after the youngest brother Krishna. As was the common practise, Krishna was married at a young age to a traditionally raised girl and upon her death with in a few years, married a second time. He often accompanied his elder brother on visits to Kathmandu and there he met a smart young girl, brought up in the modern ways of the city. It was not unusual those days for a man to have two wives and Krishna married Dibya Kumari, mother of B.P. With this marriage, the family's lifestyle changed. Gradually, their close contact with their mountain home in Dumja diminished and with it the traits and habits of the hill people too faded away. Urban mannerisms and 'sophistication' took over.

The comfortable life of the Koiralas changed abruptly and forever during the reign of Bir Shumsher. Kalidas returned home one evening after a rough day, he had to take a decision to demote one of the clerks in his office. He was called to the palace by the prime minister the next day. Bir came out of the palace, carried by a strong Magar valet on a kind of saddle especially fitted for the back of a man. Abruptly, Kalidas was rebuked for punishing an innocent man; Kalidas referred to the provision in law he relied on. Bir pulled the valet's right ear lobe, a signal to go back into the palace. Perplexed, Kalidas waited outside. Soon the maharaj returned astride the Magar, threw open the page in the law book where the disputed provision was; Bir had clearly crossed it out!

'What is the law you relied on?' he fumed.

'Your Highness, the provision was there when I decided the case; now it stands altered'.

The maharaj was infuriated.

'This *Dittha* thinks too much of himself, he is a scheming scoundrel. Tie him up and take him round the streets of all the law courts in the valley as a spectacle and then banish him out of the valley!' he commanded.

From that fateful day the family income dried up. One impassioned order of the prime minister had shattered the lives of all in the family. Krishna Prasad was also in Kathmandu at that time. He took a personal pledge never to join the government service!

'An unseen seed of revolt took root in the heart of the young man'[189].

The family now moved to Janakpur to live a life of relative contentment, cultivating land they acquired or enjoying profits through local trading. Fate was to find a more substantive vocation for the family. The so called 'great game' was being played out between the Russians and the British. During the final decades of the 19th century the British sought permission from Nepal for safe passage for their Indian troops across the eastern corridor of the country en route to the Tibetan plateau. Bir Shumsher could not refuse the

British but understood that Russia too was a major global player not to be taken lightly. He chose to procrastinate, forcing the British to rely on the alternate route via Kalimpong.

The diplomatic manoeuvre had underscored the tactical importance of the eastern corridor, so far unnoticed. The district of Morang needed proper vigilance and attention. Bir looked for an able administrator willing to take on the rigours and dangers inherent there. The area east of the Kosi River and all the way to the eastern border at Mechi was covered with the dreaded jhadi, breeding ground of the killer mosquitoes. The state had little presence and outsiders avoided even a casual visit. The unfortunate officers posted to these parts often chose to resign from their posts. Many high-level officers refused to drink the water and survived on soda water imported from across the nearby border. Those forced to serve in Morang often sought corrupt ways to compensate for the dangers they faced. The prime minister needed an officer who was both upright and efficient. Bir was advised that Kalidas Koirala was the right man. The maharaj was prepared to admit and rectify his earlier hasty decision. He reinstated Kalidas as Dittha, with a prestigious, if onerous assignment to head the administration of Morang. There was a natural feeling of resentment in the Koirala household against the cruel treatment meted out to the family earlier, and reluctance to move to Morang. Kalidas weighed his options and accepted the trust and honour belatedly bestowed on him by the maharaj and face the challenges posed and opportunities offered by the assignment that carried the authority, powers and responsibilities similar to that of a governor. Neither found cause to regret their respective decisions.

B.P. Koirala, who was born later, ruminates in his book *Afno Katha*, published many decades later, about the servile attitude of the 'rusting tradition bound' mindset of the bulk of the government servants of those days, but he was happy now to accompany his brother and learn from his tutelage and experience under the umbrella and patronage of the state.

The fortunes of the Koiralas grew rapidly in Morang. Biratnagar the industrial centre of modern Nepal just did not exist when the

Koiralas moved to Morang. Rangeli, some twenty-five kilometres southeast of where the industrial township has grown now, was the centre of activities those days. The 'Bazaar' was a little hamlet with a row of huts built of roughly hewn logs and planks with thatch or tin roofing. However, farmers brought their produce to Rangeli on bullock carts, beasts of burden or even elephants, which marked the owners as men of power and plenty. Jute was the principal crop that distinguished these parts of the country from others. The banks of the rivers and rivulets that flowed gently southwards were ideal for the raw crop to be fermented and dried in the sun. The traders bought their stock here and transported it south on bullock carts to Jogbani and to the rest of India by train or truck. From the Indian side they brought back merchandise used in Nepal.

Krishna Prasad at the peak of his youth revelled in the opportunities the new venue offered. While his elder brother managed and controlled the affairs of the state, he handled the business side. The Koirala residence was like a beehive that attracted the ambitious and industrious, rich and poor alike. They needed the help and support of Dittha Saheb Kalidas and the state mechanism under his control. They could share the profits of business with younger brother Krishna, fast learning the tricks of the trade, and always prepared to explore a new idea. Kalidas had pleased the prime minister with his dedication to and competence in duty and in return received patronage from the maharaj. One such favour was the licence to import cigarettes from India. However, by far the most profitable venture was the contract he was able to bid for and win, for collection of import and export duties on behalf of the state. Starting from eastern Nepal, the family was able to steadily expand their business and garner lucrative contracts throughout the country, in the hilly regions and the Madhes plains alike. It is true that Krishna Prasad kept his self imposed vow not to join any government service; but he was very much an integral part of the family business: blessings of the rulers as well as a favourable tilt of the administration were prerequisites for success then as it is today. The Koiralas were adept at both levels.

They had established a firm base for future expansion by the time Kalidas was given another appointment and transferred elsewhere. Krishna stayed back, grateful for the love, guidance and patronage he had received from his brother, and confident now of his ability. For some time, he had been looking for a more suitable location for his business, with better access to and from the mountains of the eastern hills, including the district headquarter, Dhankuta, and also closer to the Indian border. His choice fell on a fallow land near Rangeli called Ghoraha. He now called a meeting of community leaders and suggested they move to this location. Some of the young men agreed to take up the proposition. They readily moved with their belongings to build new homes, till new fields for their livelihood and boost trade and commerce.

'The distant dream of these young men has turned into reality today—in the shape of modern day Biratnagar,' writes B.P., with justifiable pride.

The new settlers had chosen the name Biratnagar for their adopted village as it would have been a part of the ancient Kingdom of Raja Birat. As a first step and to seek blessings for their new enterprise they built and dedicated a temple to Kali, the goddess of protection. From this spot the bazaar and township of Biratnagar has spread out and 'to this day both at dawn and dusk each day the echo of temple bells reverberate in thankfulness into the skies above'.

Meanwhile, Dev Shumsher was forced to resign and move out of the valley in 1901 after five months as prime minister. Krishna Prasad had placed great hope in the plans of Dev to promote education and learning, a prelude it was thought, for socio-political reforms. Chandra Shumsher, on the other hand was known as shrewd and cunning in achieving his goals, but equally for his competence and capabilities in managing the affairs of State. The lives of Chandra and his descendants and of Krishna Prasad Koirala and his descendants are so closely interlinked that 'the story of one will be incomplete without that of the other.'[190]

'Chandra Shumsher ruled for twenty-nine years, during this period he harmed our family more than any other. We had to bear the pain of exile for twelve years. Father was his greatest critic. Yet Chandra was a renowned maharaj but renowned in his own aggrandizement. He linked his personality with the image of the country and the State so closely that the words of Louis XIV 'the nation that is myself' can apply only to him. Later, many rulers tried hard to place themselves on that pedestal but the natural way he succeeded in doing so, who else can manage it?'

One wonders whether B.P. had the haughty quip 'Indira is India, India is Indira' in mind when he wrote these concluding lines.

Krishna Prasad knew that the ears of the Maharaj and a nod of his head were useful, often essential to facilitate the smooth progress of any new venture. He never forgot, nor was ever allowed to forget this mantra. The move to Biratnagar was a stroke of genius. Krishna rose to the pinnacle of success both in his personal and social life, and decisively in his business. His two wives, the elder more traditional, and the younger, he had chosen to wed, lived in harmony; the triangular relationship was not unusual those days. They gave birth to nine children and nurtured them to maturity, giving them ample love and the opportunity for education. Three of the boys were destined to be prime ministers. The family owned plenty of fertile land to feed the large family and the constant flow of guests, friends and followers that visited Koirala Nivas; but business was the main source of their wealth. While the contracts for the collection of state tax continued to expand, local trading and exports of farm products and cash crops to the mills of India supplemented the income. The spattering of the English he had learnt during his earlier stay in Kathmandu gave Krishna an extra edge over his competitors. He visited Calcutta often. A Nepali businessman, Subba Adibhakta, who had succeeded in reaching the very top rung of business circles in the metropolis, took a liking to the energetic young man from Biratnagar and groomed him in the business. Together, they traded in metals, successfully gauging the volatile market that World War I created. The Koirala household was flush with riches and known for their aristocratic/bourgeois lifestyle. They owned several horses of Arabic and Tibetan breed and livestock imported from different parts of India. When in Calcutta, Krishna Prasad drove swanky cars, bought suits at Rankins, ornaments and watches at Cooke and Kelvey, and sported the latest sunglasses Lawrence and Mayo had on offer.

Spurred by his success in business, his thoughts turned to improving the lives of people in Biratnagar. With full support of the community and blessings from Kathmandu, a hospital and a school were established—entirely from local contributions, a major part from the family. The school developed into one of the most sought after centre of learning; sixty students were provided free education, food and dress. Perhaps the most valuable input of Krishna Prasad to the township was his relentless initiative that led to the extension of the Indian railway line to Jogbani a few kilometres from Biratnagar, and the placement of a post office there. Gradually, Biratnagar became the busiest transit point for trade and transport between eastern Nepal and the unlimited markets of India and overseas via Calcutta.

The life of the Koirala family since they moved to Biratnagar had been filled with joy, prosperity and success. His mind was at peace. The course of such an idyllic life was suddenly diverted, and forever.

He was on his way back home astride a mountain pony, one bright autumn day. The intense heat of summer and the wet monsoon season had given way to the cooler days; the setting sun gilded the earth a golden hue. The man on the horse was content and fulfilled. A voice in the wilderness chided him.

'Why do you feel so smug about your success? What have you really achieved?' Krishna pulled his horse; there was no one anywhere within hearing distance.

A divine call, he thought, and offered a response, setting out the long list of his achievements, not without a sense of pride. The mystic voice hit back, 'All your success is for your own sake; what have you done for your folks in Dumja, and the thousands of villages like Dumja where people still go hungry and half naked?' The magical spell vanished.

Krishna Prasad returned to Biratnagar, a changed man, his mind no longer at peace. He had the long hours of the night to reflect upon his tryst with the unknown and to reveal his inner self to his wife. The next morning he called his friends and well wishers to his workplace, the 'Gaddi' as the office was referred to in those days. He conveyed his decision to work for the benefit of the people from this day on and asked them to join him in the noble journey. Most of those assembled were sympathetic but reluctant to throw in their lot; none volunteered to join.

In the days that followed, both his wives were convinced of the merit of their man's resolve. And there were just two others, his nephews studying in Banaras who backed their uncle wholeheartedly. One of them went a step forward: he felt that the last name of the family, Upadhyaya or Sharma, denoting the high caste they belonged to, was not apt in the context of the new path they were committed to. Despite the opposition of kith and kin he dropped these caste-ridden attachments and henceforth stuck only to the name Koirala. Sooner or later members of the extended family followed suit. The other nephew was Dharani Dhar Koirala, the poet and litterateur, whose famous poem *Naibedya* stirred the revolutionary spirit

It was during these eventful days that B.P. Koirala was born, when his mother was on a visit to Banaras. The year was 1914: across the oceans, Europe embarked upon the Great War.

Krishna Prasad had been able to establish a line of communication with Prime Minister Chandra. The two men shared a sense of mutual respect for each other. He often submitted Binti Patras (letters of supplication) to the maharaj couched in humble court language, full of praise, 'the people are confident under a maharaj dedicated to them, such as Your Highness, their aspirations for progress and reform in the country will be fulfilled'. In between such lines of flattery which was the expected norm, he also suggested in subtle undertones, areas where such reforms would be most beneficial for the betterment of the people. The Prime Minister often responded expressing his readiness for reforms in tune with the needs of the times and that he was pleased with the suggestions received. Chandra had permitted or supported all his former projects, the school and the hospital and the initiatives for the extension of the railway line. Now a novel request couched in a Binti Patra reached Singha

Durbar. This time the letter was signed by the woman of the house, Divya Koirala. One day she approached her husband with a proposal to form a formal group of women activists of the community for seeking redress to the social ills. She wished to approach Bada Maharani, Lok Bhakta Laxmi, wife of Chandra Shumsher, to head a women's organization to be formed in Biratnagar. Krishna gave his nod willingly. The local community too approved of the plan, with little hope of positive response from Singha Durbar, but as a gesture of goodwill. The letter was drafted with due care, each sentence and word carefully balanced, and was then dispatched to Kathmandu. The reply received no doubt after a suspenseful interval amazed all. The Bada Maharani consented to be President of the committee with Divya Koirala as the Secretary; she also offered financial assistance. The decision in Singha Durbar, for a Bada Maharani to head a committee made up of the duniyadars was unprecedented. In Morang it was received with joy and disbelief. No wonder Krishna Prasad was elated, and convinced of the liberal mindset of Chandra. The euphoria was to be tested by later events. Nor could the Women's Committee move much forward. But it was indeed a novel happening.

'In this respect,' wrote B.P. later, 'the women in Nepal were ahead of men'[191].

There may be many who see faults in the Koirala family but in the area of 'the liberation of women' the Koirala household can rightly claim to be decades ahead of their times. They mingled freely with the men folk and were involved in the decision making process. Girija Prasad Koirala fell in love with a widow Sushma, who had a child, Sujata, from her former marriage. Defying objections from some members of the family, they went away from Biratnagar and got married in a simple ceremony. Eventually, they lived in full compatibility within the extended family; if there is any other similar instance of that kind in those days, the author is not aware of it. B.P. wrote and talked about sex and the charms of women without a trace of inhibition, few in that generation could manage such openness. He was happy to see women do their own things, not follow the trodden path of convention. A niece was not a good student but showed talent in the fine arts. The elders in her family were not too keen for her to embrace such an uncertain career. B.P. encouraged her to do what she was best at. Ragini Upadhyaya stands out today as one of the finest artists in Nepal. Manisha Koirala, a granddaughter entered the glamorous world of Indian cinema at a time when acting and modelling was frowned upon by society, as a career for the promiscuous. She lived and loved the Bollywood life openly and rose rapidly to reach the top. Sushila was a simple and somewhat shy girl at the time of her arranged marriage with B.P. She grew to become a lady of real substance and poise, as strong in support of her illustrious husband as her mother-in-law had been to Krishna Prasad. After the death of her husband, she commanded the kind of respect and admiration that eludes most political heavyweights.

Back in Biratnagar, the mystic voice that had goaded him towards a new goal no doubt played upon the psyche of Krishna Prasad. His fertile mind sought other avenues to help the poor and weak.

One day he was sitting at his Gaddi, in the bazaar, as he did on most days. It was the beginning of autumn when groups of jobless labourers, the Dhakres, from the hills descend to the plains to seek some work to sustain their lives. The scene was nothing new but this day he noticed the miserable condition of the half-naked men, bent low with the heavy loads they carried, their clothes soiled and in tatters, standing barefoot in the dust and dirt, their faces wrinkled with long poverty. Krishna Prasad was stirred by the condition of his countrymen. An idea struck his restless mind.

'Call them to the office,' he instructed the clerk working for him.

The motley group entered the Gaddi carrying the putrid smells of sweat and grime. One of them was asked to exchange his clothes for a new outfit. Confused at first by such an unlikely gesture he eventually agreed. The others were also given some cash and clothes before they left. The torn and patched, lice-laced, bug-infested, dirt covered swatches that passed for human apparel was packed into a bundle with a letter addressed to Maharaj Chandra Shumsher, and sent to Singha Durbar, Nepal[192].

The riveting tale of what transpired when the parcel arrived in Singha Durbar and the reaction of the prime minister is narrated in Part II Chapter 1. In Biratnagar the governor, who was on good terms with the Koiralas, discreetly hinted they should flee the country before the formal order for his arrest reached the governor's office. The same day he took a horse and crossed the border to reach the safety of Jogbani. Some members of the family followed. As soon as the news of the escape reached Singha Durbar a fresh order was sent to arrest remaining members of the family and 'collaborators'. A few were arrested while the rest made their escape, quickly taking their own routes to Jogbani.

'Terrorized individuals descended on Jogbani where my father was. All of us went to Banaras after some time. My father rented a large house in Thatheri Bazaar. There began our twelve difficult years of living in wilderness'[193].

The year was 1917. B.P. was three years old.

The reason for sudden U-turn in the attitude and actions of Chandra Shumsher within six months of the letter of support from the Maharani was an 'an unending inconclusive dialogue' in the Koirala family.

'The opposite view held that Chandra was a ruthless ruler intent on crushing any opposition against his regime but at the same time liked to be seen and viewed as a liberal reformer...I personally believe that no dictator can be a reformist. Their reformist moves are either artificial rouge or else the output of some strong pressure'. B.P. Koirala seems to have carried this conviction, at least in his subconscious mind, throughout his revolutionary career and some believe that actions based on such an analysis never allowed a sincere reconciliation with King Mahendra first and then his son Birendra, or even with the communist leadership in Nepal.

There is an alternate view asserted with some emotion by critics of the Koiralas. Krishna Prasad had been granted a contract to collect import/export tax on goods passing through the border check posts. The root cause of Prime Minister Chandra's arrest order, they claim, was not related only to the 'parcel episode'. That the Prime Minister had received several reports and complaints pointing to serious irregularities and unlawful dealings in the process of the collection of duty...and the maharaj issued the arrest orders on this account, and was right in doing so.

However, if at all there were malpractices there is little concrete evidence to back up such allegations.

The once insignificant patch of fallow land in Ghorahi gradually grows into a thriving township while the Koiralas move on to Banaras to fuel the revolution against the Rana oligarchy from that, the holiest of Hindu cities.

Chapter Three

The Nepalese and the Holy City

'**B**anaras is not only a city, but a culture in itself—those who can sense and be part of it can experience its revealing consciousness,' said Kamal Gupt, a local scholar[194]. Brahma, the Creator of the Universe in Hindu mythology, is said to have remarked, 'You balance all the heavenly deities on one side and Kasi on the other, and the gods will be lighter.' The celebrated poet-seer Vyasa[195] established his hermitage here. Tulsidas wrote his Ramacharitamanas here. Gautama Buddha gave his first sermon at Sarnath nearby. Kabir, Ravidas, Ramanand, Munshi Premchand, Girija Devi, Sitara Devi, Bismillah Khan, Pandit Ravi Shankar, Hariprasad Chaurasia, Laxmi Prasad Devkota and a host of other great philosophers, and men and women of the arts and letters found inspiration in this holy city.

The connection of Nepal with Kasi is as old as history itself. Some of the rarest texts of the Skanda Purana preserved in Nepalese palm-leaf manuscripts, dated AD 810, are available in Kathmandu[196]. It is ordained by the scriptures that the practice of yoga and even merely spending one's last days in Kasi, will lead to moksha[197]. Even before the history of these cities were recorded with exactitude, and until the mid-twentieth century it was the ardent desire of most Nepalese to visit Kasi at least once in a lifetime or better still, to 'attain deliverance from the body' in Kasi.

Kasi has always been the centre for Nepalese pilgrims and priests, but it also sheltered those exiled from the country. 'Some days after Jung Bahadur took control of governance, he asked King Rajendra to choose a destination for him and the queen to settle down, outside of Nepal. The king replied 'there are many places of worship and for meditation in Kasi. The holy River Ganga flows and the God of

Gods, Lord Vishwanath is there. Many Nepalese people have lived in Varanasi for generations. That is where I wish to go'. This is how in 1846, King Rajendra and Queen Rajya Laxmi came to live in Varanasi with their large retinue. My great-grandfather, the Raj Purohit and his son, my grandfather were part of that retinue'[198]. Krishna Prasad Bhattarai, fondly remembered as Kishunjee, was born at an outhouse of the palace the royals built. He followed the footsteps of the family helping his father in the performance of religious rites in Banaras and Ramnagar, a town located in north Bihar across the Chitwan district at the palace of Mahendra Bikram Shah, alias Ram Raja. But once his elder brother, Gopal and he joined the Banaras Hindu University (BHU) in the 1940s, they were absorbed by the revolutionary spirit that engulfed India and joined the movement against British rule in India and the Rana oligarchy in Nepal.

The story of the Nepal royals exiled in Varanasi and the Raj Purohit Bhattarai family as part of the entourage depicts parallel tales of thousands of other Nepalese families who came to Kasi and adopted it as their home. The profession of 'purohits' was the most lucrative and prestigious occupation in Nepal, well into the twentieth century, and Varanasi was *the* city where one could train in and master the practise. Once proficient, there was no shortage of patronage whether in Banaras or on return to Nepal. Conversely, to this day if one seeks the assemblage of 108 Nepali pandits for a recitation of the Vedas, they can congregate at Kasi within a couple of days' notice.

Arun Dhital, a third-generation Nepali now living in Dudh Binayak, says,

> The holy Ganga was revered then as it is now. But those days the water was sparkling clean. Some Ganga Jal is preserved in most Hindu households; it contains rare chemical properties that keeps the water pure for months, even years. When Maharaj Chandra sailed for Europe he had huge vessels made, sent them here to be filled with Ganga Jal and took the cargo in the ship and was used for drinking purposes. The city was neat and

clean then: garbage was carted out of town to be disposed at sites assigned, not dumped into the holy river as now.[199]

The holy city still presents a stunning face. On a clear morning as the 'Sun God, Surya appears, glowing with opal fire, its rays hit the gentle waves and together they impart an orange glow to the Ghats—of magnificent architectural grandeur, rows of lofty buildings and holy sites—filled with devotees, pilgrims and visitors, and the sound of bells and conches and of religious hymns and chants 'contribute to make the complete view, one which stands quite alone, and possibly could not be surpassed in the whole world'[200]. The Nepali Temple built under the patronage of the king of Nepal in 1841, is one of the eighty-four Ghats that line the river front. The picturesque temple is fashioned after the Pashupatinath Temple in Kathmandu with pagoda roofs half-hidden by magnificent tamarind and Pipal trees with leaves shimmering in the river breeze.

Many of Nepal's political leaders have lived in Banaras, and it was one of the main venues where the anti-Rana movement gathered force; however, politics was rarely a subject of discussion inside the inner city. Here the entire population was engaged in literary and spiritual discourse and activities. Those days, the Rana oligarchy never allowed education to flourish in Nepal, so students and scholars came here. The famous poet, Devkota composed many of his poems in Banaras. Much later the Nepali Congress located its office in Dugdha Binayak, but that did not interfere with the spiritual ambience of the area—Krishna Prasad Bhattarai and his brothers were devoted Hindus very much at home with Kasi, its mores and manners. Pushpa Lall, amongst other communist leaders and even the Koiralas, lived in Dugdha Binayak for a short time but they were very discreet about their atheist views. The pivotal centre of Nepali politics was at the residence of the Koiralas located at Thateri Bazaar. And the hub of Indian politics and the Indian independence movement were in and around BHU and other parts of the city.

King Prithvi Narayan Shah

Prime Minister Bhimsen Thapa

Jung Bahadur Rana

Bhanu Bhakta Acharya laid the foundation of the Nepali language through his translation of the Ramayana

'Coronation' spectacle of Dev Shumsher

*Ranis and ladies-in-waiting. Influence of European fashion in the
Durbars of Kathmandu*

Maharaj Chandra Shumsher at work

King George VI and Chandra Shumsher

*The Koirala family in Biratnagar. Below, fourth from right: Krishna
Prasad Koirala and standing, second from right: B.P. Koirala*

Juddha Shumsher holding court

Singha Durbar

The grand shikar

Juddha (right) hands over premier's crown to grateful Padma (left)

Protest march at Hanuman Dhoka, the central square in Kathmandu

*Pushpa Lall Shreshta, founder
of Communist Party of Nepal*

*Tanka Prasad Acharya, chained
and shackled after arrest*

Prime Minister Mohan Shumsher with newly crowned boy King Gyanendra

King Tribhuwan flanked by Prime Minister Mohan and Home Minister B.P. Koirala

Prime Minister Mohan as leader of the coalition cabinet with Baber Shumsher, B.P. Koirala and Subarna Shumsher

B.P. Koirala and Ganesh Man Singh after the emergence of democracy

The author interviewing Prime Minister Krishna Prasad Bhattarai

Socio-political Ferment in Banaras and the Koiralas in Exile

Krishna Prasad Koirala with more than forty members of his family and followers arrived in Banaras in 1917. They rented a large house with two courtyards which soon turned into a venue for political and intellectual dialogue, especially for the Nepalese activists ranged against the Rana oligarchy. Amongst them were Devi Prasad Sapkota, a subba earlier in Nepal and now in exile under similar circumstances as Krishna Prasad; Surya Bikram Gyanwali who was to be one of the leading lights in the literary field; Durga Nath Dhungana, father of Daman, the Speaker of the House of Representatives in 1991; and Dharani Dhar Koirala, who composed the revolutionary poem *Naibedya*. With their support the Koirala family established a press and launched weekly and monthly publications, *Gorkhali* and *Janmabhoomi*. They highlighted atrocities and injustices of the Rana oligarchy and spread the message of rebellion amongst a large number of the Nepalese now living and working in north and east of India. However, the efforts to penetrate into Nepal were effectively blocked by the Rana administration.

There were other ways in which Chandra Shumsher blunted the political manoeuvres of the Koiralas in exile. Their properties in Nepal were confiscated, reducing the family to acute financial distress. They could not afford two square meals a day, subsisting on a simple repast of daal-bhat-tarkari (lentils-rice-vegetables) at one meal but make do with soaked grams or sattu in the evenings. Still, they made light of their hardships as their home was lit with revolutionary zeal and good humour.

Meanwhile, the massacre at Jallianwallah Bagh in 1919 aroused deep anger against the British rulers. 'Cooperation in any shape or form with this satanic government is sinful,' proclaimed Gandhi, the advocate of peaceful Satyagraha giving a new direction to the politics of India through his call for revolution. A wave of excitement and energy ran throughout Hindustan. 'It was a matter of great fortune to be able to live in India during those years, an opportunity that our life in exile provided for me'[201]. It was probably during the 1920s when Gandhi visited Banaras and inaugurated the Kasi Vidyapeeth, that Matrika and B.P. went to listen to the famed leader. His simple but compelling message called for a boycott of all British goods and institutions. B.P. stood up and declared his resolve not to attend the government school and Matrika followed. Thunderous applause followed and B.P. remembers a garland earlier accepted by Gandhi being placed around his neck. Someone at the platform then lifted the small, good looking boy and placed him tenderly on his lap; Matrika told B.P. later that this was Nehru. This was the first public expression of revolt against the colonial and dictatorial rule by B.P. at the tender age of seven or eight, and he was lauded by the spontaneous acclaim of the crowd. He was destined to experience innumerable heady moments such as this, during his illustrious career.

The Koirala family joined the non-cooperation movement. British mill-made clothes were cast off into the bonfires that lit the streets of Banaras and many cities and towns of India. Krishna Prasad took formal membership of the Indian National Congress. 'Father's political responsibilities,' writes B.P., 'were now clearly divided in two: to raise awareness against the Rana oligarchy and to support the freedom struggle in India. I perceived a necessity to establish democracy in Nepal through an awareness aroused by the freedom struggle of India.'[202]

Matrika and B.P. joined a Gandhi Ashram school located couple of miles out of town. The brothers also started attending political meetings and gatherings. But the non-cooperation movement lost its momentum, and sporadic cases of violence erupted. A shrewd reader of the mood and sentiments of the people Gandhi opted for a tactful retreat on grounds that the outbreak of violence had eroded the moral force on which the movement rested. In the meantime the Koirala family was now unable to afford sufficient quantities of even the humble sattu. Many had to go hungry for a few meals every week. And then, a difference of viewpoint emerged between Krishna Prasad and Sapkota who had inspired groups of young Nepalese in Banaras to work for social and political change in Nepal. While Krishna Prasad was committed to the Gandhian principle of non-violence, Sapkota insisted that they should adopt a policy of direct confrontation with the enemy, with no holds barred. The publication of *Gorkhali* and *Janmabhoomi* was discontinued due to financial constraints as much as the difference of opinion on strategy.

These were the toughest days for the family in exile. Krishna Prasad decided to go to Calcutta. He had often visited the city as a prosperous businessman from Biratnagar, made many contacts and, lived in great style, as a 'dandy'[203]. He was confident his old partners would help him start a new business. But times had changed. The astute Chandra Shumsher had ordered confiscation of all properties of the Koiralas in Nepal and sent warning signals to their sympathisers to avoid contact with 'the rebels'. Koirala found little response to his proposals. Some advised him to seek pardon and make amends with the prime minister. Krishna Prasad persisted: he worked as a hawker selling nick-knacks, along the burning pavements, or in and out of the Calcutta trams. At another time he found a job selling newspapers, and booklets on behalf a militant wing of the anti-British movement. He had promised to return to Banaras with a success story but with the paltry sum he could no more than feed himself. One evening, he found young Bishweshwar, at his door steps! Unable to get proper treatment in Banaras for a festering wound, Bishweshwar had been sent by his mother to Calcutta. The wound healed under treatment at a free clinic in the neighbourhood but the acute poverty persisted.

Young Bishweshwar, however, viewed poverty with an uncommon vision. People paint a very 'dark picture of poverty and exile' he writes. 'I do not know about the effect of exile on my parents and elders but to be truthful my life in exile was a time of happiness: it is not possible for me to think of that experience as years of suffering and sacrifice. During those years I could wear only two pairs of shoes. I owned no other dress than the one I donned. With the three and half rupees of monthly scholarship I earned from school, I could barely pay for my school fees and buy rice and lentils twice a day and that too not every day. I presume that is a life of suffering. But I can not view that as misery, however much I try…if someone were to take me back to my age of four and ask me whether I choose the prosperity of Biratnagar earlier or exile there after I will have no hesitation whatsoever, I will opt for the latter. The experiences of life in exile are of infinite value for me'.

B.P. was never tempted by the unlimited attractions Calcutta offered. Only when some well-to-do friend of his father or relative from Nepal took him out did he get to eat the Bengali delicacies or take a cab ride. He was taken just once to a theatre, the Corinthian, and that left a lasting impression on him. He liked to meet people though, and developed close relationships with mature men and women. And now at an age when sexuality is a natural and novel emotion, he was attracted by the shapes and forms of the female body, their charms and mysterious ways, as his writings clearly reflect.

At this time the family came across 'Raja Saheb', a grandson of Jung Bahadur, born and brought up in Orissa and a learned scholar, who later adopted the life of a yogi. A binding chemistry developed between them, as each recognized the intellectual depth in the other. The Yogi made a generous offer: he wanted the Koiralas to buy a nice piece of agricultural land for his young daughter and use it until her marriage took place. On advice of grandfather of Bishwa Bandhu Thapa, they bought a fertile piece of land near the Kosi River, not far from the Nepal border and their beloved Biratnagar.

The gypsy existence of our family came to an end for six years. Those were golden years for me—a time of peace and hope between the two wars. The land was lush with fruit plants and the greenery of bamboo and trees, when the seasonal crops turned from green to rich gold, when the brackish smell of the earth filled the air as the monsoon rains sprinkled the earth, freshly turned by the plough, when the morning sun sprayed its rays through the green leaves and the myriad songs of countless birds burst forth, when the approach of evenings was the hour of mellow *Gaudhuli*[204] and the world was lost in silken nights of colourful dreams. Where the herdsmen of the cows and buffaloes were dear friends of the children, the ponds filled with pure water and the splendour of lotus flowers, where the music of devotion in tune with the sound of drums and clash of cymbals rang out from the seats of the *yogis* early each morning. The exuberant songs of rustic young lovers matching the mood of each season rose to breach the silence as if pierced by an arrow and where every girl was a daughter of the village and each boy a son. Poverty, pain and the tragedy of death itself were painted over as an inevitable part of life and made bearable by the fairs, festivals, swings, songs and nautanki.[205]

B.P. concludes with a telling observation, 'These days men earn a great deal, innovations have made life very prosperous. But the present generation has also lost out something vital: the peace of rural life... as if a person who has reached the summit of success has missed out on the colourful experience of first love.' The canvas drawn by B.P.'s masterful strokes of the rural bliss of dehat—the sprawling flat land on both sides of the Indo-Nepal border—exemplifies his excellence as a sensitive writer, one whose diverse range of social and political writings, novels and literary work has placed him at the highest rank in this field as well.

During the six years that the Koirala household lived in Tedhi they had sufficient food and earnings for a healthy life. Krishna Prasad established a school, as he had done in Biratnagar earlier, run on the lines of Gandhian thought. Young B.P. found the atmosphere oppressive, as he did with some of the traditional practices and rituals he was obliged to follow. However, it was the all-embracing academic environment of this house in the rural hinterland that infused the seeds of intellectual stimulation and moulded Bishweshwar Prasad Koirala into an exceptional leader 'the tallest among the most celebrated Nepalese'[206]. 'The dominant element in the atmosphere of our Tadi house was politics,' writes B.P. Koirala. 'People who gathered here read several newspapers and periodicals, and forcefully expressed their views about national and international affairs during our regular deliberations...Russia, Lenin and Communism, Turkey and Kamalpasha, China and Japan were the main topics of debate, in reference to Nepal and India...in particular we eagerly supported the state revolution in Russia and felt Lenin was the Messiah of poor people like us also.' Knowledge of modern Nepalese history will be incomplete if we fail to appreciate how this man's mind functioned and evolved in his formative and indeed later years.

The entire family and most of the village followed Krishna Prasad's leadership and Gandhi's political guidance.

> [He was the] beacon of hope for our family and all the deprived and oppressed communities. My political concepts took shape under this liberal academic atmosphere; the mixture of thoughts of Gandhi and Lenin dominated the thinking; the concept of 'Vasudhaiba Kutumbakam' the whole world is one family, became the irremovable cornerstone of my belief. Under no circumstances can my mind accept that politics is merely a game of Machiavellian moves for the acquisition of power or that nationalism is the most profound principle of the human thought process. Internationalism is an essential need of the modern age, narrow nationalism is counterproductive. Many of my critics, friends and enemies have castigated me as unfit for politics of Nepal. I admit my inadequacy at what people call palace or court intrigues; but I maintain that such politics was not stable or beneficial for society in the past nor can it be so in the future.

There was one vital aspect of education that the young Koiralas could not have mastered in Tadi: the knowledge of their mother tongue, Nepali. That need was fulfilled by none other than the man who was the principal perpetrator of all their wanderings and sufferings in exile—Prime Minister Chandra. Even during the exile years each had kept a nexus with the other; Chandra often sent veiled massages to Krishna Prasad opening an outlet to seek pardon and return to Nepal; Koirala baulked. Yet, he had words of praise mixed with disappointment, 'What could that maharaj not have achieved for modernization of the country had he so wished? But he never did so.'

Chandra enquired about the well-being of the Koirala family at times and about the education of the children. Krishna Prasad reported the progress made by the school he had established but conveyed his concern that he could in no way fulfil the need of the students to learn their national language. Chandra sent a huge parcel containing three copies each of all the books and educational material published under the auspices of Gorkha Publications in Nepal. Copies of Gorkha Patra weekly too started arriving regularly to the school.

'These materials were the source of my knowledge of Nepalese literature in my formative years. Chandra also sent medicines from the Ayurvedic centre, established by Nepal government. But despite these overtures my father was adamant in the matter of asking for a pardon.'

He never returned to Kathmandu as long as Chandra was alive. Only the incisive genius of Bishweshwar could fathom and express the enigma that was Chandra, in one short sentence, 'once one meets him, nobody can forget him.'

The near-idyllic life of the Koiralas was cruelly disrupted when the Kosi River changed its course and devastated their land in 1927. They had to be on the move again and were scattered to different parts of Bihar and UP. Matrika joined a school and went on to a college based on the Gandhian principles. B.P. was determined to join a school in Banaras. He sensed a utopian character in the Gandhian way and felt that the easy rustic life of rural India could not fulfil the demands of his versatile mind and far reaching ambitions. So to Banaras he would go, to feel the thrill of pulsating political fermentation in India. B.P. assured the family that as long as he could reach Banaras he would somehow sustain himself, as his grandmother was in permanent residence there. His younger mother and sister each insisted on giving 'Bishu' (Bishweshwar) the few gold ornaments they possessed. His father wrote to some of his friends in Banaras who could help him get admission and possibly a scholarship at Harish Chandra School, the prime choice of B.P. He took a train to Banaras, elated.

B.P. Koirala, Gandhi, Marx and Democratic Socialism.

The teenaged B.P. stayed with his aged grandmother at Dugdha Binayak. Nothing was going to deny him a life of political adventure. However, the political activist in B.P. was disappointed by the Nepalese settled in Banaras. He complains that they were 'not only devoid of interest in their home country but seemed untouched by the sweeping revolutionary upheaval that engulfed India. 'Amidst such a large population of Nepalese in the city, I did not find my society'. Such an indictment may be a little naive; Nepalese people flocked into Kasi in search of 'mukti' (release) from temporal attachment or for learning matters spiritual, not political theories, or to stimulate rebellion.

It was outside of Dugdha Binayak, in school or elsewhere that 'my social being was taken over by (the politics of) Hindustan'. He was a good student in formal studies and brilliant in oratory. He went barefoot to school and donned the one set of handspun Khadi kurta and dhoti that he owned, and washed in the river every time they were soiled. Those were days when the flaunting of affluence was not fashionable and a simple life and high thinking was respected. Young Koirala made many friends and became role model for many in his school and outside. He never disclosed to anyone that his 'style' was the outcome of necessity. He visited libraries in his off time and received many books as gifts from his more affluent friends or admirers: his writing began during these early days. He started jotting down his thoughts and feelings during quiet hours of reflection. One benefactor read some pieces and sent an editor of a leading Hindi monthly literary magazine *Hans*. To the utter surprise of both, the short story found space in the following issue, to start off his journey in writing. Thereafter, his writings found space in important magazines and accolades in the literary brotherhood of Banaras and beyond. B.P.'s views on religion too had taken root early. He avoided the prescribed rituals and routines of a Brahmin, or visits to temples where possible. In this sense he remained a non-believer throughout his life. When Matrika derided his younger brother for his neglect of religious duties, calling it an insult to the gods B.P. replied: 'God resides within each man, in his heart. A deity of external creation is no God at all.' The first line of his assertion replicates a thought expressed in the Gita, 'I am seated in the hearts of all'[207]. B.P. is often called a 'nastik' He viewed his own spiritual inclination as that of a 'Bhabuk Rahasyabadi' (an emotional realist).

There is little doubt, however, as to the juxtaposition of the psyche of B.P. Koirala: it was firmly rooted in the battlefield of politics. The ideological base of his politics during his formative years, B.P. admits, was still confused, hovering between the thoughts of Gandhi, Marx and Lenin. It was at such a time in 1930, while he was still in class nine that he and Matrika 'came into contact with a terrorist organization involved in a bank robbery case' Both of them were arrested; B.P. was 'chained and locked up round the clock in a dismal cell, blocked on all sides except a small eyehole'. Fortunately, no eyewitness could identify the two brothers and both were released after about three months.

About this time Maharaj Chandra died and was succeeded by Bhim Shumsher. Krishna Prasad and his family settled down once more in Biratnagar. B.P. returned to Banaras and after his matriculation, joined Banaras Hindu University (BHU). He was often sent to run errands related to the family business to Calcutta or Bombay by his father during the vacations. It was during one such trip that he met some leaders of the Communist party. They were clearly impressed by young Koirala's intellect and started cultivating the boy—so far a Gandhian and a follower of the Congress party, but nevertheless still impressionable and open to other ideologies. These were the early thirties and the Communist party was banned in India but, they had a cell in the Engineering College and the students had built a radio set hidden in one of the rooms. 'To them, listening was some kind of a ritual which they devotedly performed. I was enthralled and delighted by this clandestine experience. Afterwards I started a socialist study circle in BHU'. Students leaning to the left joined the circle. B.P. was soon disillusioned by the Communist party. The actions of Stalin, their doctrinaire attitudes towards the liberation movement in India and their vulgar criticism of Gandhi 'were anathema to me'[208]. It was then that Jai Prakash Narayan and Ram Manohar Lohia entered his life. Like B.P. both of them were looking for a middle path between the authoritarian Marxism as shaped by Stalin in Russia and the Gandhian values and concepts that demanded a severe test on the normal nature of the ordinary man. The concepts of Democratic Socialism, largely a euro-centric ideology so far, were discussed and J.P. expressed his intention of starting, and did later lead, a new party in India based on similar goals and objectives. 'I felt I had found a man I could work under,' admits B.P. in his interview[209]. B.P. learned the concepts of democratic socialism under guidance of J.P. and in company of Lohia as long he was in India. However, it was in Nepal that he was inspired to shape the contours of 'democratic socialism suited to South Asia' for which he is recognized and honoured in his home country, and at the platform and amongst leaders of Socialist International.

For now J.P. and Lohia returned to their respective duties. B.P. completed his graduation from BHU and went on to Calcutta for his Masters degree in Arts and Law. During these years J.P. formed the Congress Socialist Party (CSP) under the overall umbrella of the Indian National Congress. B.P. joined the new formation. He had given a great deal of thought to a suitable ideology, before choosing democratic socialism as his final political platform and formally entering the hazardous arena of revolution. His sporadic legal practice, the party work and demands of his family business took him to different parts of the country including Darjeeling, Patna and of course Calcutta and Banaras, and his hometown Biratnagar. Once he went to Kathmandu on invite of Matrika, who had joined government service as a Subba. B.P. found the atmosphere in Kathmandu most oppressive. He considered joining service under the Rana government as 'immoral' and came back to India.

Devendra Prasad Singh, fondly addressed as Deven Babu, one of the activists with B.P. in the Socialist Circle at BHU and now a leader of the CSP in Bihar belonged to an affluent family, with a successful legal practice in Patna. He could foresee the great potential of B.P. for political leadership in India or Nepal and made a generous offer to fulfil the financial needs of his friend Bishweshwar, should B.P. devote his full time and energy to party work. And so began a personal friendship and a political bond that was to last a lifetime.

Meanwhile the freedom struggle in India entered a critical phase. World War II broke out in 1938. Opinion was sharply divided in the Congress. Subhas Chandra Bose took his militant path to support the Axis coalition against the 'common enemy', imperial Britain. J.P. and his followers continued to build and strengthen a militant wing prepared to launch the struggle as and when called upon[210]. The beleaguered British government under Winston Churchill sent a high level emissary, Sir Stafford Cripps, to make a firm commitment to independence post the war. Nehru and a section of the Congress who favoured a compromise solution with the British were isolated when Gandhi changed his line, comparing the British offer to a 'cheque of a failing bank', and asking Cripps and Britain to: 'Leave India in God's hands and go!' The Congress Central Working Committee CWC backed the Mahatma and launched the nation wide 'Quit India Movement.'

The Congress party was ill prepared for such a quick turnaround. The British were. All members of the CWC were arrested before they could move into action. But the CSP and its cadre were better equipped to respond to the battle cry of Gandhi. Young B.P. for example plunged into hectic activities. Starting in 1939 he was working with the trade union movement, engaged in disruptive activities. There were several groups such as the one B.P. worked with, trained for clandestine activities. Their bases were in UP and Bihar. Hit and run operations were carried out and communication installations destroyed in some areas, causing a sense of insecurity. The open border with Nepal also allowed room for a quick getaway from the jurisdiction of the Indian security men[211]. The veteran Krishna Prasad—once again living in Biratnagar—was also sheltering rebels from across the border while his son joined operations in India. Each was eventually arrested. Krishna Prasad was jailed in Nepal and died in captivity a few years later. By a tragic coincidence, the son was released from prison just one day later in India. They had not met each other for many years.

Banaras Hindu University and the Nepali Students Union

Madan Mohan Malaviya, the founder of the Banaras Hindu University, was one of the CWC members interned. The resentment in the university was bitter. Gandhi appealed to all students over the age of sixteen to join the movement and the students throughout the country got directly and physically involved in the national struggle for independence.

Malaviya had worked with rare commitment and persistence to establish BHU. The vision of Malaviya and goal of BHU was to create a seat of learning that would imbue 'the best of Hindu culture and philosophy and all that was good in the ancient civilizations of India', and at the same time expand the limited range of education set for the 'native people' by the British establishment, and introduce courses in the sciences and engineering that would match the West. The Raja of Banaras had gifted major part of the five and a half square miles of prime property to BHU the largest residential campus in Asia. The institution came into being through official enactment in 1915. Unprecedented support from the ruling families of many Indian states, corporate houses, merchants and common citizens enabled construction of buildings inside the sprawling campus grounds to house the students, the teaching fraternity, classrooms, sports fields and extensive facilities for recreation and extra-curricular activities, in gradual progression[212].

The governing body of BHU had kept the teachers and students away from active involvement in national politics. However, the arrest of Malaviya and Annie Besant, the two guiding lights of the institution, and the call of Gandhi drove the students to the streets. The Bhattarai brothers, Gopal Prasad and Krishna Prasad the Vice President of the Nepal Students' Union, the Secretary Ishwar Baral and Manamohan Adhikari were amongst the few Nepali students who did so: the rest were close to the Ranas. 'The atmosphere in Banaras was rife with anti-British sentiment. No one worried who was born where, what nationality someone held. There was this overwhelming surge against British rule'[213].

The Vice Chancellor of those years, Professor Sarvapalli Radhakrishnan, as well as Pandit Malaviya, tried to restrain the students asking them to avoid any destructive action and adhere to the principles of non-violence; but the agitations were intense and the response ruthless. Eventually, the governing body notified closure of the university until the violent activities subsided.

The situation in the rest of India was similar as Gandhi asked them to 'do or die'. With responsible leaders from the Congress arrested and jailed, unbridled mob violence erupted in many parts of the country. The government was in no mood for restraint or compromise. Well organized, rigorous and sustained action on the part of the security forces disrupted and dispersed public demonstrations, bandhs and hartaals. Jails all over India filled up. But the spontaneous uprising of common folk could not sustain in absence of a unified chain of command. Faced by multiple adverse conditions, the uprising gradually lost steam. Yet it lasted about one year and during this period 'about a thousand lives were lost and 60,000 arrested[214]'.

Nepalese activists jailed or detained in different parts of the country included the two Bhattarai brothers, Dilli Raman Regmi and Ishwar Baral in Banaras, Surya Prasad Upadhyaya, Dharanidhar Koirala, and Surya Bikram Gyanwali, in Patna, Calcutta, or Darjeeling respectively. B.P. was in Biratnagar and helped his father in arranging shelter for activists from Bihar crossing the border into Nepal. While on a trip to visit his socialist comrades in Bihar, B.P. was arrested near Patna and taken to jail in Bankepur. His friend and supporter Devendra Prasad Singh, Rajendra Prasad (the first President of the Republic of India), and Jagjivan Ram (the renowned Dalit leader), amongst many other top-ranked leaders, particularly from Bihar, were also detained there. B.P. found the experience in the British jail pleasant. The 'A'-class prisoners were given a wholesome diet, good accommodation, any books they wanted and they could converse freely with each other. 'The British jailors could be harsh at times but they were always fair'. B.P. and most of the other leaders were not released until 1945 when the world war was in its final phase, the outcome no more in doubt.

The involvement of the Nepalese in the Quit India Movement and companionship in the prisons allowed ample opportunity to relate/comprehend the constraints on liberties, hardships and inequities imposed by the Rana oligarchy in Nepal. The shared experience strengthened the bond of solidarity between the activists and leaders irrespective of race, age or nationality. Most of the Nepalese leaders released from prison, including the Bhattarai brothers and Dilli Raman Regmi were from Banaras and returned to the city. There was greater connectivity between the communities living within and outside the BHU campus now and each strengthened the resolve of the other. The older generation as well as the student community could now sense that British rule in India was tottering and the fate of the Rana oligarchy was linked with it.

'In the forties,' Banaras was evolving into something akin to the capital, the centrifugal force behind the Nepalese revolutionary movement in India,' recalls Dr Deepak Malik, a professor at BHU, still an ardent socialist, content with his Bohemian lifestyle. 'We helped the Nepalese movement, too, even with the clandestine collection of guns in the late forties. Anti-colonialism and an anti-authoritarian sentiment against the dictatorship your forefathers imposed on Nepal was the guiding mindset of the young and conscious generation those days, (yug ke vichar) and so was agnosticism. We were fond of B.P. Koirala as a fearless leader. Like us, he was not a religious-minded man but he possessed spiritual integrity, rarely seen these days.'[215]

It was no surprise then that in 1947 through a resolution of its general meeting held in Calcutta, the Nepal National Congress decided to locate its head-office in Banaras. And Krishna Prasad Bhattarai, Secretary of the Organization Department, was assigned the responsibility to head the office.

Chapter Four

The Great Metropolis

Between the fifteenth and nineteenth centuries, tales of the fabled riches of the East reached Europe. Merchants and adventurers traversed the seas in urgent quest of opportunities for trade and profit. As luck would have it, some of them entered the Great Gangetic Delta that meets the seas at the mouth of the Bay of Bengal: a lush magical paradise they'd never envisaged. Soon, cajoling, enticing the village folk, they wheedled their way upriver—doing what they could to create a base.

If Job Charnock, the English merchant who founded Calcutta in 1690, was to visit the trading settlement he founded from the mud-hut villages he first came upon, he would hardly believe the transformation. Ships and vessels from the China Sea, across the Atlantic, stately European liners and steamers from African coast towns now moved in and out carrying huge quantities of tea, coal jute, shellac and mica. By 1870, Calcutta had become one of the largest and busiest ports in the world. The money required to service the high turnover of business flowed to the city. Major banks followed, and industries, shops, malls, hotels, educational institutions and hospitals sprung up along the wide roads and splendid avenues.

Job seekers came in droves, seeking an El Dorado in the glittering city. While some found stable employment, the rest could be seen squatting outside the train stations or at open spaces in the city, breaking stones or forced to beg on the streets. They slept on the sidewalks, at railway platforms or yards, or lived in the clustered jhuggis depicted in Dominique Lapierre's *City of Joy*. In the red-light districts, there were nubile young girls abducted from faraway homes, forced into selling their bodies.

Sad and sordid as these stories are, one must still remember that these people came to the cities perhaps from even more wretched conditions.

Calcutta gave them hope, breathing space and perhaps more kindness than most cities in the world. The glittering city provided employment and opportunity to many who came to her, including awestruck natives from rural India and Nepal. They found work at the labour-intensive industries or at the harbour and port that handled about half the total imports and exports of India, or by ferrying passengers on the thousands of hand-drawn rickshaws that plied the streets. Others worked as domestic help or guards, in teashops or eating houses, or at low-ranked government jobs. The more enterprising ones set up business. These were the more fortunate for they found steady income and could send money to their families back home.

By the time the British established their Empire, not only was Calcutta the premier city of India, it was also considered the grandest city of the Commonwealth, second only to London. Credit must go to the British for setting up a public transportation network that matched the city's ambience. The tramway lines covered a great part of the city as they weaved their way at leisurely pace. The brightly painted yellow-black taxicabs could be hired at any point along the street.

Calcutta emerged as the symbol of the might of the British Empire in India, and 'epitomized the white man's domination of the globe'[216]. The glory days began after direct British rule replaced the East India Company's, following the 'mutiny' of 1857. The city was a pleasure ground of the rulers, the rich and the famous. 'Every year before Christmas, a glittering season of polo, horse-racing and social receptions drew the entire elite of Asia to Calcutta—with the latest fashions of London and Paris, and the matchless robes and jewels of the Indian royals. Excursions on splendid horse-drawn carriages along Chowranghee, stately gondolas along the Hooghly, the racing days and all-white clubs, accompanied by the colourfully dressed brass bands or the tunes of ball room music formed part of the pleasurable diversions of the Burra Sahibs and Mem Sahibs.

The bachelors could pick sprightly young Anglo-Indian beauties or find nubile lasses from the hills and dusky-skinned enchantresses in the recesses of the city.

The greatest show of the British Raj in India was staged in 1911 when the newly crowned King George V and Queen Mary visited India. Thereafter the capital of British India moved to Delhi, but that did not impede the economic growth of Calcutta, or its fame as the city of entertainment and pleasure.

Calcutta, also, commands an especial niche in the history of the revolution against the Rana oligarchy.

An Influx of Nepalese and their Role in Political Activities

There is no definitive record of the pattern, dates or any count of the flow of immigrants from Nepal to India. However, Hindustan has always been a land of escape for them from the hardships and miseries caused by the unyielding soil of the rugged mountains, the lack of opportunities for gainful employment, a feudal society, or for those in the run from the law. The contacts and relationships built between people before 1816—when large parts of present-day India were under Nepal's occupation—helped migratory trends. An increasing number from the Eastern hills went to West Bengal and Assam since the turn of the twentieth century, to find work in the tea gardens. Anonymity and opportunity for a new beginning was a great challenge and boon. Their numbers grew substantially following the two Great Wars. The Nepali language, however, was and still remains the mother tongue and a channel of endearment. And wherever they may be living, an enduring affection for the motherland is common to all Nepalese migrants.

Calcutta was an attractive destination for ambitious businessmen. Nepal's trading community, particularly the Newars, set up successful business in silver and gold, musk and other animal products, herbs and spices. Many handled the imports to Nepal of fabrics, cigarettes, and petroleum products produced or processed in the Indian or British mills or refineries. The Rana families often imported diverse items including carpets, furniture and furnishings, objects d'art, biscuits and motor vehicles from Europe. Every one of these items were transported in trains and trucks first, and finally manually carried by stout porters over the last part of the journey across the mountain passes. Most of the traders and agents were commissioned by the government and therefore loyal to the Rana rulers, but a few bold ones discreetly supported the anti-Rana political movement. Many students were drawn to the city seeking higher education. The places they gathered were fertile breeding grounds not only of erudite scholars and skilled manpower but often for political activism against British rule in India and the authoritarian regime in Nepal.

Two Nepalese students who were reared in the volatile atmosphere of Calcutta during the 1940s gained prominence in the twists and turns of the politics of Nepal for more than half a century. Their reminiscences, writings and finally interviews depict life in Calcutta during the forties, leading to the armed insurgency of the Nepali Congress and the fall of the 104-year-old Rana regime in February 1951. The activities and experience of these two students are representative of hundreds, perhaps thousands, who had taken similar routes from the interior, often remote villages and towns of the country, to the schools and campuses in India, and then the political life of strife and struggle, terms in jail and exile and finally to the trials, tribulations and triumphs of emerging democracy in Nepal.

The Democratic Front[217]

Ram Hari Joshi was born to a well-to-do zamindar family in Sarlahi. After primary schooling he went to Muzaffarpur for his matriculation and to BHU for an Inter Science degree. Though not actively involved, he was stimulated by the ongoing political ferment and spirit of revolution in Banaras. He enrolled into Bagabasi College, Calcutta, in the tumultuous year 1946, a slim, wiry, young and active lad of barely twenty.

There was a deep divide at the time between the Hindus and Muslims in India. Ever since Mohammad Ali Jinnah took leadership of the Muslim League[218] in the mid-1930s, the differences got increasingly pronounced. Gradually, the concept of a Muslim state within India began to stimulate the minds of the Muslim population. By the beginning of the 1940s, Jinnah was quick to take up the cause.

After World War II the independence of India was viewed as a realistic, indeed inevitable outcome. With the focus of fighting the common enemy diluted, the Muslim League now battled to establish a separate space in independent India. Jinnah was prepared to go to any length to carve out his Pakistan. 'We shall have India divided, or we shall have India destroyed,' he declared. In order to drive home his stand the Muslim League declared 16 August 1946 as 'Direct Action Day'. The Muslim League administration in Bengal, an exception to the other states of India where the Congress had prevailed, was headed by the energetic H.S. Suhrawardy. The action kicked off in Calcutta. His private army of strongmen organized a demonstration. Whether he intended it to be so or not, the irate mob went out of control. Bloody riots broke out. Criminal elements took advantage of the mayhem and joined in the looting, rape and arson. Over four days this great city of two and a half million people was given over to violence, torture, savagery, murder and massacre that was never witnessed before. An estimated 6,000 men, women and children, mostly Hindus, were killed. The revenge riots overtook north India where the Muslim losses were greater.

The riots overshadowed all other issues. The politics of Nepal was far from the minds of the people when young Joshi joined the college. The democratic movement in Nepal was, in any case, not an active issue, as compared to Banaras. It took Joshi some time to get adjusted to the new surroundings; he knew very few people, none intimately. Gradually he learnt about the Himanchal Chhatra Sangh, an organization of students from north India, Sikkim, Bhutan and Nepal. Many Nepalese students from several colleges were its members, but the Sangh was purely a social body looking after the welfare of the Nepalese community in particular. Politics was not on its agenda at all and few talked about it.

'Even the social agenda was put on hold due to the tension and fear that gripped the city; it was almost defunct,' recollects Joshi.

The hostilities led to all forms of violence. Nepalese men and women were not spared, particularly the women[219]. A breakaway wing of the All India Gorkha League led by D.N. Pariyar and D.B. Lama, calling itself All India Gorkha Congress, was established in 1946. They publicly announced their commitment to support the movement against the Rana regime. Engaged in social work for the welfare of the Gorkhali community since its inception in 1905, the breakaway wing now focused on providing protection to the community from the violence and assisting victims of the riots and extortions. Gradually, the Sangh started to function more actively, the social issues now getting inevitably linked with religion and politics.

Joshi gradually made contacts and developed friendships with students in the Sangh.

> ...a large number of stipend holders sponsored by the state and indebted to the Ranas. There were a few like me, who had come on our own and therefore of independent view. When I first joined the Sangh those who were close to the Rana regime were dominant. Many of my contemporaries became prominent members of Nepalese society in later life, Devendra Raj Upadhyaya, B.K. Shreshta, Dr Jaya Narayan Giri, Dr Savitri Gurung, Bishnu Prasad Dhital and Keshar Jung Rayamajhi who was a political activist, influenced by communist ideology. I was the lonely one committed to and actively involved with the democratic front, which later took the form of the Nepali Congress.[220]

While the Nepali students generally stayed aloof from politics, the student community was active.

> They were loosely divided into the democrats (Congress), the communists and the socialists. I admired the communist activists; they were very dedicated and active; they distributed al newsletter 'The Militant' and other Marxist literature clandestinely. I was also very friendly with an ardent activist

Dixit-da. He took me to the conference of the Students Union of Calcutta University, held in Baharampur. In the train compartment they were chanting slogans such as 'our war is a class war'. I was registered as a Fraternal Delegate. I presented a resolution through the Chairman that condemned the autocratic Rana regime in Nepal, approved by the meeting. The Indian Congress candidate was elected President that year.[221]

Joshi was encouraged to bring up political subjects for discussion amongst the Nepalese students in the Sangh. The activities of B.P. Koirala and his followers and Ganeshman Singh's daring escape from prison were now common themes for interaction between all Nepalese and Indians of Nepalese origin. The Sangh became more popular and held an election for the posts of the president and membership of the working committee. Joshi was elected to the Working Committee and given charge of the literary wing. He was now in a position to influence the Sangh and its activities. Then one day he was asked by an uncle visiting Calcutta to come to the house of one D.K. Shahi in Ram Mohan Dutta Road. Little did he realize that as he set foot in that house he was beginning a journey that was to last a lifetime. Shahi was the pivotal activist of the Nepali democratic movement in Calcutta and his house was like 'a home away from home for Nepali leaders visiting Calcutta, and their meeting place'[222]. On that day he met many activists/leaders of that time.

D.N. Pradhan, D.N. Pariyar, leaders of the Pravasi Nepali community and Rudra Prasad Giri, from the rich merchant family from Janakpur, were present amongst others. Everybody was attracted by B.P.'s recent appeal for all forces against the Rana oligarchy to unite. D.K. Shahi and those assembled in his house that day were seeking an opening to contact the youth and students group, Joshi happened to be the right man at the right place. He was told that a meeting held in Banaras had decided that Calcutta would be the venue for a 'great' meeting of democrats on 25–26 January 1947 with the agenda to establish a new party and asked to bring the students and young men committed to the cause.

It was not easy to persuade people to attend the meeting. The fear of retribution from the Rana rulers weighed heavily and the Hindu–Muslim fights had not yet abated. Nevertheless, my friend Jaya Narayan Giri and I were able to get together some twenty-five to thirty like-minded people. This was a significant contribution from the Himanchal Chhatra Sangh, considering that the total number of participants was somewhere around one hundred and twenty-five.[223]

Although the number was fewer than expected, the meeting remains an important milestone in the history of the democratic movement in Nepal[224].

Joshi was now 'deeply committed to the cause' despite his father's objections and advice not to neglect his education. On his way home during the mid-term break, he met Mahendra Narayan Nidhi[225] and Saroj Koirala[226], prominent leasers of the Nepali Congress. Joshi was given an assignment to distribute pamphlets urging the farmers to oppose the order of a new levy on the paddy crop at his home district. While at his job 'I was arrested and imprisoned. This was my first experience of jail, for six months; I had many more such experience later, as you know,' he said in a simple matter-of-fact tone. 'After that incident, my relations with my family soured. I lived elsewhere and did not talk to my father until 1975, when Kishanjee (Krishna Prasad Bhattarai) brought us together.'[227]

Joshi recounts these happenings at his home in Kathmandu with justifiable pride and a happy smile, nearly sixty-one years later, on his eighty-first birthday. He is fully alert of mind and offers me a cup of tea and yes, a roshogolla. He has been involved in every one of the satyagraha or revolutionary activities of the Nepali Congress, against the Rana regime at first, and then the Shah Kings after 1960. He became a cabinet minister in the Nepali Congress government-led by G.P. Koirala in 1991; but 'Gandhian' in his outlook and manners, he could not reconcile himself or fit in to the new trends of degeneration of values and self centered politics. Gradually, he moved out of the playing field, like many such stalwarts that sustained the Nepali Congress.

The Left Front

Dr Keshar Jung Rayamajhi was born into a 'rich' household in Palpa. The family's house stood out prominently amidst tiny huts scattered over the green cover of the mountain slopes. He was not destined to stay at his birthplace for long; his mother died while he was still a toddler and his father also died when Keshar was seven years old. A maternal uncle who lived in Kathmandu, an officer in the Nepal army, took him and his brother under his wing.

Keshar was admitted to the Durbar High School and then the Tri Chandra College. He was taught the usual practice of chakari and taken each morning to Baber Mahal to pay his obeisance to the Director General of Education, General Mrigendra. The young man did not like this routine but could not avoid it either. Moreover, he was haunted by the memory of the untimely death of his parents and conscious of the lack of even the basic health services where he was born. He developed a keen desire to be a doctor. Calcutta was the best known city for medical education. He was not close enough to the Rana rulers to get state sponsorship but his mind was made up, his motivation strong.

On a fine morning of 1946, with little knowledge of the hardships he could encounter in conflict-ridden India, he took off for the city of Calcutta. There were a few families who would put him up for a few days but none that could ensure him placement into the lone state-run Campbell Medical College. A frail young lad like him, an outsider without any recommendation or sponsor in Calcutta, stood little chance of gaining admission. Yet, he made persistent daily calls at the office of the head clerk of the college. 'At last, perhaps taking pity on me or to get rid of me, he suggested that I should approach an MLA by the name of Ratna Lal Brahman, popularly known as Mahila

Baje and seek his recommendation.'[228] Mahila Baje was a Nepalese also from the Palpa district. He had once defied an order forbidding the Nepalese to carry the khukuri which many Nepalese in Calcutta carried as an essential tool of guard duty. Mahila Baje had walked into the State Assembly with the khukuri proudly tucked into his cummerbund. He was duly arrested. In his defence, he pleaded that if the Sikhs were allowed to carry their *Kirpans,* then why the ban on carrying a khukuri for the Nepalese? The court was convinced. It was a landmark victory for the rights of the Nepalese in India.

Keshar Jung approached the residence of the legislator and to his surprise got an audience without much fuss. Once he sensed the burning desire in the voice of the young boy from his home district, and heard of his sorry plight in an unknown city, Mahila Baje agreed to write a letter of recommendation. But he had never acquired the skill of letter-writing and asked a colleague sitting beside him to help out. Also a member of the legislative council, the man who composed that letter was called Mujib-ur Rehman, the same Sheikh Mujib-ur, who was destined one day to be the 'liberator' and first prime minister of Bangladesh. The letter was invaluable for getting the boy entry into the prestigious college. As a special case he was also given a stipend of ₹25 per month as an entrant from the marginalized sections of the community, sufficient in those days to sustain him.

Once in college, he was inducted into the All India Students' Union, and quickly discovered that it was dominated by young and active Marxists. He was impressed by the ideology they preached. His biology professor, Hiren Mukherjee, a veteran Marxist, took keen interest in him and Keshar was also instantly impressed by the committed and articulate Marxist leader, content with his simple lifestyle and humble manners. Keshar had been guided into the communist fold, a career he had never sought or imagined, and a destiny that led him to the position of General Secretary of the Communist Party of Nepal in 1958.

The Communist Party in India (CPI) was banned during different years before and even after 1947, but the organization functioned underground, particularly in Bengal. Keshar's progression up the ranks of the party was swift. In the meantime, he had joined the Himanchal Chhatra Sangh[229] and again rose quickly to become secretary of its medical wing. He is remembered by Ram Hari Joshi as a competitor well versed in Marxist ideology who distributed communist literature from time to time, and was backed by a superior international organization network of the well-entrenched Communist Party of Bengal. On the advice and recommendation of Hiren Mukherjee, now his political guru, young Keshar took official membership of the CPI. Unlike the democratic parties, membership into the communist party originating in any country, automatically inducted the member into the fold of the International Communist Movement.

Encouraged by the senior leaders in Bengal, he and his colleagues in the student body established the Marxism Study Circle, later renamed the Progressive Study Circle, in order to avoid the constant threat and recurring instances of punitive actions it often attracted from state authorities and the right fundamentalists. The Indian National Congress (INC) was the primary driving force in the struggle against the British; but the CPI chose to follow the guidelines of the international communist movement. The dubious role of the communists in India during World War II and their connection with Russia was resented by British and Indian leaders alike. When the party formally opted to follow a policy and course of violent revolutionary activities to achieve its goals, the government issued arrest warrants on its leaders and activists. Keshar learnt the art of hide-and-fight from a young age. Even under rigorous scrutiny communist activists continued to carry out party work, adopting pseudo names, changing places of residence repeatedly, moving about incognito most times. The religious riots and violence that engulfed Calcutta were an additional hazard; but for Keshar, the experience of working amongst the injured and offering free medical service provided an invaluable platform for social work and indeed for interacting with a wide variety of Nepalese and Indian activists. He was elected the secretary of the Progressive Study Circle and its office was housed where he lived. Soon the Circle established its credentials as the meeting point of Marxists, especially those visiting Calcutta from other parts of India and Nepal. Pushpa Lall, Manmohan Adhikary, Tulsi Lall Amatya, Shailendra Updhyaya and most other renowned communist leaders, who played a prominent part in Nepalese politics well into the 1980s, passed through the portals of this Circle. The Study extended its contact in many parts of India and Nepal, 'from Banaras to Palpa, from Calcutta to Kathmandu, Darjeeling, Jhapa, Morang, and Ilaam and as far as Burma'[230].

Pushpa Lall and the Birth of the Communist Party of Nepal

The most prominent of the future leaders who interacted with the Study Circle was Comrade Pushpa Lall Shreshta. He had made a solemn promise to his brother Ganga Lall, one of the four martyrs of January 1941, to carry on the struggle against the Rana oligarchy. Pushpa Lall kept his word. He joined the movement against the Rana regime. The political dividing line between the Democrats and Communists at that time was shelved; their one goal was to bring down the regime. Nevertheless, there were a few active proponents of the Marxist ideology and literature in Kathmandu. One, Bihari Lall is credited with collecting Marxist literature from outside Nepal and teaching and propagating Marxist/communist thoughts as early as the early thirties[231]. The scarce literature and pamphlets were secretly passed from hand to hand by the activists, a majority of them from the middle class.

Post 1940, Pushpa Lall worked under the overall direction of the leaders of the anti-Rana movement quietly as was his nature and secretively as was the need of the times. He slipped back and forth between Nepal and India and made his mark as a fearless leader during the anti Rana rallies on the streets of Kathmandu valley in 1948. He then escaped to India to avoid certain arrest. In Banaras he formally joined the Nepal National Congress (NNC) as he was not in touch with the communist movement in India. He sided with the Dilli Raman Regmi faction along with other like-minded colleagues. Soon he held the post of General Secretary. It was on contact with communist comrades in Banaras and Calcutta that had found his permanent moorings. He took up the challenging task of translating the Communist Manifesto into the Nepali language. This landmark document was brought out in April 1949. Perhaps even more important input was the additional chapter where Pushpa Lall 'openly challenges' the labour policy of NNC and advocates the commitment of the Communist Party of Nepal 'to fight not only to bring down the Rana regime but against the feudal order in Nepal, as well as the Indian capitalists and Anglo-American imperialism that nurtures and supports it'.[232]

However, it was in Calcutta that the Nepal Communist Party was founded under the Pushpa Lall's leadership[233]. However, this part of history is shrouded in controversy. 'During these days,' writes Keshar Rayamajhi with obvious bitterness, 'Pushpa Lall was lost for some days. Later we heard that he and four others formed the Communist Party of Nepal.' As the driving force of the Progressive Study Circle he should at least have been consulted. Keshar debated the option of starting another party but on counselling of his Guru Hiren Mukherjee, he agreed to work with the new party for the greater cause they were fighting for[234]. One wonders, if the seed of divisive tendencies in the communist movement in Nepal was sown at this very point of its germination.

That division came to the fore when Nepali Congress launched its armed revolution in November 1950. While Pushpa Lall as President declared that the party cadre will not join the revolution under leadership of the Congress, several young communists did not want to sit idle at such a critical juncture of the nation's history. Keshar Jung was one of the most restless. Hiren Mukherjee agreed, 'If you remain aloof from such a great moment, history will curse you.' At that time All India Radio flashed the exhilarating news that the revolutionary army had captured Birgunj but tragically his friend, the handsome and brave Thir Bam Malla, was killed in action.

'If I cannot make good use of my knowledge and skills at such a time what is their purpose?' reasoned Keshar Jung. He packed a few personal belongings, his medical kit and some medicines, and headed for the war front. However, destiny took him to Koilabas, a little township at Indo-Nepal border. Rayamajhi was shocked to find the busy township deserted: a serious epidemic of the dreaded plague had driven them out. The doctor stayed back to make use of his professional expertise and serve the sick.

After 1951, his involvement with the party continued and within seven years he was elected to the highest post of the party, the Secretary General. But as the years went by, his credentials as a true Marxist were questioned by his comrades on account of his 'royalist' leanings. He was forced to relinquish his leadership, and joined the royal camp.

To the charge of being a 'royal communist' his response is: 'Even the CPN UML accepts the King now.'

Ranas Expelled from Nepal Rise and Prosper in Calcutta

It was on the platform of the affluent society of Calcutta that one powerful wing of the Rana family, expelled from the valley of Kathmandu in 1934, established its base, spread its roots and prospered. Those ousted carried their riches and were allowed to draw the salaries they received earlier, acquired huge mansions and enjoyed the same lifestyle, comforts and luxuries they were used to in Kathmandu. However, the prize and position of power they wielded was blunted and they were driven out of their ancestral homes and beloved birthplace. They never forgot the trauma nor forgave the insult. The ouster this time was a wholesale purge of families whose wealth was substantial, and contacts not limited to within the country alone. They formed a powerful combined force.

Ram Shumsher was sent to Jaleshwar as governor, the first to proceed to Calcutta and set up a permanent base. Mahavir Shumsher the other powerful and high-ranking general under previous Prime Minister Bhim, never trusted the intentions of the rulers and joined

Ram in Calcutta. They were attracted to 'Cal' in more ways than one. First, as a city unhindered by the diktat of the Nepalese court, then as a land of promise, and ample opportunities for gainful investments in trade, commerce and industry, and finally as the pleasure ground, the Paris of the East. Others who followed this path, too, never regretted their decision.

Of all the Rana members of the family who decided to make Calcutta their base, Mahavir Shumsher and Subarna, son of Hiranya, who continued as governor of Birgunj but also established a base in Calcutta, were to emerge as leaders who influenced the future course of Nepal's history.

In the initial stage of Mahavir's long innings in Calcutta, he bought and stayed in one of the mansions from his cousin Ram. It offered ample space for the comforts of the family. Soon, he purchased and moved into a new property in Alipore, a posh residential area. 'It was a large mansion surrounded by a compound of some four Bighas where we could play football or cricket, with a big lawn in front of the house'[235]. The mansions gave space for those expelled from Kathmandu to meet and plan their future life in exile, their investments and their strategy to avenge the ruling Rana cousins back home.

In 1938, World War II broke out in Europe. The German army marched in triumph across Europe in the early stages of the war and later the Japanese captured key positions, including Singapore and Malaysia. The Japanese army, joined by the Azad Hind forces, entered Burma and captured Mandalay in the early 1940s. Panic gripped the city as Japanese fighter aircrafts showed up in the Indian skies and dropped a few bombs on Calcutta, including near the famed Grand Hotel in Chowringhee. As a direct consequence, property values declined sharply particularly in eastern India. Amidst the crumbling values of real estate and the stock market, Mahavir was one of the few who intensified investments in prime real estate and large business and residential properties in central Calcutta, including Chowringhee and Dalhousie Square. He acquired controlling equity shares in banking and insurance companies, the sole ownership of

Himalayan Airways and substantial holdings in a number of public companies. When peace returned, Mahavir was established as one of the wealthiest individuals in Calcutta and indeed Nepal, barring the prime minister. He also made full use of the waiver of income tax offered by the British government to Nepalese residents in India. Mahavir was joined by Hiranya and his son Subarna as partners in this phenomenal growth. The rise of Calcutta into greater heights of prosperity, carried on its back, those who had kept faith in the city during its darkest hours.

Mahavir carried an intense desire to avenge the rulers in Kathmandu. At the same time he was intoxicated by the exuberant lifestyle and heady glamour Calcutta proffered. Also blessed with the easy charm of a playboy he became one of the leading actors of the high life. Both these interests were shared with equal passion by none other than King Tribhuwan of Nepal. Indeed, the seeds of their friendship were sown at an early age. Rana boys of similar age used to be sent to the royal palace as playmates for the young king.

King Tribhuwan had grown up to be handsome, elegant, well-spoken and an attractive man. He hated being restricted within his palace for his entertainment, wine, women, western music and ballroom dancing. But the movement of the royals outside palace gates was strictly restricted by the Ranas. There were a couple of palaces however, where restriction was not possible. One of them was Shah Mahal located across the street from the compounds of the royal palace, and built especially for one of the princesses who was estranged from her husband. Her son Samrajya was about the same age, including Mahavir, as the king. Tribhuwan visited Shah Mahal whenever possible. This palace was to attain fame, or was it notoriety. It was a favoured venue for rampant revelry and debauchery by the elite. In the 1950s B.P. Koirala as Home Minister was shocked by a scene in Shah Mahal:

> Spirits flowed like water...there was a young woman the king liked and whom he was used to meeting here; arrangements were made for providing one woman for every single and even

married man, for dancing, among other things…while the wives suffered. There were cubicles in the Durbar and before long the men paired off with the girls and disappeared into the darkness[236].

Mahavir was one of the frequent guests there before he was exiled from Kathmandu. He and the king were to renew their companionship and share these pleasures in later years in the glittering metropolis of Calcutta and add a new dimension, that of a political covenant.

An Emerging India

By the beginning of the twentieth century, extension of primary and higher education, expansion of the transportation, communication and irrigation networks, amongst other arenas of development, were creating the base for emergence of a new India. Men like Mohandas Karamchand Gandhi, Rabindranath Tagore and J.R.D. Tata gradually emerged, and challenged the claim of superiority of the white race.

Calcutta also changed gradually. The Bengali society was on the rise. They now used motor cars and yellow taxicabs and wore well-cut suits. The Saturday Club established by the Bengali gentry in 1907 grew in stature and popularity but sans the snobbery of the all-white clubs. A white Russian now entered the Calcutta scene. Born into a rich aristocratic family, Boris Lissanevitch joined the Russian army. In 1917 the Russian Revolution erupted. Boris, aged fifteen, suffered a bullet wound in a skirmish with the revolutionary red forces. He escaped under the pretence of being a student in his aunt's ballet school. After the end of the revolution and following the execution of the Czar's family, he crossed the border and reached free Europe, in the 'gay twenties', to be selected to join the Ballet Russe. He now moved from one glorious city to another in a whirlwind of rising fame, dancing with the most celebrated ballerinas of Europe. He fell in love with and married Kira, also a famous ballerina.

It was ballet that brought them to India, on the way to Shanghai and the far east. In Calcutta they spent exciting days inhaling the sights, smells and sounds of the bazaars and meeting the crème de la crème of the British and Indian high society. They completed their tour of the far east and returned to Calcutta. Boris instinctively sensed an opening and a life of imponderable excitement. In the mid 1930s the privileges of entry and membership to the British clubs were reserved for whites. But many of his friends were Indians, seeking excitement and new avenues to explore, but unlike Boris, with a healthy bank balance. The financial hub of India attracted the captains of industry, the newly rich business folks and successful professionals but of most interest to Boris, the Indian princes. Many of these rulers and princes had amassed riches and indulged in luxuries and fantasies that have inspired innumerable books. They came to Calcutta for fun and frolic.

For people like these, Boris opened The 300 Club.

Most Europeans who came to India looked for profitable trade, but none had the vision, reckless guts or gumption to create anything like Boris's club. It was to be a 'mixed' club, open till dawn, unlike the other clubs and restaurants in Calcutta that would close by midnight. Its membership was restricted to the select 300 and it soon became an avidly sought-after symbol of prestige for all races. Founding members of the club included Maharajas of Cooch Bihar and Burdwan, His Highness Gaekwad of Baroda, Sir Allen Lockhart, Sir Biren Mukerjee and J.R.D. Tata. Such a galaxy of the elite may be viewed, in other places and other times, as the gathering of the bourgeois oppressors. But at that time it served to demolish the concept of white superiority, not through any legislation or coercion but by the sheer strength of magnetism attached. Historian G.W. Forrest laments, 'the Englishman (in India) unfortunately, imitated the luxurious style of living of the nobles of the Mughal Empire.' Boris may have guessed such an outcome when he established the club but could not have visualised that 'The 300' would one day provide a space for the King of Nepal, Mahavir and Subarna to meet in secret and devise a strategy for bringing down the Rana regime.

Around the same years another stalwart of the hospitality business Mohan Singh Oberoi bought over the five hundred-room Grand Hotel and gradually nursed it back to its original grandeur. When Europe was hit by the most destructive war in world history and the hotels and clubs of Calcutta got an unexpected booty. 'Men in khaki more than made up for the lack of travellers in Mufti'. Tens of thousands of the Tommys and G.I.s from the war zones in the far-east poured into the city for their R & R. 'At the height of the war, some 4000 soldiers billeted in that five hundred-room Grand Hotel—not to mention their companions for the night. The owners took a cavalier view: the hotel was there to make money, not to safeguard the morals of the foreign armed forces. One can safely assume that other hotels, clubs and restaurants shared this booty of war.

Mahavir Enters the Elite Circle

Mahavir moved in quite naturally to become an integral part, indeed an effervescent addition, to the elite circle of Calcutta. He had the title of a general and the name of a Rana from Nepal, and wealth well above the ordinary. In addition to the prime properties, he invested in, he leased a smaller theatre, the Tiger, in Chowringhee, for night-time pleasures and relaxation. After midnight, it was used for the entertainment of his close friends and relatives.

There was no better place to be for the rich pleasure-seekers of the subcontinent than the winter festive season in Calcutta. The hours of entertainment started with the 'sundowners' and moved to dinner at Firpo's, the Princess in Grand, the Great Eastern or one of the exclusive clubs. 'The rustle of silk, the starch of the shirt, the lustre of pearls, the dazzle of diamonds, emeralds and rubies the size of pigeon's eggs…swayed to the tunes and beats of the Flamenco and Tango, Can-Can and Rumba, Latin rhythms, Dixie and St. Louis. Head Chefs from Mayfair of London to the Negresco of Nice, considered the best in the world, all came to Calcutta. After the dance and dinner the hardcore revellers moved to the bolder shows in the night clubs, Princess or Trincas. When those heady shows too were over, the night owls headed invariably to The 300 Club till the birds twittered to herald in a new day[237].

The Maharaja of Cooch Bihar (Bhaiya to his friends), Boris and Mahavir formed the trio that came to be known as the Three Musketeers of Calcutta.

One of Mahavir's passions was breeding and racing thoroughbreds, a favourite sport and pastime for the kings and princes. The Royal Calcutta Turf Club, established in 1847, had grown to be the sanctuary of the white sahibs and memsahibs. The rules of the club excluded from the stands and enclosures 'all the rag tag and bobtail of the racing world from coming and pestering trainers and touting jockeys' till the turn of the twentieth century[238]. Indian members, elite no doubt, grew slowly after World War I.

The exclusive members' enclosure offered glamorous fare. Rare and now priceless jewellery from the collection of the Czars of Russia, or Marie Antoinette, or the Nawabs of Lucknow, and from the most prestigious sales outlets and mines from the world over could be identified by the knowledgeable, amidst the latest fashion from Europe and the glittering saris and achkans.

Mahavir's stable produced winners but he was more famous as destiny's chosen punter. 'If you want to win put your money where Mahavir does' was a frequent tip the 'old hands' gave. He was joined by many reckless friends and relatives who came to Calcutta to enjoy life to the hilt, some were consumed by it. Take the case of one such romantic eccentric, the Raja of Ramnagar, and a close relative of the Ranas. This handsome prince came to Calcutta 'with a fortune of between twenty and thirty million rupees that was entirely spent in a little over three years in lavish nightly parties, fine wine and women, high-stake gambling and betting at the races'[239]. Many others like him found life thereafter mundane.

Mahavir was one of the rare few who not only revelled in this transitory life of pleasure but made full use of it. Despite letters taking forever to deliver and telephone connections dubious at best, he constantly remained in touch with several politically associated relatives in Nepal who secretly shared his misgivings about Rana misrule. He was determined to make use of his new friendships in high society and with emerging leaders in India to fuel his unrelenting quest for power and revenge.

Subarna Shumsher

As mentioned earlier, Mahavir was joined in his quest by his cousin Subarna Shumsher. The latter was still studying in Calcutta for his MA degree, when he received the shocking news of the wholesale purge of 1933. His father was appointed governor of Birgunj, the border town linking India with Kathmandu, the richest in the country. They were host to all foreign delegations, travelling between India and Kathmandu or those attracted by big game hunting in the forests of Chitwan. For twelve years Birgunj was to be their home, but in the meantime Subarna opted to invest heavily in properties in Calcutta, in conjunction with Mahavir, and together they reaped rich dividends.

Subarna resided in his Camax Street property, an imposing and historic mansion[240], in the same style and with similar comforts as in Kathmandu. However, he did not indulge in the heady pleasures of Calcutta that consumed Mahavir and so many of their ilk. He was happily married to a gracious and intelligent woman, a constant and willing companion in his work and leisure. Their residence was open to a continuous flow of relatives, guests and party men, through out his life. Meals were prepared daily, for thirty or forty guests or visitors. This number rose rapidly with his growing involvement in politics. He spent most of his spare time reading and catching up with the latest trends in politics, finance and international affairs. His grandson recalls, 'publishers used to bring to him bundles of books every week. He encouraged others to read and helped to educate many who could not afford to pay the fees.'[241] Rishikesh Shah pays a handsome tribute[242], 'Though born into a rich family wielding great power and wide authority, he was soft spoken, polite, full of humility and kindness, contrary to the traits and habits of the Rana family. Even in the midst of hectic political life he never said anything that would hurt the feelings of another. His foremost interest was to read and reflect in quiet isolation'.

Those who knew him well, share this view, although some found him to be 'reserved and taciturn' and Purusottam Shumsher thought[243] he was 'extremely selfish, secretive and of a jealous nature. However, no one can deny Subarna credit for his unremitting commitment and support for the democratic cause in Nepal.

Forming Links with Indian Leaders and the King of Nepal

Subarna applied himself diligently to cultivate contacts and friendships at various levels of the government, and political leaders of India, ably assisted by his close associates, Surya Prasad Upadhyaya and Rishikesh Shah. Each of them belonged to a respected and wealthy family back ground, alumni of premier learning institutions of India and well versed in politics of both countries. Upadhyaya was in close touch with Rafi Mohammad Kidwai and through him the Nehru family. 'Surya Prasad was the only Nepali who could walk into the Nehru household without appointment; he used to address Indira Gandhi as Indu which only her family members did'[244]. Rishikesh Shah writes, 'Shovendranath Tagore, leader of the Revolutionay Communist Party was our inspiration and a guide (for us)'—paradox as it may seem for the wealthiest Ranas of Nepal to be inspired by a revolutionary communist leader. Dr B.C. Roy was the personal physician and friend of Mahavir and Subarna even after he became chief minister of Bengal. One can conclude that while the Koirala–Ganeshman led Congress in Banaras befriended the social democrats and caught the imagination of the grass root activists, the 'Calcutta group' cultivated the upper crust of Indian politics.

Mahavir and Subarna were, however, one in their assessment that the most critical linkage for the success of their ultimate goal to dislodge the Rana regime was king Tribhuwan, and *he* remained in virtual captivity inside the Narayan Hiti palace in Kathmandu. As a hereditary monarch, viewed by a large section of the population as one with divine attributes, the king occupied a pivotal position in the fluctuating course of political evolution. When the C-class Ranas were thrown out of Kathmandu, the contact between the three had been effectively cut off. Mahavir, Subarna and many in their circle knew that Tribhuwan was eager to rid himself and the country from the yoke of the Rana oligarchy. The rift between the royals and the Rana rulers became even more pronounced after the Praja Parishad episode of October 1940. Some of those arrested and tortured admitted the involvement of the royal family in the earlier Raktapat Mandali plot to assassinate the prime minister and senior Ranas. Juddha had never expected that Tribhuwan would go to this extreme of assassination. But despite convincing proof of royal involvement, the prime minister did not dare to accuse the monarch. For days his fury was intense but he was restrained by a more pragmatic approach counselled by the sons of Chandra. In a surprising about turn, Juddha decided upon a psychological strategy to cultivate cordial relations with the palace. Two great granddaughters of the Prime Minister, Princep and Helen, were offered in marriage to younger sons of the king, princes Himalaya and Basundhara.

In another tangent of appeasement, Juddha invited the royals to join the social activities, including hunting expeditions in the Terai forests that the prime minister so enjoyed. The critical concession came though in 1941 when Himalaya and Basundhara were allowed to visit Calcutta. The opportunity Mahavir and Subarna were seeking so desperately was coming to their doorstep. This was to be the first-ever trip of members of the royal family outside the territories of Nepal for purposes other than pilgrimage.

Ironically, Juddha asked his grandson Nara Shumsher, father of Princep and Helen, to accompany the king. A little diversion from our main theme is needed here, for there are innumerable riddles and puzzles in the saga of Rana history but none as enigmatic as the life and deeds of General Nara. Gifted with an athletic frame he perfected his physique through an unrelenting regime of wrestling, body building, and football; he is rightfully recognized as 'the father of Nepalese sports' and has been honoured by an 'A'-merit award by the International Olympic Committee.

In the forties he played for the famous Mohamadan Sporting club of Calcutta. Acting like a trustee he lavished such favours and love on the team and the players that decades later when I happened to meet the goal keeper, migrated to Germany and eking out a hard living, discovered I was a nephew of Nara, he literally prostrated himself on the carpet in a spontaneous gesture, overwhelmed by his memories. Nara's high spending on his personal pleasures and interests was as uninhibited and uncontrolled as his generosity to others, at times leaving him empty handed; and on such occasions he is known to have been unscrupulous in some of his financial acquisitions. He never regretted either side of his personality!

As a favoured grandson of the ruling prime minister, he occupied a special place in the power play at the Rana court. He could plead and coax his grandfather to bestow gift or honours on those he recommended, and unlimited funds for his expenses, official or personal. As the Chief of Home Affairs he was always at the forefront of action against political activists. His commanding voice intimidated and his powerful punches often laid low his opponents in the field of sports or during political agitations. He could get away with murder, and not merely in a paradoxical sense. He personally supervised the hanging of two of the martyrs and point blank shooting of the other two in 1940. Yet barely one year after the execution *he* was the one assigned the job of accompanying the two princes to Calcutta, with the duty of monitoring and reporting their activities! A dreaded and hated figure during suppression of the peoples' andolan in Kathmandu in the forties, he led a signature campaign against the Rana regime during its last days, hustling and goading his cousins, nephews and the bhardars inside the court of Mohan in Singha Durbar. When King Tribhuwan made his triumphant return from Delhi to announce advent of democracy, in February 1951, Nara was by his side. He could have been the centre of rebuke and hatred from both or at least one side, but in fact he was liked by a majority of the Rana families of all categories and by the people in general including many who once suffered under his verbal and physical whip.

The younger prince, Basundhara, happened to be another vibrant personality who brightened the social scene wherever he went. A charming playboy, like his father, and father-in-law Nara, Basundhara was blessed with the added gifts of a sense of humour and humility, a rare quality indeed amongst the princely order. There is no reason to doubt the stories of their wild escapades and amorous encounters, fully supported and financed by the now affluent Mahavir, and aided, abetted, and joined in by the Indian Maharajas, Boris and the rest of the revellers. The more important outcome of their visit to Calcutta was the reopening of channels of contact between the palace, and Mahavir and Subarna. It was not a channel of easy access but crucially important in the days ahead.

Mahavir and Subarna Visit Kathmandu

The two princes returned to Kathmandu and no doubt briefed their father about what they had learnt in Calcutta, at least on the political front. Nara's report to his grandfather may well have been selective even on political matters but certainly avoided their amorous escapades. Meanwhile, Juddha was getting weary of the heavy burdens he carried as Prime Minister for more than ten years now. He was planning a retired life and in 1945 made his grand exit. The new Prime Minister Padma Shumsher promptly announced his intentions for economic and political reforms. Generally recognized as the most 'liberal' of the Rana Prime Ministers, Padma was aware of the democratic credentials of Mahavir and Subarna and invited them to return and take up important assignments in the government, and to counter a host of cousins holding critical positions in governance but opposed to the liberal reforms, in deed looking for ways to banish the Maharaj. Padma desperately needed support for implementation of his plans and programmes, and appointed Subarna as his advisor. He relied heavily on this nephew, with an added experience of Calcutta, especially for setting a guideline for economic and industrial growth in the country. An Industrial Council was constituted as suggested by Subarna and he was appointed its Vice President. He visited key industrial centres of growth in India and produced a policy document to suit Nepal. However, implementation of the programme was hindered by the hardliners, the rising tide of political convulsions and the process of constitutional reforms that kept the prime minister preoccupied.

Subarna's contacts and good relations with the Government of India were invaluable in giving shape to the new constitution. On recommendation of Subarna, the NNC leadership readily accepted Sri Prakash Gupta a known advocate for progressive political reforms, as the coordinator of a three-member advisory team for Nepal. Intense lobbying and discussions followed, between the 'reactionary elements within the Rana family and the priestly establishment'[245] on one side, and the liberal elements such as Subarna on the other. Subarna sensed that unless Padma acted boldly and decisively, the hardliners led by Mohan and Baber will prevail. He advised Padma to act promptly, but the prime minister was 'not convinced, or too timid to take decisive action.'[246] Subarna suspected danger to his life. With regret, he took leave of Padma and made his way back to Calcutta in late 1947, a permanent break from his link with the Rana administration. Subarna was also chosen during his stint in Kathmandu, as one of the delegates of the Nepal government for the first Asian Conference held in Delhi. Prime Minister Nehru is quoted to have declared in front of the delegation, 'I would be happy if you were to be the finance minister of my government'.

In 1946 King Tribhuwan expressed his wish to visit Calcutta for a medical check up and Padma was happy to oblige. A ruling monarch of Nepal set foot outside its territory for the first time, along with Himalaya and Basundhara. The entourage was headed by General Bahadur, fourth in the line of succession in the Rana hierarchy. General Kiran Shumsher, son of Juddha and half brother of Bahadur from one of the several ranis of Juddha, and Daya Bhakta Mathema, principal secretary of the King were other high-ranking delegates in attendance. Calcutta was the final destination. 'It was not a state visit but we were looked after well.'[247]

We lived in a large mansion of one of the Maharajas of India. There was no strict restriction on His Majesty meeting the Nepalese in Calcutta, but whenever Mahavir, Subarna or other such 'suspect' visitors were with His Majesty the intimidating rotund figure of Bahadur was a constant vigilante. Although a voracious eater, he was strict in matters of Hindu dietary code and generally avoided late night duty. Kiran remained in attendance of the Royals. One of several 'C'-class sons of Juddha, he was soon influenced by Mahavir and Subarna. It was from those days that he became secretly linked with them and remained loyal to King Tribhuwan: he persuaded many of his brothers and cousins to adopt this line. This was the reason he was rewarded and designated as the First Commander in Chief of the Nepal army after democracy.

The royals were allowed greater scope for free movement as wished by Prime Minister Padma. They went shopping, to cinemas, races, clubs and restaurants. But Mahavir and Subarna were 'black-listed' following negative reports from Daman Shumsher, the Nepalese Counsel General in Calcutta. Indeed no one from Kathmandu would like to be seen with us openly in fear of incurring the displeasure of the Ranas back home. The guards and attendants in the entourage always nearby ostensibly to meet His Majesty's every requirement, were in effect to report back any suspicious move. Kiran may be lax in his observations but he could not very well ask others not to remain alert!'

Devious means had to be worked out to arrange any clandestine rendezvous. The 300 Club was the perfect venue. Boris was known for his generous hospitality and happy to help his friend Mahavir: all the amenities of the club were laid out for the gracious king whenever he wished. One evening Tribhuwan entered the men's washroom, a few minutes later to be joined by Mahavir and Subarna, the guard stranded outside. The king then presented a gold cigarette case to Subarna with the letter 'T' and '1.9 4.7' inscribed inside. Future messages to Subarna and Mahavir were to be deemed authentic if signed just 'T'. The cigarette case remains a valued possession of one of the grandsons of Subarna.

There is ample evidence to assume that the Calcutta visit of Tribhuwan established some channels of contact between the palace and Mahavir/Subarna, and that Boris played a major role in this action. However, no one had yet revealed any direct connection between the king and high-level leaders from the Indian government.

An interview with Inger points to such a link. Boris and his second wife Inger closed down the 300 Club and moved to Kathmandu in the early 1950s where they established the Royal Hotel, at Bahadur Bhawan *(now the office of the election commission)* across the street from the royal palace, fitted for a relatively comfortable accommodation for western tourists. Boris is talked of as the 'father of tourism in Nepal'.

Boris passed away in 1985. Inger remained in her beloved Kathmandu. Decades later but still a sprightly eighty-two, I called upon her, with a slim hope that she may have known about King Tribhuwan's secret movements in The 300 Club. 'No, Sagar,' she responded, 'I was not married to him then'. We continued to reminisce of the good times in Kathmandu for another hour before I took one more chance: 'Did Boris help Tribhuwan meet or pass messages to the Indian leaders? Surely he must have talked to you later, in Kathmandu, some times!' She pondered now, travelling back down memory lane and then excitedly gushed out,

> Oh, yes! Once…much, much later during the panchayat time he did talk of an evening at the 300. Tribhuwan and his son came to the club with the bulldog-like Bahadur in tow. After one drink at the bar Boris invited them to his apartment on the third floor, but not Bahadur! The three went up, leaving Bahadur befuddled. As soon as they went up, they came down, from the kitchen side stairs onto a side street. An ordinary car was waiting and they were taken to the Government House. They delivered a letter from Tribhuwan addressed to Nehru, talked with some high-level Indian official and returned to the

apartment, up from the side stairs. They then went down and Bahadur was *fuming*, but had no inkling of what had transpired! These were Boris's words and believe it or not, he related this story in Kathmandu in front of Bahadur! Bahadur did not find it amusing; he just turned from black to blue...'

Laughter returned to her once more as in older times.

While Mahavir and Subarna were actively cultivating key contacts for the assault against the Rana regime, the Koirala camp moved separately for the same purpose, their activities aimed at galvanizing the grassroot activists for the party. After the end of World War II and the victory of the Labour Party in Britain, B.P. sensed that the time was ripe to launch a concerted move for a united assault on the Rana citadel. On 4 October 1946, he made a call for the unity of all anti-Rana forces to come together for this common goal. The Calcutta group no doubt considered their options. Mahavir and Subarna always believed that a militant and direct approach was needed, the *Satyagraha* type of approach advocated by Gandhi and adopted by the Koiralas was considered unsuitable to combat the conditions in Nepal. Moreover, they were confident of the strength of the critical connections and alliances built by them over the years. They decided to consolidate their own area of strength, and command a militant cadre-based political organization that could in due course launch an armed insurrection into Nepalese territory. 'The king is with us. Why should we mix with the riff-raff?' Mahavir once remarked[248]. Meanwhile, in January 1947, the group led by B.P. Koirala formally launched a party naming it the Nepali National Congress (NNC).

Genesis of the All India Gorkha League and the Jana Mukti Sena

Mahavir and Subarna provided some financial support to leaders of the new party but continued to operate as a separate unit. Subarna contacted different groups of Nepalese communities in India, the Pravasi Nepali, with a view to induct them into a militant wing. The

Pravasi migrants also referred to as the Gorkhalis or Lahures have a long history. As early as the first decade of the century they were beginning to mobilize themselves as an active community group especially in the northwest. A publication, *Gurkha Saathi*, had come out some years before the Koiralas turned against the Ranas. Its issue dated 15 October 1907 contains an article addressed to Prime Minister Chandra 'so wise a Maharaj' and pleads 'with your orders prohibiting this publication's circulation in Nepal...and the loss your people suffer in not being able to read a newspaper' whereby 'our lives and property are set in danger[249].

An institutional framework was set up when Gorkha League was formally established in 1921 at Dehradun, a popular base for many Nepalese. Thakur Chandan Singh its leader was a law graduate, working as a registrar in the court of the state of Bikaner, a coveted post in those times. However, the growth and progress of the Gorkha League was disrupted by the onset of World War I when he and many of his colleagues joined the Indian army. After the war he joined and rose rapidly in the ranks of the Indian National Congress INC in the Garhwal area bordering Nepal, and simultaneously took up the challenge of rebuilding the organization of the Gorkha League with fresh input from the retired army men. Influenced by the freedom struggle in India, their focus gradually turned to the oppressive conditions and injustices their own people friends and relatives back home were enduring under the autocratic Rana rule. A quarterly publication Northern Star was launched; it projected the socio-economic issues of the Nepalese community in the region but news and views critical to the Rana regime, and call for reforms also featured in its columns. Its readership extended to all areas where the Nepalese were living but entry was forbidden inside Nepal. North Bengal and Assam were the other prominent areas of Nepalese settlement. Dala Bahadur Giri emerged to head the organization in Darjeeling. In 1936 another publication, *Gorkha Sansar*, this time in the Nepali vernacular was launched from Darjeeling. The Rana rulers pressed upon the British government in India to ban these publications and influenced their cousins living in India to try and distract its key functionaries by offer of well-paid jobs. However, it was the onset of World War II and recruitment of most of its leaders and workers into the regular army and the Azad Hind Army of Subhas Chandra Bose that the League became dysfunctional, and its assets were handed over to a purely social, non-political body.

Although the League ceased its political activities, the consciousness it generated remained alive in many parts of the subcontinent, and in Burma, Hong Kong, Singapore and wherever the Gorkha Army men were stationed. After peace returned the population of Nepalese in India rose rapidly, in line with the robust growth of tea gardens, orchards, commerce and industry in India. The more educated and conscious civil society in Calcutta, north Bengal and Assam resumed active participation in mobilisation of the socio-political consciousness in the community. A large number of Pravasis from different parts of India assembled at Siliguri in 1943 for a meeting. It led to formation of All India Gorkha League in May 1945. A working Committee was formed and Dambar Singh Gurung was elected President and Ranadhir Subba[250], its Vice President. The League diversified its activities in other parts of India as well but its main focus remained in north Bengal and Assam[251].

The League's activities covered social as well as political issues. The call for creating a 'Gorkha Land' within the state of north Bengal emerged around these years. The Government of India, GoN and the INC were against such a 'secessionist' move. The Rana rulers were quick to notice this rift and managed to influence many leaders of Gorkha League to support them against the common 'enemy' the GoN and INC leadership. One section, especially in the lower ranks, however, remained active in raising their voice against the acts of oppression and injustice in Nepal. A new dynamic force emerged to energize these activities. They joined the Azad Hind Army on an understanding that after defeating the allied forces in Burma, Assam and north eastern states of India they would proceed to Nepal and raise arms against the Rana regime. They marched in unison with the Azad Hind army under Japanese command.

By the spring of 1944, many parts of Burma came under Japanese control and they penetrated into the Indian territories. The fate of the war was, however, settled in other theatres of war, in Europe, Hiroshima and Nagasaki. Netaji himself is presumed killed in an air accident. The Azad Hind soldiers and officers were taken prisoners, including a contingent of the Nepalese. The INC leaders recognized that the Azad Hind was committed to the cause of freedom of India. Indeed Subhas Chandra Bose, fondly remembered as 'Netaji', was revered in Bengal as much as Gandhi or Nehru in the rest of India. The Indian leaders made a strong plea for their release, Nehru personally pleading their case in the law courts. They were freed after a few months. While the Indians dispersed in the vast expanses of the subcontinent, the Nepalese officers and soldiers settled down mostly in Assam, north Bengal, and Garhwal and remained in close contact with each other and the Gorkha League.

The Government of India established a separate security force under Rtd General Mohan Singh to absorb the fighting force of the Azad Hind. Hundreds of Gorkha soldiers and officers were also recruited and one of its prominent leaders was Major Purna Singh Khawas. In the meantime under the urgings of Subarna Shumsher a break away wing of the Gorkha League made a formal declaration to cooperate with the party to be formed, at an early date, with the common goal of an armed struggle against the Rana regime. In April 1947 Purna Singh received a message from Subarna Shumsher inviting him to Calcutta and asked him and his men to join the revolutionary forces. General Mohan Singh readily consented and indeed exhorted his men to 'grasp the opportunity to serve the motherland, which comes but once in the life time'.

Subarna had arranged for an office and residential quarters for them in Chowranghee in the heart of Calcutta, and the work of fresh recruitment commenced in earnest. A majority of those who joined the group belonged to the ethnic hill communities of Nepal[252]. A meeting called at a secret venue in Calcutta and attended by a large number of eager men, leaders of different communities and retired army men decided to form a secret militant revolutionary force. A formal meeting held in June 1948 formally declared formation of

Jana Mukti Sena, 'peoples liberation army' and constituted a working committee with Major Purna Singh as its Chairman. Their training in the science of war and experience in the fields of battle were to prove vital in providing a degree of professional input into the Jana Mukti Sena[253].

Subarna Shumsher had attended the meeting as the Chief Guest. He financed all activities of the Mukti Sena and promised supply of arms and ammunitions when the time of action was at hand.

Subarna, meanwhile, contacted his young nephew Thir Bam Malla one of the sons of the Raja of Galkot in western Nepal to join him in Calcutta. A captain in the Indian army outfit, he resigned from service and dedicated himself to the cause he shared with his uncle. By all accounts he was a popular, able and gifted leader of men. He worked as a link between Jana Mukti Sena and Subarna with an additional responsibility for procurement of arms. Under the guidance of Subarna, the Jana Mukti Sena worked as a separate unit, with 'military precision'. Political and military training was imparted at secret camps. Six target venues in Nepal were identified for preliminary reconnaissance activities, Biratnagar and Dhankuta in the east, Bhairawa and Palpa the west, and Birgunj and Kathmandu in the central region. Small groups of activists and volunteers were assigned to travel in disguise to their respective destinations. Besides the military reconnaissance work their job was to contact supporters and look out for well wishers or sympathizers of the cause. They crossed the plains and the hills, rivers and forests, posing as porters, traders or travellers in transit. These were the first such clandestine planned forays into 'enemy territory.'

The Birth of the Nepal Democratic Congress, August 1948

Meanwhile NNC was facing a serious rift. B.P. and Dilli Raman Regmi headed two rival factions, each claiming to be the authentic face of the party. It was under these circumstances that Mahavir and Subarna decided to establish a separate party, Nepal Democratic Congress. The NDC was formed in August 1948, with Mahendra Bikram Shah as its president and Surya Prasad Upadhyaya the general secretary; Mahavir and to an increasing degree Subarna continued to remain the driving force in the decision making process of the new outfit.

The party established its clandestine branches in several border towns and in Kathmandu, all the time avoiding the intelligence network of the state. In India they could function openly as long as they avoided acts of violence. Calcutta remained the centre of operation but the head-office was shifted to Patna where Surya Prasad Upadhyaya resided. One branch was opened in Guwahati, Assam, home of large number of ex-army personnel and tea garden workers from Nepal. In January 1949 the first party convention was held in Guwahati. Party members and sympathizers from different parts of Nepal, distant towns and provinces in India, and from Burma converged to this otherwise quiet township. A special feature of the Convention was the active participation of a large number of women, the ethnic hill community now residing in northeast India and from the eastern hill districts of Nepal. It is claimed that this was the largest gathering of Nepalese people at a political meet, to date. The Jana Mukti Sena worked in close collaboration with the party organization and its policy guide lines.

On another front Sunder Raj Chalise, one of the most trusted assistants of Subarna[254], was assigned the delicate task of infiltration into the interiors of the country and to fan anti-government sentiments. He led the main group accompanied by Major Purna Singh inside Nepalese territory. They crossed the border at Gorakhpur and gradually moved to Palpa and after a tortuous trek of many days, fraught with the risk of detection and arrest, reached Kathmandu. All along the route they met with old colleagues and friends and recruited new entrants into the newly formed party. In the valley they met up with another group deputed by the party to enter through the central route of Birgunj. A third group was sent to Biratnagar and covered the eastern hills under the guidance of a local unit leader. In the capital, the activists were kept in hiding through the efforts of Badri Bikram Thapa, a teacher to a number of army officers and soldiers. Chalise was the lynch pin and coordinator of the operation.

Slightly built and agile he was well known in Kathmandu but moved secretly often in disguise, reaching like a beaver into the recesses of the administrative network. Crucially, he was able to pass messages and get back response from the palace, a task that required a delicate and sensitive handling. Daya Bhakta Mathema was the link from the side of the palace but there may well have been others, who may never come to light. On completion of the mission most of the freedom fighters returned to India but a few stayed back. They were scattered in key transit points leading from the Indian border to Kathmandu or principal townships in the west and east Nepal. Many of them were women, who worked undercover, as fruit or vegetable vendors. Others feigned to be salesmen, ran paan shops or tea stalls. Some stayed in their friends homes and helped with clandestine manoeuvres. These contacts were to prove an invaluable asset when the insurgency commenced in 1950.

In Kathmandu, the new Prime Minister Padma's visible leanings towards the liberal elements emboldened and encouraged a number of prominent personalities. Mahavir and Subarna moved with plan and purpose to cultivate the support of these elements. Kiran was already on their side and he was able to gradually influence some key members amongst his own 'C'-class brothers and half brothers numbering eighteen strong! Toran Shumsher was another senior officer in the army who was to side with the revolutionary elements. About half a dozen 'A'-Class Ranas formally pledged to 'oppose and fight the feudal autocratic regime with a view to bring about a fully responsible democratic government under the constitutional leadership of the king of Nepal', and joined the Nepal Democratic Party[255]. The most sought after target of Subarna was Field Marshall Rudra Shumsher, governor of Palpa. Some of his sons readily joined the party. In 1949 the party discussed the possibility of persuading King Tribhuwan to secretly move to Palpa. Field Marshall Rudra was prepared to host the king. But he wanted concrete evidence of the king's support before he could commit his backing. Tribhuwan was not willing to risk such an adventure.

One wing of the Jana Mukti Sena led by Nirmal Lama was keen

to launch an armed action into mid-west Nepal. The party leadership tried to convince them that adequate preparation was lacking and time not yet ripe. However, about a dozen daring men defied the central order and decided to take their lonely course, collected what little weapons they could muster and reached their chosen destination Syangja through secret routes. Helped by local friends they attempted to recruit new activists and collected spears, khukuris and flint guns. Calcutta felt that sooner or later, the Rana government would discover their movements. Nirmal was summoned to Banaras. The rest were barely able to slip away before the state security force reached their hideout.

Letter of Support from King Tribhuwan

The Nepal Democratic Congress had made notable progress, in several fronts. The King remained sympathetic to their cause. Mahavir and Subarna felt 'they knew how to manipulate the system internally.'[256] Yet the realization must have dawned, that the sum total did not amount to sufficient strength to launch a frontal attack on the Rana citadel. The Rana rulers had managed to retain the unwavering loyalty of the Nepalese army and of the civil service. Acutely conscious of the Chinese moves north of the Himalayas and its occupation of Tibet, the Government of India was negotiating for a treaty of peace and friendship with Mohan Shumsher, who had succeeded Padma (1945–48) and so was not willing to offer more than moral support to the democratic movement. Similarly, the royal family was not willing to go beyond their private sympathies, and risk exposure.

A major shift in the equation was required to move the revolution forward. Subarna in particular was wise and shrewd enough to understand that the party was short of a network of dedicated and agile political activists and local leaders inside Nepal, an essential prerequisite for the final thrust; he knew that this was an area of strength of the NNC under the dynamic leadership of B.P. Koirala and the fearless and unflinching Ganesh Man Singh holding a special place in the hearts of the residents of Kathmandu. Indian leaders were therefore pressing both sides to start a serious dialogue for unity. Subarna had already sent and received some feelers aimed at unification of the two parties. But his instinct told him that big brother India would be the key player in the final act. He therefore asked Surya Prasad Upadhyaya to use his links with Kidwai and find out from Prime Minister Nehru what his bottom line was.

'Rafi Saheb came back after a few days with the message: you will get the support of Nehru if you convince him fully, and not merely by words, that the king is behind you.'[257]

The long-standing friendship with Tribhuwan and the channels of contact they created through Mathema seemed worthwhile. Even then, the task of getting a message conveyed to the royals in Kathmandu was by no means simple. Fortunately Sunder Raj Chalise was one such emissary who could be trusted completely, and was possessed of the necessary courage and tact for the dangerous and delicate mission, to reach Kathmandu undetected and relay the message to the King through Daya Bhakta Mathema and/or one of the princes. And so he was again sent to Kathmandu. After some anxious weeks, Mathema personally came to Calcutta and delivered Subarna a letter addressed to Prime Minister Nehru and a copy for future use of the party. It was typed on the official letterhead of His Majesty with the Royal seal and dated 30th March 1950. The letter starts with 'My dear friend' in Tribhuwan's hand. It recounts the in-type excesses of the authoritarian Rana regime and its cruel treatment of the citizens 'including the person who is carrying this letter' and seeks Nehru's help in the efforts made by the people of Nepal to overthrow the Rana regime. The king reiterates his wholehearted support for the cause of democracy and places his full signature. I was permitted to go through the original copy of the letter on promise that the source will remain undisclosed.

The letter arrived at an opportune time. During the last months of 1949 and the beginning of 1950, B.P. Koirala and Subarna had met each other several times with the purpose of working out the modalities for a merger[258]. Each realized the compulsions to combine their strength in order to launch an effective challenge upon the Rana citadel. Two weeks after the King signed the typed letter the merger between the two parties was formally concluded in Calcutta and the Nepali Congress commenced its long political voyage.

Chapter Five

Maharaj Padma Shumsher (1945–1948)

After the grand exit of Maharaj Juddha, Padma Shumsher succeeded him as prime minister in a volatile Nepal. The new maharaj was cast in a totally different mould. He was overshadowed by Juddha's powerful personality. Furthermore, he had to contend with the combined force of Chandra's three astute sons Mohan, Baber, Keshar and the bullying Bahadur following him in the Roll of Succession.

Before he became prime minister, Padma had remained a relatively ineffective figure despite his high rank of mukhtiyar or C-in-C. He had few friends amongst the Ranas. His father, Prime Minister Bhim (1929–32) had promoted and groomed his C-class half-brothers and neglected Padma. The purge that removed the C-class Ranas from the Roll in 1934 included Padma's half-brother Hiranya, one of the most powerful amongst those thrown out. Hiranya's last words before his departure were prophetic: 'I have not much to say now to anybody else, but do tell that so called Commander-in-Chief Padma that henceforth he will be like a vulture with clipped wings.'

Padma's isolation was aggravated by the strained relationship with his only A-class son, Basanta.

Mohan, now the top man in the line of succession, inherited the incongruous title of C-in-C and with it, the direct command of the civil administration. Baber, next in line, became the Jungi Laath, controller of the military and security wing. Keshar continued to place greater stress on his scholarly pursuits and built the Keshar Library, which was the largest private library in Asia, till he died in 1964. As per his wish, he was sent to St James's Court as the Ambassador from Nepal.

The collective strength of the three brothers needed no demonstration. Padma knew he could not undermine them. Bahadur, eldest son of Juddha, went to Bishalnagar Palace to offer his customary allegiance to the new prime minister, but with the strong presence of his brothers. While sending his *Haziri* he told the messenger to 'remind your master that there were seventeen Shumsher brothers who ousted Prime Minister Ranodip in 1885. And now we are eighteen brothers'[259].

Yet, the most daunting challenge for Padma lay beyond the family circle; the forces of change and the spirit of revolt were simmering perilously close to boiling point.

Padma was, however, clear in his mind that the country should move in a new direction, that of a more liberal political order and socio-economic progress. After Juddha announced his abdication and left Kathmandu, the newly crowned maharaj announced in a public address: 'The ruler is the servant of the people. I consider myself to be your servant.'[260]

It was a dramatic and timely departure from the posture of his predecessors. However, he was shedding tears as he spoke, a weakness that never deserted Padma and one that earned him few admirers and even fewer supporters.

It will be unfair to judge Padma's term in office merely on the basis of his emotional personality, unbecoming of a prime minister. To his credit, his liberal views were genuine, although some critics point out that he took the liberal course and initiated reforms in fear of the looming danger of imminent revolution or to counter the ambitious intent of his hardliner cousins. Yet, the swift move towards reforms, is proof enough of his sincerity of purpose. Twelve days after assumption of office he convened a public meeting at Tundikhel and delivered his state address in which he outlined his vision and commitment: liberalization of education, effective measures for speedy growth of the developmental process, liberal political reforms increment in the pay scales of civil and military service. These promises were not mere sops. Concrete steps were taken to implement them.

His promise to increase pay scales of the lesser ranks in the civil service and provide rations to the security personnel at a subsidized rate was speedily met. However, the intent to mobilize economic growth could not move much beyond the planning stage[261]. Kept constantly engaged by political agitations and hampered by harassment by his cousins holding top positions in governance, he called back his more trustworthy and like-minded cousins and nephews from India, including Hiranya, Mahavir and Subarna.

Promotion of Education

The prime minister did deliver concrete results on his commitment to promote institutions of education and literary activities. Padma was the second Rana Prime Minister (after Dev) who believed that an educated populace was not necessarily a danger for longevity of the Rana regime but an essential prerequisite for growth and development of the nation and perhaps longevity of the regime. He had to choose the right person to take on this task, someone in agreement with his views in the first place, and with necessary knowhow for the job in hand. Mrigendra was brought back to head the Department of Education. He was sent to India to observe the policies and methods adopted there. The education system in India was based and structured on the English model. Mrigendra soon discovered fundamental differences in its application in India. The British never intended to energize the mind of the 'natives' in the same way as the students in Britain. Instead, a majority of schools and colleges and their curriculum were designed to produce 'babus' or clerical manpower, to help the British run their administrative network. Furthermore, education was out of reach for a great majority of the children in rural India either on account of the distance between school and home or due to acute poverty. Contrary to popular belief, 'when the British departed in 1947 they left behind a rural population that was ninety-nine per cent illiterate,' writes Adrian Sever.[262] On the lookout for a more appropriate educational model for Nepal, Mrigendra came upon the Gandhian model of 'basic education' which was introduced in the 1920s along with the call for boycott of all things British, including their educational institutions[263]. Inspired by ancient Vedic culture, these institutions were located in sylvan surroundings, called for an austere lifestyle, practise of Yoga and value of labour. Classes were held outdoors, often under a tree. The medium of education was the local language in the lower classes, but English was also taught along with other general subjects. In addition, the charkha or spinning wheel, carding and weaving of indigenous khadi cloth formed a daily routine. Crucially, the fees were much lower and therefore affordable for the millions of youth living in the villages.

Mrigendra's recommendation to follow the Gandhian model was readily accepted by Padma. The new system was introduced slowly into some of the existing schools. Tulsi Mehr, the exponent of Gandhian thought and Khadi use in Nepal[264] was happy to be involved in the new programme. However, resistance came from an unexpected direction—influential groups of teachers and the educated middle-class turned against it. They may have felt that the Gandhian tenets ignored modernism or the 'western' style of education more suited to advance the political changes that they aspired for. Groups of teachers and students in the Durbar High School and Tri Chandra College and from institutions in other parts of the country led the protests for retaining the western model. The Gandhian model had to be abandoned. Mrigendra was allowed to retain the model in four schools and they were still running along the Gandhian style until the 1950s.

The drive for expansion of the existing education network continued in earnest. The three short years of Padma's reign saw the emergence of more new schools, public reading rooms and libraries than the sum total of all the decades of the past. The policy to allow schools to be established and managed, independent of state interference opened the floodgates. The young and educated class in Kathmandu eagerly applied themselves to take full advantage. A school for the Dalits and another for the elderly were also opened through active efforts of Nutan Thapalia[265], a valiant attempt to break free from the stranglehold of archaic discrimination. However, the government still wanted to have some involvement in the schools. The Department of Education deputed one headmaster for each new or old school with a view to assist and support the schools and to maintain some conformity in the pattern of education imparted. The teaching fraternity did not see it that way[266]. The newly emerging schools were funded by the locals and many of the teachers worked without pay. They felt that the independence such a management ensured and the enthusiasm it generated would be violated by the intervention of an authoritarian regime. Following a widespread opposition led by Bhuwan Lal Pradhan, the prime minister ruled that the schools that did not wish to accept the headmaster appointed by the state would not be compelled to do so, but the state was willing to provide the service to those that wished. Many well-known schools that operate today including the first one for women the Padma Kanya and the Patan High School whether established through state sponsorship or public initiative, trace their origin to the conducive atmosphere of those years and occupy prime locations in the capital today.

Rapid Revolution Overtakes the Reform Process

The prime minister took concrete steps to fulfil his promise of constitutional reforms. Not a facile exercise at any time. In the 1940s it was an enormous challenge[267]. Padma moved quickly, requesting the Government of India and the INC leaders to send constitutional jurists and advisors. No doubt he had hoped that such a prompt action would convince the Nepalese people about his sincerity of purpose and thus prevent politics of confrontation. Yet the revolutionary fervour was moving faster. Indeed, the ship of Rana oligarchy was now being rocked and jostled like never before since Jung took the helm nearly one hundred years ago. The rising tide of revolution eventually overtook Padma's attempts at reforms and at the same time swept aside its architect.

As Padma embarked upon his plans for political reforms, Ganesh

Man was in Calcutta. He was familiar with the city from his college days and he found some shelter with the Newari traders who had their bases in the city. But he had to remain alert: if the Ranas were to get even a whiff of his whereabouts they could ask the British to seek him out, and repatriate him to Nepal. He roamed the streets of Calcutta, restless and aimless, for many frustrating weeks. He had to put aside for the time being his ambition and purpose to 'lead the revolution from India'[268].

He then noticed posters in the city inviting men to join the Indian Air Force and promptly decided to try a period of military training, while avoiding detection. He took the long rail trip to Lahore, passed all the tests for recruitment but his height let him down. Ready to return disappointed, he learnt that the musical group in the Airman's Club was looking for a Tabla player, and Ganesh Man was talented and enthusiastic exponent; the jovial young man became a popular member of the music group. He remained a cadet of the air force for close to a year. But his tempestuous nature rubbed against military discipline; as he was being berated by his trainer, Ganesh Man forgot his rank and knocked out the corporal![269] He now went back to civilian life and explored new avenues to expound his views. The Nepalese in east India he sought out showed honest hospitality but little enthusiasm for political lecturing or dialogue. By this time Padma had adopted a more liberal policy, and the British authority in India was on a decline: chances of arrest in India were remote. He could move freely and made frequent trips to Banaras, Calcutta, Darjeeling, Kalimpong, Sikkim and similar hubs of Nepalese settlement. His name and exploits were now the stuff of a legend with the Nepalese. Ganesh Man was encouraged by the younger generation and student communities. They did not carry the burden of fear and suspicion that made the older generation hesitant to come close to the rebel from Kathmandu, whereas the student groups readily invited the celebrated leader to speak to them. He was a natural and entertaining speaker at such informal gatherings: he had now found his moorings.

'The disappointment and sadness that grew inside me from those whom I knew earlier, was erased by the unknown students I now met, they filled me not only with new energy and commitment but provided a new dimension of self-belief and confidence. The door of new opportunities was open to me now—for carrying out a revolution'[270].

B.P. Koirala and the Socialists

The activists in Banaras, too, could move freely now. B.P., the brothers Gopal and Krishna Prasad Bhattarai, Man Mohan Adhikary, Dilli Raman Regmi and Ishwar Baral, were 'products' of Banaras who returned to their city after spending time as prisoners in different cities of India. While in jail, they had cultivated personal friendship and political association with socialist leaders like Jai Prakash Narayan, Ram Manohar Lohia and Devendra Prasad. B.P. shared space with Dr Rajendra Prasad, Jagjivan Ram, Satya Narayan Sinha amongst other top leaders of India inside Bankepur prison. Political prisoners were treated well in the Indian jails that provided ideal conditions for reading and deliberations between like-minded colleagues. The contact and friendship forged was to pay rich dividends in the future. Some of the more memorable writings of national or regional leaders have emerged from the prison cells of India and of Nepal, considered to be a 'political learning school' those days.

When B.P. was released in 1945, 'the communists were trying to get me to join them, and they visited me daily, morning and evening. Man Mohan Adhikary was the most persistent visitor—but by then I had become a proper anti-communist. I criticized them strongly—they got exasperated and started opposing me'[271]. He had to go to Bombay once more to tame the insidious lifelong enemy within his body, his cancerous throat. He spent a few anxious months there and had to undergo an operation. On release he returned to Banaras. 'He had been told by the doctors that he may not live long and so he immersed himself in hectic activities.'[272]

B.P. remembers how 'everyone knew Juddha Shumsher was a harsh bull-headed ruler incapable of understanding the changed situation. Padma Shumsher, on the other hand, was a more flexible man—I even wrote to him suggesting that he begin the process towards democracy by allowing people to engage in politics'[273]. He was also convinced that independence of India was near, the time was ripe to make a concrete move. His contact man in Banaras was Ishwar Baral. Under B.P.'s direction Baral encouraged the student community and the Nepali residents to establish an organization with twin objectives, to mobilize activities targeted to end British imperialism in India and the Rana regime in Nepal. The All India Nepali National Congress was established in January. Its president was the ailing and elderly but steadfast Devi Prasad Sapkota. The vice president, Bal Chandra Sharma, and secretary, Krishna Prasad Bhattarai, ably supported him. Gopal Prasad was at that time the more active of the brothers and made significant contribution, in mobilizing media contacts. A similar committee was also formed in Calcutta. They were the stepping stones that led to the eventual formation of the Nepali National Congress and then the Nepali Congress.

Around the same time the rift within the All India Gorkha League reached a breaking point. The central command continued to align with the Rana rulers, in return for their support for the demand of Gorkha Land within the Union of India. In reaction a strong wing of the League led by the president of the Calcutta branch submitted an official letter to the head office in Kalimpong urging support for the ongoing struggle of the people against the authoritarian Rana regime. D.B. Pariyar and D.K. Shahi were the prominent members of this group. The Calcutta branch had assisted large numbers of Nepalese and Indian families to escape the carnage of the Hindu–Muslim riots and commanded a substantial following. But they failed to get a satisfactory answer from the head office. A meeting of members called in November 1946 reached a unanimous decision to form a new party, the All India Gorkha Congress, with the objective of providing social service to the community but also with the unstated commitment to join and support the movement to dislodge the Rana regime in Nepal[274].

Call of B.P. Koirala for United Action, October 1946

In 1946 when Padma was trying to grapple with the intricacies of the constitution-making process, another new British prime minister, Clement Atlee, was working out the manner and modalities of handing over the power of governance in India to its people. Taking stock of the national and international situation, B.P. issued a statement in October 1946 published in *Amrit Bazaar Patrika*, The *Searchlight* and some other publications. It pointed out that with the conclusion of World War II the end of British colonial rule in India was imminent. This was the right time for all Nepalese to foregather, intensify the struggle and make the final push against the autocratic Rana regime. He made a public appeal through the media for all Nepali organizations and individuals to contact him and demonstrate solidarity and support for the common cause. The response was overwhelming. K.P. Bhattarai was one of 'the first to respond. Not only me, but Bharat Shumsher who was a student in Bombay at that time also wrote to say he was ready to join—despite the fact that his grandfather, Baber Shumsher, was the Commander-in-Chief in Nepal, and second man in the Rana hierarchy'[275].

B.P. followed up on this appeal and contacted important personalities and leaders in different parts of India. One of the most admirable qualities in the man was his natural grace and politeness that cut through all pride and prejudice based on rank or race. He was willing to visit any leader, king or pauper, friend or foe without the least concern for 'prestige'.

B.P. travelled intensively, to Dehradun, Darjeeling, Patna, Banaras and Calcutta and met with local leaders and those who slipped away from Nepal to meet him. The key figures of that time were Ganesh Man and Dilli Raman Regmi, and of course, Mahavir and Subarna. Regmi was a senior leader who had taken part in the Quit India movement and spent three years in prison. He was a learned man, an authority on history and politics. Ganesh Man had called upon him in Banaras and suggested forming of a party. But he cited ill health and was not prepared to risk arrest and repatriation to Nepal.

'I did not see the commitment, energy and spirit required for a great leader. I returned to Kalimpong, disappointed'.

The meeting of B.P. and Ganesh Man preceded a show of one-upmanship before it was finally achieved. Ganesh Man admits: 'I definitely felt I was a bigger leader and my going to meet B.P. would be an insult'. On strong persuasion of K.P. Bhattarai he eventually reached Calcutta. B.P. too was cautious in his approach. So they met at a common ground, a hall where many other Nepalese and Indians were assembled to hear B.P. speak. Ganesh Man reached the venue first accompanied by D.B. Shahi and settled himself comfortably on a couch. B.P.'s arrival was greeted by the whole assemblage rising to salute and applaud the leader. Ganesh Man did not budge from the seat unwilling to accept a lower status. B.P. stood up with a pleasing smile walked across the hall and offered a humble namaskar. 'I know all about you, I have wanted to meet you for a long time. Now that wish is fulfilled. I will speak with you separately', these were B.P.'s first words. 'Even his humility did not move me,' says Ganesh Man, many decades later.[276] B.P. addressed the gathering. The bottom line of his message was that it was high time to establish a new party. The British would leave soon but one could not wait for it. 'A few minutes back, I had never expected that this chit of a man with spiny legs would speak so clearly about the complicated affairs. Koirala jee, left me thoroughly impressed, I decided in my mind right there and then, whatever happens, I must support this man.'[277]

That same evening, the two of them and B.P.'s brother Tarini met at a cramped room in Khalsa Hotel. B.P. convinced his new partner that it was not yet possible to operate from Nepal. Even in India international support could be expected only for a peaceful struggle and finally that the diverse communities living in the isolated parts of Nepal should be involved and feel connected to the struggle, even if that took a longer time. It did not take them long to agree that a new party should be established at an early date. B.P. had already made arrangements for the venue, the Khalsa School premises in Calcutta and the dates of 25–26 January 1947. Ganesh Man agreed readily.

B.P. was equally impressed by Ganesh Man. 'Indeed, he was the best catch as far as I was concerned.[278] The three went to a simple but clean Punjabi restaurant for the meal. B.P. was never extravagant with money but he always dressed smartly and liked to dine well, Ganesh Man noticed.

Gifted with a sharp intellect, B.P. could impress, enchant and disarm people by a mix of his humility, charm, and sincerity. He was at home with the humblest of surroundings and at the highest forums of global leaders. His erect figure and chiselled features attracted many admirers of both sexes. Ganesh Man, on the other hand, was stocky but powerfully built. His willpower and indomitable courage were matched by unshakable moral moorings, native wit, infinite goodness, humility and sense of humour. History is witness to the fact that each possessed outstanding leadership qualities that are not readily found for generations.

B.P. sought to meet Mahavir and Subarna, natural allies in the move to dislodge the Rana regime. 'But Mahavir was a whimsical man. He lived ostentatiously in palatial surroundings and was proud of his wealth.'[279] A meeting was finally scheduled at Mahavir's mansion. 'After keeping me waiting for quite a while downstairs' writes B.P., a message came and he was finally taken up to Mahavir. The meeting was short, perhaps terse but his purpose was partially served. 'My brother Subarna and I have agreed that we will match whatever amount I give. So, you go ahead with your work'. However, the Ranas were not willing to accept the line of non-violent struggle, and were convinced that insurgency and armed insurrection inside the country was an essential prerequisite to bring down the Rana oligarchy, backed by the contacts and linkages including with King Tribhuwan, and the organization Mahavir and Subarna had built.

Making contact with the Nepalese living in India was one part of B.P.'s initiatives. Another was to seek support from the Indian leaders. He wrote to Jai Prakash Narayan, Vijayalakshmi Pandit, (sister of Nehru), Acharya Narendra Dev and Ram Manohar Lohia, amongst other leaders to seek their advice and support for the formation of a new party. His long association with the independence struggle and years in jail together brought some dividend now. They expressed their moral support to the new party and continued to extended direct or indirect assistance in its future activities[280].

The Nepali National Congress Comes Alive

With these preparations done the meeting to form a party was called and held in January 1947 at the Khalsa College premises. A large number had converged to Calcutta from far away too, both from Nepal and India. The attendance was smaller, about 100 people, but with firm resolve and true dedication to the democratic cause. Those from Nepal were hesitant to venture inside the venue, unwilling to be marked by the regime back home[281]. The delegates represented all castes, creeds and age groups, mainly from the lower-middle and middle-income group. All India Gorkha League had been invited and they agreed to merge into the new party. The meeting was inaugurated by D.R. Regmi who was vying for the position of the President. However, on recommendation of Ganesh Man, Tanka Prasad Acharya, languishing in the dark cells of Kathmandu jail was unanimously elected president and proposal of B.P. as acting president was greeted with hearty cheers. Even without any post Ganesh Man was accepted as the second man after B.P. Balchandra Sharma got the position of Secretary General and Krishna Prasad, Secretary of the Organization Department. D.N. Pradhan and D.B. Pariyar representing the minority and Dalit community and from the Gorkha League were elected unanimously to the Central Executive Committee.[282] B.P. persuaded Ganesh Man to withdraw the name Nepal Praja Parishad, and the new party was named Nepali National Congress (NNC). Several issues were raised and discussed openly in the meeting but resolved in a dignified and friendly manner. The only bitter note came from Regmi. Not satisfied with his position of Chairman of Department of Publication, he left Calcutta abruptly carrying deep resentment that was to remain a constant blemish in the party.

A resolution adopted outlined two primary objectives of the new party:

- To establish a constitutional monarchy under the leadership of King Tribhuwan, and a government responsible to the people, in Nepal.
- To assist the independence movement in India.

The formal inauguration of NNC was a major milestone in the historic struggle against the Rana regime. The news reached out to the youthful students in the colleges and universities, the socialists bred through the rigours of struggle against British rule in India, the ethnic hill communities settled and working in the northern hill states, the workers, traders and professionals living in urban centres, and the freedom fighters who had faced the wrath of the Rana rulers in their own den in Kathmandu or other parts of Nepal. The overall impact was widespread and penetrated deep into Nepalese territory and more importantly, into the psyche of the people and of the Rana rulers. Though the group led by Mahavir and Subarna Shumsher had not joined the new party, they contributed liberally, providing much-needed monetary assistance to facilitate the meeting, a preliminary step towards an eventual merger. The socialist leaders of India had been and remained actively involved in the programmes and activities of the party.

The news infused fresh impetus into the movement for democracy, and confidence in its ultimate success. There was a steady rise in the flow of people who left Nepal to join the activists in India or to meet with the leaders who were now household names. Kedar Man Byathit and Laxmi Prasad Devkota amongst a group of renowned academicians and poets, Pushpa Lall Shreshta who was to lead the communist faction in the anti-Rana movement as well as Surya Prasad Upadhyaya an influential future-leader in the Nepali Congress were part of this exodus. Most of them were from the Kathmandu valley. Many others stayed back to discreetly stoke the fire of revolution inside the country.

Until this point leaders of the NNC including B.P. had viewed direct confrontation, peaceful or otherwise, within the country as impractical. Providence was to open up this option within three months of the formation of the party and it emerged from the Koirala headquarters, Biratnagar.

Girija Prasad Koirala and the Labour Strike in Biratnagar

Prime Minister Chandra Shumsher had driven out most of the adult members of the Koirala family in 1917. Yet neither Chandra nor his successors could extinguish or even diminish the ever-rising spirit of revolt that was silently sweeping through the country. As the men in exile fanned democratic sentiments amongst the Nepalese in India, those who stayed back including younger brother Girija in Biratnagar were destined to raise a potent force to carry the battle to the Rana rulers and the institutions that sustained their authority.

The mills established in the late 1930s by Juddha operated successfully well into the 1970s and provided gainful employment to many people. By the end of World War II, more than twenty large- or medium-scale industries (by Nepalese definition), were operative in an area of perhaps ten square miles in Morang district, with more than twenty thousand employees on the payroll. The benefits these industries brought cannot be minimised. But they also provided natural platforms for seeking rights and privileges of the 'proletarian' and emerged as a breeding ground for unrest. While the mills were planned and constructed to match the best in South Asia and with high-quality machines from Europe, the management failed to look into the upkeep of the mills and the interests of its employees. Profit became the guiding motivation of some of the directors, such as the Chamadias, originally brought in from India to share in equity participation and management of the most prestigious company, Biratnagar Jute Mills.

Girija Prasad Koirala was employed in a clerical position at the Cotton Mill, at a young age. He was frail but by no means docile. 'He was a pampered child and grew to become an adamant man who liked to push everybody else around.'[283]

I was a very spoilt child. I also stole some money kept by my mother in her room once. I used to be punished but everybody liked me. My first school was Adarsha Vidyalaya started by my father. At first it operated from a room in our house. When it moved out it adopted a Gurukul system. We were taught to wash our own clothes, prepare the meals and so on, and always wore Khadi. Then in Banaras school father took me to a meeting place being addressed by Gandhiji. I was disappointed at first: he came not astride a horse but walking and looked most unimpressive. He talked humbly but with such great passion that he changed my thinking.[284]

But, obviously, not all his beliefs! 'Once a Haji Saheb, a renowned Muslim teacher, came to Biratnagar and was invited to our house. He came riding a splendid horse. He was seated grandly, on a decorated chair, while all the others sat on the floor. I wanted to be like him. Instead, we fell into great poverty when father and the rest of the family were driven out of the country. We had to borrow money constantly. It was so demeaning. So from childhood I had just one ambition, to earn money.'

There were other fields where Girija was far removed from the thoughts of the Mahatma. 'In school we were taught and made to perform the daily rituals and prayers. This was my greatest worry. A rebel at heart, I used to rattle the hand bell, finish the rites in a jiffy and escape quickly.' From an early age he was a rebel. When he first joined college in Kathmandu, unaware of the dress code, he wore a loose shirt and pyjamas, his usual attire in the Terai. A few days later, during one of his frequent visits, the director general, Mrigendra, saw the young man and reprimanded him, asking him not to enter the premises dressed so shabbily. 'I had passed all the tests needed to join the college and yet this man wants me out, because of how I was dressed. I decided I would not follow his diktat, hiding when he visited. I carried on like this until the very end of my college days.' One can sympathize with the young rebel's angst. But his sense of resentment at the norms of a dress code in educational institutions, expressed on a TV series in 2007, when he had headed a government for more than a decade, does betray a hint of naiveté.[285]

At the Morang Cotton Mills, Girija was given a clerical post. Yet, he was often ordered to perform the tasks of a peon—to carry furniture or loads of office material—which the young man resented. One day he refused to follow the manager's order. In order to avoid a confrontation, others would cover up for him; but his stubborn character soon became known to his fellow workers and his political lineage was well established.

Another stalwart revolutionary, Manmohan Adhikary, worked as a chemist in another mill. His commitment for change and determination to oust the Ranas was as intense as Girija's. Nobody at that time would have imagined that both these employees of the Biratnagar Mills would one day be prime ministers of the country. Unlike B.P. and Girija Koirala, Manmohan Adhikary and others like him remained steadfast in the Marxist ideology. A science graduate from BHU, he had been a regular member of the Communist Party of India and worked with the labour unions. Once he joined the chemical factory in the mid-1940s, his experience and aptitude played a vital role in mobilizing labour unity in Biratnagar. Girija on the other hand, was not politically inclined to begin with. I asked him how it was, that he got involved in politics. He had no hesitation in answering; his memory and intellect were both sharp, even in his mid-eighties[286].

It was pure chance, providence. My father and brothers, B.P. in particular and Tarini were of course totally immersed. I worked in the Mill. The conditions were terrible, rough clothes, dirty environment, rude managers. So there was a seething discontent amongst the workers. The issue of strikes was being discussed and suddenly, the emergence NNC became the tipping point. There was no detailed planning. It just happened so quickly in a few days, and at the gathering that was arranged, they chose to make me their leader. I was quite unprepared.

The proposal to form a labour union had been discussed for many months. The preliminary demands would include official recognition of the union, a 35 per cent raise in salary, an eight-hour work day and proper working conditions for all employees. A meeting of all employees was called for 4 March 1947, in the Jute Mill area. On this clear and bright spring day some twenty thousand people gathered to be part of the historic occasion. Girija was asked to take the chair. He had no experience of such a position and he had never addressed a gathering of any kind before. When he rose to speak he was frozen, hardly able to utter anything sensible. As it was, since the details of the demands were worked out, not much needed to be said in the meeting[287].

Girija Prasad Koirala entered the pages of history that day. From January 2007 when the monarchy was abolished and until Dr Ram Baran Yadav was elected to be the first president of the Democratic Republic of Nepal in July 2008, he functioned both as the head of the state and the prime minister of the country. As President of NC he was heading a three-member 'High Level Committee' with the objective of taking the peace process to a logical conclusion. The other members were Pushpa Kamal Dahal 'Prachanda', General Secretary of Communist Party of Nepal, Maoist and Jhala Nath Khanal, General Secretary of the Communist Party of Nepal United Marxist Leninist. He died while still on the saddle, his leadership in Jana Andolan II had been inspirational.

Back in Biratnagar the mill management was unwilling to meet the demands. Gradually, the nature of the movement changed, the procession moved out to the city area, and was joined by the townsfolk. On another front, the NCC leaders were watching the developments in Biratnagar very closely. B.P. was not one to lose sight of such an opportunity especially one that was brewing in his home town; he had been waiting for exactly this sort of a spontaneous uprising. The party announced full support to the labour movement. B.P. promptly reached his home town, drawn as always by the centre point of political tumult. Similarly, Manmohan Adhikary persuaded the communist leaders from India to send volunteers to Biratnagar. The agitation now took on a distinctly political colour. The speeches at picketing points and slogans of the surging demonstrations were directed against the Rana regime, its feudal order and its excesses. In Kathmandu the rulers realized the matter was serious. More than one hundred well-armed soldiers were dispatched. They had to trek the length of the postal route along the mid-mountain terrain that took more than two weeks. Matrika Prasad Koirala, was still in government service and on a temporary assignment in Darjeeling. Not yet a member of the party, he was near Biratnagar at this point. He met B.P. and warned him that the Rana administration had plans to arrest the high-ranked leaders of the NNC and the labour movement, and advised some to avoid arrest: he retraced his steps back to Darjeeling[288]. But B.P. stayed back. Soon several leaders and activists were indeed arrested. A batch of six prisoners was taken to Dhankuta, on orders from Kathmandu no doubt, a full day's climb north, and from there along the same Postal Route towards Kathmandu. Amongst the six, B.P., Girija and Manmohan were destined to be prime ministers of Nepal. Tarini lived to see the fall of the Rana regime but fell victim to a bullet during the Panchayat time. *The Gorkha Patra* reported the incidence in its usual derogatory style, 'six culprits engaged in instigating the coolies against the state were arrested'. Back in Biratnagar the agitation continued, and was joined also by women from the Koirala family led by Divya, mother of B.P. All those perceived to be leaders, including the women, were arrested and later detained or lodged in the local jail; but at the same time most of the demands of the labour union were conceded. The strike in Biratnagar was over. But the sparks it emitted were soon to spread along the entire kingdom.

The Prisoners' Trek

The six prisoners taken from Dhankuta to Kathmandu trekked across one of the most beautiful stretch of the Himalayan foothills; anyone who has covered this trail during the lovely month of March is unlikely to forget it. Yet the political impact of the trek is of greater topical significance here. There were some porters with them and ten to fifteen soldiers, assigned to guard and escort them. B.P. recalls the trek with fondness and gives it ample space in his recollections. The major-in-charge of the prisoners told them not to speak to each other. But soon it was apparent that this order was not to be taken literally. Indeed the whole group conversed freely during the trek. By the end of his journey B.P. notes, 'We developed a type of camaraderie with the guards. We walked together, enjoying each other's company'. Such a relationship was no doubt a reflection of the benign attitude of Prime Minister Padma.

The news of the uprising in Biratnagar and the arrest of the leaders was covered extensively by the Indian media and had travelled fast throughout the kingdom. After they started their trek along the Postal Route the ultimate destination was evident. And 'it was quite a sight when all of us hit the trail together', it aroused waves of curiosity and interest that the Ranas had not bargained for. Growing number of villagers gathered at key stations along the way to meet the leaders. Conversely, it was a rare opportunity for the latter to place their views before the simple folks. 'Those three weeks created quite a political impact in the hills. Earlier, our contacts had been all in the plains', B.P. admits. For the first time they registered the levels of deprivation the hill people suffered, 'in some places, you found them using fern stalks as a vegetable'. This first tryst of B.P. with these harsh mountain terrains left a lasting impression and in later years helped him formulate the concept of Democratic Socialism in context of South Asia, and Nepal in particular. These thoughts, anointed as 'B.P. Baad' by his followers, influenced and inspired generations of democrats in Nepal, and gained global acclaim.

After more than two weeks the prisoners reached Charikot and crossed the very spot Indra Bahadur Raya and I were gazing at, sixty years later, from across the river Sunsari in Sindhuli district[289]. 'Some of us walked many miles to reach the nearest suspension bridge to cross over to the other side and meet them or watch from close range. I remember Koirala was wearing a clean, white shirt and dhoti and he was very good looking, and smiling most of the time even as a prisoner. He was from our own village and so were his brothers; we were told they were prepared to fight for us and go to jail for us. We carried fruits and milk products for them.'

Three days later the trek ended in Kathmandu. The prisoners were taken straight to prison. They were to remain in custody for a year while the rebellion raged outside.

Nationwide Satyagraha Movement, April 1947

The labour strike in Biratnagar was the first open, direct and organized public agitation against the Rana oligarchy. Once the uprising subsided and the leaders were imprisoned, the action moved to Calcutta. As directed by its Executive Committee, the NNC sent a message to the prime minister demanding release of all political prisoners with an ultimatum to launch a Satyagraha throughout the country starting mid-April, the first day of the Nepali year 2004 B.S., if the Rana government failed to comply. In the absence of B.P., Matrika was suddenly elevated to the centre stage of Nepali politics as the acting president of NCC.

The Rana Durbar was now divided between Padma's more liberal followers and the hardliners led by Mohan. The latter prevailed and the government ignored the demand of the rebels. A convention of the NNC was called in Darbhanga, across the southeastern border, and well over a hundred members turned up. The enthusiastic gathering decided to launch a non-violent satyagraha simultaneously across some twenty towns in different regions of the country. These were the tense and testing days, both for the freedom fighters and the Rana oligarchy.

The satyagraha was directed by Ganesh Man Singh in Ilam and the eastern hills manned mainly by the indigenous Kirat people, by Matrika Koirala in Biratnagar, by K.P. Bhattarai in Birgunj and by other key leaders of the time in different townships. Spontaneous uprisings sprung up in some districts including Palpa. In most of the towns the demonstrators were arrested within a few days, often beaten up and locked up in the local jails.

Decisive Satyagraha in Kathmandu

None of the known NNC leaders from the party was assigned to direct or lead the Satyagraha demonstrations in Kathmandu. However, the nationwide Satyagraha movement stimulated and stirred the secret informal groups 'operating underground and waiting for the right opportunity to emerge in open confrontation'. That opportunity and time was now at hand. Kathmandu rose in strength. The leaders of the anti-Rana movement operating from India not only Ganesh Man and the Bhattarais of the NNC but Subarna and Mahavir too directed their followers to assist the movement. But the steering wheel was operated by the command structure in Kathmandu and guided by those who had stayed back in the lion's den to wage the battle[290].

At ten in the morning on the appointed date, 17 Baisakh 2004 (early April 1948), three separate groups gathered at the centre of each of the three cities and marched through the main bazaars. They carried placards handpainted secretly with 'Nepal National Congress' scrolled across them. There were only a limited number of marchers in the beginning. They chanted precise slogans, carefully rehearsed in advance:

- Inkalab Jindabad (long live revolution)
- Nepali National Congress Jindabad
- The Taj (crown)—we have not aimed at
- The Raj—we do not aim
- Release political prisoners
- Civic rights must be granted
- The guns we do not fear
- To face death we are prepared

Besides these officially coined slogans, some sections of the crowd chanted 'Maharaj Padma Jindabad' showing some soft sentiments towards the liberal elements in the regime and perhaps with some hope of leniency from the state authorities.

It was the first time the people of the valley had witnessed such a demonstration, though many had heard about and some seen similar

activities in India. Soon excitement gripped the populace and the
protestors were joined by many common citizens who had been long
time sufferers from the repressions and injustices of the rulers. Young
men and women emerged from the lanes and the by-lanes. Within
half-an-hour the procession had swelled beyond all expectations.
The rulers were taken by surprise, and the administrative machinery
and security force were unprepared. The relatively smaller number of
demonstrators in Patan and Bhaktapur were dispersed, some brutally
assaulted. The leaders and those who still persisted were arrested and
taken to different detention centres. But in Kathmandu the numbers
were vast and no one dared to intervene. The rally moved around
the streets and lanes of the city merrily, free of intervention, for
many hours, cheered by the onlookers on the side streets and from
the balconies and windows of the quaint houses.

It was only after the rally moved out of the inner city towards
the palace of the prime minister some two or three miles away
that the state forces made their move. The rulers assembled in a
hurry and called upon their ace striker Nara Shumsher to manage
the surging crowd, the same general chosen a decade earlier for
the task of executing the four martyrs. He in turn, chose another
similar figure, trusted and admired by the rulers and dreaded by the
agitators, to assist him—Colonel (later General) Chandra Bahadur
Thapa, whose powerful burly figure matched his intimidating voice.
He could be as ruthless as his superior in command that day, as they
had been during similar hours of crisis in the past and were to be
in future encounters. Nara Shumsher was driven in one of the few
automobiles to ply on the streets of Kathmandu[291].

A lorry full of armed police followed him. Onlookers and casual
supporters began to disperse; the core body remained firm. The
policemen carried heavy batons and some held iron rods or fire arms.
Nara himself led the charge, revolver held threateningly aloft. The
leaders up front bore the brunt of the vicious attack; some suffered
broken limbs, others, bloodied foreheads. Nara spotted Pushpa Lall
Shreshta, brother of martyr Ganga Lall, and threatened to shoot
him 'as I killed your bother'. 'Fire if you dare,' Pushpa Lall shot

back. Nara hit out with the pistol butt knocking out Pushpa. But obviously he did not have orders to shoot. Little Nutan Thapalia and his friend were spotted jumping and pumping their fists in the air, 'You tiny rascal, who taught you to join this gang?' Nara bellowed, his habitual stutter more pronounced. 'We used our own brain; we came to do what we can for the people' they taunted. In the meantime, the policemen had encircled the leading group and dragged and shoved them onto the open-bodied lorry.

There were a few brave women Satyagrahis and their stories merit special mention.

Sahana Pradhan[292] was born in 1927 into a family of eight. She belonged to a well-to-do middle-class family of high-caste Newars. They ran an exclusive business importing and selling paints at a prime business area of Asan in mid-town Kathmandu. Her mother died when Sahana was five and the family decided to move out. Burma, they were told, was a good country for business and they knew some people there. The Pradhans established a prosperous business in Burma until the Japanese attacks and bombings devastated their residence and wrecked their business. They had spent six years there. Says she, her voice still pained by the memory:

> Those were the most precious years of my life; I went to school with my sister Sadhana, and when I returned to Nepal I had completed the eighth class. If we had remained in Nepal we would have been illiterate, quite ignorant of anything but the chores of domestic work. On our return to Kathmandu our brothers joined the Durbar High School; we sisters were packed off into the family home, not permitted even to touch books; that was the norm of the society those days! This is how we wasted a couple of years, all the time pleading with the family to find some way to allow us to continue with the education.

Sahana and Sadhana later got married to Pushpa Lall and Madan Bhandari respectively, the two outstanding leaders of the communist movement in Nepal. Leaders in their own right, both sisters outlived their illustrious husbands. Each has held/holds important posts in the government and in the United Marxist-Leninist (UML) central leadership.

A week before the date fixed for the satyagraha, Prem Bahadur Kansakar came to meet the two sisters. He was the leader of the movement in Kathmandu and asked them what their goal was and what they could do for the country. 'Our goal, we declared, is education for us women of the country and to eradicate all forms of discrimination imposed on women.'

'Then join the andolan,' he said, 'and we will fight for you also.'

We looked at each other, Sadhana and me, and did not take long to agree readily. That is how our career in politics began.

We were given the task of writing the slogans on the handbills and placards. We worked through many nights secretively. On appointed date, several groups started off from different parts of the city in early morning and converged around Tri Chandra College clock tower at ten. Each of us women hid two or three hundred handbills inside the folds of our long cummerbunds. I led the group from the College and Sadhana from Saraswati Sadan across the street. The well-known rotund figure of Rudra Raj Pandey, the principal, came to persuade us to refrain, 'This is not the right way, my dear,' he said in his gentle way. We, too, replied politely but firmly that the world had changed, and marched forward. The principal was aghast. That is where I first met Pushpa Lall. Gradually, different groups converged and turned into a massive gathering; we marched around the Rani Pokhari and inside the inner city, and then moved out towards Padma Shumsher's palace before Nara Shumsher and his troops arrived and started the beatings and carnage.

The police did not touch us women. Nara Shumsher roared at us, 'Do you know what will happen to you?' We remembered the courage and bravery of the four martyrs, and stood our ground. The men all around us were bleeding maimed or had fractured bones; all of us were shoved into the open body of a lorry and driven to the barracks of the guards of Mohan Shumsher in Maharajgunj. There were eighty-two of us cramped into the dark confines within. It was already about ten in the night by the time we were locked in. The next morning we were relieved to see many senior leaders in the cell.

Agitations and rallies in Kathmandu and other parts of Nepal continued unabated despite widespread arrests and imprisonment. The Indian media and the Nepali leaders in India combined their weight to urge the Indian government to pressurize Padma. The liberal faction in the Rana hierarchy pointed out that the Satyagrahis had actually praised Padma, and if these very people were brutally treated the image of the maharaj would be tarnished and the reforms sidelined. On another front the hardliners were not willing at all to concede to the demands of the 'ragtag scoundrels, mostly Newars' as viewed by the hard core Rana Generals. Padma, as was his nature, chose the middle course. He called a public meeting at Tundikhel and called upon the public to terminate the agitations, and ordered the security forces that should the 'rowdy mischief-makers continue such disturbances arrest and bring them to our brother, Commander-in-Chief Mohan, or in my presence, without any beating or bodily assault'. Padma had hoped that the agitations would slacken on account of the conciliatory approach, but it had the opposite effect. The troops sent to intervene were loudly warned by the rally leaders against use of violence, as was the order of the maharaj. Each succeeding day the crowd got bolder and bigger, the noise louder. The combined roar of the huge assemblage inside the narrow streets of Kathmandu resounded and reverberated throughout the valley, penetrating deep into the Rana palaces.

The youngest grandson of Baber Shumsher, Sagar, was about nine years old at this time. Around four in the afternoon, he was at play at the palace grounds of Baber Mahal. He sensed an unusual sound, like the rumble of thunderclouds far away. Curious, he moved towards the main gate of the palace, Aath Paharia dai, his personal guard, by his side. 'What is it?' the boy queried. An evasive answer followed.

The matter was too sensitive, complicated to explain. At the main gate the sound was like the roar of thunder before it strikes. But it was obvious now that it rose from a huge crowd, the Kangresis, he had heard about obliquely. His mind raced, so did his lithe body, towards the palace at full speed, barely conscious of the curious, stares of the palace guards and servants scattered on both sides. Once inside, he slowed down and gathered his thoughts; he saw glum and worried looks of the family members and the serving maids alike. Gradually, it dawned upon him that resounding sound he had heard was the war cry of a revolution.

The elders met regularly now assessing the situation. The crowds were swelling by the day and it was not in distant parts and the border area but right at their doorsteps. The prisons and detention centres were filling up: people were courting arrest in large numbers. The rulers were forced to act; the hardliners too had no answers now, Padma had to make his decision.

Those held and locked up in different cells were brought to the compound of Padma's Bishal Nagar Durbar in groups. The women were standing a little apart. 'Many generals in their impressive military attire,' says Sahana, 'were gathered together and looking towards us.'

Why you women, too, are involved in this?' asked one of them.

'Men and women are equal and we joined because we cannot even go to school for our studies,' Sahana replied.

The generals looked at each other. 'We will think about this,' one of them assured. 'Give us your word then,' Sahana requested. They were bemused and consulted each other. Mrigendra, the Director of Education, was also there. 'All right, we will make some arrangements within fifteen days.' And indeed within fifteen days especial classes for girls in the mornings were started at the Durbar High School.

After about an hour the maharaj came out of his palace followed by senior members of the Rana hierarchy, the bhardars and invariably the high priest. Padma asked what their demands were. The spokesperson Tanka Bilas replied, 'we want the political prisoners released and civil rights guaranteed' Commanding General

Bahadur Shumsher could not tolerate the tone of the speaker 'Give me your permission maharaj, these people should be beheaded', in spite of the decisions reached earlier. Padma cut in, to shorten the ordeal and close the proceedings, 'I will release all present here today, and gradually all other political prisoners. I promise to consult my advisors including constitutional experts from India and within twelve days announce the reforms—you people can go home now'.[293] The valiant men and women knew this was a major victory. All prisoners except three were released that evening. Tanka Bilas Karmacharya, Shambhu Ram Shreshta and Tilak Shahi, seen as dangerous leaders, were chained and sent to the central jail, to remain there for three more years, until the end of the Rana regime.

Reforms of Padma Shumsher: 16 May 1947

Meanwhile, neighbouring India was going through a historic transformation. The last viceroy of India, the dynamic Lord Mountbatten, was installed on the viceregal throne in New Delhi the same month as the labour strikes and agitations in Biratnagar. Simultaneously an interim Government of India was formed with Nehru as the prime minister. Mountbatten had come to India with a clear brief to close the chapter of colonial rule in India. Neither Padma nor his hawkish cousins could be unaware that this momentous shift of power in the region would create a ripple effect in the subcontinent.

Prime Minister Padma was hopeful that a phased representation of the common people in governance would help create a harmonious environment. By the first week of April he had formed a Constitution Reforms Committee. He was expecting the team of legal/constitutional experts from India to arrive soon. Padma therefore promised to announce the agenda 'within twelve days'. He sent a personal message to the incumbent President of the NNC, Matrika Koirala, to withdraw the andolan in order to facilitate the reform process, and a request to Prime Minister Nehru to persuade them to do so. Matrika and Ganesh Man called upon Nehru. They were assured that India was sending a learned man, Shri Prakash, as a constitutional advisor[294].

The Satyagraha was withdrawn on 2 June.

The Indian government moved rapidly to send the advisory team to Kathmandu. Padma recognized the importance of the emerging free India and the role it could play in brokering the deal between the Rana regime and the rising force of the people of Nepal. From the day the Interim Government of India, later to be the Republic of India, came into being it has played its hand in influencing, at times forging at others, forcing compromises or agreements between the conflicting powers in Nepalese politics. But neither the Rana rulers nor the leaders of the NNC in India those years can realistically be blamed for their inability to foresee at that time the permanent impact such a move would leave in the equation of Indo-Nepal relations. To what extent the involvement of the succeeding governments of India in Nepalese politics has benefited or hampered the interests of its neighbouring countries, or its own, is a moot point that will be debated for ever.

Before the arrival of the monsoons, the maharaj announced his plan to usher in reforms. Some major areas were highlighted in his public pronouncement: widespread education, including female education, grant of civil rights within the scope advised by experts invited, independent judiciary, yearly budget, municipality elections in Kathmandu, followed by Panchayat elections at District and village levels. As an immediate measure of good will all political prisoners arrested during the Satyagraha were released. Padma now proceeded to expedite the constitution of the high level Constitution Reforms Committee. He nominated Senior Commanding General Bahadur to lead it. Members nominated were balanced between the liberals and the hardliners, included the sons of Mohan and Baber, and two capable bhardars with legal back ground. In the pivotal position of secretary, Padma selected a third-generation young man from the Bir family, Subarna Shumsher (not of Calcutta). His junior status and affable manners helped him garner acceptability from all wings of the family. A keen student, with a Masters degree in Political Science from the University of Allahabad, he proved his worth by the manner in which he steered the draft through his elders of strong and conflicting views. The key members of the committee worked diligently to prepare the draft, aided by the expertise of some of the keenest minds on issues of constitutional affairs, from India.

Jayatu Sanskritam, Mid-June 1947

As the monsoon rains spread across the subcontinent the rulers had to contend with a students' movement, the Jayatu Sanskritam Andolanan. Its effects were far-reaching and merits more space in the history of the democratic movement.

The Rani Pokhari Sanskrit College was housed in the imposing building of Durbar High School. Although its use as a language of common parlance gradually declined in most parts of the subcontinent and is all but extinct, Sanskrit is invariably used in recitations of the scriptures, an essential feature of the Hindu faith; it was generally a compulsory subject for lower classes before 1950.

However, until 1947, the Sanskrit students had to go to Banaras for their middle- and higher-level examinations. Their sojourn brought them into direct contact with the Indian independence movement. Besides, the head office of the NNC was located in this city. The 1946–47 batch visiting Banaras was excited by the news that a public meeting was to be held and renowned political leaders were scheduled to address the meet. Many were keen to attend but dared not disclose their intent even to each other in fear of the Rana rulers in Kathmandu. Shribhadra Sharma decided that he would quietly slip away on his own. When he reached the venue he discovered that more than a dozen of his colleagues were there, each venturing out individually like Sharma. A natural bond of solidarity and comradeship developed between them. Amongst the speakers, B.P. Koirala impressed the students most, as he did where ever he addressed a gathering. The meeting was the first of its kind for the youths, and filled them with excitement and revolutionary fervour.

That very year the exams could not be completed due to the outbreak of Hindu–Muslim riots, and they returned home grudgingly on the assurance that henceforth they would be allowed to appear for the exams in Kathmandu. However, this was not to be, due to negligence by the high school management. Discontent was rife. By this time the labour stir in Biratnagar, followed by the nationwide Satyagraha had already given a new dimension to the anti Rana movement, and greater confidence to the students. They talked openly against the Rana oligarchy on their way to Banaras, a three-day trek, bus and rail journey. After the exams some of them visited the NNC office and took membership of the party.

Back in Kathmandu they met regularly. They decided to raise their voice against the step brotherly treatment meted out to the Sanskrit department. They wanted subjects such as history, politics and economics to be supplemented in the course, increase in the pay scale of teachers to match the English teachers, and the establishment of a Sanskrit University. Political issues were kept at bay, at least for now, so the whole body of Sanskrit students was involved. Some two hundred students worked speedily and quietly, avoiding detection by the state authorities. A letter containing the demands, with well-reasoned rationale was submitted to the Director General of Sanskrit, Hem Raj Pandey known throughout the country as Mahila Gurujyu. A brilliant scholar and thinker but a hardliner to match or surpass the staunchest members of the Rana family, he remained at the very top in the team of advisors of succeeding prime ministers, often wielding authority far beyond that of a counsellor. A request for a response within the week formed part of the students' demands. In the meantime, a thousand handwritten pamphlets explaining the just cause of their demands were distributed inside and at selected venues outside the campus, other schools, the lone college, reading rooms, legal and administrative offices, military personnel, temples and rest houses attached to them. Students from other institutions also helped distribution. Surprisingly, no arrests were made, but Mahila Gurujyu did not deem it fit to respond to the letter. Gurujyu chose a policy of procrastination, in the hope that the protests would fizzle out in time. The seven days elapsed.

The students were prepared to face the challenge. They started picketing the two entry points of the campus, a few students at a time. On arrest, which was inevitable, another group would be posted. Mahila Gurujyu was forced to act. He reached the campus with the police contingent led by the well-known bully Chandra Bahadur Thapa. However, on this day, the reputation of the two was not going to deter the students! United in purpose, by no means insignificant in numbers, the students surrounded the fuming Gurujyu. In order to avoid total confrontation the leaders eventually decided that some of them would court arrest, but urged the rest to continue the stir the following day. Those arrested were released by nightfall when the curfew was in force, as was the usual practise. The students could not return home and had to spend the night in an open *Patee* nearby, hungry and cold, but buoyed by the successes of the day. The next day they met up with the other colleagues and decided to go to the prime minister's palace to plead their case directly. Treated with apparent compassion and sympathy in the beginning, Padma suddenly changed his attitude when some other Ranas came to advise him. He abused the young men for their impertinence and warned them with dire consequences if they continued with their agitations in support of a 'dead language'.

Padma moved into his palace as the winter sun ebbed. The students moved out, slighted by the insult; but the more perceptive of them were convinced that the PM had unwittingly given them the weapon they needed to fan the fire of discontent. The cause now was not limited to the reform of the education sector. The new mantra would be, Sanskrit is the language of the gods, the cultural heritage of the country, backbone of the Hindu faith. The prime minister insulted all Nepalese by calling it a dead language; he wants to curtail its growth, in favour of the language of the Firangees (a derogatory term for the 'impure' white race). That evening the students planned the strategy for the following days, based on the new theme. Early in the morning when most people went for their holy dip or visited the temples they would spread this message amongst the devout and at the same time seek *Bhiksha,* alms, for their moral cause and struggle. In the afternoons they would move in groups staging demonstrations on the streets and at road junctions, and in the evening each would visit friends and relatives from their respective districts in civil or military service residing in Kathmandu. The news of the past couple of days had spread quickly and when the students moved in the mornings for seeking alms, they were themselves surprised by the generous response: they did not have to worry about their meals any more. Within a few days the struggle took on a moral turn and attracted the religious fraternity and a much wider circle that included civil society, government employees and even sections of the army.

Baber Shumsher submitted a report to the maharaj and to Mukhtiyar Mohan Shumsher: discontent had seeped even into the rank and file of the army. It appears Padma felt quite demoralized by the turn of events, so Mohan and Baber had to take the lead. There was a general consensus amongst the decision makers that the requests of the students were not unreasonable, and the original letter was written in a polite language and not as demands. Why should the teachers of Sanskrit, working the same hours and in the same campus be paid less than half of the English teachers? How come Sanskrit students alone still needed to travel to Banaras for their exams? Some of the Rana families were genuinely sympathetic to the poorer Sanskrit students and often helped them in kind or cash. It was agreed that the genuine grievances should be met. The students were called to Mohan's Laxmi Nivas palace. But now the students were suspicious and adamant. After a great deal of cajoling they were eventually persuaded by one Sur Shumsher, who had always helped the students monetarily and otherwise, to come to the palace. Shribhadra narrates how polite and indeed humble Mohan and Baber appeared. But Mahila Gurujyu raised objections. He was unwilling to condone the indiscipline and rude behaviour shown towards him. He would not agree to release these very culprits. He would not drink a drop of water in Nepal if they were released! Mohan had to plead with all the powers of persuasion at his disposal, just as the leaders of the stir needed to do with the still agitated students, before both sides agreed to a common formula. All demands of the students that could be implemented immediately were met, the rest to be followed up sincerely. Hurt by the decision, Gurujyu left for

Banaras soon after and remained there till Padma left Nepal.

The promise to get the Sanskrit course of Nepal recognized in Indian colleges, or that of establishing a Sanskrit University was not easy to meet quickly. As time passed the more aggressive group of students led by Kamal Raj Regmi wanted to start another phase of agitation. Shribhadra warned that such a hasty action will not meet with similar popular support, and in any case the rulers were unlikely to be caught napping as on the previous occasion. The hot-blooded youths were, however, not to be dissuaded. The leaders were dragged in to action. As feared, the administration had planted informants inside the campus and the plan to boycott examinations was quickly reported. The students were divided; many wanted to continue with their lessons and not loose precious months of their studies, an inevitable consequence. Only thirty-eight were prepared to stay the course. They were quickly arrested and asked to leave the valley. Their immediate goal could not be met, but providence had planned a different direction for them. They decided to meet in Banaras: crossing the border through different routes to avoid detection they re-assembled in Banaras. They met B.P. Koirala and many of them joined the party full time. The NNC made arrangements for some to continue their Sanskrit studies in Banaras; others preferred to join the Regmi group, and the rest went back to Nepal. The well-knit group was dispersed.

However, most of them got involved full time or part, in the movement against the Rana regime, in their respective districts. Politically conscious, with a good education to back them, and anointed by the scent of revolution, they were to provide critical leadership and impetus to the struggle for democracy.

The importance of this episode is recognized by B.P. Koirala in his *Atma Brittanta*.

> After they were evicted from the hostel, the students joined the Nepali Congress—Kasi Nath Gautam, Shri Bhadra, Rajeshwar Devkota and some others. Once they settled down to work secretively in their respective districts, the Nepali Congress,

perhaps for the first time, took the shape of what can be termed a national organization. They formed the nucleus of leadership of the Nepali Congress in the mid-western hill districts, and after 1951 reached the highest echelon of national leadership in the party. Another group, including Kamal Raj Regmi joined the Regmi group in the Congress and later worked under command of the communist leaders[295].

In Banaras Kamal had attained the degree of *Shashtri* from BHU. Simultaneously, he had been drawn into the communist fold. 'Although working secretively they were well organized and gave us communist literature to read,' he says.

> A Hindi book, *Life of Mahatma Lenin* captured my imagination. A quote from it is still etched in my memory. 'Exploitation is a poisonous boil on the body of the human race. If not operated quickly it will destroy the whole body.' But since the communist party was banned in India, I moved with the Regmi wing of the Nepali National Congress but propagated Marxist ideology. In fact quite a few of us in the Regmi group including comrade Pushpa Lall operated in this way. But when I heard about the escape of King Tribhuwan to India and the declaration of an armed revolution I decided it was time to return, and for action.

Mahila Sangh, July 1947

Around these years the women of Kathmandu started a move to form an organized body to claim their rightful equal place in society, and contribute their combined strength to the anti-Rana movement. The social norms of the times, as noted earlier, restricted and confined the women to household chores. Those who did venture out of this social bondage were few and far between. So far, the women had formed secret groups in different parts of Kathmandu and to an extent in Biratnagar. But with the success of the Satyagraha movement in the country and Kathmandu in particular, they decided the time had arrived for them to act. It was the turn of another remarkable lady to come to the fore. She had faced the terrible trauma of her husband challenging the might of the Rana regime headlong, and in the process suffered terrible ordeals. He had placed his life at stake more than once. He was now fighting the battle from across the border. Mangala Devi might have taken some inspiration from her husband Ganesh Man, but the decision was hers and hers alone, to plunge into the battlefield of rebellion, shedding fear and caution aside.

A few months after the demands of the Satyagraha were conceded, the women who had earlier been part of the secret groups working against the Rana oligarchy, including the Pradhan sisters, met at a secret venue in Kathmandu. In this meeting, (July 1947), exclusively of women they decided to form an association, later to be named Nepal Mahila Sangh (NMS). They agreed to carry out a membership drive to start with and worked with missionary zeal. Many girl students and teachers volunteered to join. When the number added up to more than a hundred they met again to give a formal shape to the organization. Mangala Devi was elected its chairperson and adopted the name of Nepal Mahila Sangh. Their twin objectives were to fight for equal rights for women, and join the men folk in the battle to bring down the Rana regime. Through the ups and downs in the political struggle for democracy, and controversies at times, Mangala Devi led this organization until her death a few years after that of her husband. NMS has in built a nationwide network and continues to work for the goals of equal rights and for consolidation of democratic tenets and values.

The New Generation

A few young men in the new generation of the ruling Ranas and the bhardars returning from the schools and colleges in India were now mingling with the politically conscious and active groups outside the confines of the palace walls. Life within the palaces and mansions provided all comforts, but for the emerging generation the lifestyle was oppressive. Bharat Shumsher was to emerge as a mercurial political leader in the party politics post 1951.[296]

The birth of Bharat, the first great-grandson of Maharaj Chandra in 1928 was celebrated with gunfire and fireworks in Kathmandu. He remembers very little of his two infant years in Singha Durbar before the family moved to Baber Mahal, but he recalls he had five nurses at different ages of his young life. The last one and his senior nanny, were as dear to him as his mother, for it was them that reared the child through happy times and illness, as was the common practice in the Rana palaces. Except for 'Darshan (salutation) time' twice a day, there was hardly any contact with parents or grandparents.

Early life was filled with fun, frolic and lot of sporting activities. Schooling was at a bungalow inside the compound. Teachers at Baber Mahal attained national recognition later. There was strict discipline in the daily routine, imposed with heavy hands that went against the very grain of Bharat. 'It is difficult to make people outside the palaces visualize the experience. The head of the family had unquestionable authority over the properties and the household, and often exercised these powers arbitrarily. We grew up under the theory of "spare the rod and spoil the child". Everyone was compelled to observe and suffer through all the archaic rites and rituals, use cow urine or dung to purify oneself, accept injustice, discrimination and prejudice— unfortunately they still persist in society.' His narration of life in the palaces is largely accurate, but it was not different from most other households in the subcontinent those days.'[297]

Bharat's rebellion was against the very social order of those times and he was a vocal and active atheist. He started attending the Tri Chandra College in the mid-1940s. He expressed his angst and 'rebellious' views, often in anger, with his classmates or teachers and in his written work. In one of his essays in an examination he depicted Lord Krishna as a liar, and the principal villain of the Mahabharata war, backed by some telling narratives in the epic. The chief examiner, Balakrishna Sama, 'buried' the paper amongst his valuable 'collections' and several decades later presented it to the documentation centre of Madan Puraskar Pustakalaya.[298] Even today such writings invite trouble.

Bharat was also gifted by a keen intellect and worked hard. When a senior teacher admitted that there was not much more he could teach Bharat in Kathmandu, he was sent to Patna for his higher studies and then St Xavier's College at Bombay for a BA Honours. Nepal was a land of rare beauty those days. But it was also a land sealed off from the wonders of science and technology, and without a fresh wellspring of thoughts and philosophies, Kathmandu remained stagnant, bound within a Laxman Rekha drawn by feudal society and an authoritarian state. Those who managed to get out of this prohibitive boundary were indeed fortunate. In the liberal and cosmopolitan environment of Bombay and under a professor who happened to be an atheist the angry young man of Baber Mahal spread his wings and turned into an eternal rebel[299].

Bharat's letter to B.P. Koirala in 1946, expressing his commitment for a united action against the Rana regime, was the natural reaction of a rebel.

First Officially Sponsored Literary Symposium, Spring 1947

Mrigendra found his second son Jagadish more understanding. He was not demonstrative like his elder brother and immersed himself in the literary field[300]. His desire to attain greater freedom in this field was tempered by more strategic approach. He cajoled and worked with his father to meet his end. A proposal to construct a building for the literary activities was mooted by academics and the literary circle, including Jagadish. Against general expectations, it was approved by the government. A new building was constructed at the complex around the Rani Pokhari. The Saraswati Sadan, located right in front of Tri Chandra College, was the first building in reinforced concrete in Nepal. The first major public function staged in the new building was the historic Literary Symposium of 1947. Few had thought that the prime minister would give consent to such a risky programme but Jagadish persuaded his father to approach the PM. Mrigendra in fact was more willing than his son could imagine, and Padma nodded his approval. Jagadish was nominated to coordinate the activities of the Symposium. Laxmi Prasad Devkota, a respected and popular teacher at Baber Mahal then, poet laureate of the country in history, helped with all aspects of the programme.

The space for staging the function was made available free of charge but there was no financial support. To meet the expenses, an entry fee of ₹16 was fixed for the front seats, which covered the costs of those who could not pay. So the front rows were occupied by the affluent, Ranas, bhardars, officers and their kin; not too serious about the literary content, yet happy to be active in and enjoy this new adventure. To the surprise of the organizers almost 150 participants trickled in to fill up all empty spaces. Renowned poets and litterateurs recited their best creations. They had waited for such a public exposure and open function for long years. It continued well beyond the stipulated time. The overall performance, even if punctuated by some subtle or bolder notes of dissent, was well received by the establishment. By the next year 1948, Mohan had taken over from Padma as prime minister. Despite the more restrictive approach of the new maharaj, he permitted a repetition of the symposium. This time the socio-political content of the recitations was more pronounced and vociferous. Jagadish recited his poem entitled 'The Female Bird in a Cage', its theme sympathetic to the cause of repressed women. When one of the participants was in midst of a piece critical of socio-political exclusion, Mrigendra walked in. An uneasy hum greeted the director general. The recitations got more pointed now and challenging. Before the function could turn nasty Surendra Bahadur Shah, an army officer[301] sang a tuneful ballad that had the audience clapping and dancing. Normalcy returned. But the next morning, people discovered that the life-sized statue of Juddha Shumsher,[302] at the heart of the city, was wrapped in a white saree. Onlookers flocked to watch the titillating spectacle before the offending wrapping was hastily removed. Jagadish was summoned by the prime minister, and in the presence of his father, severely reprimanded. They were commanded not to allow any similar literary functions in the future.

India Awakes to Life and Freedom

The midnight of 15 August 1947 is a historic hour in world politics, made memorable by the stirring words of prime minister Jawaharlal Nehru. The world could feel the awakening of freedom resonate through the All India Radio, and the people of Nepal, too, remained awake to hear it. Only a few months earlier Maharaj Padma had removed all restrictions on Nepalese citizens from possessing a radio set[303].

In many of the towns, especially in the Terai, people rejoiced. Photographs of the Indian leaders were displayed to demonstrate solidarity and a sharing of joy. The local leaders of NNC encouraged celebrations in schools and colleges, at street corners and junctions in many towns. The three townships of Kathmandu valley were once more in the forefront. This time the largest gathering was in Patan, primarily on account of Tulsi Mehr Shreshta. He now enjoyed full support of the state and operated from his office on the banks of the River Bagmati. Besides the promotion of the homespun khadi, his most notable contribution to society was in the area of fostering harmony between the Hindus and Buddhists. His commitment to practice of non-violence, and simple living, free from the egoistic desires of the senses, attracted the faithful of both religions in equal measure. They were used to satsangs, discourse, hymns and prayers well before the 15th August. One day ahead, on the 14th, the gathering was so large that the police force thought fit to disrupt and disperse this purely religious event using batons and arresting the faithful chanting their prayers, 'Hare Ram, Hare Ram' and marching slowly in peace. Tulsi Mehr was worried and unsure about a similar programme scheduled for the next day when the stirring speech of Nehru excited the residents of Kathmandu. Even before dawn, small groups of the young and old began to gather outside his house. Buoyed by the news from India, the younger ones urged and persuaded him to lead the march. The religious texture of the programme now inevitably combined with the celebrations of the independence of India. Tulsi Mehr reminded the enthusiastic crowd of the need to remain strictly peaceful, disciplined in word and action whatever the provocation. As they started the march the numbers swelled and by the time they reached Patan Durbar Square the gathering was huge. Innocent boys like Siddhi Lall Singh too mingled in the procession. The police force sent to control the crowd was reluctant to use force, deterred by the serene figure in the lead. The military men now arrived in truck loads. They surrounded the marchers and started firing in the air filling the square with dark smoke. All but some twenty front-line leaders remained unmoved, and they were arrested and taken to the police station in Kathmandu. They were locked up in the dark, wet and dingy rooms along with other prisoners from the valley. Gradually, most of the prisoners including Mulmi were released but the leaders were detained in the lockup for an indefinite period. After a couple of weeks the health of Tulsi, a strict vegetarian, began to deteriorate; he was treated with Ayurvedic medical herbs by a fellow prisoner and another noted leader Siddhi Gopal Vaidya. Rudra Lall Mulmi[304], an ardent follower, was given a letter for delivery to Mahatma Gandhi. 'Gandhiji promptly penned a letter to the prime minster' asking for a show of leniency and adequate medical facility. A few weeks later the prisoners were released, gradually.

The independence of India was viewed in a different light within the Rana palaces. In Baber Mahal, one could see grave and unsmiling faces of the adults. The seniors in the family were summoned by the prime minister and went out early. Inside the household the elder generation of the ladies foregathered in our grandmother's room. They moved silently and quietly. The youngsters were not allowed in the room. We went around the palace looking for someone who could explain the sombre mood. The 'Didis' from grandfather's chamber were gathered in a hushed huddle, in the ante room. 'Have the Bara Sahibs really left Hindustan?' the younger one asked nervously. 'Yes! Now the Indian Kangressis will be the rulers of India, and stronger here,' the senior Didi Pansy responded. The unspoken concern was common. One can assume that a similar mood prevailed in grandmother's room, and inside every Rana palace including Singha Durbar.

Koirala Released, Division in Nepal National Congress, 1947–48

By this time, after the incarceration of B.P. and other prominent leaders of the party, Matrika had resigned from the government job and elected to be the acting Chairman. B.P. Koirala and the group of six prisoners arrested nearly six months back in Biratnagar were not released from confinement even after those arrested during the Satyagraha were. During this interlude Matrika Prasad, resigned from the position of acting Chairman NNC pleading ill health, and Dilli Raman Regmi was elected to carry on the responsibility for one year. Meanwhile B.P.'s health was deteriorating, the cancer in his throat playing up again. Ganesh Man and others in India pressed Indian leaders to put their weight behind the effort to get him released. At the behest of socialist leaders, Mahatma Gandhi wrote a letter to Prime Minister Padma expressing concern about the health of Koirala and in September he was released. B.P. went to Bombay and got admitted at the Tata Cancer Hospital. After the treatment he hastened to Banaras: he had received several reports that Regmi was not behaving well with the rank and file of the party cadre. B.P. writes that he found Regmi take little interest in galvanizing the party and there was a 'poisonous propaganda campaign against me by a group and focused on building up Regmi'[305]. Each leader now claimed to be the acting president, leading to a vertical split in the party. Most active leaders including Ganesh Man Singh and K.P. Bhattarai and the younger lot joined the B.P. group whereas Pushpa Lall Shreshta, who later joined the communist front, Prem Bahadur Kansakar and the older generation of leaders sided with Regmi. Ganesh Man tried to bridge the gap and so did the leaders of the Indian Congress. Tanka Prasad Acharya, who was still the official president of the party, managed to smuggle out a letter from his prison cell to each warring group, pleading unity. The Kathmandu group of Praja Panchayat that had mounted the Satyagraha sent their leader Surya Bahadur Bharadwaj with a delegation to patch up the differences. Subarna Shumsher requested both leaders to meet him at his residence for the same purpose and had also invited Dr Ram Manohar Lohia in the scheduled meeting. But Regmi failed to turn up at the last hour although he had reached Calcutta. All attempts at reconciliation failed.

Proclamation of the Constitution by Padma, 26 January 1948

In Kathmandu, Maharaj Padma was working hard to persuade his own flock to reach a consensus on the contents of the new constitution. The combined strength of Mohan, Baber, Bahadur and the high priests ensured that the 'the rules of succession of His Majesty, the King and His Highness the Maharaj shall continue as before—and shall for all time be inalienable and unalterable'[306]. They resisted the suggestion that came from the Indian advisors to include a provision that the constitution be drawn up 'with the ultimate aim of responsible and representative government' despite the innuendo that the recommendation had come directly from the Prime Minister of India[307]. But by now there was a significant block of the younger generation of the Ranas and bhardars, who were inclined to tilt in favour of the more liberal approach espoused by Padma, and supported by the advisors from India. Padma had chosen Krishna Shumsher one of the younger sons of Chandra as his hazuria general; others with similar bent of mind were Mrigendra, Vijaya, younger son of Mohan and crucially Subarna Shumsher, the Secretary of the Reforms Committee. The wing of Mrigendra in Baber Mahal was often their meeting place.

The constitution gave recognition to a range of fundamental rights and civil liberties including freedom of expression, of assembly and worship, and for establishment of a largely independent judiciary, a Public Service Commission and an Election Commission. All citizens were to be treated as equal in law. While the prime minister retained the prerogative to appoint the judges, the Act made a major concession by making the tenure of the judges of the high court permanent except on grounds of 'proven misbehaviour or incapacity'. Article 38 made it incumbent upon the maharaj to get a statement of revenue and expenditure presented at the legislative assembly each year. Through what amounted to directive principles, speedy justice, universal adult suffrage and free primary education were set as its goals.

The prime minister invoked 'our heritage and culture' in introducing the panchayat system of government, not far from the model of Gandhi, 'a village state with each village governed according to the will of its citizens, all of them voting'[308]. The Act provided a three-tier model with the village or town Panchayats elected through adult franchise, whose members then elected the District Panchayat members from within their ranks, and similarly the national legislature named Rashtriya Sabha composed of forty-two members were elected by the electoral college of the District Panchayats; an additional twenty-five were nominated into this legislative body by the maharaj. An upper house named Bhardari Sabha completed the bi-cameral legislative council. The formation of political parties was banned. And crucially, all bills passed by the legislature required sanction of the prime minister's seal before they carried the force of law (Clause 37). In addition, the prime minister retained the right to declare National Emergency at his sole discretion and 'assume all and any of the powers vested in any other body or person' (Clause 46.i) The concluding Clause 68 contained a redeeming feature, it opened the gates for introspection, and option to 'extend, modify or restrict' the provisions after seven years, or earlier[309].

Moderates felt the document reflected 'balanced democratic trends of the region with the traditional structure that prevailed in the kingdom'[310]. It was a 'landmark document in many respects, it granted fundamental rights to the people, even if in a diluted form'[311]. Judgemental assessment of critics apart, the constitution gained practical relevance when the NNC accepted it as an instrument which laid the ground work for a compromise, and future reforms, and on this basis withdrew the agitations.

One part of the promised reforms was speedily implemented, in June 1947. The election to constitute an 'autonomous local council' somewhat in line with a municipality, was held in Kathmandu. There was great enthusiasm. A large turnout of 77 per cent elected counsellors from each of the twenty-one wards, and several candidates including those leaning towards the Congress or pro-democratic changes in general, contested and some were elected.[312] For the first time, elected representatives of the sat together with the Rana rulers as participants in the decision-making process. The proceedings of the legislative council, with the prime minister as the chairperson, were conducted in a peaceful and disciplined atmosphere[313].

Assassination of the Mahatma, 30 January 1948

Just four days after Padma proclaimed the constitution, the news of the assassination of Mahatma Gandhi shocked communities throughout the world. In many parts of Nepal spontaneous peace processions were taken out. The Government of Nepal declared a two-day holiday. In Kathmandu the mourners carried a photograph of Gandhi around the three cities requesting shopkeepers and offices to remain closed in remembrance of the Mahatma. This was the first 'bandh' to be undertaken in the country; peaceful and spontaneous. The hymn of 'Ishwar Allah Tere Naam' so close to the heart of the Mahatma was sung along the route as the procession moved to Pashupati temple. Prayers were offered and mantras chanted as the photograph was reverently placed in the crystal clear waters of the gently flowing river.

Gandhi never concealed his sympathies for the democratic movement in Nepal yet the Rana rulers were sincere in their grief of his assassination, at least in Baber Mahal. Father had called a family meet at his large office-cum-sitting room: he gave us the news, his voice sombre. Senior Didis were also seated. Then mother walked into the room. When she heard the news she moaned 'Hey Ram' and sat down heavily on the nearest seat. She was aghast when told that the killer was a Hindu fundamentalist. A few of the ladies, including my mother and sister, in her late teens, were sobbing softly at times. For the first time I was able to learn about the great man

and his deeds. I also learnt that the Mahatma's last two words were
'Hey Ram'.

Padma's Tearful Departure, Reforms Abandoned in Mid-Stream

Out in Banaras and Calcutta a drama of a different nature was being
enacted, on the very day of the assassination.

In his *Atma Brittanta*, B.P. discloses another attempted plot to
assassinate the top hierarchy of the Rana rulers. 'Basanta Shumsher
(the lone 'A'-class son of Padma who was accused of a similar plot
during the reign of his grandfather Bhim) had a democratic mindset
and helped me significantly later. But at that time (1948) I did not
know him; he sent a message that he wanted to meet me'. By common
consent the two met in Banaras in January. They hired a boat, and
floating down the holy river Ganga, safe from any other intrusion,
Basanta came straight to the point. His father, the prime minister, was
a weak man, but they were united in their purpose for liberal and
democratic reforms. But as long as the hardliners held top positions
in the government no change was possible. They must be eliminated,
and the only way to do so was to 'finish them off' in one go. If you
can arrange for five or six grenades, I shall do the job.' He would get
the grenades to be thrown in the gathering of the senior Ranas who
'come to the chakari' in the prime minister's residence each evening,
after his father moved out at the appointed time. B.P. agreed readily,
and asked Basanta to meet him in Calcutta in about one week, the
time needed to procure the explosives. As the winter sun was about
to set over the holy river, the boat brought them back to the Ghats
and the two parted, the lanky frame of Basanta sliding away silently
into the crowd, his head half covered by the shawl he always threw
over his salwar-kameez or even more formal attire.

B.P. left Banaras the same night, for Delhi. His friend Ram
Manohar Lohia had arranged for him to call upon Mahatma
Gandhi. At some length he briefed Gandhiji about the situation
in Nepal and about the struggle to dislodge the Rana regime. It

was evident he was seeking some positive response. 'I cannot help you,' Gandhi responded in sad tones 'When my own people do not heed me why will the Ranas listen to me?' 'I do not seek any material support,' B.P. persisted 'but we need your sympathy and moral support. You are not only a leader of India but a beacon for wherever there is exploitation'. 'Wherever there is a struggle against injustice, exploitation and repression, it will have my support,' the frail old man of peace assured him.

When he came away from the meeting that evening, B.P. briefed Lohia about what transpired, and then about his talk with Basanta in Banaras. Lohia duly delivered the explosives to him in Calcutta. Koirala recalls the venue, a paan shop in the city, where he had asked Basanta to meet him on 30th January. B.P. arrived some minutes earlier carrying the heavy bundle by his side and waited impatiently, eager to hand over the lethal explosives. It was late afternoon when All India Radio broke the stunning news: Mahatma Gandhi was shot and killed in Delhi. 'I was engulfed by a sense of gloom. I realized at that moment the great devotion I felt for Gandhi. I thought the world had come tumbling down.' Basanta arrived soon after and 'I gave him the bundle.'

The day the apostle of peace, whom B.P. so admired, was murdered on the green lawns of Birla House, a plot was set on course for assassination of the Rana rulers in Nepal. This episode also poses a question mark on the sincerity of B.P. and the NNC in projecting its image as a follower of peaceful andolan, as against the stand of Mahavir and Subarna who opted for armed insurgency and made preparations to that end. B.P. is reported to have confessed in later years that his posture of non-violence was a matter of convenience, rather than conviction[314].

Basanta returned to Kathmandu soon after he received the hand grenades. B.P. waited 'every day for news of the blast from Kathmandu'. This particular blast never happened, nor did Basanta deem fit to contact B.P. Instead within one month of the rendezvous at the paan shop, Padma made his tearful departure from Kathmandu. Years later, following the revolution of 1951, at an informal gathering,

B.P. asked what had happened to his 'plan'; Basanta replied smoothly that he had handed over the grenades to another member of the Rana family, Nara Shumsher, who in turn told Basanta after a few days that it was not the right time for such an act. Could it be that those targeted got wind of the plot and pressured Padma to quit without delay, within less than three weeks of return of Basanta the lynchpin?

In light of these revelations, the alleged 'pressure' applied by Mohan and his associates to force the resignation of Padma gathers another dimension. The view held by some that the plot was disclosed by someone to the hardliners, that the incriminating evidence emboldened them to exert the final pressure that eventually persuaded Padma to relinquish his post, within less than three weeks of the return of Basanta cannot be ruled out. The real truth may never come out.

Whatever the cause or compulsions, Padma abandoned his responsibilities in Nepal and departed from Kathmandu on 21 February 1948. He held on to his position of Prime Minister and appointed Mohan as the acting prime minister. Within three years of Juddha's regal farewell, the citizens of Kathmandu lined the streets to view a second prime minister leave the capital before his time. This time the scene was different. Head bowed down, hands folded, and tears running down his cheeks, this was a rather pathetic departure. The crowd was bemused. Those who were initially optimistic of Padma's attempts at liberal reforms felt let down, the reform measures including the proposed constitution were abandoned in mid-stream. The well-meaning but timid man chose to settle down with his family in the safe havens India offered in Ranchi and was to be stuck with the derogatory nickname of 'the weeping maharaj'.

Chapter Six

Maharaj Mohan Shumsher (1948–1951)

Prime Minister Mohan Shumsher took effective control of the state without delay or dithering, once Padma's formal resignation letter reached King Tribhuwan in end April 1948. A lavish ceremonial procession in the streets of Kathmandu heralded the Sindure Jatra of the last Rana prime minister. The new maharaj honoured his brother Baber, second in command now, with an unusual but coveted title of 'Minister'. Keshar stood by their side and Bahadur was happy to see a firm hand and a well-knit team in command, in place of the 'timid' Padma. By now their younger brothers and sons were also matured after several years of experience in governance. The formidable stalwart Mahila Gurujyu, Hem Raj Pandey, returned from Banaras to join the team he trusted to govern well and deal firmly with the anti-state elements. A significant portion of civil society expected them to manage state affairs wisely and with a greater degree of competence. Satya Mohan Joshi, still agile in his mid-nineties now, a budding junior clerk in the employ of the government those days, and Nutan Thapalia, the energetic activist against the Ranas[315] admitted that they had initially expected as much 'but they turned out to be hawkish and a damp squib'.

I targeted Satya Mohan Joshi, a veritable encyclopaedia in matters of Nepali culture, often referred as 'Shatabdi Purush' for interview. On account of his his remarkable memory, knowledge base and experience in government, his views are respected. Similarly, Nutan Thapalia was a young activist those days and known as a selfless democrat.

Mohan and his supporters were not unaware of the difficult national and international challenges they faced. The dice was loaded against the regime, but they were determined to give it a final roll.

In the initial months they moved ahead with a new confidence, vigour and resolve, visible in their body language and mannerisms. Their strategy for survival, nay revival of the regime was to be quite different from the reformist line of Padma. Mohan surmised that if he could stimulate economic growth, control rise in price of essential commodities and maintain good relations with India: he would be able to suppress the rowdy rebels. In his first public address he promised, 'I will give you rice at one Mohur (half a rupee) per Mana (half a kilo),' a catchy phrase that summarized his plans for economic growth. The new rulers had failed to surmise the mood of the people and the drift of the changing times.

The tensions that were building up outside the palaces were the natural topics inside the compound walls. The chakariwallas were from the middle class who went to colleges, were serving in the army or held position of some authority in the civil service. The other groups gathered in conversation were, Aath Paharias, Chhetri soldiers from the hills now residing in rented rooms in the valley, the valets or gardeners who were invariably Newars of the valley mainly from the farming community, and the cowherds and stable boys, the rustics from the mountain districts. The measures announced by the maharaj may have pleased a section of the salaried class and some of the urban elite, a minute percentage of the population. But the overall reaction was not positive as the rulers had hoped. Economic relief promised by the state was viewed as cosmetic by the influential civil society. And ire against the Rana regime was ignited by the discriminatory laws, rules and norms, and the excesses and tyranny of the rulers. The quest was for liberty and freedom, and for political empowerment of the people, which Mohan was unwilling to concede.

Mohan took concrete steps to woo India. He was quick to offer and dispatch a contingent of the state troops to India to support the takeover of Hyderabad. While the governments of each country was still assessing the bi-lateral policy options in the changed scenario within South Asia, the regional and indeed global power equation took on a major shift. In January 1949 the Communist forces occupied Beijing and in October a huge and vociferous crowd hailed Mao Tse-tung as he proclaimed victory of the revolution and the formation of the People's Republic of China. India now needed to view Nepal in a different light. As for Nepal if the clout of its principal source of support was diminished when the British left India, the rising power of China and its expansion into Tibet allowed Mohan some space to negotiate with the new rulers of India. Indian sympathies no doubt leaned on the side of the political activists ranged against the Rana regime but it could not afford to antagonize the government of Nepal. In fact it went one step further, and invited the new prime minister on a state visit to India. Mohan accepted readily and left Kathmandu in mid-February in 1950. The red carpet welcome in New Delhi by Nehru, and the twenty-one gun salute which greeted the guests were followed by lavish receptions wherever Mohan went. The leaders of NNC as well as the Mahabir–Subarna group who commanded the Jana Mukti Sena were told not to indulge in any hostile or provocative act during the course of the visit, and strict vigilance was kept to ensure no such obstruction took place. The level of welcome and honour that greeted Mohan during this visit exceeded those extended to any of Mohan's predecessors on Indian soil. In fact India was keen to enter upon a treaty with Nepal, and an agreement through which it could address its security concerns. In return she was willing to offer a hand of friendship to the Rana government. It is believed that at a one-to-one meeting between the two prime ministers, the two agreed on a new formula for Nepal that would allow Mohan to continue as prime minister provided he ushered in liberal political reforms and allowed representation of the people in the cabinet[316]. Whether or not such an understanding, a formula termed by Nehru as a 'middle way', was reached during Mohan's visit, soon crystallized into a policy guideline of India. In return Mohan promised to enter into a new Treaty of Friendship that would safeguard India's security interests in Nepal. The Indo-Nepal Treaty of Peace and Friendship was signed in Kathmandu in July 1950. The contents covered primarily issues of trade, commerce and transit between the two countries. The security concerns of India were met by a separate letter, an appendix to the treaty that came to light many years later. The relevant clause allowed the signatory countries to take 'effective counter measures' in the event of 'a threat to the security by a foreign aggressor'. The Treaty has been tagged as 'uneven' criticized and opposed often bitterly by political parties and pandits as diminished sovereignty. But the parts covering trade and transit, have been altered more often in favour of Nepal and in implementation, for example, of the clauses related to ownership of property or employment in each other's territory Nepal has gained a favoured position. While India remained the primary focus of the foreign policy the prime minister 'made overtures to the western powers to keep Nepal's former position intact'[317]. A concerted effort was made to secure membership of the United Nations but each attempt was frustrated by the diplomatic manipulations and pressure of India and Veto by USSR when required, in the Security Council. Britain remained a sincere friend of the Ranas till the very end and the rising power of USA, and Switzerland emerged as new partners in economic cooperation.

On the domestic front Mohan strived to pacify influential members of the Rana family who had migrated to India during the reign of previous rulers. A few of them responded but the major players such as Mahavir. Subarna and their followers remained unconvinced by the placating gesture. Mohan also disappointed relatives and the bhardars, inside the country. Age had caught up with him and some odd idiosyncrasies afflicted his mind and body.

Observations from some of the young 'insiders' of those days, reveal the extent of the malaise. Late Meen Shumsher narrates without any ill will:

> We were bemused and taken aback by the prime minister. His span of attention was minimal. He would doze off frequently even while the senior members of the Bhardari Sabha were debating important matters of the state. He spent the majority of his waking hours in the bathroom washing himself, in the dining hall or playing 'Shatranj' (chess) games with his male retainers and chakariwalas. We were ordered, even the youngsters, for Chakari every afternoon, made to hang around

in the cold passages of Singha Durbar twiddling our thumbs for hours. I think he was suspicious and did not want us to gather or meet in separate houses. Our movements were watched and reported. He was barking up the wrong tree— as he soon discovered: the royal family eluded his spies and suddenly ended up in the Indian Embassy.

Khagendra K.C., Baber's personal secretary and confidante, lamented: 'During the last part of his reign Maharaj Mohan was suspicious of everybody; even your grandfather Baber, such a staunch supporter.' Bharat Shumsher covered the whole ruling lot: 'Those were old men of another age; they were totally out of sync with the times. They had no idea what was going on outside their immediate vicinity, what the people felt or how the rest of the world was moving'.

Despite these debilitating views Mohan was committed in purpose to ushering in economic progress. He constituted a National Economic Planning Commission and assigned it the task of drawing up a fifteen-year plan that would meet people's 'basic needs' through development, extension and improvement of 'water resource, hydropower, agriculture, industry, mines, forests, transport, education and health'. His capable and dynamic son Vijay was appointed to head the high power Commission and an experienced technocrat Sardar Bhim Bahadur Pandey as secretary.[318] The Commission recommended division of the fifteen years into three equal phases, the format drawn obviously from the Russian or Nehruvian model. 'Merely the name of Five Year Plan does not lead to automatic success,' writes Pandey 'we had to face far too many problems. The Commission was critically constrained by the lack of information including the quantum of annual state revenue, an exclusive domain of the prime minister, not revealed even to Vijay[319]. There was scarcity of trained man power, public awareness, communication, transport and connectivity, statistics and of finance'. Besides, the prime minister, taxed by the political unrest that was spreading fast, had little time for other matters.

Nevertheless, the Commission worked diligently to submit a

comprehensive plan that allotted top priority to hydro power. After surveying several rivers running down the central part of the country, the Kali-Gandaki was identified as the most suitable source. On recommendation of Robert Kilburn the 'Chief Engineer', the lone British advisor stationed in Kathmandu, with his ever cheerful wife always by his side, a British firm was assigned the task of detailed survey: it recommended construction of a 2.2 MGW hydropower station. It would supply electricity to more than a dozen districts including Kathmandu and irrigate large swathes of central Terai. Road construction and malaria eradication formed part of the project package. Sale of electricity, at the prevailing rate of six paisa per unit, would result in substantial increment in the annual revenue. The proposal recommended the estimated cost of eighteen to twenty million rupees be covered by part of the thirty-three million rupees paid by the British government in recognition of the war efforts of Nepal during World War II. The prime minister approved the proposal without delay but before launching the project Mohan thought he should consult the resident Ambassador of India C.P.N. Singh. Singh persuaded the prime minister that India was planning a major power project in Bihar that could supply electricity to adjoining Indian states and to Nepal at two paisa per unit. The Kali-Gandaki project would be a major folly. Without cross checking the facts the gullible prime minister dropped the project, castigating the planners for their incompetence.

The concept of 'foreign assistance' emerged after the end of World War II. It was propelled by the Marshall Plan (1947) designed to help countries aligned to the Allies rebuild their economies destroyed during war time. The Four Point Programme of President Truman created a fund of hitherto unimagined US$19.35 billion[320] in early 1949 as aid to 'underdeveloped countries' the world over. The Cold War gave a new dimension to the north–south international co-operation. Nepal was active in seeking its share from this bounty. Diplomatic relations were established with the USA and France. One of the Rana palaces, Ravi Bhawan, was hired to house the US Programme. The Swiss government agreed to help draw up a development plan for the country—a particularly appropriate decision on account of its credentials as a non-aligned country and similarity of its topography.

Activities under both these projects commenced after the fall of the Rana regime, less than two months later, but the process of 'opening up of the country' was ushered in earlier. An attempt made to meet the promise of 'one Mana rice at one Mohur' through import of rice from other countries could not be sustained for long due to the exorbitant costs of transportation but a mid-term plan was drawn up for the development of Chitwan and the Rapti Valley as the 'future food grain bowl of the country'. But the price of food grain was governed by factors beyond the control of the state. The construction of the Kathmandu-Hetaura motor road later to be renamed Prithvi Raj Marg, started during that time. Tribhuwan International Airport in Kathmandu was built with financial aid from India and the Indian Ambassador Sardar Surjit Singh Majithia, an amateur pilot who took keen interest in aeronautics, was an enthusiastic promoter of the project. Once the airstrip was ready it was the Beech Bonanza VT-CYZ of the Majithias, piloted by Surjit's nephew Dalip that made the first landing on 23 April 1949. Other airfields were constructed, albeit not cemented, in Bhairawa, Biratnagar, Simara and Pokhara. Wireless transmission stations were established in about thirty districts. For the first time, permission was granted to foreign, mostly European teams for mountaineering, and climbing the Himalayan peaks.

Admittedly, the benefits of these measures hardly scratched the surface of poverty and backwardness in the country. Even as late as 1952, there were only 321 primary schools and a total of 8,500 students and 95 per cent of the population was illiterate[321]. Women trekked for several hours up and down rugged mountain trails to collect water, allopathic medical care and cure was practically non-existent, mother and infant mortality common; there was no electricity except for a limited number of elite households in a few major cities, little employment other than the daily drudgery of subsistence farming. Yet each community learnt to maintain and share their scarce sources. There was social and gender discrimination no doubt, but rarely any violence or crime. The communities still lived in relative harmony and peace.

Maharaj Mohan and his advisors in 1948 thought happiness lay in the affordable market price of commodities while all along the principal cause of discontent against the Rana regime lay elsewhere. The impetus of the revolutionary activities emerged not from the impoverished populace. The Koiralas, Adhikarys and Bhattarais, and the socialists from Banaras belonged to the upper middle-class, the Parihars, Pradhans and Subbas had lived in comparative comfort for generations in northeast India or the Doon Valley. Mahavir, Subarna and their ilk in Calcutta or Darjeeling were the super rich seeking revenge for the way they had been evicted from Kathmandu. The (Ganesh Man) Singhs or Shreshtas, Regmis, (Tanka) Prasads, Acharyas or Sharmas, too, did not belong to the impoverished or illiterate lot. Similarly, motivated young men who rose against the Rana oligarchy, from the eastern or western hills or the southern plains belonged largely to the educated middle income groups. The poets and writers were reasonably well off but their minds wanted to express their musings and their fingers itched to ink them.

Mohan failed to identify the epicentre of the ire or else thought he could control it through stern measures. He was to find out sooner than he or the opposing forces could guess that the tremors were gaining rapid force and the century old hold of the Rana oligarchy was slipping fast and would succumb within three years of his grand Sindure Jatra.

Praja Panchayat Commences Agitations, Autumn 1948

Mohan was intent on demonstrating his strong hand without delay. NNC was declared 'illegal' even though they had kept the agitations on hold after Padma's reforms. He showed little inclination to activate the provisions of the constitution scheduled for implementation in mid April 1948. A few 'representatives of the people' from different parts of the country were inducted in the Bhardari and Rashtriya Sabha. But they were select followers of the rulers. Similarly, 150 village panchayats said to have been 'elected' owed their allegiance to the Rana administration. The Indian prime minister repeatedly 'advised the Government of Nepal, in all earnestness, to bring themselves in line with the democratic forces that are stirring the world. Not to do so is not only wrong but also unwise from the point of view of what is happening in the world today.'[322]

However, the opposing rank was also in disarray. The division in the NNC had led to inertia, disappointment and delusion, and Kathmandu remained aloof, sorely disappointed.

On the first day of the Nepali Year 2005 (mid-April 1948), a young man called Balamukunda Singh got up on the steps of the platform in Bhugol Park located in centre of Kathmandu, and started to address the assembled group, a signal to demonstrate right of free expression offered by the constitution. He was promptly arrested and imprisoned. The promise of Padma had been formally broken by the new prime minister. The idea of forming a third group took root, to wage the battle from inside the recesses of the cities of the capital, as they had done before. A group of activists and leaders of the three cities in the valley met regularly and secretly inside a dilapidated hut, as the monsoon rains pelted outside. A strategy for the struggle had to be evolved. They decided to wage the struggle on the strength of their own steam. It was for the other democratic forces to assist where they thought fit. During a series of meetings that followed Gopal Prasad Rimal argued forcefully that their demands be focused upon and limited for now, to attain the freedom to exercise the civil rights conferred by Padma's constitution, and movement be in line with the non-violent satyagraha. The proposal found consensus. An eleven member committee was constituted to coordinate the activities, under the leadership of Rimal. A vigorous but low key drive to induct new members proved effective.

The Vijaya Dashami, considered an auspicious day, was chosen to start the Andolan. Nepal Praja Panchayat (NPP) came into being that day 12 October 1948. A large crowd had assembled at the Bhugol Park. Ceremonial red 'Tika' was applied on the foreheads of the speakers: Tripurabar Singh and Vijaya Malla, the speakers for the day.

They explained that the andolan was targeted to ensure guarantee civil rights conferred by the Constitution promulgated by Padma, and will be peaceful. No arrests were made that 'auspicious' day, wisely chosen.

The news reached the Rana hierarchy. Once more the dependable Colonel Chandra Bahadur Thapa was selected to persuade the leaders to postpone the agitations. The leaders of the movement were now better versed in legal/constitutional issues. They countered that a written order cannot override the provisions of the constitution and the functions planned will remain within the framework of liberties granted by the constitution. 'Rule of Law' must prevail in the country. It was perhaps the first time such legal terms were heard, and the powerfully built colonel was out of his depth! The leaders were detained and not allowed to leave till the end of the day. The next morning a delegation of the party went to the gates of Singha Durbar and requested an appointment with the prime minister. Hours later an officer was sent to meet them. The discussions followed the same pattern as with the colonel. It was obvious that the rulers were determined to disregard the vital provisions of the constitution. The state machinery was ordered not to deviate from this line.

After a few days the street agitations were launched. Huge crowds assembled, some ready to join the andolan, others eager to watch the proceedings. The speakers were explaining carefully the fundamental concepts of rule of law, the provisions of the constitution, and the right of the people when the police force intervened. The speakers and the Satyagrahis were arrested and detained. But similar programmes were staged at regular intervals of two or three days. The crowds were not deterred and in fact grew in number, and with it, the response of the administration hardened. Even the onlookers were dragged down from inside the houses. Pre-emptive arrests were made at the hint of the slightest suspicion, and the victims included students and the teaching community in particular, considered to be the main culprits.

B.P. Koirala Enters Kathmandu in Disguise

The leaders of both the NNC and NDC were watching the developments in Kathmandu intently. They ordered their followers in the valley to support the andolan. The driving wheel of the andolan remained all the time with the NPP leaders. They strongly refute the reports in some Indian media and accounts of historians suggesting they were guided by other leaders stationed in India. The strength of each of the Congress factions lay in some dedicated young activists in different districts of the country and along the Indo-Nepal border, contact with Indian leaders, an amateur fighting force of the Mukti Sena, and the financial clout provided by Mahavir and Subarna; but they had no experience of the nuances of an andolan from the heart of the capital. B.P. Koirala was aware of the shortcomings and decided to go to Kathmandu 'because a lot of irresponsible things kept happening in Kathmandu and it was important to explain things to the people'[323] a rather ambiguous statement. B.P. explained to his colleagues that the nature of future activities of the party should be determined after talks with the leaders of NPP. Since Ganesh Man was too well-known in Kathmandu it was decided that B.P. and K.P. Bhattarai should enter the valley and remain there in disguise, with Kedarman Byathit as the guide and companion. After a 'dramatic and romantic sojourn'[324] of several days they reached Kathmandu safely, in the beginning of November. The andolan was in full swing.

They moved house daily to avoid detection Starting with Tripurabar Singh and Rimal they met several activists each day but B.P. was 'quite disheartened by the intellectuals of Kathmandu, and still that feeling persists.'[325]. Soon, Bhattarai went back to Lucknow 'as he had nothing more to do here', another curious observation. Although, one cannot find any record or reference of discord between Koirala and the NPP leadership, there is little praise for each other. Queried about this dichotomy Nutan Thapalia admits cautiously,

> Not really, but you are right about your doubts. We, too, were not told at that time why there was no joint action. But in the years that followed, the truth emerged slowly. Koirala wanted

the Satyagraha postponed and launched after more thorough preparation, and jointly. But Tripurabar contended that people were already in jail and the agitations in full swing. It is not wise or possible to postpone it. Besides, they were quarrelling with each other in India whereas we were facing ruthless persecutions here and could not afford to be divided or diverted. Let them spend their energy in 'organization' and in bickering but here in Kathmandu it was time for action. Our decision to launch and continue the Satyagraha was well founded.'

It seems one main aim of Koirala was to try and meet Prime Minister Mohan in Kathmandu. For this purpose he tried to send the message through a Nepali source and even met with the Indian Ambassador Surjit Singh Majithia, entering the Embassy secretly. The message to Mohan for an appointment had a rider, a promise not to arrest B.P. for twenty-four hours after they met. Mohan was not inclined to any precondition or promise; B.P. not prepared to take this risk. Thereafter the search for the intruders was intensified, soon enough his hiding place was located, and arrest followed.

The andolan continued at the same tempo after B.P.'s arrest. The relentless drive to arrest and lock up of citizens, often on mere suspicion, was unprecedented. The prisons and detention centres in the valley filled to choking point. The leaders of the Praja Parishad jailed since 1941, followers of B.P., Regmi or of NDC, the communists, and of course the NPP Satyagrahis were crammed in the central jail. They shared one common goal, termination of the Rana regime; and this bond of common purpose 'removed the drudgery of boredom and purposeless existence and filled them with energy.

In the real world outside the jail, sustaining the struggle was getting tough. Handful of leaders somehow managed to avoid arrest and still operate from secret hideouts. They were able to persuade groups of volunteers to march in protest a few times every week but the numbers were dwindling fast. The common people were intimidated and reluctant to risk the terrible consequences. Nevertheless the Satyagraha had lasted some five months. By the beginning of January the few leaders who remained outside felt the street protests could no longer be sustained. The last group of Satyagrahis marched out once more and announced that for the time being the agitations will be halted, and then courted arrest. The remaining leaders still free decided to join the revolutionaries or party of their choice in India.

'Thereafter, one does not find any revolutionary activity initiated in the name of Praja Panchayat' confesses Bhuwan Lal Pradhan.

The contribution of Praja Panchayat Andolan was of critical importance to the eventual success of the long drawn out struggle against the Rana regime. The NNC was so fragmented that B.P. had shared his concerns about the 'survival' of the party, with his senior colleagues Ganesh Man and K.P. Bhattarai.[326] Official formation of NDC further divided the democratic force. The Ranas were encouraged by the disarray in the enemy ranks in India. They were buoyed up further by the benefits of support from the Gorkha League operating from Darjeeling. The perceived good will of the Government of India was an additional factor that led the Ranas to intensify the crack down at home. Yet the common citizens of the valley of Kathmandu had raised their voice and standard of revolt for five cold months of winter against the might of the Rana oligarchy The andolan convinced Koirala in the damp, freezing prison cell, that Kathmandu is a critical factor for the success of the revolution.

I Suffered As Much As It Is Possible for a Human to Suffer: B.P. Koirala

The wrath of Mohan Shumsher and his government turned to B.P. Koirala. Following his sudden arrest on a freezing day of December, he was taken straight to Singha Durbar, wearing a thin jacket over the 'bhoto suruwal', and no shoes. They chained him around the body, shackled the feet and wrists and left him near midnight standing on the flat cold stone slabs of the guard room, windows wide open. No quilt or bedding was given for three days and nights. 'I did not know that humans were ever kept that way.'

After a few days he was taken for interrogations. Hari Shumsher was again appointed the chief interrogator and judge, rolled into one. He sat himself comfortably on a large chair, Chynata Gurujyu representing the priestly order and Sardar Ratnaman, grandfather of Ganesh Man Singh, close by. Grilled about identity of his accomplices B.P. replied: 'I have sworn to God not to reveal their names and I will not break my word'. As he was a Brahmin he could not be whipped or tortured. Hari Shumsher was a man of big build, with huge appetite for food and women. He was haughty, but not always unkind. He asked the Gurujyu what should be done: 'he is a Brahmin and we are Chhetris whose responsibility is to protect them'. But the response surprised him: 'that distinction is valid only as long as a Brahmin performs his bounden duties'. Hari Shumsher stuck to his own views and desisted from coercion.[327]

B.P. was led to a 'dungeon'. There was a smoky lantern, unseasoned damp wooden bedstead, and bluish wet algae on the wall. A hole in a corner with a metal plate at a slight angle was the toilet; there was no water. All waste was supposed to end up at the pit below the toilet but there was no passage for discharge. The cooking utensil was 'a battered container' used as a lota in the women's lavatory. The firewood was not sufficient to cook the food: 'the water barely came to a boil'. 'Left alone I began to wonder about the extent to which a man can suffer in this life'. B.P. rubbed the floor with manacles for hours each day in a hopeless attempt to escape. 'All I achieved was a great shine in the metal'. He could meet or even see anyone other than the guard. No books, of course, and not even a scrap of paper.

After a month or so he managed to befriend a Tamang soldier who used to wash clothes outside the cell. On assurance of help after his release, the guard helped smuggle massages through to his colleagues in India and get reply; but the news of NPP Andolan weakening and Subarna Shumsher and his new party 'attacking me severely' depressed B.P. The bitter winter turned to warmer weather, but soon the mosquitoes started their invasion. The tension was intense. 'I thought I would go mad and die—and so I decided to go on a fast'. The first two or three days were excruciating. Then the longing subsided but he suffered from severe diarrhoea and pains.

By about the tenth day the news spread throughout the country and was covered by the Indian media prominently. There was consternation against the death of a Brahmin amongst the ladies in the palaces. A high-level meeting was convened that decided to send the two brothers Tarini and Girija, still in detention since the Biratnagar labour. They were told that B.P. was in a critical state. The dungeon like cell shocked the brothers but when assured that B.P. was not as serious as made out the three agreed that the fast should continue. People may or may not like the Koiralas but none can deny their toughness and fortitude. Indra Bahadur Thapa was now sent to the prison. 'Your death will merely mean that the dust that needed a broom to sweep has been blown by the wind' B.P. was told. But the bluff did not work. And now B.P. felt stronger, his pain subsided. 'Thus, I remained for about twenty days—only drinking water.'

The Indian Ambassador, Sardar Surjit Singh Majithia, hinted diplomatically to the sons of Mohan and Baber, at the golf course or bridge table, that it was not a good idea to prolong the tussle with an adamant and desperate prisoner! Well-formulated requests and messages reached Mohan and Baber from the Indian leaders, including Nehru. At long last he was transferred to better quarters but still inside the Central Jail, and was given a change of clothes. Arrangements were made for his aged mother Divya, wife Sushila and young son Prakash to come to Kathmandu from Biratnagar. On the twenty-fourth day B.P. fainted. On gaining consciousness he found he was given saline. Visit from the family members took place late in the evening. If tears were not shed, that effort was surely more painful.

The prime minister now allowed the ladies to meet him. The Koirala women are as strong willed and proud as the men folk. Divya had been in touch with Mohan's mother many years back. She was not about to bend or beg now. Mohan lost his temper: in such a situation 'your son will die,' he threatened. 'I cremated my husband in this place and I have come now to cremate my son. Do not threaten me.' Divya shot back. One can take a safe bet that

Mohan had never been confronted in this manner in his life, by his subject, and a woman at that.

On the twenty-eighth day, an order for release was signed. The gentle Dr Siddhi Mani Dixit who had pleaded with Mohan for a soft line now offered a glass of fruit juice. The fast was broken to the relief of all.

After he recovered B.P. sent a message to the prime minister seeking an appointment. Mohan agreed and was greeted with proper courtesy. Mohan was seated on a chair flanked by his two sons. A rug was placed on the floor for B.P., as was the normal order. 'And so, is it true that you are planning to take over the government and the throne?' Mohan asked. 'No, your highness will remain in place. But we have to have civil liberties—and this government must be answerable to the people.' B.P. answered. 'That is for me to decide. I have not released you under pressure from any quarter.' Those were the final words of the Maharaj. The two were to meet again in three years, in a different world, Mohan might have felt. He was still the prime minister but Koirala faced him straight and erect, in negotiations for a joint coalition government.

B.P. left for India the next day. The wisdom of Mohan's rigid stand, backed with tough measures in the following weeks and months, was debated then, and continues to be a point to ponder about, even today. A conciliatory line then might have led to a smoother transition of power, one in which foreign interests or royal ambitions would have lesser space to play. B.P., too, is known to have made a remark many years later. 'If I had known the tree (of the Rana oligarchy) would fall so quickly, I would not have pushed so hard'.

Compulsions for Unity of the Democratic Forces, 1949–50

It was the sweltering summertime of 1949 when B.P. returned to India. There was a steady decline in the fortunes of NNC. True, most influential leaders and activists had joined the Koirala camp but Regmi had drawn a substantive following especially from Kathmandu, and most of the leftists including Pushpa Lal Shreshta, nominated as the General Secretary. The 'comrades' were carrying on clandestine activities of the banned communist party in India, under cover of the Regmi group, little known to the leaders[328].

Those backing the anti-Rana movement had expected NNC to fully back NPP Satyagraha in Kathmandu. Even when B.P. was arrested, the party remained moribund, other than the routine activities in the safe havens of the border towns in India. Only after their leader had suffered for several weeks 'as much as it was possible for a human to suffer' a General Meeting was called on 1 March 1949 in Darbhanga which decided to launch a nationwide stir starting 1 June! B.P. was released at the end of May. The very purpose of the stir fizzled out. If NNC thought that the Satyagraha type of non-violent movement was no longer effective, the party was unable to articulate these views clearly, far less convince those who were in the middle of the fray, marching on the streets of Kathmandu or locked up in its jails.

Even after B.P. returned to India that summer the party appeared unsure of its course. He did meet Prime Minister Nehru, and then issued a statement that the Prime Minister of Nepal had made a commitment that he would soon initiate measures for political reforms. Mohan shunned any such gesture. Indeed there is no record of Mohan making such a commitment. Koirala's narration of their final meeting suggests quite the opposite. The statement of B.P. proved to be an embarrassment. In August 1949, Koirala eventually issued another statement declaring that the Rana government had backed out on its commitment.

One can assume that long months of introspection preceded such a change in direction and move nearer the line of armed revolution, of Mahavir, Subarna and their party. The move led to the long-awaited amalgamation of the two parties. Both sides were aware of the strength and shortcomings of each other. The NNC was led by charismatic leaders, commanded a dedicated political workforce, impelled by youthful exuberance, combative character and capacity of sacrifice. And after the entry of the youth leaders from the western hills following the Jayatu Sanskritam Andolan (Kashi Nath Gautam,

Shribhadra Sharma, Rajeshwar Devkota, for example) and of the volatile Dr K.I. Singh and his followers, B.P. could rightly claim 'our party character began to reflect more and more of Nepal as a whole.' But in the past couple of years the party was sharply divided and there was a chronic shortage of funds.

In the meantime, NDC moved forward under a clearly defined plan of action, driven by the conviction that armed revolution was essential to bring down the Rana regime. They had established a link with the palace. Some influential leaders especially from Kathmandu had bolstered their strength. On the flip side, the NDC was finding it difficult to maintain control over the Jana Mukti Sena. The armed insurgency into Nepalese territory required larger stock of fire arms, an area where the linkage of B.P. with the socialist government in power in Burma could, and did in fact prove productive.

The need for the two parties to come together, combine their strength and knit a united strategy was obvious and essential. The Indian leaders pressed their Nepalese comrades to unite at all cost. J.P. Narayan and Lohia, pressured their socialist comrades. Lohia in particular went to far corners of northern India to address public meetings called by NNC and was arrested more than once, for leading march rallies demanding the release of prisoners in Nepal. On the other side, Rafi Mohammad Kidwai, a close confidant of Nehru, pressed NDC and encouraged both sides to expedite the process of unification.

First Formal Approach for Unification

The ice was broken when Mahendra Bikram Shah, President of NDC and its General Secretary Surya Prasad Upadhyaya visited Patna to meet NNC leaders and propose unification. Each party had earlier vented bitter criticism at the other in their own ways and style. Now, an 'urgent' telegram from B.P. reached Ganesh Man in Raxaul, asking him to come to Patna forthwith. No reason was cited. B.P. was known for his meticulous planning in preparation for such a sensitive dialogue. Subarna was known to be even more thorough in this respect, weighing and planning each move carefully. The two leaders may have been in direct and single point contact with each other earlier, and worked out the modalities of agreement that they then tried to convince their respective parties to accept.

Ganesh Man was in the midst of a crisis at Raxaul when he received the telegram. They were woefully short of funds even for two square meals for the a few party men posted there. While strolling in deep thought along the railway station a chance meeting with a businessman brought relief; he offered what was in his wallet: a token twenty rupees, but with promise for more in future. And that was sufficient for the humble rations for a month for the freedom fighters and the 'luxury' of cigarettes for some, as a change from the usual pull of bidis!

Ganeshman clambered into a cramped and crowded night train headed for Patna. For four or five stations he could only stand, hemmed in, pushed and shoved. When he did find a seat the enemy was the bitter cold wind of winter gushing furiously through the open windows of the moving train. Ganesh Man had given his shawl 'to a poor man from the hills shivering with the cold' couple of days back. So the grandson of Sardar Marich Man Singh, affluent bhardars in the court of the maharaj of Nepal, now second in rank in the NNC leadership, squatted on his 'haunches atop the seat, and clasped both arms around my knees' to try and ward off the cold. After sometime he dozed off, an enviable ability that never deserted him.

A Dialogue for Merger at Patna

Early in the morning the train reached Patna station. Never would Ganesh Man have guessed that he was at the starting point of a new kind of pilgrimage that day. One that would relieve him and his dear and dedicated friends cum freedom fighters from the state of penniless wanderings, having to scrounge and scratch for a square meal; and more important, a beginning which would help set up a mechanism that would dismantle the might of the Rana regime, within less than twelve dramatic months.

A cycle rickshaw took him to Cozy Nook where B.P. stayed when in Patna. In the forties and well into the sixties the Rest House offered the ambience akin to a club or a 'coffee house' for the Nepalese in general and the revolutionary elements in particular. Patna, the capital of Bihar, was a halting station for all Kathmanduites travelling to different parts of India, The Ganga spread wide and broad and flowed gently around the city and then took a sweeping turn east to give it a serene beauty. Many noted leaders of independent India hail from Bihar and amongst them Devendra Prasad, the mentor and later a colleague of B.P. was a resident of Patna, and often the Nepali Congress leaders found asylum and warm hospitality at his ample family residence. 'Deven Babu' offered unwavering support to the NC and the cause it espoused. Surya Prasad Upadhyaya alumni of Patna University resided in Patna. Indeed, the head office of NCD was located here. The city was also a preferred stop-over point for the Shah and Rana families. The host for many of them was one Radha Krishna Jalan, a Marwari gentleman of immaculate taste and rare wisdom. Quila House the family mansion perched atop the bend in the Ganga and housed a collection of antiquities that matched many museums in the country and hosted rulers, politicians and art lovers of all shade.

B.P. and Ganesh Man the two comrades-in-arms settled down to the serious business at hand. B.P. revealed that M.P. Koirala, the President of the NNC, at that time had also arrived in Patna, and NDC had made a formal approach for the merger of the two parties. President Mahendra Bikram Shah and General Secretary Upadhyaya had placed a 'condition', of Shah to be the General Secretary in the new formation. Ganesh Man was elated, for in that case the choice of the President would naturally rest with the NNC. The talks resumed the following day. Three principal issues were discussed during the series of meetings that followed. Naturally, the Chairman's position was of utmost importance. Ganesh Man argued that an active and dynamic leadership was essential and put forward the name of B.P. It was agreed without much debate. The name of Shah for general secretary was confirmed and consensus was reached that each party would submit names of four persons for membership of the Central Working Committee (CWC). The issue of the party's flag was also decided in favour of NNC. After some heated discussions about the name of the new party, in which B.P. seemed to take scant interest, a compromise was reached on Nepali Congress. Overall, B.P. and Ganesh Man were satisfied by the outcome of the talks. Little did they suspect that the terms agreed upon would be gradually chipped and chopped, and eventually the balance would tilt on the side of the 'crafty' Subarna'[329]. The next morning the representatives of NCD came back somewhat embarrassed, to suggest that someone other than B.P. would be preferred as president. That was the directives from Calcutta! Naturally, there were angry responses, Ganesh Man again to the fore. After some time the name of Matrika Koirala, current president of NNC was suggested by Surya Prasad and the elder brother was present at the meeting. It was a trump card that could not be bettered. Despite continued wrangling the issue was settled when B.P. gave in. Matrika has his own version: except for the 'closest' coterie (whom he describes at another instance as 'sycophants') of Bishweshwar, the field workers were in my favour. The supporters of B.P. shied away from this test'.[330] Bitterness and differences of this nature between the step-brothers threads its way through the history of their lives and that of the Nepali Congress.

Matrika was not only friendly but more 'manageable' as far as Mahavir was concerned. And both of them proved to be closer and more acceptable to King Tribhuwan than with the other leaders of the NC in later years. Many keen observers believe that the government of India too and the leaders of the Indian National Congress, other than the socialists, preferred a more 'mature' leader in Nepal who would be closer to them. The resolute, dynamic and charismatic leader B.P. Koirala came off second best, on this front.

Once the major issues of contention were resolved the details and mechanism of the merger were worked out: the current presidents of each party, Matrika Koirala and Mahendra Bikram Shah, would issue separate statements, declaring that the two parties agreed in principle to unite and merge to achieve the common goal of terminating the

104 years of Rana oligarchy and for establishing a democratic order in Nepal. 8th April 1950 was scheduled for the formal merger.

The Merger at Tiger Cinema, Calcutta, April 1950

The news strengthened the resolve and confidence of forces lined against the Rana regime. The fear element that gripped the people at the time of inauguration of the NNC three years ago was much reduced now. Some three hundred activists converged to Calcutta and attended the meeting as delegates. The venue for the meeting was the Tiger Cinema, the playground of Mahavir, at the centre of Chowringhee. During the three days, 8–10 April 1950, the still-elegant street was abuzz with the animated chatter and bustle of the Nepalese people.

Ram Hari Joshi noticed a handsome and well-built young man welcoming and seating the guests with military precision—he was Thir Bam Malla[331]. It was the first occasion Ganesh Man saw Subarna Shumsher. Subarna was to start off the proceedings by proposing the name of Mr Shah to chair the meeting, and Ganesh Man to second the proposal. It was surely the first time the quiet and reticent Subarna was addressing such a large and important gathering. According to Ganesh Man: 'When he climbed to the platform his legs were shaking ... his head was lowered like that of a shy bride. His hands and lips were quivering as in severe cold ... what kind of a leader and politician will such a man be?' Ganesh Man thought silently.

The proceedings then continued along the lines agreed upon earlier: the name Nepali Congress, Matrika Prasad to be president and Mahendra Bikram General the secretary. Then B.P. went up to the platform to announce the choice of a flag and he suddenly proposed the flag of NCD for the new party! Ganesh Man was aghast. B.P. explained patiently that a couple of days back Subarna had taken him to a four-storey building in 13 Theatre Road, where the rooms were packed from top to bottom with flags: the red stripes at the top and bottom with the white in the middle having four little stars in red. The logic of Subarna was clear; large sums were invested in these flags, kept ready in anticipation and preparation of the final move into Nepalese territory. 'Let us not waste all that.' B.P. could not counter the logic and had consented to the proposition. Now, Ganesh Man, too, was quiet, and persuaded the dissenting group to support the resolution (the red stripe on top denotes the armed revolution, the white in the middle peace, and the bottom red socio-economic revolution to follow).

B.P. felt that the name of the party and the symbolic value of the flag were peripheral issues, and that the leadership would be sorted out in time in line with the contributions made, abilities displayed and trust earned by individual leaders. For him, the core issue was the ideology adopted and policies and programmes inscribed in the party manifesto. B.P. drafted this first manifesto of the new party[332] which in time developed into an ideology and line of thought that came to be recognized as 'B.P. Baad'. The Nepali Congress has retained the fundamental twin goals set out in that manifesto to this day.

- A democracy where sovereign authority of the state is vested on the people and a government elected by and responsible to the people.
- A society built on the principles of justice and socio-economic equality.

The mechanism and modalities for attaining these goals have been modified in line with the dynamics of unprecedented changes that emerged during the decades of the last half of the twentieth century and the beginning of the twenty-first. There is room for criticism that the party has from time to time strayed from the route charted, under the pressures and compulsions of the globalization process and coalition politics, but the fundamental principles and the twin objectives set in April 1950 remain intact.

Preparations for the Final Assault

The manifesto of the party made it clear that the goal of the revolution would not be limited to reforms in the existing political system but a final struggle for rule of the people under the constitutional leadership of Shree Paanch Maharajdhiraj, His Majesty the King. However, there was a serious debate about the strategy: 'armed struggle' or 'through constitutional and peaceful means and the support of the people'. The issue was put to vote. Matrika in the chair had always followed the Gandhian line of peaceful Satyagraha; but B.P. was open now to the alternate line of armed struggle in the Nepalese context. Eventually a compromise phrase 'by all available means' was adopted by a clear majority. All options were now open and due respect had been given to the sensitivities of the Government of India, from where the party was being launched.

A Central Working Committee (CWC) was formed with Matrika Prasad as President, Mahendra Bikram Shah as General Secretary, Krishna Prasad Bhattarai as Assistant Secretary and Subarna Shumsher Treasurer. B.P. and Ganesh Man from the NNC, and Mahavir Shumsher and Surya Prasad Upadhyaya from the NDC were the other 'heavy-weight' members who dominated the decision-making process of the party. In the first in camera meeting of the CWC, some members of the NDC proposed 'individual terrorism' against the Rana rulers, till such time as the party was ready to launch a nationwide insurrection. 'I vehemently opposed this idea. Terrorism and conspiratorial violence would not be conducive to people's participation ... I carried my view without division.'[333] Future events show that this decision was overridden in practice within the year. But at this point in time, a Supreme Command Council of three was constituted, headed by the President Matrika with B.P. and Subarna as members. Ganesh Man needed no official rank. He was confident his personality and background as a fearless leader from Kathmandu would give him sufficient clout[334]. The head office of the party was to be located in Banaras. The skilful K.P. Bhattarai, a born and bred Banarasi, was placed in charge of the head office. The main responsibility for making all necessary preparations for an armed insurrection was assigned by common consent to B.P. Koirala, Subarna Shumsher and Surya Prasad Upadhyaya, with its secret office in Patna.

There was no dispute amongst the leaders that the main thrust of the revolution would emerge from an armed struggle inside the country. Both NNC and NDC had set up their branches at key townships south of the border in Indian territory, hugging the entire southern length of the country. The workers could and did saunter across and carry out party activities with relative ease. The nationwide Satyagraha launched by the NNC in April 1947 had spread the message of revolution and built up pockets of clandestine resistance groups in the Terai, and freedom fighters in several districts in the interior. The Praja Panchayat agitations of 1948 in Kathmandu had demonstrated the festering discontent amongst, and inherent potential of its residents. The Jana Mukti Sena under Subarna, albeit, limited in number and fire power, was prepared for an insurgency across the border. The Indian government had clearly expressed its inability to supply arms and ammunitions for use against a neighbouring sovereign state. Despite the declared policy of a non-violent struggle B.P., as early as 1947, had worried that someday an armed insurrection could be inevitable, and a sufficient stock of armaments an indispensable prerequisite. And to meet this contingency he had sought advice from his socialist friends J.P. Narayan and Lohia. They suggested that the then ruling socialist party in Burma could be of help and that they would put in a word. The occasion of the Asian Conference of Socialist International in Burma opened up an opportunity for dialogue on this subject[335]. B.P. was able to meet the Prime Minister U. Nu. 'They assured me that our revolutionary struggle would have their full support.'[336] When B.P. relayed the news of his Burma mission to his colleagues on his return to India, 'I felt as if half the battle was won,' thought Ganesh Man.

The time was now at hand to activate that pledge. It was 1950. Two men were chosen for a trip to Rangoon to approach the leaders of Burma. Bhola Chatterji, an active journalist from Calcutta, a trusted friend and admirer of B.P. and a respected comrade in the socialist ranks was one of them[337]. Thir Bam Malla was the other. They were to liaise with the Burmese leaders, inspect and select the consignment of firearms. Mahavir Shumsher had willingly offered the services of the fleet of Himalayan Aviation for this mission, or for future use. Chatterji and Malla made their trip to Rangoon and brought the good news that the Burmese were willing to supply two plane loads of armaments, one as a free contribution and the other at cost price. The next hurdle was to find a secret air field for the planes to land. The Government of India could not permit landing of the lethal consignment at their commercial airports. Once more J.P. offered a solution: an airfield not far from Patna, built during World War II but not in use after that. The long flight from Rangoon to a little known airfield in southern Bihar, avoiding detection by the Indian air surveillance network was no mean task but daredevil pilots of the Himalayan airways led by Captain Brejeski took up the challenge. Two DC3 aircrafts landed amidst the unruly growth safely. B.P. and Subarna were waiting to take possession of the valuable cargo. It was loaded into waiting trucks and within half an hour headed for their respective destinations. The consignment had arrived none too soon. A few days later, on 6 November 1950, King Tribhuwan made his dramatic move and with his family entered the gates of the Indian Embassy in Kathmandu. The NC hastily ordered the invasion to commence on 12th November, a couple of weeks ahead of its plan.

Missions to Palpa and Kathmandu, in Quest of King Tribhuwan

The task of assembling men and material was complete, to the extent possible. The uprising of the people, it was hoped and assumed, would follow the entry of the armed rebels into Nepalese territory. B.P. and Subarna, in charge of planning the strategy, knew that now it was the king who could tilt the fortunes of the impending battle either way. A public announcement by the king, or at least a firm commitment for support of the revolution, could mobilize the restless masses into action. But he could not very well make such a gesture from the palace, surrounded as it was by officers and agents loyal to the Rana rulers. Means had to be devised to get him and, if possible, other members of the royal family out of the palace and to a venue safe enough for him to act. A plan was drawn up to convince Tribhuwan to move out of the palace on some pretext, to be met by a group of activists at a predetermined venue in the valley and escorted to Palpa. Field Marshal Rudra, the governor of Palpa, had promised to join the revolutionary forces 'subject to the consent of His Majesty'. The first move on the game plan pointed to Palpa. Someone needed to reach Tansen and convince the grand old man. Once escorted to Tansen, the royals had to be housed and hosted well, with respect and reverence due to the monarch, and protected by the troops under Field Marshal Rudra. There, he would sign a proclamation, Lal Mohur, abrogating the authority to rule the country granted to Jung Bahadur and his successors, some 100 years back. On abrogation, the supreme authority of the state would automatically revert to the monarch. Through the same document the king would pledge to constitute a government to be formed through due democratic process and his commitment to reign as a constitutional head of state. Simultaneously the revolutionary forces would move in to take control of the districts of the country in the name of the king.

A top-level leader was needed to assume this responsibility and to take the risk of passing through the network of government agents along the hazardous route. B.P., as in most such cases, volunteered and made the trip to Tansen, guided by Rudra's son Gopal. He returned safely to convey the good news of the solemn commitment of the field marshal to support the cause of democracy and play host to His Majesty the King when the time was at hand.

The next move led to King Tribhuwan. The obvious choice for such a mission would be Mahavir or Subarna, on account of their personal relations. However, reaching Kathmandu undetected through the dense malarial forest of the Terai and a treacherous trek across the high mountain ranges was not their cup of tea. M.P. Koirala agreed with this view. Ganesh Man was the unanimous choice. Once this decision was reached, the terms of reference of the mission were widened in scope and reach. The primary objective was to make contact with King Tribhuwan and convince him to agree to the plan. The second task was to get in touch with the Indian Embassy and take the Ambassador into confidence, perhaps seek his advice and cooperation. Third renew and consolidate bonds and the links with supporters in Kathmandu.

Thus so far the goals were realistic. However, the final task was more than hazardous. It was reckless and not in line with the policy guideline set by the CWC. The festival of Indra Jatra was approaching. To commemorate that day, ruling members of the Rana family and their relatives assembled at the Hanuman Dhoka palace to watch from the balcony a festive procession of the Living Goddess Kumari moving along the street below. Three mammoth wooden chariots would be drawn by the devotees and merrymakers, each carrying a 'living deity' dressed colourfully in the finest brocade gowns and heavy makeup. On this day, Ganesh Man and his team were to approach the old palace, mingling with the procession and launch a sudden attack on the unsuspecting Ranas. Such an operation required a sufficient number of trained hands with firepower to match. The team led by Ganesh Man comprised Sunder Raj Chalise for the political work and five combatants from the Jana Mukti Sena, including Major Dil Man Singh Thapa, a veteran of the Azad Hind force and Kulman Singh, a retired British Gorkha Subedar. Both were trained veterans in similar operations. In addition, four sturdy porters cum guides carried one Bren gun, two machine guns, a wireless set, six revolvers and twelve hand grenades[338]. However, there was a gross underestimation of the treacherous route and the enemy strength. The mission was a nightmare from the start. Monsoon rains hit as soon as they entered the Terai forests.

'The forest was so dense that you required a lantern even in the day time. The clothes and blankets got heavy soaked with constant rain. In between we had to cross rivers, mostly chest deep but some deeper; so we had to swim across, pulling Sunder Raj Chalise on a rubber tyre we carried, as he did not swim.'[339]

A few days into the trek, they came across a wide river with strong currents, impossible to cross. The food was practically finished, except for a couple of bottles of brandy. Suddenly they heard some rustling noise inside the forest. Fortunately, it was an elephant with a mahout atop. They pleaded with him to get them across but he was adamant, noticing the guns they were carrying. Finally, the brandy persuaded the mahout! They climbed onto the bare back of the elephant, with Ganesh Man tumbling down once but eventually made it across the raging river. Nearing the mountain ranges was a relief and in a small bazaar in the foothills, a Newar shopkeeper and supporter, proved to be a blessing! After more than a week the team ate a proper meal.

There were still high mountain ranges to be crossed, with a different kind of misery. Leeches attacked from the ground and larger species dropped from the trees. After another few days of torture, at last they reached Banepa, a township, one day's walk from the valley. The town is a centre of the Newar community: the Bade Shreshtas, Nepali Congress supporters for several generations, happy to offer safe shelter and warm hospitality to their hero Ganesh Man.

After a day or two of well-earned rest, food and Raksi they were ready to move. Six years after he had made his improbable escape Ganesh Man landed in his beloved Kathmandu. 'My head was high when I felt that I had come back with the same resolve and determination that had driven me to break the shackles of the jail to free myself and escape. As I touched the grounds of the valley I did not sense that I had come here as a revolutionary in secret hiding, but as a conqueror!'

A feeling of exhilaration continued as he roamed the well-trodden streets and lanes. But he could not stay at his home which in effect he had left more than a decade back. So he relied on Chalise to make all the contacts. The guns and equipments including the radio set had to be kept hidden. Subarna Shumsher had sent a letter each to his relatives Pratap Bikram Shah and Toran Shumsher Rana both colonels in the Nepal army who were secretly aligned to the NC. Their home and grounds were now offered for any purpose thought fit.

Meanwhile, the team had split into different groups to avoid detection. Ganesh Man was hosted by a dedicated cadre. His house in

central Kathmandu seemed safe from the security people and allowed
him to meet those willing to take the risk. Ganesh Man sensed
that the state machinery was fully alert and active in maintaining a
check on any movement directed against the regime. Indeed even
contact with the palace or the Indian embassy proved difficult. As
they pondered, the memory of the sweet store, 'Maharaj jee ko
mithai pasal' suddenly flashed through his mind. The shop owned
by Maharaj jee—an immigrant from Rajasthan, was located at a
crossroad at the very heart of the city; people from far and near
visited the store for the delicious mithais and for sharing news and
views, rarely possible elsewhere. Crucially they were suppliers to the
royal family, the top Rana palaces and the Indian Embassy and so
had access to all three that no one else possessed. B.L. Sharma, one
of Maharaj jee's sons had been denied admission into the Thapathali
English School since he did not belong to a bhardar family. However,
taught through generations to keep his bitterness well concealed he
was as popular in the Rana palaces as with the royal palace and
King Tribhuwan in particular. With the Indian Embassy, the family
had a natural affinity. Gradually Ganesh Man and Chalise, frequent
visitors to the shop when in Kathmandu, persuaded B.L. to act as a
go-between: his relations with the Embassy ran much deeper than
the supply of *mithais*, as will be narrated later[340]. The message he
brought back from Ambassador C.P.N. Singh was disturbing, that
the government suspected Ganesh Man and his team to be hiding
in Kathmandu. Indeed every house suspected of compliance with
the mission from Calcutta came under constant surveillance. The
plan of lethal attack on the Rana big-wigs on the Indra Jatra day
had to be aborted.

One last goal of the mission was still possible. The contact man
suggested by Subarna for reaching King Tribhuwan was Dittha (later
Subba) Daya Bhakta Mathema, trusted palace secretary. Chalise
approached him and requested that His Majesty be humbly briefed
about their arrival in Kathmandu and their plans. After a few days
Mathema informed Ganesh Man at a secret venue that His Majesty
was suffering from an attack of severe gout and in no condition to

take on the trek to Palpa. However, he was fully supportive of the revolution. As a token of his commitment Tribhuwan acceded to another request from Chalise and wrote a letter in his own hand expressing satisfaction in and willingness to support the activities of the Nepali Congress. Mathema let Chalise read this letter but took it back with a promise that he would hand it over personally to Subarna in Calcutta[341]. The promise was kept at some future date. It was a valuable possession that persuaded several key personalities including members of the Rana family and bhardars to join the NC.

As for the flight to Palpa, despite his ill health if a helicopter could be arranged through the government of India, His Majesty was willing to proceed. Ganesh Man viewed the response as reasonable in view of the hazardous nature of the land route and sent the message to Calcutta. But it was not realistic to expect the Government of India to fly in a helicopter to the palace grounds of the King and whisk him off to another destination in Nepal! Perhaps even before the letter reached Calcutta whereabouts of those involved in the mission was revealed under torture by someone in the know. Chalise, the officers of the Jana Mukti Sena, Toran Shumsher and Pratap Thapa were picked up in quick succession. The arms and wireless set were also found, vivid and irrefutable proof of the conspiracy to assassinate. Ganesh Man was still undetected as he had changed his night halt frequently or roamed the forests around the holy shrine of Pashupati and similar areas all day and most nights. Eventually realizing the futility of the exercise, he decided to return to India. Three other Newars volunteered to accompany the leader. Posing once more as traders of live water buffaloes they reached the border at Thori, near Birgunj, after days of trekking, hungry and aching in every part of the body. They saw the Indian border across a rivulet not too deep or wide. Ignoring the sound advice not to linger Ganesh Man entered a local pub in the bazaar! The thought of a Newari meal with buffalo meat, rice and Raksi tempted them. That was the folly. The security forces at the border area had been alerted and one of them recognized Ganesh Man. All of them were arrested and taken back to Kathmandu.

The identity of many committed supporters of NC had been compromised and key functionaries were imprisoned. Instead of energizing the people the ill-conceived mission dampened their spirits. Perhaps the most damaging outcome was the loss of confidence of the royal family on the competence and capabilities of the Congress.

There may be another reason for failure of the mission. B.L. Sharma confesses he was no more than an energetic and tactful salesman until the Indian Ambassador called him to his office. 'After that whenever I went to deliver the mithais he told me about the authoritarian rule of the Ranas, the values of democracy...and all that. Then one day he told me how the king was kept like a prisoner in the palace. Would I like to help in releasing him from this bondage?' Slowly the plot was revealed, of starting a regular airline service connecting Patna and Kathmandu and then one day to whisk the King away to Delhi. B.L. was indeed fond of the kind and gentle Tribhuwan and agreed to do what he could. On the guidance of C.P.N., he went to Chakari of Vijaya Shumsher, cultivated his good will and one fine day made a 'humble request' for appointment as sales agent/representative of Indian National Airways. Vijay smiled and nodded. Sharma smoothly took out a silver coin from his pocket, placed it on his folded palms and extended with due reverence, for Vijay to touch the coin; and that gesture was the sign of approval. Soon thereafter, a weekly service commenced. 'But attempts to bring the king to the airfield and quickly board him at the last minute of take-off could not materialize; the Ranas placed capable and trusted soldiers to guard the airfield at the time of landing and takeoff.'[342]

It will not be amiss to speculate whether the strategic design of C.P.N. Singh to take the king to Delhi jeopardized the attempt of Nepali Congress to take him to Palpa and scuttled the mission of Ganesh Man.

Ganesh Man and some twenty-five others arrested and jailed in Kathmandu were charged with treason, attempted murder, or as accessories in the plot. They were not the only prisoners facing trial. From the time Mohan Shumsher embarked upon the hardline policy, the incidence of arrests and imprisonment had taken a steep upturn. The holding capacity for prisoners in jails, police cells and improvised detention centres could not cope with the numbers and a new jail house had to be constructed. The Nakkhu jail was quickly built outside the city area of Patan, even Nakkhu was packed to capacity by the end of 1950. More than five hundred and twenty-five political prisoners were identified and listed by name in the three cities of the valley and two adjoining districts by one of the inmates[343]. A special judicial commission was constituted by the prime minister to try the political prisoners and submit the findings to the prime minister's court of hearing, Ijlas for a final decision. Hari Shumsher was once more assigned the task of conducting the trials with his assistants. Under their coaxing, interrogations, threat and torture not many secrets remained undisclosed, including the complicity of the royal family.

Most leaders arrested, including Ganesh Man, had admitted their personal involvement in the plot but their strength and resolve was truly tested during the course of the interrogation and torture. In the eyes of the rulers this Newar was a known criminal, and had dared to lead a team of conspirators in an attempt to eliminate members of the Rana family indiscriminately. There was little reason for compassion. Ganesh Man recognized Hari Shumsher sitting on a sofa 'like a monster of the nether world, his burly figure covering its entire width'.

Ganesh Man quoted in *Ganesh Man Singh: Mero Katha ka Panaharu* by Mathbar Basnet.

Two men were standing on either side of the sofa, the chief interrogator Mahat, and Upendra Purush Dhakal, personal secretary of the prime minister. Mahat conducted the interrogation in a polite manner, but Ganesh Man responded in a condescending and belligerent tone, refusing to name any other colleague in the plot. Hari Shumsher, was getting increasingly agitated as 'the Newar criminal continued his cocky posture'. Soon he could not restrain himself. Shaking with rage he began a tirade of vulgar abuse in his booming baritone, expecting the prisoner to cow down. But this was no ordinary prisoner. Ganesh Man responded without fear, addressing Hari Shumsher as 'thou': the general had never been insulted in this manner before. Furious beyond words he shouted at the guards to use the lashes. The long whips were soaked in water so that they bit deep into the skin. It is said that Ganesh Man withstood the lashes longer than any known prisoner in Nepal. When he fell to the ground and lost consciousness; Mahat and his assistants had to intervene and remind their master, that the prisoner was near death. Hari Shumsher returned to his senses and ordered the end of proceedings for the day.

The semi-conscious victim was dragged to his cell. The guards were sympathetic; indeed admiring of the bravery. The following day news of the terrible treatment, and the victim's steely resolve did the rounds amongst the rulers and found some admirers even there. Mohan who spent long hours in his ritual worship each day ordered cessation of the interrogation. It is said that Hari Shumsher was reprimanded. After that day the tone of the interrogation was 'softer than butter'.

At the end of the trials, Hari Shumsher recommended death sentence tor Ganesh Man, Chalise and six others, and life imprisonment or lesser sentences to the rest of those held guilty. The decision was forwarded to the prime minister's Ijlas for his final endorsement. Mohan wanted Tribhuwan to place his seal, as per law and precedence. The king took his time. And time was of critical essence. The political climate was heating up, ready to boil over. Mohan was pressing hard for the king's seal. The king faced a terrible option. One would be an act of treachery against his own supporters, the other lead to grave risk to his person, members of his family and the institution of Monarchy. Tribhuwan made no move until his final plunge to take refuge into Indian hands.

Ganesh Man and his fellow prisoners remained in jail, unable to be part of the dramatic activities outside, fuming and exasperated, until the Rana regime was in its final throes. But the popular title of 'iron man' was coined on account of this feat of defiance to the terrible ordeal.

The Bargania Convention

The first General Meeting of the NC after it was founded in April that year was held inside an old rice mill in the hot, humid and dusty town called Bargania across the Indo-Nepal border in September 1950. Some two hundred delegates and supporters attended the meeting. Unlike the comforts of the Tiger Cinema, this venue gave a more 'socialist' flavour to the meet[344]. B.P. Koirala had prepared a base paper that spelt out the subjects for discussion and decision. Armed revolution was recognized now as unavoidable and imminent. A war time council had to be formed. The enigmatic character, Dr K.I. Singh represented the mid-western region of the country and his performance was the main attraction for the participants. Donning his signature Montgomery cap and with his handlebar moustache he delivered a powerful and witty speech and projected himself as the right choice to lead the armed revolution.

The two-day convention passed a resolution that the Nepali Congress would soon commence revolutionary activities inside Nepal to liberate the country from 'Ranarchy'. The action would not stop until the Rana regime was brought to its heels. It was agreed that in an armed revolution of this nature, one person should be given supreme command so that timely decisions could be taken. K.I. Singh's claim was not taken too seriously. The proposal of B.P. Koirala was strongly opposed by one section of the participants. Matrika Koirala once more emerged as the compromise candidate, with a title of 'Dictator'.

The King Makes His Move into the Indian Net

While brave declarations for armed struggle were being made in Bargania preparations for the final assault were still incomplete. The armaments required for the assault were still in the pipeline, in faraway Burma.

As narrated earlier, the cache of arms did land in a dramatic fashion near Patna. But before they could be transported to the battle front, the border towns where the Jana Mukti Sena men were waiting, King Tribhuwan made his move, out of the Narayan Hiti palace, and straight into the waiting arms of C.P.N. Singh in the Indian Embassy. The king had taken permission from the prime minister to go out for a picnic with his family, to Nagarjun reserve forest to the northwest of the valley. One crisp and cold winter morning, on 6 November 1950, the royal motorcade moved leisurely towards Nagarjun. But as they approached the gates of the Embassy in Sheetal Nivas palace at Maharajgunj, Tribhuwan was glancing anxiously to his left. To his immense relief, he saw what he desperately hoped for...a predetermined signal from inside the compound. On the king's indication the vehicles veered suddenly to the left, the gates of the Embassy opened in the nick of time to allow entry, and were quickly closed again, leaving the guards attached to the royals and the Embassy stranded outside. This much is recorded history. The long planning that preceded this smooth exercise is coming to light in bits and pieces but will probably never be fully revealed.

Nepal was passing through a volatile political upheaval with an unpredictable future. The Chinese entry into and occupation of Tibet added to the security concerns of India and the strategic importance of Nepal as the buffer state south of the Himalayan divide. India was keen to see that its influence in Nepal would remain undiminished, if possible more pervasive. The sympathy of India's leaders may have been for 'fighting to end a feudal economic and political structure, a medieval economy and a Rana autocracy.'[345] However, in practical terms, 'Nehru was a tower of strength for our movement, but he rendered only moral support' and the Government of India was not prepared to 'provide us a single piece of arms and gave us no material support.'[346] Furthermore, Nehru repeatedly told NC leaders directly or through his emissaries: 'You may have your agitations, Satyagraha and minor skirmishes; we will then put necessary pressure on the Ranas to ensure democratic changes' or words to that effect.

There was no difficulty for India in maintaining regular contact with the Rana rulers in Kathmandu or the leaders of Nepali Congress in India. Both were courting the support of the neighbouring superpower. But King Tribhuwan had never been allowed to meet Nehru or the other top leaders of India. Similarly, contact between the king and the Congress leaders was near impossible; secret messages were exchanged on the rarest of occasion. However, the content of letters that have come to light and observations of those in the know give ample evidence that the king relied a great deal on the 'friendship' of the Indian prime minister and support of the Indian government to topple the Rana regime. Conversely, as the dialogue between Rafi Ahmad Kidwai and Surya Prasad Upadhyaya reveals, the government of India understood the crucial space of the monarchy in the politics of Nepal. Not knowing which way the dice would fall India did not totally undermine the Ranas either, as was evident from the high-level reception laid out to Maharaj Mohan during his official visit. India wanted to keep all three centres of power in Nepal balanced and within its sphere of influence. The three-pronged diplomatic manoeuvre was used with subtle variations to ensure that Indian interests in Nepal remained protected. But it required tact, delicacy and shrewd manipulation to meet the goal of creating a clear but secret line of communication with the king, surrounded and isolated as he was inside the Narayan Hiti palace.

The first Ambassador of free India to Nepal was an aristocratic Sikh, Sardar Surjit Singh Majithia. He is known to have been in secret contact with the 'palace' but mainly he interacted with the government in power with distinction and natural flare. But he was not the right man for devious moves to penetrate inside the royal palace. Delhi was able to locate just such a man to replace him.

Chandeshwar Pratap Narayan Singh (C.P.N.) replaced Majithia in the summer of 1948. He did not emerge from the college of diplomatic service; he was a member of the Bihar Assembly and Vice Chancellor of the University in Patna, handpicked by Jawaharlal Nehru for the post.[347] C.P.N. was a frail Hindu widower with a slight stoop and spoke in muted tones. Whilst booming laughter had been second nature to the Sardar, a permanent scowl hovered over C.P.N.'s grim visage, humour clearly very far removed from his repertoire. In stark contrast to the well-cut western suits, immaculate

Jodhpuris, stylish achkans and colourful turbans of Majithia, C.P.N. invariably donned a Gandhi cap and white homespun khadi. While the manners of the latter were often condescending, the aristocratic Sikh was possessed of a natural charm. In fact, the new ambassador gave the creeps to the Rana rulers and was not popular with other Nepali people. As his devious activities came gradually to the fore, both King Tribhuwan and B.P. were constrained to make derogatory remarks about him. In short, he represented the diminishing breed of Indian diplomats who by their air of superiority often grated on the sensibilities of people from neighbouring countries. But C.P.N. was working for and accountable to the Government of India, and to his masters he delivered an outstanding service that few could have matched. But the manner in which the objective was attained may well have soured and damaged the harmonious tenor of friendship between the people of the two countries.

The primary task assigned to Singh was to prevent Tribhuwan from moving into the fold of the Nepali Congress and to escort the Nepal monarch under protection of the Indian mission in Kathmandu to the 'safe haven' of the Indian capital. He invested his undivided attention to this goal as he settled himself in the imposing Sital Nivas palace, a residence provided to the Embassy of India during the interim period of transfer of the former British embassy property to the Republic of India.

C.P.N. had brought with him one S.K. Sinha as his personal secretary. It appears the secret nature of his mission was shared only with him and Pratibha his daughter. A regular flow of communication with the palace was needed and B.L. Sharma had been groomed to take that position.

The king was pleased with the link with the ambassador. But at the same time the palace found other channels to remain informed of the happenings outside the palace walls. There were the secretaries and officers working in the palace and a few high-ranking Ranas who passed on the secrets of the Rana palaces to the royals. The three princes made their own contacts. Collectively and individually they would converse with employees working in the palace at all

levels. Priests, soldiers, dishwashers, stable boys, gardeners, barbers…
men of all vocations were carefully selected, and the trusted ones
not only fed the royal family with information from outside, but
facilitated clandestine meetings with some rebel leaders or at times
used secret routes into the palace for an audience with the king.
Tulsi Lal Amatya, later to reach the highest rung of leadership in
the Communist Party of Nepal, was one of them. He was helped
one dark night to climb over the compound wall and then guided
inside the palace for an audience.[348] This was a rare case but there
may have been others that may never come to light.

There was one case, however, where politics had nothing to
do with the breach of the palace wall. Krishna Bahadur was the
private guard or 'Athpaharia' posted in Baber Mahal. A strongly
built good-looking soldier, he was not very talkative and usually
had a faraway look. He used to take his 'long leave' in odd seasons
and there were rumours that he did not go home, some five days'
trek east, during that time. The reason became clear later. He waited
patiently near the palace during the dark phase of the moon, and
when all was quiet silently approached a point along the northern
wall of the compound where there was a drainage channel. He waited
for a lantern to be raised from one of the windows of the palace
couple of storeys high and that was the signal to indicate absence
of the night guards, and for Krishna to crawl through the hole and
move to his lover's call. A rope was dangled from the window and
Krishna soon found the warm embrace of his lover. She was one
of the many pretty chamber companions of Tribhuwan, but one as
promiscuous as the king and possibly more daring! Several times in
the past years the lovers had made a similar rendezvous, reminiscent
of Romeo and Juliet. This particular week though, one of the other
jealous maids leaked the secret. At dawn, Nara Shumsher moved
thundering in with the guards and search dogs, marched down the
corridor and soon into the room. The canines sniffed at a sandook,
a large wooden chest, and Krishna was pulled out from inside the
chest by the scruff of his neck. With Nara and the dogs barking in
tandem, he was dragged down the corridor, out of the palace and

straight into the dungeon of the central jail. The love scene apart, the incidence was an unprecedented breach in the palace security apparatus.

If this was a tragic romance there was another, happier and more celebrated one. The entry of Erica into the life of Tribhuwan and political ferment of Kathmandu started in the late forties. Erika Leuchtag, a German orthopaedic/physiotherapist, had been engaged by the royal family of Patiala for her professional services. She received an invitation from the Government of Nepal to come to Kathmandu for similar work: the patient was Her Majesty the Senior Queen Mother. Against the advice of many well wishers, Erika ventured into the remote country and soon fell in love with the Himalayan capital, the royal family and the handsome, King Tribhuwan. From the very first evening she was invited into the Royal palace she was a hit. Upon bidding of Tribhuwan, she soon started to teach western ballroom dancing to the king. The treatment of the Senior Queen receded to a secondary concern. 'His body was superbly muscled and as graceful as that of the dancing deity Natraj,' she writes. He opened his mind to her and she learnt that the Ranas ruled Nepal and the king was no more than a glorified prisoner in the palace—desperate to get out of their clutches. Between them they coined a name for Prime Minister Mohan, Gobbles! Erika had met Surjit at the Patiala Palace and she quickly renewed friendship with the Indian Ambassador. She told him Tribhuwan was not a debauch, a lecher, or a drunkard as painted by the Ranas, and made a passionate appeal to somehow get him out of the clutches of the Rana rulers. 'At least talk to him and may be take his message to Pandit Nehru'. Surjit eventually agreed to do so. 'When I took this news to the king all the bitterness and frustration of his life seemed to explode in that one spasm of joy.'

Neither Erika nor the Ambassador knew how they could meet in secret, but Tribhuwan did. One dark evening, the king visited his brother's mansion in Chauni. Inside, he quickly changed into a farmer's robe, put on a wig and disguises he kept handy for such cases, exited out of a secret back door to reach the cover of a grove of trees, where Surjit waited for him. Neither revealed to Erika what they discussed. There is little doubt too that the jovial Sardar ventured on such a risky meeting merely on account of the pleas of an emotional Erica.

The new Ambassador C.P.N. Singh, however, pried open a more regular and direct route of contact. Singh moved a gear higher to persuade B.L. Sharma to carry written messages on scraps of paper placed underneath the bottom layer inside the sweets packages: it ensured more regular and direct communication. He followed up on this move with a more audacious scheme.[349]

Recollects Mathema:

> The airfield at Gaucher had been completed and a few private planes had already landed. His Majesty showed keen interest in taking a flight around the valley, the Government of India offered a plane and the prime minister could not refuse such a simple request. But he sent two of his trusted generals to accompany the royal family on the flight. The Ambassador escorted their Majesties and the princes aboard but somehow managed to keep the two generals out! The next half hour, the plane flew around the valley. They had plenty of time to talk to each other and exchange private notes...I could sense in the following days that something was brewing.

Certainly a plot was brewing, one that reached its climax one month later, when the King of Nepal and all members of his family except the child prince Gyanendra took shelter in the Embassy of India.

'The Matter Has Gone Out of Our Hands'– B.P. Koirala

That same fateful morning of 6 November, B.P. happened to be in Patna. At his room he had secretly installed a broadcasting and receiving set, with two operators in service. From here, they could monitor the wireless transmitters from the Indian Embassy in Kathmandu; so Koirala was one of the first to hear the news 'the King has entered the Indian Embassy in Kathmandu and taken refuge with his entire family' B.P. was stunned. 'Now the matter has gone out of our hands!' he blurted out…'the king is under India's control'[350].

King Tribhuwan and the Royals in the Indian Embassy no doubt felt exhilarated now that they had at long last escaped from the clutches of the Ranas. But his feelings were different once he went to Delhi and returned to Kathmandu 'triumphant' as he disclosed much later.

> The moment I landed at the Palam airport I knew how matters stood. I had become a pawn in the hands of the Indian prime minister … I was segregated from all contact with leaders of the Nepali Congress. Now I am home. I have brought with me one Indian gentleman to work as my private secretary and two officers of the Indian army to look after my security. They are the special gifts of Pandit Nehru. I did not have the heart to reject. I foresee many more such gifts to come. I am no more under the bondage of the Rana prime ministers. But am I free? Am I not under the tutelage of the Indian prime minister?

But then to his credit, Tribhuwan was not innocent or unaware of the inevitable and natural compulsions of state to state relationships, as his final remarks reveal. 'The Indian Ambassador had given me many assurances about the altruistic motives of the Indian prime minister, but he could never dampen my suspicion that the Indian prime minister could never be a friend of Nepal, at the expense of being a patriot of India. Later, circumstances drove me to the extremity.'[351]

In Patna, B.P. consulted the socialist leaders and issued a statement pointing out that Mohan Shumsher's government had lost its legitimacy following the escape of the ruling monarch from his palace in protest of the Rana regime. As predicted by the veteran Indian leader, J.P. Narayan, the statement and the news of the king's escape were relayed simultaneously worldwide. The NC leaders now remained in constant touch with each other, and decided to launch the attack without delay. The aeroplanes of Himalayan Airways were once more pressed into service. 'The quiet peace of the valley of

Kathmandu was suddenly shattered by two aeroplanes hovering high over the city. Frightened if bombs would start to drop many people took shelter inside the nearest buildings. A large number of white leaflets were sighted floating down from the sky.[352] The leaflets declared that the invasion would begin on 12 November and called upon the people to join in the movement of liberation or exhorted the army to support the Nepali Congress. In his palace Baber Shumsher 'was out on the balcony looking straight up at the aircraft gawking, his mouth open' before Bharat arrived and took him inside.

Besides Kathmandu, leaflets were dropped in some other cities, including Biratnagar and Birgunj. Some weeks later, the Nepal Democratic Radio station started broadcasting from Biratnagar. The news service and the aircrafts flying free and defiant over the fields and mountains, helped boost the morale of the party cadre, the fighting forces and supporters throughout the country. Crucially they convinced the people at large that yes, the Rana regime was vulnerable. The element of fear that had cowed down the people for more than a century was evaporating[353].

The entry of the king and his family into the Indian Embassy/ territory may have dismayed B.P. and the NC, but it jolted them into action and lighted the spark for the armed revolution to commence in earnest.

Tremors in Singha Durbar and on the Streets of Kathmandu

The epicentre of the shock was, however, located in Singha Durbar. The news reached the prime minister and Baber at about the same hour of the morning. All those holding key positions in governance were summoned. It is said that the prime minister was furious: the royals had deceived him. The option of storming the embassy was discussed but rejected quickly. So a letter was sent addressed to His Majesty, to be handed over to Ambassador Singh. The reply was quick and forthright. Once the royal family entered the premises of the Embassy, the Government of India was bound by international convention to offer them political asylum and all courtesy due to them. Mohan now sent a high-powered delegation consisting of Vijay Shumsher, known to have maintained good connections with the Indian mission, and his cousin Arjun, whose mother was the sister of King Tribhuwan. They, too, returned with a negative outcome. There was a clear indication for Mohan and his court that neither the king nor the Indian Ambassador was willing to compromise. The royal family would remain inside the embassy premises and not respond to any pleading or force. The next move belonged to the Rana rulers. Even at this stage they were not prepared to surrender: a new king must now occupy the throne of Nepal, which could not be left vacant, according to well-established convention.

At the break of dawn the next morning, the clear call of a trumpet from the top of the Dharara tower pierced through the thick fog that covered the valley. Kathmandu knew that a historic decision was at hand. Orders were passed for all *'Bhai bhardar, santa mahanta, sahu mahajan ra sarkari karmachari'* (members of the Rana family, the bhardars, officers of the state, high priests and men of God, traders and businessmen), to assemble in Singha Durbar. After the early morning meal all those included in the vague sounding order dressed in their formal best, moved towards the imposing Singha Durbar, in small groups, deep in private deliberation or hushed conversation. The pride of the new part of the city was this freshly tarred boulevard leading to the massive, ornate gates. A grassy strip ran along the centre, with rows of Crape Myrtle (Asare) trees that flower all at once in pinks or purples during the monsoon months. But that November morning, as the invitees marched its length, the bare branches spread starkly under a foggy sky, matching the state of mind of the rulers and their followers. They approached the imposing facade in front of them with trepidation. Their destiny and that of the nation stood on the cross road of uncertain future.

The venue was the large 'first' open courtyard paved neatly with sturdy local stone slabs. The cold morning air had given way to the rays of the sun as the invitees filtered in, in an orderly manner, taught to them since childhood. The prime minister and the top brass were in council inside the palace.

In due course the maharaj appeared at one of the bay windows, the second-in-command, Baber, standing beside him.[354] In the hushed silence that followed, the prime minister explained briefly and in a grave tone how the royal family had taken refuge in a foreign embassy, leaving only a four-year-old grandson behind. 'What should we do in this situation?' he asked. Few dared to express an opinion, except those already tutored about the line: installment of the boy prince as the new king. Before any other unwanted interruption, the yes men started their tirade against 'a king of Nepal taking shelter at an Indian Embassy'! The official line was clear: according to the traditions and established conventions of the kingdom, the throne could not remain vacant for long, and so Prince Gyanendra should be crowned. Some 258 participants signed the blank paper willingly, obediently or under duress. Baber, as the leader of the Bhardari Sabha, presented the document to the prime minister with the desired text duly inserted. Later that afternoon Prince Gyanendra, barely four years old, was led by Mohan, to be crowned king of Nepal. Gyanendra appeared to enjoy his day.

While the vast majority of those who attended the function that day in Singha Durbar signed the memorandum, a group of some ten or fifteen, A-class Ranas included, avoided the process. It was an ominous sign, perhaps not noticed in the scurry and scramble of that day, but one that re-emerged with vastly increased numbers of signatories and telling effect some weeks later.

The eventful day was followed by days of intense and often volatile debate in Singha Durbar. The Indian Ambassador made repeated demands, often crossing the line of diplomatic or even common etiquette, to facilitate King Tribhuwan fly to Delhi with his family 'for medical reasons'. Mohan made frantic diplomatic efforts in London and Washington through his trusted brother Shankar, Nepalese Ambassador at the Court of St James's, and the British Ambassador Faulkner in Kathmandu, to get recognition for Gyanendra as the new king. But the Government of India came out openly on the side of King Tribhuwan. Deputy Prime Minister

Sardar Vallabhbhai Patel, the strongman who pressured the Indian princely states to amalgamate into the Republic of India, declared: 'The king of our neighbouring country has sought sanctuary in our Embassy. How could we refuse? Those who are wielding real power in Nepal today have installed the king's four-year-old grandson on the throne. They want us to accept this position. How can we do so?'[355] Nehru persuaded the Anglo-American lobby to refrain from any hasty step. Russia had earlier used its veto at the Security Council to block Nepal's membership into the United Nations and now lobbied strongly to counter the move for recognition of the new regime. Ambassador Faulkner, a sincere supporter of the Ranas, was given a patient hearing by Foreign Secretary Bevan but told that India and others were objecting strongly. 'If we and India do not agree it will be Nepal who will suffer.'[356] Pakistan was the only country that recognized King Gyanendra.

Meanwhile, the beleaguered Mohan summoned the ruling hierarchy, the C-class Ranas, and the high-ranking bhardars to Singha Durbar every day at ten in the morning and allowed them to leave only at nightfall. The Rollwallah Ranas, with a few experienced bhardars gathered on the top floor with the prime minister presiding over the meeting. The C-class Ranas were confined in the hall downstairs all day 'often without even drink of water'[357]. The antagonism and bitterness between the two groups intensified.

Even at these crucial meetings, Mohan was given to spells of dozing off and Baber conducted the meetings. Mahila Gurujyu skilfully put forward the view that if Tribhuwan was allowed to go to Delhi the Ranas would have lost a decisive battle. The 'Rajya' would soon be lost. Another powerful Mahila, Bahadur Shumsher, vehemently supported the Gurujyu. Baber, another Mahila endorsed the view, with his weight of experience and seniority. Mohan nodded in agreement. None opposed the view with conviction. Ways to prevent the departure were discussed. Radical options such as launching an attack on the Embassy were discarded but the suggestion of digging up the airfield during the darkness of night was gaining support. As the heated discussions raged on for days, a short and curt message was received from Delhi. 'All facilities should be offered for His Majesty to come to Delhi, otherwise international relations will be complicated.' 'The entire mood changed,' recollects Himalaya. 'There was no way such a stern warning from India could be ignored.' As a last-ditch move Mohan negotiated and secured a promise from his Indian counterpart that the king, when in India, would not be permitted any activity aimed against the Nepal government. With that face-saving compromise Mohan promised safe passage of the royal family from the Indian Embassy to the aircraft.

On 11 November 1950 the royal motorcade of eight vehicles moved from the Indian Embassy, not stealthily this time but at a leisurely pace and under full protection of the state, with C.P.N. Singh seated beside the king. The streets were lined by a large number of onlookers cheering the king. Some shed tears, others were unhappy with the idea of the royal family surrendering to Indian favours. Tribhuwan waved to the cheering crowd, and his limousine stopped at times, so that the people could greet him. He promised and consoled those he could speak to, explaining that they would come back shortly. As the airplane was taking off the large crowd raised resounding cheers: 'Shree Paanch Sarkar ko Jaya'. When it crossed the mountain ranges to the south the crowd milled around, gathered again and moved towards the city centre. People joined the rally as they entered the city centre, shouting slogans against the Rana regime. This was the starting point of non-violent agitations in Kathmandu.

At mid-night 11th November the Nepali Congress launched the armed offensive along the border towns down south. The sudden entry of the royal family into Indian hands had upstaged the plan of the NC leadership. But they were determined to involve the masses and connect them with the ultimate victory. They decided not to be limited to sporadic insurrections as Nehru wished, but launched offensive with all available men and firearms at their command and disposal.

Kathmandu heard the news relayed by All India Radio of a warm reception to the royals at the Palam Airport, headed by the

Indian prime minister. There was new hope and excitement that night inside the houses and in the lanes and by-lanes of the country.

The crowds in Kathmandu started moving and milling around in the streets again the next morning, buoyed by the news of the invasion down south. Those who had led the Praja Panchayat movement a few years back now emerged to mobilize the activists. The Rana rulers activated their security units to stem the tide: suspects were arrested throughout the valley. But the uprising now was spontaneous and the numbers grew rapidly. 'Each day demonstrators roamed the streets shouting slogans 'Sree Paanch Tribhuwan Zindabad', corner meetings were held, speeches delivered, all the time avoiding the police units and at times confronting the police men, stone throwing from one side, lathi charge and arrests from the other. There was no let up for weeks..

After about three weeks, while some of the young men were basking in the warm winter sun in mid-town Kathmandu, an automobile drove through the main street, quite a rare sight those days when the public was not allowed to own one. The car belonged to the Indian Embassy. S.K. Sinha, in his smart attire emerged to casually tell the crowd gathered around him that a British delegation was coming to Kathmandu, to assess the feelings of the people. They will land at the airport the next day. The subtle hint was obvious. Then he sauntered a few blocks of the New Road to reach the mithai shop of B.L. Sharma. In the privacy of a room he was specific: 'Get people to the Gaucher tomorrow and demonstrate your solidarity to the king and your opposition to the Ranas.'

The news spread like wildfire through the three cities. Next day a large crowd estimated to be more than twenty thousand by some, converged at the airfield. A lorry full of women protestors reached there, amongst them was Mangala Devi, the mercurial wife of Ganesh Man. The airfield those days had no permanent structure to protect it. No one had expected this kind of a situation. The contingent of police force deployed was wholly inadequate to control the situation. By the time the plane landed in early afternoon the airfield was surrounded by a seething mass of excitable people, demanding the return of Tribhuwan, shouting slogans against the Ranas and yelling 'British mission go back!' at the top of their voices. The lines were well rehearsed. Ambassador Faulkner had come to receive the guests, a three-man team led by Easter Denning. In an attempt to escort the guests out of the airplane and into the waiting vehicle, the policemen tried to disperse the crowd. Unable to push their way through, they resorted to baton charge and blank fires in the air. The crowd was beginning to disperse when a woman came to the fore. One Shanta Shreshta 'appeared to take on the true avatar of a Goddess Bhagwati in ire'. She dared the policemen to fire at her, moving towards them belligerently. But the order was to avoid shooting and as they hesitated the other women and then the men followed, blocking the guests' route. There was no way the vehicles could move out of the melee. Meanwhile Shanta was struck by a baton blow; she fell to the ground bleeding and lost consciousness. Her companions were still obstructing the Embassy car. At last the visitors alighted. Denning promised to report the facts accurately to the government back home and on that note they were allowed to proceed to the Embassy.

The Rana rulers had hoped that they would be able to convince the British evaluation team that there was little opposition to the accession of Gyanendra. The outcome was just the reverse.

Inside Singha Durbar, the breach between the A- and C-class Ranas was widening. The vulnerable state of the regime encouraged desertion. A couple of days after the British mission left, a few of the C-class Ranas, now in their early twenties, suggested that the revolution was gaining strength and time had come to open negotiations with the rebels. A rather pompous A-class son of Juddha castigated his step brothers/cousins deriding them as 'sons of slaves'. It proved to be the trigger point. A number of Ranas not in the Roll of Succession resigned from their respective official positions. The next day a few joined the agitators in the streets led by Balakrishna Sama, calling for the return of King Tribhuwan.

Outside Singha Durbar Tulsi Lal Amatya, a teacher at a local school in Patan and the one who had secretly met King Tribhuwan in his palace, had been trying to cultivate the support of Dimon Shumsher, the author of *Basanti*. A couple of weeks after King Tribhuwan entered the Indian Embassy he ultimately persuaded Rana, still a lieutenant in the army, 'to go find out the view of the other side.' Dimon went the next morning, to a meeting. In a small dark room in Itumbahal, Kathmandu, a group was talking in Newari which he did not understand, except the word 'juloos', a protest march. He was told after the meeting, that the next morning he was to lead the juloos from Itumbahal for a major gathering around Tri Chandra College. Dimon was not in a position to retreat, 'I decided to take the plunge.'

The next morning with a few Nepali Congress flags we started to move towards the tower. I was in the lead, my heart pounding loudly. The crowd outside the college was gathering and a police force headed by Chandra Bahadur nearby. 'We eyed each other, without emotion. All of a sudden I saw Balakrishna Sama was at the head of a large group, with a sprinkling of Rana cousins converging from another direction. Suddenly slogans of "Mohan be warned, Tribhuwan will come back," were heard. The anger locked up in thousands of hearts now erupted into a furious crescendo; a strange excitement I'd never felt before now seized me. The next thing I remember is strong arms gripping me. I was arrested and taken to Singha Durbar; all the Newars were taken to the central jail'. Ranas were given special treatment even as prisoners. Even if chained and shackled, the metal had to be silver!

Dimon was locked up alone in a dark cell, cold, threatened to be hanged, and scared. But soon 'Sama ji' and some others were brought in. They assured and convinced him that no such thing will happen. 'The Congress is winning. The king is on our side and India is with us. Mohan cannot harm us. The Rana regime will soon pass into history.'"

In mid-town Kathmandu the police force was breaking up the crowd and in the melee an elderly man, Nhuccheman, was hit by a baton. He fell unconscious and later succumbed to his injuries. The next morning his body was carried in a procession for holy cremation... from mid-town Kathmandu, 'the huge crowd of more than fifty thousand moved out to the Tundikhel grounds and turned south towards the central jail. As the first rows of excited, shouting agitators neared the jail, gun shots coming from the palace of Hari Shumsher located nearby felled a few in the lead…the crowd dispersed.'[358] Two of those injured did not survive. The rising tide of anger against the Ranas outweighed the fear.

The agitation gathered momentum in the days that followed. It was around this time that racial divide between Newars and the Brahmins who formed the bulk of the agitating crowd and Chhetris from the outskirts, Kaanth, came to the fore. Many of the kins or mates of the Chhetris were guarding the Rana palaces or facing the rebels in battle in the Madhes. Encouraged by some members of the Rana family perhaps, the Kaanthes formed mobile groups, virile in nature. With khukuris bared they started roaming the inner city streets after sunset, terrorizing the Newars. The name 'Khukuri Dal' was coined at that time[359].

Despite this aberration the andolan continued unabated so did the arrests. Names of five hundred detainees imprisoned in the valley of Kathmandu and two neighbouring districts at different times between 1949 and 1951 have been listed (Bhuwan Lal Pradhan) and no doubt many more have not come to light.

Birgunj Falls to Invading Forces

The Nepali Congress had planned to launch offensive into the Nepalese territory by the end of November. By that time the cache of arms including those flown in from Burma could be transported to reach the border towns in India where the Mukti Sena contingents would be waiting. But the news of the king's escape into the Indian Embassy 'impelled us to go into action immediately.'[360] If the Nepali Congress was to have a voice in deciding the fate of the country, prompt action was essential. Thus the planes had flown into Nepalese air space to drop the hand bills. On 11th November the king and his entourage took the flight to Delhi and on the same day the Mukti Sena under the command of different leaders of the NC made a move towards the border towns, in trains, trucks buses or bullock carts, hitch-hiking or marching, they assembled across nine target towns in the Terai region 'the soft underbelly of Nepal.'[361] The zero-hour for each contingent to strike was the midnight of 11th November.

Only a sketchy and, at times, conflicting record of the number of invading forces and the arms they carried survives. But by all accounts they were poorly equipped for such an operation at such short notice. Birgunj, the junction connecting Kathmandu and India, where Subarna Shumsher once worked as governor, was the prime target. The most trusted lieutenant of Subarna, Thir Bam Malla, was selected to lead one contingent based in Patna. Their target was the well-guarded residence of the governor of Birgunj, Som Shumsher. Another contingent based in Calcutta was under the command of a veteran from the Burma war, Purna Singh Thakur. They were in a jolly mood enjoying the festival of Diwali at their camp in Calcutta when urgent orders were received to depart forthwith and reach Birgunj by 11th night. They were assured that necessary arms and ammunitions would be waiting for them at Raxaul, and their mission was to capture the army barracks in Birgunj, couple of miles inside Nepalese territory. A few minutes before the train reached the station they pulled the chain to halt the train and jumped out into the darkness, dressed in black. But then 'a sum total of three rusty machine guns, four revolvers and a dozen hand grenades made available, were in no way sufficient to attack and capture a well-trained and equipped company of 130 state troops. But this was no time to argue.'[362] So they moved forward. But the delay caused had also blunted the advantage of a surprise attack at night and in the pre-dawn hours the army men were up and ready. The attack was repulsed; some men were wounded and one succumbed to his injuries. Two were taken in as prisoner. An order for a retreat took the men back to Birgunj town where the NC had a strong following.

There they heard the good and the tragic news. Thir Bam Malla and his men had reached the governor's quarters in time, surprised and overpowered the sleeping guards and army men and took the governor prisoner. After the guns were silent and dawn broke through, the frightened civilians were venturing out of their houses; they needed to be assured of their safety. Thir Bam stood on a high ground to address the people and as he was doing so, a gunshot from an unknown army man hit the brave heart. He was taken to a hospital in Raxaul and there life ebbed out of the handsome man in the prime of his life.

The men under Thir Bam now joined the Calcutta contingent at Birgunj town. They had brought with them as a bonus, a few firearms captured at the governor's place. The locals contributed a few more. The hungry freedom fighters were fed well by the party organization and given a place to rest for a few hours. Then they resumed the attack on the barracks. But they were no match for the strength of the state forces. All they could do was fire blanks and fire crackers to give the impression of a large attacking force. But a miracle was required to capture the enemy stronghold. And a miracle came their way.

The 'Director' of the Liberation Army, M.P. Koirala, was on a reconnaissance flight over Birgunj and Simara that afternoon. The pilot flew low over Birgunj, Matrika delighted to see so many houses flying the Congress flags. What was seen from the barracks was more important. An airplane VT-COZ zooming low over and past them, with the distinctive red and white NC flag whirling in the wind! The two prisoners inside the barracks were quick-witted. They convinced the army men that having marked the place, other planes would follow with powerful bombs and disseminate the barracks. Blow them into smithereens. Of course, there was still time to surrender and save precious lives, including 'ours'. After a brief session of consultations 'a white flag aloft, they emerged from their barracks and surrendered to the rag tag, ill equipped freedom fighters'.

The capture of Birgunj, providential as it may be, brought more than just a victory. When the Koiralas and Subarna Shumsher entered the barracks the following morning they found and took into possession one Bren gun, twenty-nine Sten guns, some 200

Mark303 rifles, nine revolvers, a large cache of ammunition, a radio set, sufficient military rations to feed a company for three months and three and a half million Indian rupees in cash. 'We could now arm our people with the captured hardware. Earlier, we had nothing but fire crackers as weapons', confesses M.P. Koirala. Krishna Prasad Bhattarai who led the invasion of Udayapur jointly with Rudra Giri relates a similar tale, 'the assurance that we could take as much arms and ammunitions as we wanted, turned out to be merely a bluff to encourage us. We got nothing more than two sten guns and one hundred rounds of ammunition for one hundred and ten rag-tag recruits under our command'[363]. Such revelations beg a question about the two Dakota loads of military hardware from Burma.

A more far-reaching benefit of the fall of Birgunj was the international media coverage of the startling victory. The numerous armed raids inside Nepal came as a complete surprise to Delhi[364]. It is said that Prime Minister Nehru was furious, but the rest of India rose in one to salute the stunning triumph of the revolutionaries.

'Nepali Congress Forces Take Birgunj' declared *The Statesman* in its front page bold headline. Other premium newspapers reported along similar lines, with jubilant undertones and sympathy towards the cause of the rebels, the same cause that had brought freedom to their country. Indeed such a trend in coverage was one of the crucial stimulants that generated sympathy towards the NC and persuaded many Nepalese living in India to join the struggle: Yog Prasad Upadhyaya, later to be home minister in the coalition government of 1991, Ram Hari Joshi and Keshar Jung Rayamajhi are some who rushed post haste for the border towns.

Young men who had little or no connect with politics too, started to join the revolution from schools and colleges, farmers, employees from different professions including for example a soldier on leave after fighting on the Kashmir front, a policeman from Ranchi, workers from the tea gardens of Assam and Darjeeling, migrant labourers from Dehradun, Himachal or Bengal. Nepalese from all walks of life came alone or in groups. In Banaras, young men started walking in and registering their names as volunteers at the NC office.

Hem Raj Adhikary[365] was one of them who volunteered to go to the battlefields.

Inside 'Liberated' Nepal

An eyewitness depiction of a 'battle' inside Nepal typifies the kind of engagements in the interior.

> At dawn the trumpets blew in maddening sharp shrill tones and within a few distinct seconds the whole town was awake and on the uneven house fronts stood thousands of, unslept people with patches on their many coloured clothes. The mountaintops look hazy. It is difficult to say what is rumbling behind the hills. A young lad hurls himself at a ditch and digs furiously at the mud. There he has a gun and a long string of fresh cartridges. 'Down with the Rana regime … Down … Down … Jaya for the King … Jaya'. The shout rends the air. It echoes and reaches the mountains re-echoing all around.
>
> It is biting cold. Yesterday evening when I was here, the town was already occupied by the Congress Advance forces, with the active ardent and enthusiastic help of the local inhabitants. The town had its band of Congress workers who had kept the ground prepared. At dawn today, the 'regulars' arrived to establish an administration. Within three hours of their arrival the town was properly manned. Rana authority was completely wiped out. The remaining army personnel and civilians have joined the new administration. By two o'clock the town is almost normal. The flag of the Congress flies and shines against a blue cloudless sky. The Congress volunteers, some with a new shining gun march by. People smile and offer food to them. Their initial shock and bewilderment at the suddenness of the revolution has subsided. They are obviously intrigued, surprised and flabbergasted that their own sons are working underground to burst into a bloody revolution like this.
>
> By our Special Correspondent, somewhere in Nepal.
>
> 18 November 1950

The Crucial Struggle in Biratnagar

In most other major fronts of attack the state forces had held out. Birgunj was recaptured by the state forces within the week. 'The end of November was not very hopeful for us, with reversals at several points. Our original plan to bottle up Kathmandu had failed.'[366]

Biratnagar, the bastion of the Koiralas, was the second important target. It is a fortnight's march from Kathmandu and with a natural defence of the Kosi River on one flank. 'Prime Minister Nehru had greatly helped the revolutionary cause in Nepal through seemingly an innocuous decision that India will not allow movement of troops, either of the state or the revolutionary forces, through Indian territory to reach one part of Nepal from another.'[367] It prevented the Nepal army from use of the Indian railway to move their troops but the NC men in civilian clothes could not be spotted. But the preparation for the first round of attacks at the nine 'underbelly' targets was not adequate[368]. The offensive on Biratnagar was headed by the eldest of the Koirala brothers Keshav, with Bishwa Bandhu Thapa as second in command. Thapa had left BHU to join the battle. B.P. remained in Patna to manage the nationwide operations. Girija was arrested some four months earlier while inciting people against the Rana regime, and detained in an army barrack in Biratnagar. He was now determined to get out and join the action outside. He complained to the jailor that the toilet was too dirty, and was permitted to use the open area amongst the shrubs. One evening hoodwinking the guards he slipped away from the opposite side, in his shorts. The guard realized and raised the alarm when Girija was a good distance away. The irate guards followed, blowing whistles, shouting and firing blank shots in the air; they were catching up on the gangling young man when fortunately he found a haystack to quickly hide himself. Girija made good his escape when darkness fell. He was warmly welcomed by his brothers and colleagues, and quickly immersed himself in the battle.

If external circumstances had propelled Girija into leadership of the labour movement in Biratnagar some three years earlier, the manner in which he now jumped into the vortex of action was entirely his decision, his will. During the turbulent, hectic and controversial course of his long life he showed an extraordinary blend of courage, energy and stamina. His constant mobility and ability to never forget people he met enabled him to be recognized as the chief architect of the organizational network of the Nepali Congress, the main source and vehicle of his political strength and success.

'We were about fifty men in the first Biratnagar attack,' recollects Bishwa Bandhu Thapa.[369] Many of us were political workers with little training in warfare and the rest were partially trained. The main bulk of our soldiers were Rais and Limbus. We had one sub-machine gun, some rifles and revolvers and the rest were country made guns. We captured the Land Office, where we found some money, and the jail, without much resistance; we released the prisoners. But by this time, the Governor Uttam Bikram Thapa, an able man, had shifted all the arms and ammunition of the barracks to his residential compound, which became his bastion. As soon as we commenced our attack we realized that they were too strong. They had a Bren gun and machine guns, plenty of rifles and hand bombs and about three hundred soldiers; we came under heavy fire and two of our people were killed and more injured. We had no option but to retreat. We then moved east to Jhapa, a three days' march, to capture the Rana outposts there. But again we were repulsed by a hail of bullets from the administrative office: men to my left and right were hit and I was forced to retreat to a bunker. We lost three brave men in this encounter'. The remaining men returned to their bases or found secure hideouts; some crossed the eastern border to Naxalbari in Bengal.

The Supreme Command Council of Matrika, B.P. and Subarna Shumsher recognized that they had met with reverses in important theatres of engagement, including Birgunj, Bhairawa in the west and Biratnagar. It was imperative now to capture a major township. With a strong contingent of the national army firmly stationed, Birgunj was unbreachable for the time being; the Nepali Congress had not even been able to launch a credible attack on Bhairawa. They decided to hit Biratnagar once more with a strengthened force.

The Mukti Sena commanders, Major Puran Singh and G.B. Yakthumba, advised that more men could be diverted from other theatres of engagement and drawn from the new recruits to supplement the existing manpower but they needed more weapons to breach the strong defence set up by the governor. In his memoirs M.P. Koirala reveals that at this juncture he approached Rafi Ahmad Kidwai and Shri Krishna Sinha, governor of Bihar. They 'somehow arranged' 100 pieces of rifles. This revelation contradicts B.P.'s assertion: 'we had received not a single piece of arms from India'[370]. On strength of other credible sources including Bhim Bahadur Pandey and a spate of interviews/conversations that include two luminaries in the Indian establishment (2009) closely associated with Indo-Nepal affairs (who prefer not to be quoted) one can conclude that Nehru did arrange supply of arms to NC secretly but in a controlled manner, through his 'trusted men in the provinces' and probably only after the first round of attacks had been repulsed by the state.

Be that as it may, on 10 December, the Jana Mukti Sena, equipped with superior arms and a greater number of men attacked Biratnagar again. They took control of the area outside and beyond the governor's residence and set up their base camp at the premises of the Biratnagar Jute Mill some ten kilometres away. They housed their cadre and the fighting force and stored their weapons safely. The Guest House of the Cotton Mill nearby was used to set up a rebel radio transmitting station. Bhola Chatterji helped its operation. In the absence of a professional broadcaster Tarini and sister Vijayalaxmi relayed the news and views of the party. The transmission covered a large part of the country including the capital and instilled fresh confidence amongst the people that the Rana regime was now vulnerable.

The governor had already drawn in all security forces stationed in Biratnagar to bolster the defences of his compound now standing as the final bastion of the state. The rebels laid siege to it, all guns pointing towards the enemy camp. It lasted almost a fortnight. We 'fired away 11,000 rounds on the night of the attack'[371]. The besieged governor ordered a counter attack but they fired mostly blanks as it was they who were short on ammunition now. The governor had contacted the high command in Kathmandu through a transmission set and asked for urgent reinforcements and was told it was already on the way. Two contingents were indeed dispatched, one along the postal road to the north and the other along the southern plains of Nepal. Even in ordinary circumstances the trek is of at least ten days. Now the rebels harassed them on their route. Governor Thapa sought help from the eastern headquarters at Dhankuta, one day's trek north, but they were facing their own problems. Nonetheless, the besieged garrison defended its position stoutly. B.P. and Girija now hurried back from Patna to their home town. B.P. and Tarini with some of the more eager combatants advanced on open ground (now named Shaheed Maidan) towards the compound, asking the rest to give fire cover. It was a reckless approach. 'We were greeted by a spray of bullets. Fortunately, there were some logs lying on the ground, and everyone dived for cover. We were pinned down there for hours and retreated one by one after dark.'[372] All such frontal attacks from the open maidan were repulsed with accurate firing from the well protected positions. The fluctuating battle was watched by the local people each day, from a safe distance, of course. But people were not yet fully prepared to rise en masse against the formidable forces of the Ranas.

Different experiments to assemble powerful explosives failed, even killing a Mukti Sena soldier during the trials. At last someone came up with a novel idea of converting a bulldozer into a tank. An experienced handyman used to repairing vehicles achieved the improbable task. On the thirteenth day of the siege, the makeshift tank moved into town drawing great cheer from the onlookers. It lumbered its way across the open area of the governor's compound with sharp shooters inside. This time the bullets from outside bounced back. The tractor-tank breached the side wall of the compound. A loud cheer arose from outside. The governor ordered a white flag to be raised. It was a major breakthrough for the Nepali Congress.

Some poignant tales of hatred, cruelty and revenge as well as restraint and compassion intersperse the two-month-long armed conflict. The Mukti Sena men had been enraged by the ruthless acts of the state; one of their colleagues was tortured, killed and the body thrown for the birds of prey and animals to feed[373]. Another was shot after the white flags were raised. So when the Mukti Sena men entered the residence of the governor they were in no mood to forgive those inside. 'The floor was filled with blood when we entered the house'[374]. 'One of the sons of the governor was shot in the legs and another shot dead when he ran out of the house. Yakthumba and his men were after the blood of the governor. When B.P. rushed in, 'I saw the governor, his wife and daughters, and some others in the courtyard trembling with fear ... Yakthumba was beside himself shouting that the governor must be cut down ... I pushed him away from there. In his fury, he hit a wooden pole with his khukuri and it got stuck and remained there, shaking. That is how agitated he was.' B.P. insisted that whatever the provocation, once the enemy surrenders he must be protected.

Once Biratnagar fell, the revolutionaries moved up north to Dharan, the headquarters of eastern Nepal. With its central location and the fort-like mansion of the governor, Khem Shumsher, the town combined for a formidable defence and grandeur. His daughter Preeti, recently married, her husband, a Raja from UP and their newborn daughter Madhu were on a visit. 'The entire hillside going up to the mansion was full of orange and holy *rudraksha* trees, and festive decorations to welcome us.'[375] The governor is a virtual ruler of the district. However, Dharan was in imminent danger. For the past few months contact with Kathmandu was virtually cut off 'even the soldiers had not received their salaries and could not be fully trusted'. The Jana Mukti Sena moved in after they captured Biratnagar. 'All we could do was to stack sandbags; even windows in our bedroom were blocked. Madhu, her nurse and a milch cow were secretly sent off to a relative's house.' The attack came at noon.

We heard loud war-like sounds. The Rais and Limbus were descending from the hills, faces covered with sindur, shouting and screaming, sweating and fuming menacingly, like red demons, some carrying guns and others with their khukuris aloft. Father had instructed the soldiers not to resist, and to keep the large entrance gate closed, but to open it if the leaders asked to meet him the governor. That is how we surrendered. However, we were neither threatened nor harmed.

Yakthumba was very considerate: he asked his assistant to meet 'my mother's needs and left our room'. Khem Shumsher, too, offered due hospitality during their stay in Dharan. 'Later in Kathmandu, Maharaj Mohan asked my father why we had surrendered so meekly. Obviously the old man had no idea what we went through!'

In neighbouring Dhankuta, the Thapa brothers[376] remained loyal to the state till the last days. But there was no trace of state security force here. 'The Congress was viewed by the innocent people as brigands. So on news of their approach everybody locked their front doors and remained ensconced inside. The bazaar was empty.' says Krishna. 'Then they came…we could hear them raising slogans against the Ranas and calling out 'Nepali Congress zindabad.' They were flummoxed when they saw all the doors locked up. They shouted orders to open the door. Few dared to face them. Some ran off from the back door. The telephone operator in Dhankuta ran so fast that when he stopped to rest, he fainted and died! Another man fell and fractured his leg. The leader of the group sent from Biratnagar was Tarini Koirala. There were a few local lads of course who had joined the Congress. When they reached our house they started knocking, with belligerent threats. There were less than ten of them but they had khukuris and weapons. I heard gun shots. Only another brother and I were in the house, the servants had gone away. So we ran off, out from the back door, on our way to Muga which we could defend. It took us two days to get there, avoiding the state soldiers with orders to shoot at sight any trespasser and crossing the Tomar River at midnight, using some logs and wooden planks. Our brothers had heard that I was shot dead and greeted us emotionally. That was how the Congress movement moved from village to village'.

Pitched Battles in the Eastern Hills and the Call for a Ceasefire

The victories in eastern Nepal and capture of Biratnagar, Dharan and Dhankuta were facilitated by interception of the reinforcements sent by the State from Kathmandu in between. Bhojpur is situated in the Mahabharata range about midway between Kathmandu and the eastern border of Nepal. Its headquarters, Bhojpur Bazaar, nestles atop a plateau some 1,500 metres above sea level. It commands a full view of the plains below. A full day's descent takes one to the River Arun to the east or the Sunkosi to the west, flowing south past its base, which is also the starting point of the Terai plains. The Ranas were well aware of its strategic importance. As soon as they sensed the possibility of armed insurrection of the Nepali Congress, the mukhiyas, birtawalas and zamindars wielding authority and enjoying privileges bestowed upon them by the state were summoned to designated venues, in their respective regions. Bhojpur was one such venue. Powerful functionaries of the area assembled at the governor's office-cum-residence. They were briefed by the governor about the 'anti-social, anti-national activities of a few miscreants who would be dealt with severely by the state': they had been summoned to draw a plan of action to protect government offices and civil installations of the state. On initiation of the governor the responsibility of protecting the main offices of the district was divided amongst those present. Each of them, one should understand, could commandeer scores of raitis—the working people.

The governor and the Rana rulers had assumed that those who derived their authority and privileges from the state would be its allies. This was a major miscalculation, especially in the case of the ethnic hill communities. Many of them were retired men from the British army, veterans of the World Wars and well exposed to the norms and values of the rest of the world. The rulers did favour them with privileges but then set a 'rank bar': they could not rise above the rank of subedar major. Many of those invited by the governor to support him were secretly against the Ranarchy. One, Narad Muni

Thulung, a retired British Gorkha soldier, had joined the Nepali Congress years before the launch of the armed revolution, and worked in secret to induct his people into the ranks of Nepali Congress, while he remained in the good books of the governor, as a competent English teacher. Now, eighty-seven able-bodied men, loyal to him assembled to 'protect' the offices of the district headquarters. While Thulung engaged the governor in minor matters at his residence, his followers captured all important offices without a shot being fired. Thulung reached the town centre in triumph, to address a mass public meeting organized to celebrate the capture of the district[377].

The rebel group was able to capture cash and some military hardware stored in various offices. Bhojpur remained in firm control of the rebels throughout the remaining days of the revolution. It served as a secure base for party men escaping to evade the counter attacks by the state, in disrupting the line of communication of the state forces, and to dispatch help and support around the neighbouring districts. It also assumed the role of a recruitment base for a rising number of volunteers into the Liberation Army.

One such stout volunteer was Bal Bahadur Rai[378]. He joined the Nepali Congress in Bhojpur with 'almost three-hundred-strong men ready to go to the battlefronts'. They were divided into smaller groups and sent to capture their home districts. 'A contingent of forty or fifty of us marched to Okhaldhunga, my district, with Muga Dhan Rai in command, and with twenty rifles and ammunitions.' After three days' trek north, and under cover of night they launched a surprise attack 'firing all at once'. The governor and men under his command ran off without resistance. However, the state sent a strong and well-armed force within a week and recaptured the position. Some twenty men were killed and the rest including Bala Bahadur escaped, reaching the safety of his home. The civilians, the Newars in particular, were beaten up or arrested and tortured by the state force. Many ran off to Bhojpur and 'I, too, reached that sanctuary.'

The unit of the state army that recaptured Okhaldhunga was part of a larger contingent sent to Biratnagar. Captain Khadga Bahadur Karki, a trusted and brave officer was in command, and started off confident that they would overrun the 'rag-tag rebels' scattered in different hill towns. And indeed they did succeed to some extent. But they were met with stiff resistance at Bhojpur. They realized now that in the last two or three weeks the Jana Mukti Sena had been significantly strengthened by the arms captured at several outposts, more effective distribution of the original arms cache collected in India, flown in from Burma or received later from the Indian government. At the same time, the spontaneous support from the local populace added to their numbers and fed them with vital information about the movement of the state forces. Captain Karki found that even before they reached their target destinations for the day, they were being harassed and hounded by the rebels at places and at hours when they were least prepared to respond. The attack on Bhojpur was blunted as many units such as that under Karki could not reach there.

The news of victory or success of the Congress including in key towns like Biratnagar, Dharan, Udaipur and Bhojpur energized the revolutionary forces. A call was sent out for each household to send at least one volunteer to assist the Liberation Army, with whatever weapons they possessed, khukuris, swords, country-made flint guns, and response was good 'raising our strength to almost 2,000'. They moved to Okhaldhunga again and commenced attack on the night of Aunsi, the darkest phase of the moon, from three sides, 'with loud, blood-curling cries of Shree Paanch Maharajdhiraj ko Jaya!', 'Nepali Congress zindabad! After one day of stern engagement they were able to recapture Okhaldhunga, this time they held the district for good. A provisional district government of the Nepali Congress was formed as directed by the high command, a general policy of the party nationwide.

'Some army men of the state were now in flight, at times leaving behind precious arms they had brought from Kathmandu. 'We chased them to some distance and then started our move west, with Kathmandu as our final target'. By the beginning of the New Year 1951, the greater part of eastern Nepal was in the control of the Congress command rather than of the state. But the retreating state forces still regrouped at key defence positions in the undulating mountain ranges and resisted the advance of the Mukti Sena. It was during one of these encounters that Captain Karki and a small group he was with, were isolated, surrounded and disarmed. Asked to put his arms up and accept surrender of forces under his command the captain refused; he was shot dead at point-blank range[379].

The Jana Mukti Sena men were now welcomed on their route to Kathmandu, given shelter and offered what little food they could afford by villagers. A few young men in most of these villages were ready to join the advancing army. They moved rapidly to Ramechap District where the governor sent a letter of surrender. But in Sindhuli a resolute governor, Mintu Jung Rana, and his men defended their position bravely, finally to capitulate after two full days of brittle resistance. Now the Mukti Sena was moving towards Dhulikhel one or two days' march to Kathmandu. 'There we got the orders for a ceasefire'. Prime Minister Mohan Shumsher had acceded to the reinstallation of King Tribhuwan and formation of the coalition government', Bal Bahadur concluded.

The Western Front and Palpa

Biratnagar in the eastern and Birgunj in the central sector were the most crucial of the nine towns, targeted by the Supreme Command of the NC in the first wave of their invasion. In the western zone Bhairawa was the prime target, a prize that NC failed to capture. A communiqué issued by the Nepal Embassy claimed, without much exaggeration: 'The invaders have been repulsed by the state forces from Bhairawa with severe losses'[380]. After four hours of fierce battle, Dr K.I. Singh, the leader of the attack, was forced to beat a hasty retreat. He then set up his camp some distance away from Bhairawa but was driven from one place to another by the men commanded by another capable Governor, Nir Jung Rana.

The main reason for the poor show in this sector was the bitter rivalry between K.I. Singh and Gopal Shumsher, son of Rudra. A message from King Tribhuwan assuring that he was on the side of the Nepali Congress had at last persuaded the grand old man Rudra Shumsher to extend full cooperation to the democratic movement, in 1950. Matrika Koirala had appointed Gopal 'Commander in the Palpa-Butwal-Bhairawa sector, while K.I. Singh was designated the Military Governor of Bhairawa[381]'. This modality resembled the Political Commissar and the Military Commander in communist Russia. But here the terms of reference and the chain of command was ill-defined and in any case subject to differing understanding or interpretation at the different theatres of engagement. Similar division of work or designation of titles may have been resolved amicably between compatible leaders in other theatres, but in this sector the two were divided in approach and temperament.

Gopal set up his headquarters in Nautanawa, a few miles inside the Indian border.

His base was thus safe from the state forces while he could send his men to attack the enemy inside Nepal. Furthermore, thousands of ex-Gorkha Army men were living here, so new recruits could be drawn from this source. Communication with the Supreme War Council of the Nepali Congress was much easier from here and any supply of additional material could reach the railhead in Nautanawa promptly.

K.I. Singh on the other hand set out separately with a small group of his followers and a few rifles, in the manner of Robin Hood, to roam and scour the neighbouring villages to collect, borrow or commandeer men, money and materials for the 'cause'. In a letter addressed to Matrika, the President, dated 24 November 1950, Gopal complained, 'There is a total lack of discipline in the party here. Workers and colleagues take scant heed of the order, instructions or humble request of the commander, and against the principles of democracy operate as over-commander of the commander'[382]. K.I. Singh on the other hand felt he was operating as a military commander under authority issued directly by the central command and saw no compulsion to take orders from a man who 'remained cloistered in the safety of Indian territory and had no courage to lead the men into the battlefield'. Each leader operated and engaged the enemy in the battle separately and success eluded the diluted forces.

The setback in Bhairawa sector had a numbing effect on Palpa. Tansen remained strangely quiet during the first weeks of the revolution. Some local leaders of the Nepali Congress had been arrested earlier, the rest were expecting the Mukti Sena to capture Bhairawa and then move to Palpa. On the other hand Prime Minister Mohan, certain that Rudra and his family had moved irrevocably to the side of the NC, sent a senior cousin, General Prachanda Shumsher and an able and experienced soldier/diplomat Col Chhetra Bikram Rana from Kathmandu to Palpa, with a crack force armed to the teeth. They camped well protected at a separate mansion in Tansen. They were given full authority to handle all political, military and administrative matters and instructed to keep Rudra and his household under strict vigilance. The governor and his household remained in virtual house arrest thereafter and the troops under his control immobile.

The Communist Party of Nepal in the Revolution of 1951

It was left to Kamal Raj Regmi, under the flag of the Nepali National Congress led by Dilli Raman Regmi, to tackle Palpa. Kamal Raj had 'made up his mind to be part of the revolutionaries in battle'. He was one amongst a large group of students who took the train to Patna the headquarters of NC. Most in the group joined the party and moved to different theatres of war as ordered. 'But eight or ten of us, committed to the communist ideology were eager to go to the front but not as members of the NC'. Pushpa Lall and the CPN had refused to participate in the revolution but permitted its cadre to be 'involved in the revolution to support the demands of the people'[383]. Matrika, the Supreme Commander, refused to accept the condition.

Regmi and his colleagues now took the night train to Raxaul where they met some communist leaders, including Pushpa Lall and Tulsi Lal Amatya. Kamal was advised to go to Kathmandu and help the comrades there, but the route was heavily guarded and impossible to penetrate. So he proceeded to Banaras, to meet his

Indian communist colleagues as well as Dr Regmi and decide upon his next move.

Dr Regmi told the young man that his party, the National Nepali Congress had made 'a decision to make its contribution to the revolution through non-violent means...and our party cadre worked in different districts of Nepal accordingly'[384]. Kamal Raj could operate under the NNC flag. So Kamal Raj, twenty-two years of age, braced himself to return to his hometown to wage the battle. The challenge was daunting. Even reaching Tansen was a formidable hurdle. A message was sent to Tansen to help Kamal somehow evade the state guards and the intelligence network and reach his destination. He took the train to Nautanawa and there to his relief, and pleasant surprise a long-time colleague was waiting for him. Lal Prasad Chitrakar was a natural mimic and comic. He was known affectionately as 'Lale Joker'. So it was this childhood friend, well-versed in theatrical camouflage, who turned Kamal Raj from a well-turned-out Banarasi youth into a poor Brahmin farmer from the hills engaged in selling milk! Lale Joker was now helping a country bumpkin return to his village after visiting his brother working in Nautanawa. Lale pleaded and cajoled, chatted and joked through a maze of state officers at several check posts to deliver his valuable bumpkin to the house of an activist and local leader in Tansen Bazaar, at the hour set, after sunset, but before the evening curfew time.

In the following days Regmi explained to his trusted communist comrades the reason he was 'coming to Palpa with approval to launch our unarmed revolution in the name of the NNC. Let us take out a peaceful procession with the three starred flag of that party'. Kamal Raj led a group and started the march the next morning.'[385]

The hours and days before the move are of severest stress for those involved in a 'peaceful' andolan, time to prepare the mind and body to march into the unpredictable whims of an autocratic regime. Who is going to take care of the loved ones? How do you firm up their and your own resolve? Then before you leave the young one comes up to you holding back tears, or the wife with pleading eyes. You wonder whether you are selfish, to so hurt these innocent lives. Then you tear away, with a little prayer perhaps or a red tika. You join the group and begin to march, some holding the flags. Men and women in the bazaar watch in grim silence. You look up straight and walk, as if in a trance, waiting for the armed men to appear. You are tense, scared. Do not believe those who say they are not. Will there be a baton charge or merely follow up on the order of arrests? Surely there will be no bullets flying around! Then you see the armed men approaching; the moment is upon you and the fear is gone. You are on your own and ready to face whatever comes your way.

On a bright and sunny day in the first week of the new year 1951 (Pousha 19 B.S. 2007), Kamal Raj led the protest march in mid-town Tansen. There were less than a dozen men, all from the Newar community, except Kamal Raj. The sounds of 'Down with the Rana regime' and 'Inqualab Zindabad' vibrated along the bazaar. As Kamal Raj started to deliver his speech the policemen converged and arrested the protestors. Kamal Raj recounts, 'As we were being led towards the police office Colonel Chhetra Bikram came up the incline puffing and breathing heavily. We explained which party we represented and the peaceful nature of our protests. Against all our expectations we were allowed to continue with the march.' Elated, they resumed the march, now joined by a spattering of additional men. As they passed the governor's palace, the younger generation of Rudra's family was seen waving and cheering from the windows. The marching men reached the sprawling grounds on the high plateau where the army barracks are located. Both sides refrained from confrontation. As the jubilant protestors dispersed for the day, the last rays of the setting winter sun painted the snow peaks to the north pink.

The followers of the Nepali Congress, overcome by a strange slumber so far, gathered hurriedly that evening and decided to join the protest next day. The manner in which the protestors were allowed to march emboldened the towns folk to join the march. There was a perceptible rise in the number of participants. The flags of the Nepali

Congress were now fluttering together with those of the NNC. Kamal Raj was addressing the assembled crowds at street corners, the tone and content of his speech distinctly revolutionary, his attack directed against the 'feudal society'. The Nepali Congress speakers were no less virulent but spoke against the Rana regime and called for the return of King Tribhuwan and for democracy. They demanded the release of political prisoners who had been jailed earlier—most of them noted NC leaders. By the end of the day they were released, including senior and respected leader Bhola Nath Sharma, after more than a year in prison. The order for the restriction on the movements of the aged Governor Rudra Shumsher and members of his family was also lifted.

Around this crucial point of time, Rudra Shumsher and the state troops under his command moved to the side of the revolution. The psychological effect of this action was felt throughout the country. By daybreak on the third morning the crowd on the streets of Tansen was massive. Hectic consultations between principal actors in Palpa and wireless contact with Kathmandu led General Prachanda Shumsher to hand over the weapons brought from Kathmandu to Rudra— an act of virtual surrender to the revolutionary forces. Kamal Raj and his men got wind of the transfer of weapons and felt he and his followers had been betrayed. They gathered in large numbers around the palace and demanded that the arms be handed over here and now to the revolutionary forces and not be passed from one set of Ranas to another. People found some logic in this point of view. The situation grew tense with the crowd growing restless, milling around in anger and confusion. Someone then came up with a mid-point solution, that a 'People's Government' be formed to take custody of the arms. Kamal Raj was in a minority amidst the common men, traders and the Nepali Congress men now gathered in the melee, and knew the Nepali Congress would be dominant in the new composition. Reluctantly but wisely, he agreed to the formula. Bloodshed or even a serious division within the ranks of the revolutionaries would have diluted the gains of a unique victory. The 'peaceful revolution' of Palpa was a single exception amidst the armed revolution of the Nepali Congress.

A provisional government was formed with the Nepali Congress leader Bhola Nath Sharma as the chief minister and Rudra Shumsher as military governor. Regmi and his men refrained from taking any position in the provisional government. There was much bitterness about the composition of the ministry and Regmi refused to join in until some of his key men too were offered suitable positions. This took place some weeks later.

The fall of Palpa was a 'turning point' of the armed conflict but there was more than one reason for the surrender without a bullet fired, none arrested or jailed. Prachanda was the eighth in the Roll of Succession, and Chhetra Bikram an astute and experienced officer, son of Governor Uttam Bikram who had stoutly defended Biratnagar against heavy odds. As soon as they had received intelligence reports that a home-based revolt was imminent in Tansen, the general, and his deputy had sent a wireless message directly to the prime minister's office asking for instructions on how the uprising sans arms was to be handled. There was no response. They were left in the lurch, forced to take their own decisions. Prachanda's high rank gave him access to vital information on the latest happenings in Singha Durbar and Uttam had his own links. They deduced that what they did in Palpa was of limited consequence. The fate of the Rana regime and future of the country was being decided in New Delhi. Why should they then stick out their necks against the rising power of the future when even Mohan was making his deal? Let peaceful co-existence prevail in Palpa. The crack troops sent from Kathmandu under them was reined in. The deductions of a Rana General and his second in command stuck in the remote district of Palpa were remarkably astute and clairvoyant about the ongoing moves in Delhi.

The Decisive Hand of Delhi

On reaching Delhi, King Tribhuwan was lodged at Hyderabad House a well-appointed mansion off India Gate, used for high-ranking state guests. His trusted private secretary, Daya Bhakta Mathema, was in Calcutta, recovering from an operation; 'but as soon as I heard the news of the departure of the Royal family for Delhi, I took a flight to the capital city. India was intent on supporting the freedom movement in Nepal since 1947, as was His Majesty. But within a few days in Delhi, I realized that the Indian government had its own agenda. I was allowed to visit His Majesty; he was royally treated of course, but other than that, he was...well, in 'Guest House arrest'. They decided who could call upon him and who could not.'[386].

In order to enforce its 'agenda' set by Jawaharlal Nehru, Ambassador C.P.N. Singh had succeeded in playing a devious but skilful game that brought King Tribhuwan to Delhi. The game was exposed by a careless conversation between Nehru and C.P.N. on the wireless picked up by Kathmandu Radio and heard clearly all over Nepal. The prime minister commended his ambassador for execution of this intricate task. Known for his measured diplomatic utterances, General Daman Shumsher, Consul General of Nepal in Calcutta those days, writes that while the Nepalese people were grateful to India for 'liberating the popular and beloved king from the clutches of Rana usurpers' they also felt 'an uneasy chill in their hearts to find a great county like India perpetrating undiplomatic activities in a small country like Nepal'.

With the king under their protection in Delhi, Nehru and the Indian establishment felt content. They could now engineer the agenda of the 'middle way', advocated by Nehru, and worked out in greater precision later. He had also cautioned the leaders of the Nepali Congress against launching a major insurgency from India into Nepal. That would be an embarrassment to Delhi, and Nehru in particular: one of the tenets of the non-aligned movement conceived and led by a triumvirate of Presidents, Tito of Yugoslavia, Nasser of Egypt and Nehru, was non-interference in the affairs of another country. Nehru wanted the Nepali Congress to merely create a condition of unrest, 'Then we will manage the rest'. But the Nepali Congress, jolted by the alarming news of the king's entry into the Indian Embassy mobilized their entire strength. The capture of Birgunj had been a great source of celebration for the Nepali Congress and the news flashed with elation by the Indian media; but Nehru was 'furious'. And the fall out of this displeasure had to be borne by the leaders of the Nepali Congress. As narrated earlier, a handsome bonus of military hardware and cash worth thirty-five lakh Indian rupees had fallen into the hands of the Nepali Congress when they captured Birgunj. While the arms were distributed at the fields of engagement, the Nepali Congress leadership decided to carry the cash to Delhi to be handed over to the monarch now residing in Hyderabad House for safekeeping. Matrika, B.P., their sister Vijayalakshmi and the Shumshers (Subarna and Mahavir) took a plane to Delhi from Patna with this valuable booty. When the plane landed in Delhi it was surrounded by gun-toting security forces; while the other passengers disembarked and went their ways, the five leaders were detained inside the airport premises and treated like a 'band of thieves or criminals'. On being told that they wanted to hand over the cash to the king as a custodian, the security men responded in a condescending manner that the property robbed from the state of Nepal would be taken over by the Indian government as it was brought inside India illegally. The authorities ensured that the process of taking full count of the cash, locking them in a container and sealing it with signatures of both sides lasted all night. Tired and furious the NC leaders were released before daybreak next morning. For two days they could not meet Nehru and eventually he 'condescended' to see the two brothers, separately. Matrika in particular had to face the brunt of Nehru's fury. Nehru even threatened to lock them up. Eventually, as was his nature, he cooled down, and explained the delicate position of India in the international forum. But the trip had been humiliating and futile. They were not allowed to meet the king, and Nehru refused any material support for the revolution, though he did not ask them to withdraw it.

They went back chastened to their respective fields of operation. The news from the battlefronts was no better in the month of December. The downturn in the fortunes of the Nepali Congress was a fresh impetus for the Rana hierarchy. The army, police and the civil administration had stood firmly with the state, Birgunj was easily recaptured and most other important towns had repulsed the attack of the rebels. True, linkage with some districts was difficult but now planes were hired to drop bundles of banknotes to these isolated positions[387].

Prime Minister Mohan approved of a proposal to send a high-level delegation to Delhi to assure the Indian government first that within days, his government would introduce new reforms to allow a significant induction of the representatives of the people including the Nepali Congress into the governing process and second, carry a proposal to form a 'Regency Council' to act on behalf of the monarch, meaning Gyanendra, until such time as the issue of succession was resolved. In the last week of November, the witty Keshar Shumsher, now ranked third in the Roll of Succession, accompanied by Vijay Shumsher, each with full command over the English language were sent to Delhi for a dialogue with India. On reaching Delhi they made an immediate impact. 'The noise of the Indian press,' they declared, 'is louder than that of the guns of the Nepalese rebels', a statement that even B.P. admitted later was in fact true. But then the Indian establishment was not ready to take the bait. They were not as impolite to the senior representatives of another country as they had been to the Nepali Congress leaders a couple of weeks back. The delegates called upon the prime minister and met with other senior ministers and put forward the new proposals of their government. But they were denied the opportunity to meet King Tribhuwan even though his sister was married to Keshar. They cooled their heels and waited for a breakthrough for more than a week.

On 6 December 1950 Nehru clearly stated his government's policy on Nepal in the House of Parliament:

> As the House knows the King of Nepal is in Delhi with two other members of the Nepalese government. Needless to say, we pointed out to the ministers that we desire above all a strong, progressive and independent Nepal. In fact our chief need, and that of the whole world, is peace and stability. We have tried to advise Nepal to act in a manner so as to prevent any

major upheaval—a middle way which will ensure progress of
Nepal and introduction of some advance towards democracy.
We have searched for a way, which would at the same time
avoid total uprooting of the ancient order.[388]

A couple of days later, without any reference to the proposals brought
from the Government of Nepal by Keshar and Vijay, a memorandum
of a five-point proposal unilaterally drawn up by the Government of
India was delivered to them. The contents went against the interests
of the Rana rulers. To add to their consternation, Britain, long-
time friends of the Ranas, was constrained to abandon their initial
intent to recognize Gyanendra. The mission returned to Kathmandu,
downcast.

The Five-Point Proposal

The five-point proposal set the tone for the formula finally accepted
in January 1951 by the three protagonist power centres. Ironically,
the arrangement came to be known as 'The Delhi Compromise'.

- Tribhuwan to be reinstated as the king of Nepal.
- Formation of a cabinet led by the Rana prime minister but
  inclusive of representatives of the people.
- Release of all political prisoners.
- Right to form political parties to be recognized.
- Members of a constituent assembly elected on the basis of
  adult suffrage to draft a new constitution.

The proposal to reinstate Tribhuwan was particularly agonizing to
the ruling Ranas. Serious objections were raised by the still-dominant
hardliners at Singha Durbar. Vijay was again sent as head of a
delegation to Delhi with a counter-proposal that recommended the
early election of a Constituent Assembly which would then decide
whether Tribhuwan or his grandson Gyanendra should continue
as king. Nehru refused to meet the delegation. Indeed he made a
stern statement in Parliament that warned of the possibility of a

grave situation regarding peace and security for Nepal should the Government of Nepal fail to address the issue of political reforms satisfactorily and in good time.

The situation inside the country was even more fragile for the fortunes of the Rana regime. By the beginning of 1951 the Jana Mukti Sena had scored a series of victories not only along the border towns but even in the middle hills. The reports in the Indian press left no doubt that the negotiations in Delhi were heading towards a formation of a Rana–Congress coalition government with Mohan as the prime minister and five ministers from each side, in a cabinet of ten.

In Singha Durbar, the Shumshers, Jungs, Narsings or Bikrams, as well as the bhardars could sense the approach of impending change. The group of A-class Ranas who had secretly joined the Nepal Democratic Congress in Calcutta in 1949, felt the time had arrived to make a concerted move. 'We began to probe into the minds of those who were showing disenchantment, seeking out the most vulnerable links in the chain. Many C-class sons of Juddha including Kiran and Surendra, even the mercurial A-class grandson Nara, and Nirpa Jung who was brought up in India were the first to find common cause with our stand'. Gradually the group expanded; they started to meet secretly at different private residences, to deflect suspicions. Himalaya suggested that the division of 5-5 was fair but since Mohan did not hold the confidence of all the Ranas, he as prime minister should nominate two but the other two should be elected by all Ranas present. A consensus was reached on this basis and a letter drafted accordingly. 'We went from house to house to get it signed by as many as possible. Surprisingly even the dreaded Bahadur and the younger Subarna handpicked by Maharaj Mohan as advisor in matters of the constitution signed it. The number reached 120. Nara was chosen to carry it for submission to the King in Delhi, and through him to GOI.[389]

From the vortex of the revolutionaries Bhuwan Lal Pradhan writes, 'These acts of desertion made at a time when the fall of the Rana regime was certain, lays bare the selfishness of those who throughout their lives had taken all the special benefits available to them under the protective umbrella of the all powerful family oligarchy and then abate their links with that very family when it was obvious personal gains could be derived no more.' Much later, during his retired life in Bangalore, a physically enfeebled ex-Maharaj Mohan observed, 'India was against me, the king was against me and naturally the Congress, and finally even my own kith and kin who benefited so much from us betrayed us...so I had no choice but to give in. But you will agree that the cost of change could have been much more damaging to the Ranas as well as the country, had I remained adamant.'[390]

The beleaguered prime minister called a meeting of the Ranas and the bhardars. The same congregation of haughty courtiers who had demanded the ouster of King Tribhuwan less than a hundred days earlier now entered Singha Durbar. Some inwardly happy and others in a sombre mood placed their signature on a document that in essence surrendered the unfettered authority of governance that the Rana rulers had exercised for more than a hundred years. The next day, on 8 January, Shree Teen Maharaj Mohan Shumsher Jung Bahadur Rana, now a lone, weary, outmanoeuvred and politically defanged prime minister, issued a proclamation that accepted all conditions of the five-point proposal, with the addition of a few minor procedural directives. The government sent orders to the governors and military commanders posted in all the districts to avoid military confrontation with the 'antinational' elements, but in any case not to open fire except as a last resort of self-defence.

Matrika Koirala camped at Gorakhpur, learnt about the declaration of Mohan through an Indian newspaper. As the 'dictator' of the revolution he made his resentment clear. The party should have been consulted before any such declaration, which in any case should have come from the king and not the prime minister. Though he had no quarrel with the theory of equal distribution of ministerial positions between the Ranas and 'the representatives of the people' the very name of the Nepali Congress the rightful representative was missing. It was an act of betrayal against the people[391]. To the dismay of the Nepali Congress camp, King Tribhuwan issued a statement in Delhi, welcoming and giving his stamp of approval to the announcement. B.P. was in Biratnagar, unaware of the rapid turn of events elsewhere when he saw pamphlets being dropped by a small aeroplane flying over the area. He picked up one that landed nearest to him, as must have been done by tens of thousands of the people over the hills and plains of the country. He read the statement of the king and his appeal for the Rana government and the Congress to hold a ceasefire and work together. B.P. was livid. 'What right does he have to do this? He has not even given the order to fight so how can he demand a ceasefire?' he fumed and in his rage ordered the gun man next to him to shoot at the aircraft. He retracted from his spontaneous outburst in time[392]. The Nepali Congress decided that unless their demands were met they would continue with the military action within Nepal. The leaders assembled in Patna and were conferring on ways and means to move forward when C.P.N. Singh reached the city. He invited Matrika, B.P. and Subarna to meet him. 'There he was, talking as an emissary of India and also that of the King of Nepal!' rues B.P.[393]. His Majesty, they were told, had asked that a tri-partite meeting be held at an appropriate venue. B.P.'s suggestion of Kathmandu was rejected on grounds of guarantee of security and Biratnagar which was in control of Nepali Congress was shot down as there was no proper venue to house His Majesty in that town. So it was to be Delhi and reluctantly they agreed. 'With our hands tied up...we reached Delhi,' writes Matrika. There they learnt that Nehru, on whom they had placed their hopes, was in London to attend the Commonwealth Conference. His acceptance of the statement of Mohan and of the King was relayed to them. Soon India as well as Britain issued statements welcoming the message of the king.

Meanwhile in Nepal, while the state army avoided confrontation, the Liberation Army continued to 'capture' several districts in different parts of the country, with no more than token resistance. In each place, a provisional government was formed and in essence, the administration of practically every district outside of the Kathmandu valley, barring notable exceptions like Bhairawa in the west and Jaleshwar in the east, was assumed by the Nepali Congress-led teams. The Nepali Congress declared a ceasefire on 16 January more than a week after the Nepal army had placed their guns to rest.

In Delhi, they demanded that the 50 per cent representation from the 'people' in the cabinet, as proposed in the five-point proposal should be nominees of the NC, and key ministries such as home and finance, headed by them. Negotiations followed in earnest thereafter, with India as the self-appointed arbitrator. Prime Minister Nehru headed his team, with the Foreign Secretary Girija Shankar Bajpai and C.P.N. Singh as the main assistants. Visitors to King Tribhuwan were screened and 'security personnel' always placed in close attendance. The Nepali Congress leaders were taken to Hyderabad House once for an audience and no more. The Ranas and the Nepali Congress leaders were never allowed to meet across a table. Both sides were invited at the public function to celebrate 26 January at the open grounds of Rajpath. During a casual encounter B.P. made a special point of wishing Vijay Shumsher but that was the end of their contact. It was C.P.N. Singh who moved from one to the other, or invited the leader he chose, to meet him separately; B.P. considered to be an 'impetuous and excitable' man as compared to the more reasonable elder brother 'who understands Nepal's politics', was often excluded and invited only in meetings called by Nehru. After a few weeks of such unsubtle diplomacy B.P. heard one day. 'It had been done.'

The Rana–Nepali Congress coalition government, with the king presiding as the 'constitutional' head, was a non-starter from its very inception. The manner in which Delhi manipulated the deal rankled the sensibilities of King Tribhuwan and the Congress leaders, and the Rana rulers were of course the most aggrieved of the three. C.P.N. Singh, true to his Machiavellian temperament, continued to act in an exemplary show of bad taste even after the coalition government was formed. B.P. remembers, 'At that juncture (coalition government) the man who represented India had a very narrow outlook with a feudal background. I told him that he did not function as the representative of India, but of the Muzaffarpur District Board (he was the chairman of that board once).[394] The Communist Party of Nepal castigated the Delhi compromise as a deception. The Rashtrabadi Gorkha Parishad, the principal opposition party of those days, accused the Nepali Congress of being a dalal (broker) of India. Who then was left to appreciate the intervention of the Government of India? India, thereon, was viewed as an interfering bully instead of a benevolent elder brother. It is such a pity, since the ardent and vocal support of the people of India and its media had hastened the emergence of Nepal out of the morass of an outdated family dictatorship.

The Final Curtain Fall

The proclamation of Maharaj Mohan was received coolly by the residents of Kathmandu. The contents of the document did not convince the politically alert civil society that the Rana rulers had indeed surrendered to the demands of the people. Mohan Shumsher was to continue as prime minister. Was this then, the end goal of the revolution? Most people did not believe that the process of the transfer of power would be facile. Those waging hard battles in their respective areas of engagement felt let down. In the districts several groups of the Liberation Army, joined now by increasing numbers of the local adventurists did not surrender their weapon and continued to loot and plunder. The unpredictable maverick Dr K.I. Singh openly defied the party orders and continued to wage battle in the western parts of the country.

Five prisoners were locked inside an especially secure cell appropriately named 'black hole' in the Central Jail of Kathmandu. Four leaders of the Praja Parishad, including Tanka Prasad and Ramhari Sharma, convicted in 1940, and Khadga Man Singh, the only man of the Prachanda Gorkha group who had managed to survive the inhuman conditions since 1932. Several other regular cells housed some three hundred political prisoners convicted of 'lesser crimes'. The news of the general amnesty took a few days to reach them. The relief felt in personal terms was matched by a sense of satisfaction that their years of struggle and suffering had not been in vain. Release order came for those housed in the central jail excluding Khadga Man Singh. The Praja Parishad leaders and some others in the outer cells refused to leave without the veteran Khadga Man. The Rana rulers were in no condition now to withstand such a pressure. By the end of January they were all released. 'Thousands of jubilant men and women had assembled outside, in the Tundikhel grounds to greet and cheer us,' recollects Ramhari Sharma, now past eighty, his deep grey eyes far away. He remembers they were lifted by unknown people and carried to the New Road gate and asked to address the crowd but then 'all I remember is my neighbour, taking me home in his car. Other leaders too reached their respective homes. It was about eight in the evening and it was pitched dark'.

There was a strange lull in the rallies and protests in days that followed their release. Sharma explains the reason: 'Imagine how we felt to be free of the heavy iron shackles cramped in the darkness of those cells, and then meet our families after ten long years. You know, I had to be introduced to my daughter!' But there were other reasons. Other principal leaders including Tanka Prasad Acharya had reached Delhi to stake claim in the coalition government. They found that the Nepali Congress had assumed the exclusive right to nominate its nominees for the ministerial posts. All eyes and ears had turned to the Indian capital. Nepal entered a phase of arrested animation.

Ganesh Man Singh and his colleagues held in Singha Durbar learnt about the message of Mohan sooner. He was told the king, and then the Indian government welcomed Mohan's proclamation. Ganesh Man was agonized. Why should the Nepali Congress on the brink of total victory condescend to accept that same dictator as prime minister? He was some what relieved when Nara Shumsher came on a visit and told him that the president of the party Matrika had rejected the arrangement of coalition government as unacceptable, through a statement in *The Hindu*. But on a cold and freezing day, the first of Magh (mid-January), a festive day for the Nepalese the NC President took a U-turn: he announced a ceasefire through the All India Radio and appealed to all party men and commanders to support the peace process. Ganesh Man felt that 'the revolution was aborted'. He sent a message to the leaders that he opposed the Delhi compromise, and after his release rejected the offer of a ministerial post in the cabinet. It took all the powers of persuasion of not only the collective leadership of the party but even King Tribhuwan, for him to digest the internal and external compulsions that led to this decision and eventually to be part of the team again.

The leaders of the Nepali Congress were busy working out the logistics of the transition of power. A peaceful atmosphere in the valley was a prerequisite for the return of the king and his entourage as well as the Nepali Congress leaders. The loyalty of the state army and of the civil administration towards the new government-in-making or indeed towards King Tribhuwan could not be taken for granted. A trusted follower of the royal family, Col Yog Bikram Rana was summoned to Delhi during the first week of February and assigned the delicate task of paving the way for a smooth transition. Although his sympathies and loyalty lay with the king, he was not inimical to the interests of Mohan and the ruling Ranas. He was in touch with them and was no doubt aware that at this point of time the perception of fear was far greater amongst the Ranas. The position of the once all-powerful prime minister was unenviable.

> He used to go for leisurely strolls in the gardens of Singha Durbar or a ride in his limousine in the late afternoons everyday. He stopped doing so after 8 January—the day he announced acceptance of the Delhi compromise. Chakaridars, who had attended his palace for their entire adult lives, started to desert him in ones. By the beginning of the month of February, Singha Durbar looked deserted…like a cemetery where only ghosts of the past lingered. The selfish Chakaridars moved quietly and scurried out of the palace like rats do from a granary, once all the grain is emptied. Mohan Shumsher was seen strolling alone deep in thought along the long open balcony on the

top floor of Singha Durbar where the national flag flutters, his bushy moustache untended, bent over in dark mood—like an old, lone tiger walking about inside the cage of the zoo.[395]

The Triumphant Return of King Tribhuwan

Yog Bikram reached Delhi and called upon His Majesty at Hyderabad House. He briefed the king carefully about the conditions in Kathmandu and the Rana palaces, and then sought and carried an assurance from the monarch for the guarantee of safety for the Rana rulers. Tribhuwan was understanding and gracious in response. 'I am not angry with Mohan. It is on Jung Bahadur that I ought to place the blame. Mohan merely carried out my orders.' There was discernable relief on Mohan's weary face when he heard these words of assurance[396]. The prime minister summoned his brother Keshar, now in command of the army, and directed him to follow the suggestions of Yog Bikram. Trusted generals and senior officers were briefed to follow the instructions from Yog Bikram and assigned duty inside the Royal palace. Those who had shifted their allegiance to the new order, such as Nara, Kiran or Toran, were handpicked for critical positions or duties. Nara was to escort His Majesty when he alighted from the aircraft in Kathmandu.

The date for the return of the royal family was scheduled for 15 February. The Congress leaders in Delhi were informed a few days ahead that the royal entourage will reach Kathmandu in the afternoon in an aircraft made available by GoI. Ganesh Man and the NC group in Singha Durbar had expected that they would be released soon after those in the Central Jail were set free. But instead they were transferred to the Central Jail and remained there for close to a month. Many speculate that the Rana rulers kept them as prisoners as a last desperate card in hand. Only two days before the 15th, Ganesh Man was told that they were free to go home. A general amnesty had been declared. In order to avoid crowd stampede, they will be released one by one. The 'iron man' at last walked out into the bright midday sun. 'I was breathing the air of Kathmandu freely under an open sky after ten years. Never before had I felt the beauty and joys of Kathmandu as I did on that day.' The people were now gathering rapidly to felicitate their leader, round the Khari tree at the mid-point of Tundikhel, the symbol of the authority of the Rana oligarchy. A Newar, a mere plebeian, had challenged and brought down the citadel of the Ranas. The next few hours witnessed a public spectacle and celebrations in the Tundikhel and on the streets of Kathmandu as never seen before. The sounds of 'Bir Ganesh Man Zindabad' rent the air. It was to remain his constant inspiration till he took his last breath in September 1997.

Two days later the royal family was to return to the capital, followed by leaders of the revolution. Kathmandu was decorated with festive banners and flags and welcome gates all the way to the Gauchar airport.[397] Loud cheers went up as the aircraft entered the valley and touched down. King Tribhuwan was at the height of his popularity those days, as a monarch who risked the throne in support of the democratic cause. He emerged from the aircraft immaculately dressed in the traditional Nepali style. He raised his right hand, holding a roll of paper, indicating a draft of the new constitution that would free the country from the oppressive Rana regime. One of the cameramen captured the historic picture that was to remain the symbol of the advent of democracy in Nepal for many decades. The royal cavalcade moved to the palace, between rows of cheering crowd, and amidst flower petals, vermillion and auspicious offerings and chant of 'Maharajdhiraj ko Jaya'. Some hours later, the Nepali Congress leaders emerged from another aircraft to be similarly greeted by the ecstatic and more boisterous crowd. The words of the chant were suitably altered to 'Prajatantra amar rahos' (may democracy thrive forever), and 'Bir Bishweshwar zindabad'. The victory parade lasted till late in the evening.

Within the next two days the details of the new arrangement were finalized. The decision about the prime minister (Mohan), ministers, five from the Rana side and five from NC, had been reached in Delhi. The Ministry of Home went to B.P., Defence to

Baber, Finance to Subarna and Industry and Commerce to Ganesh Man. The 'lesser' ministries went to the rest. Two from the Rana side were nominated by Mohan; two others, one Rana from outside the Roll of Succession and one from amongst the bhardars were elected, by general consensus, but did not necessarily owe allegiance to Mohan. For the order of precedence the Nepali Congress claimed the second position, since the prime minister was a Rana. Baber Shumsher pleaded that as a senior minister, a title he held earlier for two years, he should not be denied the rightful honour. The matter was resolved amicably when B.P. graciously accepted 'the wish of an older man'.

On 18 February 1951 (the seventh day of Falgun 2007 B.S.), King Tribhuwan delivered the historic proclamation. In essence the monarch:

- Abrogated the authority bestowed by King Surendra Bikram in 1846 upon Jung Bahadur, to rule as prime minister until his death and thereafter in perpetuity to his family.
- Declared that hereafter governance of 'our subjects' be carried out according to a republican constitution drafted by a constituent assembly to be elected by the people under adult franchise.
- Constituted a Council of Ministers consisting of representatives of the people 'commanding their trust, in order to advise and assist us in carrying out the functions of the state, that will be responsible to us and hold their respective offices in accordance to our wish, until such time as the constitution comes into effect.'

It is to be assumed that King Tribhuwan derived his authority on the basis of the ancient theory of the divine rights of the king, which his predecessors had claimed. The evolution of the political history of Nepal hovered fitfully around this issue until 2008.

Notes

1   Thapar, Romila, *A History of India: Volume One*, New Delhi: Penguin Books India, 1990.

2   Chinmayananda, Swami, *The Holy Geeta*, Sri Ram Batra, Central Chinmaya Mission Trust, chapter IV, verse 13.

3   Whelpton, John, *History of Nepal*, Cambridge University Press.

4   Gurung, Dr Harka, *Nature and Culture: Random Reflections*, Kathmandu: Saroj Gurung, 1989.

5   Rana, Jagadish, *Nepal: A Concise History of the Cultural Scenario of the Himalayan Kingdom*, Nirala, 1996.

6   Tuker, Sir Francis, *Gorkha: The Story of the Gurkhas of Nepal*, Pilgrims Publishing, 2009.

7   Regmi, Mahesh, *An Economic History of Nepal: 1846–1901*, Nath Publishing House, 1988; Stiller, Dr F. Ludwig, *The Rise of the House of Gorkha*, Human Resources Development Research Centre, 1995 and *The Silent Cry: The People of Nepal, 1816–1839*, Sahayogi Prakashan, 1976.

8   It was only in 1955 that an adult man, Crown Prince Mahendra, succeeded his father, King Tribhuwan.

9   Acharya, Baburam, *Shri 5 Pratapsingh Shah*, Kathmandu: Pilgrims Publishing, 2013.

10 Tuker, Sir Francis, *Gorkha: The Story of the Gurkhas of Nepal*, Pilgrims Publishing, 2009.

11 Sever, Adrian, *Nepal under the Ranas*; United Kingdom: Asia Publishing House.

12 Landon, Perceval, *Nepal*, Constable and Company Limited, 1928.

13 Tuker, Sir Francis, *Gorkha: The Story of the Gurkhas of Nepal*, Pilgrims Publishing, 2009.

14 Records of letters and reports are available in the British Embassy Library, Kathmandu.

15 Interview with Surendra Chaudhary whose ancestors fought in the war, 8 November 2009.

16 Tuker, Sir Francis, *Gorkha: The Story of the Gurkhas of Nepal*, Pilgrims Publishing, 2009.

17 Capital of the Kaurava and Pandava rulers in the epic Mahabharata.

18 Raj Guru and Mukhtiyar, 1837–38.

19   Whelpton, John, *A History of Nepal*, Cambridge University Press, 2005.

20   It was the caption besides a large portrait of Wellesley in Victoria Memorial, Calcutta.

21   Spear, Percival, *A History of India*, Penguin Books, 1965.

22   From records of correspondence and news cuttings of those times at the British Embassy, Kathmandu.

23   Kaini, Bhiravraj, *Nepal ma Krishi Vikas*.

24   Rose, E. Leo, W. Fisher Margaret, *The Politics of Nepal: Persistence and Change in an Asian Monarchy*, Cornell University Press, 1970.

25   Selection and translation by author.

26   Dixit, Kamal, *Janga Bahadur ko Belayati Kapy*, Nepal: Jagadamba Prakashan, 2046 B.S.

27   Sever, Adrian, *Nepal under the Ranas*, United Kingdom: Asia Publishing House.

28   Tuker, Sir Francis, *Gorkha: The Story of the Gurkhas of Nepal*, Pilgrims Publishing, 2009.

29   Present districts of Kailali, Kanchanpur, Banke and Bardia.

30   Percival Landon, who inspected some of the priceless items.

31   A bejewelled headdress with long, flowing, snow-white plumes from the bird of paradise.

32   Described in full in a report to Jung by Siddhi Man Singh.

33   Tod, James, William Crooke, *Annals and Antiquities of Rajasthan*, vol. 1, Oxford University Press, 1829.

34   Rana, Greta, *Hidden Women: The Ruling Women of the Rana Dynasty*, Roli Books, 2012.

35   Dixit, Mani Kamal, *Jung Gita*.

36   Rana, Pramode S.J.B., *A Chronicle of Rana Rule*, Kathmandu: R. Rana, 1999

37   Born out of wedlock and/or in cohabitation with 'non-marriageable castes' according to the Hindu code in practice.

38   Agnatic system of succession.

39   This palace was later converted into the official residence of the monarchs of Nepal and remained so right up to 2006, when Nepal was declared a republic.

40   Grandfather of B.P. Koirala.

41   Koirala, B.P., *Afno Katha*, Shajha Prakashan, 2014.

42   A railway line was constructed to connect Calcutta with Darjeeling. From here the land route via Sikkim to Lhasa passed through lower altitudes and easier terrain. The caravans of mules and then yaks could reach Lhasa in three weeks, whereas the Calcutta–Kathmandu–Lhasa trail took six weeks.

43 Sever, Adrian, *Nepal under the Ranas*, United Kingdom: Asia Publishing House.

44 Rana, Purusottam S.J.B., *Shree Teen Haruko Tahya Brittanta*, Part 1, Kathmandu: Bidyarthi Pustak Bhandar (second edition published B.S. 2059).

45 'Antarashtriya Manchama Prithvi Bahadur Singh', translation by Gajendra Bahadur Singh.

46 Dixit, Kashinath Acharya, *Bhaeka Kura*, Kathmandu: Johripal, B.S. 2031.

47 Dixit, Mani Kamal, *Chandra Jyoti*.

48 Tuker, Sir Francis, *Gorkha: The Story of the Gurkhas of Nepal*, Pilgrims Publishing, 2009.

49 Sever, Adrian, *Nepal under the Ranas*, United Kingdom: Asia Publishing House.

50 He did produce one son out of wedlock but ensured that both the maid and the son remained low-profile.

51 Descendants born out of wedlock.

52 Rana, Pramode S.J.B., *A Chronicle of Rana Rule*, Kathmandu: R. Rana, 1999.

53 Letter from Lord Curzon, Viceroy of India, to King Prithvi Bir Bikram Shah, 24 July 1901.

54 Sever, Adrian, *Nepal under the Ranas*; United Kingdom: Asia Publishing House.

55 In the week-long hunt, some five hundred elephants helped King George alone 'bag' eighteen tigers, eight rhinos, some bears, leopards and 'lesser' game.

56 Only five maharajas among the princely states of India were entitled to the maximum honour of a twenty-one gun salute.

57 Sever, Adrian, *Aspects of Modern Nepalese History*, Vikas Publishing House.

58 Spear, Percival, *History of Nepal*, Penguin Books, 1965.

59 *Reminiscence of Mrigendra S.J.B. Rana* (author's father), not yet published, is with the author.

60 Sama, Balakrishna, *Mero Kavita ko Araadhana*.

61 Those not permitted by the scriptures to don the sacred thread.

62 *Reminiscences of Mrigendra S.J.B. Rana* (author's father), not yet published, is with him.

63 *Kunwar Ranaharu ko Brihat Banshavali*, Panchayan Publishers.

64 The army handled both external and internal security those days.

65 Vadivelu, A., *The Ruling Chiefs, Nobles and Zamindars of India*, Madras: G.C. Loganadham Bros., The Guardian Press, 1915.

66 Sever, Adrian, *Nepal under the Ranas*; United Kingdom: Asia Publishing

House.

67   Shah, Rishikesh, *History of Nepal.*

68   Professor Bhadra Ratna Bajracharya, scholar on Buddhist religion and President of Lotus Research Centre and College, Interviewed on 1 April 2010.

69   Dr Ramesh Dhugel.

70   Spear, Percival, *A History of India.*

71   Pradhan, Bhuwan Lal, *Nepal ko Janakranti.*

72   From the *Memorial Issue of Tulsi Mehr,* edited by Jeevan Chandra Koirala. Interview with Rudra Raj Mulmi, 16 March 2010. Born in 1921, Mulmi came in contact with Tulsi Mehr at the age of eighteen and has served ever since as an executive secretary or office bearer of organizations established or promoted by Tulsi Mehr.

73   Rana, Pramode S.J.B., *A Chronicle of Rana Rule,* Kathmandu: R. Rana, 1999.

74   *Reminiscence of Mrigendra S.J.B. Rana* (author's father), not yet published, is with the author.

75   Sever, Adrian, *Nepal under the Ranas,* United Kingdom: Asia Publishing House.

76   Acharya, Dr Raj, *Prime Minister Bhim Shumsher and Nepal of His Days.*

77   Dixit, Kasinath Acharya, *Bhaeka Kura.* This portion has been translated by the author.

78   Interview with Dr Ramesh Dhungel, a grandson of Janak, 30 December 2008.

79   Rana, Pramode S.J.B., *A Chronicle of Rana Rule,* Kathmandu: R. Rana, 1999.

80   From records at the British Embassy, Kathmandu.

81   Interview with Himalaya Rana, August 2008.

82   In conversation with the author decades later, in the mid-sixties.

83   Adhikary, Dr Surya Mani, *History of Democratic Rebellion in Nepal.*

84   Singh, Khadga Man, *Twenty Years in Jail.*

85   Ranga Nath was released through the intervention of one of his benefactors after three years.

86   Khadga, Man Singh, *Twenty Years in Jail;* Dr Rajesh Gautam, *Prachanda Gorkha: A Study.*

87   Rana, Pramode S.J.B., *A Chronicle of Rana Rule,* Kathmandu: R. Rana, 1999.

88   Sama, Balakrishna, *Mero Kavita ko Araadhana.*

89   Ibid.

90   *Reminiscence of Mrigendra S.J.B. Rana* (author's father), not yet published,

is with the author.

91 Shumsher, Brahma, *The Earthquake of 1990*. He was assigned the task of reconstruction and rehabilitation.

92 Summarized from accounts of Purusottam Rana, Pramode Rana and Balakrishna Sama.

93 Lt Gen. Sir Francis Tuker.

94 Sir Geoffrey Betham, British resident of that time.

95 Prabhakar Rana, great grandson of Dev Shumsher, interviewed on 29 June 2008.

96 Bada Kaji was the highest position in the civil administration, outside of the Rana hierarchy.

97 Sever, Adrian, *Nepal under the Ranas*, United Kingdom: Asia Publishing House.

98 Ibid.

99 Tuker, Sir Francis, *Gorkha: The Story of the Gurkhas of Nepal*, Pilgrims Publishing, 2009.

100 Sever, Adrian, *Nepal under the Ranas*, United Kingdom: Asia Publishing House.

101 Interview with Kunda Dixit, author/publisher.

102 Pradhan, Bhuwan Lal, *Nepal ko Janakrantik Andolan 2007 (People's Revolution of Nepal 1951)*, p. 81.

103 Compounder is the designation given to an allopathic medical practitioner, who is short of a degree of a doctor. The royal palace and each of the high-ranking Rana palaces maintained one allopathic and one Ayurvedic medical room, each well stocked with essential medicines and operated by a compounder and a Vaidya Raj (an Ayurvedic doctor). As mentioned in another Chapter, there were only two qualified doctors in Kathmandu, possibly in the whole of Nepal, until well into the late forties!

104 Sama, Balakrishna, *Mero Kavita ko Araadhana*. The extract has been translated by the author.

105 From records at the British Embassy, Kathmandu.

106 Sever, Adrian, *Aspects of Modern Nepalese History*.

107 Basnet, Mathbar Singh, *Ganesh Man Singh: Pages of My Story*, Part I.

108 Then the largest and one of the most affluent princely states in India.

109 Sever, Adrian, *Aspects of Modern Nepalese History*.

110 Ibid.

111 Vadivalu, A., *Ruling Chiefs and Nobles of India 1816*; Sir Walter Lawrence, *Ruling Princes and Chiefs of India*, Lahore: Sang-e-Mil Publications.

112 Author is the Founder President of the Handicraft Association of Nepal, founded 1968.

113 Interview with Hari Bahadur K.C., March 2010.

114 Sama, Balakrishna, *Mero Kavita ko Araadhana*, 'Nirashabadi ra Koeli', poem no. 79.

115 *Reminiscence of Mrigendra S.J.B. Rana* (author's father), not yet published, is with the author.

116 Satya Mohan Joshi, interviewed on 12 August 2007. He was a young civil officer in 1940s and is now a respected senior citizen.

117 Slightly less spectacular than that of the maharaj.

118 See Part II, Chapter Two for details.

119 Rose, Leo E., Margaret W. Fisher, *The Politics of Nepal*.

120 Minister in current equation.

121 Even in the palaces of Kathmandu many children learnt and chanted these verses before they were introduced to the Nepali or English alphabets. The author was one of them.

122 Pandey, Sardar Bhim Bahadur, *Nepal of Those Days*, pp. 116–133.

123 Sharma, Ramhari, *Atma Brittanta*, 2001.

124 Pandey, Sardar Bhim Bahadur, *Nepal of Those Days*, Part II.

125 Some of the stores in Asan and Bhotahity area still survive, a few still deal in educational material.

126 Pradhan, Bhuwan Lal, *Nepal ko Janakrantik Andolan 2007 (People's Revolution of Nepal 1951)*.

127 Basnet, Mathbar Singh, *Ganesh Man Singh: Pages of My Story*, Part I.

128 Passel, Michel, *Tiger for Breakfast*.

129 Now converted to museums.

130 Resting place open on three sides, an essential feature of the Newari cities.

131 Interviews starting March 2008.

132 Two round baskets hanging from each end of a bamboo pole, carried across the shoulders.

133 Interviews starting October 2007.

134 Translated as, 'the tale of a sin'.

135 See Part III, Chapter Six for narration of that part.

136 Interviewed on 14 October 2007.

137 A loose set of pyjamas and an overlapping shirt.

138 Fisher, James F., *The Living Martyrs*.

139 Where he was adopted by the ruler.

140 Bhageshwar Pageni, about Martyr Dharma Bhakta, as told by brother Dhruba Bhakta.

141 Told by Ramhari Sharma.

142 Sanat Shah, husband of grand daughter of Ram Raja, believes Ram Raja had contributed ₹100,000 to the party.

143 Basnet, Mathbar Singh, *Ganesh Man Singh: Pages of My Story,* Part 1.

144 Rana, Hemanta Shumsher, *Nara Shumsher J.B. Rana: A Biography.*

145 Pradhan, Bhuwan Lal, *Nepal ko Janakrantik Andolan 2007 (People's Revolution of Nepal 1951).*

146 Rana, Purusottam Shumsher, *A Chronicle of Rana Rule,* pp. 163.

147 Interview with Dimon Shumsher, who was one of the officer and a reluctant observer.

148 Late General Meen Shumsher Rana, son of Juddha, interviewed on 1 March 2010.

149 Gautam, Dr Rajesh, *Democratic Revolution of Nepal and Ganesh Man Singh.*

150 From interview with Ramhari Sharma.

151 Adhikary, Dr Surya Mani, *History of Democracy in Nepal.*

152 Interviewed on 21 May 2009.

153 Sama, a short version of Shumsher, also bears the connotation to 'Samata' or equality in Sanskrit.

154 Pradhan, Bhuwan Lal, *Nepal ko Janakrantik Andolan,* pp. 184–85. Pradhan was also a prominent member of the group.

155 Interview with the author.

156 Late General Meen Shumsher, interviewed on 1 March 2010.

157 Satya Mohan Joshi, who was a junior officer at that time, in an interview with the author starting 12 August 2007. Joshi has now earned recognition and respect from all segments of society as an unbiased and fearless leader in the cultural field.

158 *Some Reminisces, Some Thoughts.* The part played by him in the communist movement is covered in the Chapter The Great Metropolis.

159 Pande, Bhim Bahadur, *Tyas Bakhat ko Nepal, (Nepal of Those Days,* Part I).

160 Ibid.

161 Ibid.

162 11 per cent Dalit population, according to a recent census.

163 Tikaram Gahat Raj, interviewed on 31 October 2007.

164 Not allowed to don the sacred thread.

165 Interviewed in November 2008.

166 Now preserved as a model of Newar architecture and culture.

167 Interview at the NC District Office, Pokhara, 28 October 2008.

168 Interviewed on 6 October 2007.

169 Kshetri, Dr Dil Bahadur, *Documents on Nepal: A Collection of Correspondence with British India – Treaty of Commence with Raja of Nepal 1790.*

170 Business office.

171 1 Maund equals about 40 kilos.

172 *Kantipur Daily,* 8 August 2009, translation by author.

173 Bhim Bahadur Pandey.

174 Pageni, Bhageshwar, *Pashchim Nepal ma Prajatantrik Andolan (Democratic Revolution in West Nepal).*

175 Ibid.

176 Bahadur, Khagendra B.C., *Private Secretary of Baber.*

177 Interview with Purusottam Shumsher, grandson of Rudra, author of several books including *Shree Teen Haruko Atma Brittanta* in two volumes, 28 November 2008.

178 2011 report.

179 Interview 30–31 July 2008.

180 Bal Bahadur Rai: A respected leader of the Nepali Congress with an impeccable record, he was elected member of the short-lived Parliament in 1958 and after the restoration of democracy in 1990 he reached the position of deputy prime minister on two occasions.

181 Until Chandra Shumsher discontinued the practise of grant of birta land.

182 The part of Mughlai Thapas is based on interview with two of the seventh generation of Thapa brothers, Rtd General Krishna Narain Singh and Ajit Narain Singh, a leader of the Nepali Congress in Dhankuta, 16 November 2009.

183 Kayasthas are Vaishyas.

184 Interview with the author, 29 January 2009.

185 *Life Story of Ram Lall Golcha,* compiled by Hulas Chand Golcha.

186 Interview with the son Bishwa Bandhu, 14–15 November 2008.

187 Bauhunia Variegata.

188 Koirala, B.P., *Afno Katha.*

189 Ibid.

190 Ibid.

191 Sharma, Ramhari, *Atma Brittanta.*

192 Kathmandu was more readily addressed this way until the 1950s.

193 Sharma, Ramhari, *Atma Brittanta.*

194 Singh, Rana P.B., *Banaras: Cosmic Order, Sacred City, Hindu Traditions.*

195 Composer of the Bhagavad Gita.

196 Singh, P.B. Rana.

197 Freedom from the cycle of birth and death.

198 From an unpublished autobiography of Krishna Prasad Bhattarai.

199 Author's interview with Arun Dhital, October 2008.

200 Havel E.B., *Benares: The Sacred City;* Edwin Greaves, *Kashi: The City Illustrious.*

201 Koirala, B.P., *Afno Katha.*

202 Ibid.
203 *Portrait of a Revolutionary: B.P. Koirala*. Bhola Chatterji's recorded interview with B.P. Koirala.
204 When the cattle returned home.
205 Translation by the author.
206 Chatterji, Bhola, *Portrait of a Revolutionary*.
207 Chapter XV, verse 15, 'Sarvasya chaham hridisannibishto'.
208 Koirala, B.P., *Atma Brittanta*.
209 Chatterji, Bhola, *Portrait of a Revolutionary: B.P. Koirala*.
210 Surendra Mohan, *In Evolution of Socialist Policy in India*, published on the occasion of Socialist International Council Meeting, New Delhi November 1997.
211 The story of J.P. and Lohia in Hanuman Nagar on the Nepalese side of the border is narrated in Chapter Five.
212 In 2007, BHU had more than 125 teaching departments and close to 16,000 professors, teachers, and students.
213 Gautam, Dr Rajesh, *Karma Yogi Krishna Prasad Bhattarai*.
214 Spear, Percival, *A History of India*, Penguin Books, 1965.
215 Interview at BHU, 13 October 2008.
216 Lapierre, Dominique, *Freedom at Midnight*.
217 Contents covering the lives of Ram Hari Joshi and Keshar Bahadur Rayamajhi that follow, are derived largely from interviews with each during December 2006–January 2007, and books entitled *Kehi Samjhana, Kehi Chintan*, by Rayamajhi and *Nepal ko November Kranti* (Nepal's November Revolution) by Ram Hari Joshi.
218 Founded in 1905.
219 Pradhan, Dharma Narayan, *Ma Ra Mero Anubhuti*, pp. 24–26.
220 Joshi, Ram Hari, Nepal ko November Kranti, Antarrashtriya Manch: Kathmandu. Interview Ram Hari Joshi on Baisakh 2048 (B.S.)
221 Ibid.
222 Joshi, Ram Hari, *November Revolution of Nepal*.
223 Ibid.
224 Covered in detail in Part III, Chapter Six.
225 General Secretary and a respected leader of NC in later years.
226 Brother of B.P. Koirala killed in the insurgency launched against the Panchayat regime.
227 Interview with the author.
228 Interview with Keshar Jung Rayamajhi
229 Ram Hari Joshi's account.
230 Surendra, Dr K.C., *The Story of Communist Revolution in Nepal*.

231 Ibid.

232 Ibid.

233 Lall, Pushpa, *Nepal ma Communist Andolan ko Sanchipta Itihas* (A Concise History of the Communist Party in Nepal).

234 Interview 1–2 February 2008.

235 Siddhi Rana, son of Mahavir, during the course of several sittings with present author in Kathmandu and Calcutta.

236 Koirala, B.P., *Atma Brittanta.*

237 Passel, Michel, *Tiger for Breakfast, Bachi J. Karkaria To a Grand Design: The Reminisces of the Generation.*

238 The Royal Calcutta Turf Club, W.G.C. Frith.

239 Passel, Michel, *Tiger for Breakfast.*

240 Originally built and owned by a renowned British nobleman, a friend and contemporary of Lord Curzon.

241 Acharya, Dr Yagya Nath, *Subarna Shumsher and the Democratic Movement.*

242 *Punarjagaran Weekly,* Commemorative Issue on Subarna Shumsher.

243 *Shree Teenharu ko Atmabrittanta* (True facts of the Maharajas of Nepal) Part II, pp. 265.

244 Rukma Shumsher, son of Subarna, during interviews and interactions, starting 21 August 2008.

245 Sever, Adrian, *Nepal under the Ranas.*

246 Sunder Raj Chalise, a close confidant of Subarna, reveals in a recorded interview with Dr Yagya Nath Acharya in Subarna Shumsher and the Democratic Revolution.

247 Late Daya Bhakta Mathema, in interview with author 4 June 2008.

248 Rukma Shumsher.

249 Bahadur, Dr Ksetri Dil, *Compilation of Documents on Nepal,* original translation.

250 Later to play an important and controversial part in Nepalese politics.

251 In 1947, President of the League was nominated in the Constituent Assembly headed by Baba Saheb Ambedkar.

252 G.B. Yakthumba and C.B. Bantawa from this group attained the post of Inspector General of Police after 1951.

253 Most of the contents related to Jana Mukti Sena are derived from *Jana Mukti Sena: An Unwritten History* by Shyam Kumar Tamang and author's interaction with G.B. Yakthumba.

254 He was attached to the family for two generations.

255 Included amongst them were Basanta Shumsher and Himalaya Shumsher who provided much support in the creation of this book.

256 Claims Rukma Shumsher during an interview.

257 Ibid.
258 Basnet, Purrusottam, *Desanter Weekly, Kathmandu, 2053 B.S. Bhadra 23* and *Contours of the History of Nepali Congress.*
259 Interview with Prabhakar Rana, his grandson, 29 June 2008.
260 *Gorkha Patra,* 29 January 1945.
261 Pandey, Bhim Bahadur, *Tyas Bakhat ko Nepal,* Part IV.
262 Sever, Adrian, *Aspects of Modern Nepalese History.*
263 Kripalani, J.B., *Gandhian Thoughts*; Shiller, *Gandhi: A Memoir.*
264 Vide Part II, Chapter Three.
265 Pradhan, Bhuwan Lal, *Nepal ko Janakrantik Andolan.*
266 Interview with Nutan Thapalia.
267 India took almost four years to complete the task, starting 1947.
268 Dr Rajesh Gautam, p. 66.
269 Basnet, Mathbar Singh, *Ganesh Man Singh: Pages of My Story.*
270 Ibid.
271 Sharma, Ramhari, *Atma Brittanta,* p. 30.
272 Dr Tulsi Giri in conversation with the author, 18 August 2009.
273 Sharma, Ramhari, *Atma Brittanta.*
274 Pradhan, Dharma Narayan, *Ma Ra Mero Anubhuti.*
275 Gautam, Dr Rajesh, *Karma Yogi Krishna Prasad Bhattarai,* p. 19.
276 Singh, Mathbar, *Mero Katha ka Panaharu,* Ayam Prakashan Pvt Ltd., Part I, pp. 231–235, Second Edition: B.S. 2058.
277 Ibid.
278 Chatterji, Bhola, *Portrait of a Revolutionary: B.P. Koirala,* p. 62.
279 Mathbar Basnet.
280 *Atma Brittanta,* pp. 32–38.
281 Ibid.
282 Pageni, Bhageshwar, *Democratic Revolution in Western Nepal.*
283 Bishwa Bandhu Thapa, interview 9–10 September 2008.
284 Interview with the author, 19 November 2007, while Koirala was prime minister.
285 A television series broadcast on Kantipur TV on the life of G.P. Koirala relayed first during summer of 2007, and the interview of 19 November 2007, form the bulk and direct source of this narrative.
286 Interview by the author on 19 November 2007.
287 Pradhan, Bhuwan Lal, *Nepal ko Janakrantik Andolan 2007,* p. 221.
288 Koirala, M.P., *A Role in the Revolution.*
289 Part III, Chapter Five.
290 Details of this Satyagraha movement are derived from Bhuwan Lal Pradhan's *Nepal ko Janakrantik Andolan 2007,* and Nutan Thapalia and

Sahana Pradhan, all three activists of the Satyagraha.

291 All automobiles imported and brought into Kathmandu were carried manually by teams of porters across the mountains to Kathmandu.

292 Interviewed on 20 June 2008.

293 Pradhan, Bhuwan Lal, *Nepal ko Janakrantik Andolan 2007*.

294 Gautam, Dr Rajesh, *Nepal ko Prajatantrik Andolan and Ganesh Man Singh*.

295 Major contents of this section, Jayatu Sanskritam, are derived from a booklet by that name, authored by Shribhadra Sharma, and interviews with Sharma 30 August 2006 and Kamal Raj Regmi on 6 October 2007; sadly, Shribhadra Sharma passed away in 2009.

296 Conversations and interviews with Bharat Shumsher regarding this book started 27 September 2004.

297 In interview with Dr Rajesh Gautam, *Democratic Revolution in Nepal, Rebellious Bharat Shumsher*, 2006.

298 Dixit, Kamal Mani, *Khurpa ko Bind*.

299 Himalaya Shumsher, a batchmate of Bharat at St Xavier's.

300 Some of his books have received wide acclaim and national awards, including the highly coveted Jagadamba Prize for his *Narasimha Avatar*.

301 He rose to the rank of commander-in-chief in the early sixties.

302 The statue still stands at the centre of the New Road roundabout.

303 *Gorkha Patra*, 8 August 2003.

304 Interviewed, 16 March 2010.

305 *Atma Brittanta*.

306 The Government of Nepal Act, 1948, Article 3.

307 Parmanand, *The Nepali Congress Since Its Inception*.

308 Kripalani, J.B., *Gandhian Thoughts*.

309 Those familiar with the Panchayat system introduced by King Mahendra in the 1960s will recognize the close proximity.

310 Dr Regmi, *A Century of Family Autocracy in Nepal*.

311 Parmanand, *The Nepali Congress Since Its Inception*.

312 Gupta, Anirudha, *Politics in Nepal: A Study of Post Rana Political Developments and Party Politics*.

313 The author in indebted to late Subarna Shumsher for his multifaceted input during our numerous meetings.

314 Gupta, Anirudha, *Politics in Nepal: A Study of Post Rana Political Developments and Party Politics*.

315 Interview on 12 August 2007.

316 Bhim Bahadur Pandey, arguably the closest counsel of Vijay Shumsher, who managed most of the affairs of state on behalf of his aging father. *Nepal of Those Days*, Part IV, p. 170.

317   Gupta, Anirudha, *Politics in Nepal: A Study of Post Rana Political Developments and Party Politics.*

318   Pandey, Bhim Bahadur, *Tyas Bakhat ko Nepal,* Part IV.

319   The first ever budget of the country 1951–55, aggregate revenue 29,081 million Nepalese rupees and expenditure 24,627 million.

320   Pandey, Sardar Bhim Bahadur, *Nepal of Those Days,* Part IV, p. 140.

321   Raeper Houfton, *People' Politics and Ideology,* and Whelpton.

322   Speeches of Jawahar Lal Nehru. Publication Division, Delhi, 1954.

323   *Atma Brittanta.*

324   Ibid.

325   Ibid.

326   Dr Rajesh Gautam, p. 95.

327   This account has been put together from the narration in *Atma Brittanta* and a chat with a member of the Juddha family who prefers to remain anonymous.

328   Kamal Raj Regmi, Interviewed on October 2007 and March 2008.

329   Basnet, Mathbar Singh, *Ganesh Man: Pages of My Story,* Part II, p. 9.

330   Sharma, Ganesh Raj, *M.P. Koirala: A Role in a Revolution.*

331   Joshi, Ram Hari, *November Revolution of Nepal.*

332   Full text in *Nepal Ma Prajatantrik Andolan* by Bhaweshwar Pageni, p. 73.

333   *A Role in the Revolution* by M.P. Koirala.

334   Basnet, Mathbar Singh, Part II, p. 20.

335   Chatterji, Bhola, *Palace, People and Politics.*

336   *Atma Brittanta.*

337   He later took part in the attack on Biratnagar, and is an author of several books and writings related to B.P. Koirala, the Nepali Congress and Nepal.

338   Kumar, Shyam Tamang, *Jana Mukti Sena: An Unwritten History.*

339   Basnet, Mathbar Singh, *Ganesh Man: Pages of My Story,* Part II.

340   Sharma, B.L., *Rashtrapita Tribhuvan Ra Ma.*

341   Bhuwan Lal Pradhan, p. 406.

342   B.L. Sharma, interviewed on 10 September 2008.

343   Bhuwan Lal Pradhan.

344   Joshi, Ram Hari, *November Revolution of Nepal.*

345   From an article by Subarna Shumsher, *Amrit Bazar Patrika,* 24 August 1950.

346   B.P. Koirala, quoted in an interview with Bhola Chatterji, 'The Three Kings and a Commoner', Sunday, 19 June 1977.

347   *Hindustan Times,* 14 June 1948.

348   Bhuwan Lal Pradhan.

349   Daya Bhakta Mathema interviewed on 04 July 2008.

350 *Atma Brittanta.*

351 Tuladhar Daman Raj, *Contemporary Nepal: An Experience in Democracy*, pp. 272–23. Excerpt from Tribhuwan's 'exhortations' during an audience granted to Tanka Prasad Acharya, President Praja Parishad and Daman Raj Tuladhar, Secretary, at the Royal Palace, March 1951.

352 Abridged version of accounts from Satya Mohan Joshi, Nutan Thapalia, Khagendra Bahadur K.C. in separate interviews.

353 Parmanand, *The Nepali Congress Since Its Inception.*

354 Himalaya Rana.

355 *Hindustan Times*, November 10 1950.

356 Annual Reports on Nepal, kept at the British Embassy, Kathmandu.

357 Purusottam Shumsher.

358 Bhuwan Lal Pradhan.

359 After the fall of the Rana regime they were to join a political party Nepal Rashtrabadi Gorkha Parishad.

360 Koirala, M.P., *A Role in a Revolution.*

361 The Statesman, 12 November 1950.

362 Tamang, Shyam Kumar, *Jana Mukti Sena: Euta na Lekhieko Itihas* (An Unwritten History).

363 Prasad, Krishna Bhattarai, *Mero Ma*, p. 167.

364 *The Statesman.*

365 Author of *Aaja ko Nepal* (Nepal of Today).

366 M.P. Koirala.

367 Prasad, Krishna Bhattarai, *Mero Ma*, p. 35.

368 The desired result was achieved only in Birgunj and Kanchanpur in ther west.

369 Interviewed, 12 September, 2009.

370 Chatterji, Bhola, *Palace, People and Politics.*

371 Bishwa Bandhu.

372 *Atma Brittanta.*

373 Tamang Shyam Kumar: *An Unwritten History.*

374 Bishwa Bandhu.

375 Interviewed with Preeti Singh.

376 Read Part II, Chapter Two for their interview.

377 Adhikary, Hem Raj, *Aaja ko Nepal.* pp. 279–81.

378 Interviewed on 30–31 July 2008.

379 Later, his son, Beni Bahadur Karki joined the Gorkha Parishad party and was elected to the House of Representatives in 1958. Following the coup of King Mahendra in 1961, he was imprisoned. On his release, he joined his leader Bharat Shumsher in the merger of the Gorkha Parishad with

the Nepali Congress and remained with him during their life in exile in Calcutta. After the restoration of democracy, he was elected Chairman of Rashtra Sabha, the Upper House of Parliament.

380 *The Statesman*, 16 November 1950.

381 Bhageshwar Pageni.

382 Pageni, Bhageshwar, *Democratic Revolution in Western Nepal*.

383 Rawal Bhim, *Communist Revolution in Nepal*.

384 Article by Dr D.R. Regmi, *Revolution of 1951 in Palpa*, Editor Kamal Raj Regmi.

385 Buddha Ratna Shakya.

386 Interviewed on 4 June 2008.

387 Bhim Bahadur Pandey, Part IV.

388 Parliamentary records, speeches of Pandit Nehru.

389 *The Himalayan Times*.

390 Talking to the author's brother, Jagadish Rana.

391 *The Hindu*, 11 January 1951.

392 Interview with Daya Bhakta Mathema.

393 *Atma Brittanta*.

394 Chatterji, Bhola, *Palace People and Politics*.

395 Translated by the author from *Tyas Bakhat ko Nepal* by Sardar Bhim Bahadur Pandey, one of the few courtiers who did stick by the Rana regime until its final fall before being part of the resurging new order.

396 Yog Bikram in an interview with Bhim Bahadur Pandey.

397 Later named Tribhuwan International airport.

Acknowledgements

For many years, Kamal Mani Dixit and Satya Mohan Joshi had suggested and urged me to write about the Rana regime and the democratic movement. I need to commence my expression of thanks with them. The first serious stirrings for writing the manuscript for this book entered my mind after restoration of democracy in Nepal, April 2006. As it would be my first such attempt, I tested myself by writing a piece about Jung Bahadur and requested my brother Jagadish, author of several publications, to read and share his comments. After a cursory glance, he sternly advised me to do the homework first. That homework, followed by jottings and writings, has lasted these eleven years, independently, but with constant advice from my niece, Rachana Rana Bhattacharya, a writer, critic, designer, all rolled in one. Her encouragement, including the first edit, has kept me alert and active to keep working on the manuscript and related work. She is the foremost in my list of acknowledgements. I am similarly grateful to my friend, Kunda Dixit, who advised and helped edit and condense my much-longer manuscript to a shorter version while still retaining the interesting anecdotes. Rupa Publishers India have now shaped and polished it to a fine finish. My words of appreciation and gratitude are due to all of them. My whole family and in particular, Brinda, my wife; daughter Usha and two sons, Upendra and Udaya, have always stood by me whenever the need arose—and often there was a need.

Pictures that appear in the book are a select few from the incredibly rich collection of the Madan Memorial Pustakalaya, Jeevan Rana, Tanka Prasad Foundation, Sushil Koirala, Manju and Jharendra Rana, and Durga Prasad Joshi of Snapshot Studio. I thank them for their kindness and ever helpful contributions.

In my search and exploration, I have relied heavily on interaction and one-to- one interviews with a large number of family members, political leaders, freedom fighters and social activists, Marxists, Nepali Congress or the Panchayat stalwarts, as well as unknown villagers who were part of the socio-political evolution in their time. With some of them it was much more than an interview, it was hours and days of sharing past memories. These anecdotes have been mentioned in the chapters of Part III, and posthumously or alive, I offer them my sincere gratitude for the invaluable input and fascinating experience.

Index

300 Club, 242, 244, 251–252

Adda, Khadga Nishana, framework of, 65
Adhikary, Hem Raj, 364
Adhikary, Krishna Lall, 80
Adhikary, Man Mohan, 136, 236, 269
Adi Bhakta, 143
Administrative network, 12, 30, 107, 259, 265
Administrative Reforms, 64–67, 119
Adrian Sever, 60, 65
Afno Katha, 198
All India Gorkha Congress, 230, 270
All India Gorkha League, 230, 253–257, 270
All India Nepali National Congress, 270
All India Students' Union, 234
Amatya, Tulsi Lal, 236, 348, 376
Amrit Bazaar Patrika, 271
Anglo-Afghan war, 72
Anglo-American lobby, 355
Anglo-Indian beauties, 227
Anglo-Nepal cooperation, expansion of, 71
Anglo-Nepal Treaty of Friendship, 71–75
Anglo-Nepal War, 15–20, 26, 184
loss and humiliation suffered, 18
Angoor Pari (angel of grapes), 51
Animal husbandry, 29, 112
Animal sacrifice, 69
Annexation of villages, 16
Anti-authoritarian sentiment, 224

Anti-colonialism, 224
Anti-Rana movement, 75, 92, 168, 210, 228, 236, 296, 326
communist faction in, 275
Arbitrary restrictions, bondage of, 179
Armed revolution of 1951, strong component of, 171
Arya Samaj, 75, 77, 133
movement, 77, 130
reformist tenets of, 77
Aryans, migration of the, 3
Ashoka, 7
Asia Minor, 3
Asian Conference of Socialist International, 334
Athleticism, 20
Atlee, Clement, 154, 271
Atma Brittanta, 295, 307
Authoritarian regime, 87, 128, 228, 267
Azad Hind Army, 255–256, 239

B.L. Sharma, 341, 347, 350, 357
Bada Gurujyu, 78
Bada Hakim, 141
Bada Kaji, 103
Badrinath, 34
Bagari music festival, 52
Bagmati river, 135
first iron bridge over, 18
Bahadur Shah, 12–13
Bahadur, Rana, 13–15
Bajpai, Girija Shankar, 388
Balakrishna Shumsher (Sama), 91, 126–127, 152

Balamukunda Singh, 318
Banaras Hindu University (BHU), 195, 209, 222–224
Baral, Ishwar, 223
Bargania Convention, 344
Basanti, 137–138, 359
Basnet, Mathbar, 22
Basundhara, 249
Bedabhakta, 93–94
Begum Hazrat Mahal, 39
Banaras, xiv, 12–14, 19, 22, 27–28, 69–70, 80–81, 129, 138, 143, 145, 163, 177–178, 180, 194–195, 203, 206–213, 217–220, 222–224, 228–229, 231, 236–237, 246, 260, 268–271, 277, 291–292, 294–296, 303, 307–308, 310, 317, 333, 363, 376, 402
Banaras Pandits, 69–70
Bengali society, 241
Bhabuk Rahasyabadi (emotional realist), 219
Bhandari, Gagan Singh, 20
Bhanu Bhakta Acharya, 121
Bharadwaj, Surya Bahadur, 156
Bhardari Sabha, 19–20, 103, 115
Bhardars, council of, 13
Bhattarai brothers, 223
Bhattarai, K.P., 209–210, 224, 270–272, 363
Bhattarai, Muralidhar, 131
Big-game hunting, 97
Bikram Rana, Col Yog, 391–392
Bikram Shah, Mahendra, 209, 257, 330, 333
Bikram, Chhetra, 378, 380
Bi-lateral policy, 311
Bill of Rights, 129
Binti Patras (letters of supplication), 203
Biratnagar, 163, 196, 276, 365

crucial struggle in, 365–374, 365
Birgunj, 360, 362–363
Birtawals, 46
Bishnu Prasad Dhital, 127
Bishu (Bishweshwar), 213, 217
Bom Bahadur, 28–29
Bose, Subhas Chandra, 221, 255–256
Brahmanic code, 8
British Connection, 62–64
British invasion in Tibet, 63
British monarch, 64
British–Nepali cooperation and friendship, 49
Buddha Dhamma Uddharak Sangh, 76
Buddhism, 5
Buddhist Dhamma, 76
Buddhist missionaries, 7
Buddhist monks, resurgence of, 157
Buddhist stupas, 7
Buffer state, 63
Burton, Richard, 39
Byathit, Kedar Man, 130, 275

Canning, Governor General, 36–37
Capital punishment, 141, 150
Caste and occupation, divisions of, 168–171
Caste barriers, 135
Caste divide, 31
Ceasefire, 371–374
Celibate Buddhists, 76
Central Jail of Kathmandu, black hole in, 389
Chaar Khal Adda, 114
Chakari, 116, 129, 137–138, 233, 307, 313, 341
Chakariwals, 123
Chalise, Sunder Raj, 258
Chamadia, Seth, 192
Chandra Man, 106, 145, 149
Charms of women, 204

Charnock, Job, 225
Chaurasia, Hariprasad, 208
Chhetra Bikram, Colonel, 378
Chhetris, 4–5, 17, 98, 121–122, 169, 177, 186, 323, 360
Chitrakar, Lal Prasad, 377
Choudhury, Surendra, 184
Churchill, Winston, 221
City of Joy, 225
Civil Rights Committee, 130–131, 133–134
Clemency, 29
Closed-door policy, 175
Colonial dictatorship, 75
Colonial rule in Hindustan, 9
Colonial rule, bondage of, 62
Communist Manifesto, 237
Communist Party in India (CPI), 234
Communist Party of Bengal, 235
Communist Party of Nepal (CPN), 152, 172, 236, 376–380, 389
    birth of, 236–238
Community collaboration, 171–177
Congenial relationship, 17
Congress Socialist Party (CSP), 220
Consolidation of authority, 61–62
Conspiratorial violence, 333
Constitution, Proclamation of the, 304–306
Constitution Reforms Committee, 289–290
Constitutional bodies, 110
Constitutional monarchy, 95, 275
Cooperative movement, 110
Corinthian Theatre, 179
Cottage industries, 113
Council of Nobles, 20, 24
Council of State, 29
Court of Nepal, 29
Cripps, Sir Stafford, 221
Cross-border trade, 176

Cultural heritage, 7, 293
Custodian of the law, 168

Dalan, Pustak Padhne, 180
Dalit community, 168, 181, 274
Dashrath Chand, 142, 144–145, 149–151
Daudaha Sawari, 97
Daya Bhakta Mathema, 259, 261, 380
Decisive Hand of Delhi, 380–384
Deities and motifs, 134
Delhi Compromise, 384–389, See also Five-point proposal
Delhi Coronation Durbar in 1913, 72
Democratic movement, history of, 232, 291
Democratic Socialism, 218, 220, 281
Democrats vs. Communists, 236
Despotic oligarchy, 46
Devendra Prasad, 220, 223, 269, 329
Devkota, Laxmi Prasad, 128, 208, 275, 300
Devkota, Rajeshwar, 327
Dhakal, Upendra Purush, 342
Dharma Bhakta, 143–144, 149
Dharma Patra, 61
Dharma Shastra, 31
Dhital, Arun, 209
Dhungana, Durga Nath, 211
Dhungel, Janak Lall, 89
Dictatorships, 115
Diplomatic
    courtship, 74
    initiatives, 16
    manipulations, 313
Direct Action Day, 229
Divine directive, 27
Divya Upadesh (wise directives), 11
Dixit, Acharya, 87
Draconian instruments, 118

Dudh Kosi River, 185
Duff, Sir Beuchamp, 72
Duke of Wellington, 28
Duniyadars or Raitis, 21, 29, 50, 80, 82, 89, 116, 129, 204
Durbar High School, 50, 123, 125
Durbar Squares, 134
Durbar Tulsi Lal Amatya, 358

Earthquake of 2015, 18
East India Company, 9, 15–16, 37, 108, 175
expansion policy, 188
interests of the, 36
rising presence and power of, 26
Economic exploitation, 173
Ek Paap ko Katha, 137–138
Election Commission, 304
Enlightenment, 4
Ethnic communities, 122, 129, 174
External relations, 103–105

Facile movement of men and material, 110
Fateh Jung Shah, 22–24, 40
Father of tourism in Nepal, see Lissanevitch, Boris
Feudal society, 173, 227, 299, 379
First War of Independence, see Sepoy Mutiny
Five-Point Proposal, 384–389
Foreign policy, 26, 33–36, 313
Forrest, G.W., 242
Freedom movement, 74, 131, 142–143, 179, 186, 381
Friendship gesture, 63

Gaanth Gaddi, aiming at, 95
Gaekwad of Baroda, 242
Gandaki river, 5, 166
Gandhi Ashram, 212
Gandhi, Indira (Indu), 246

Gandhi, Mohandas Karamchand (Mahatama Gandhi), 78, 92, 131, 241
assassination of, 306–307
and Democratic Socialism, 218–222
line of peaceful Satyagraha, 333
thought, 215
Ganesh Man, 271
Ganga Lal, 132–133, 149–150
Garat, Bijuli, 55
Gaunda, 30, 165–166, 172, 179, 182
Gautama Buddha, 208
Giri, Dala Bahadur, 254
Girija Devi, 208
Girvanayuddha, 14–15, 18
Golcha, Hulas Chand, 191
Golcha, Ram Lall, 192–193
Good governance, guidelines for, 32
Gorkha army, 10, 16, 171, 255
serious setback, 14
Gorkha Land, 255
call for creating, 255
support for demand of, 270
Gorkha Language Publication Committee, 126
Gorkha League, 254, 256
Gorkha Nepal army, 10
Gorkha Patra, 53, 128, 217, 280
Gorkha Sansar, 254
Gorkha troops, recruitment concessions, 49
Gorkha, Johnny, 104
Gorkhali Fauj (Gorkha army), 13, 35
Gorkhali, 211, 213
Governance, machinery of, 29, 65
Grand Council, 53
Great Earthquake and Sweeping Purge of 1933, 97–101
Great Gangetic Delta, 225
Gruelling, 10, 149
Gupt, Kamal, 208

Gupta, Mathura Prasad, 179
Gurkha Saathi, 254
Gurung, Bakhan Singh, 171
Gurung, Bakhat Bahadur, 170
Gurung, Dambar Singh, 255
Gurung, Tirtha Bahadur (Colonel),
   171
Guthi, Satyacharan Malami, 78
Gyanendra, King, 355, 384
   accession of, 358
Gyanwali, Surya Bikram, 211, 223

Halo Andolan, 181
Hamlet, 179
Hans, 218
Hari Maya (God's love), 51
Hari Priya, 44
Hazuria General, 54–55, 61, 65, 97,
   304
Henry VIII of England, King, 97
Hill Districts, 167–168
Himalayan Airways, 240, 351
Himalayan Aviation, 335
Himalayan foothills, human
   settlements in, 3
Himanchal Chhatra Sangh, 229, 235
Hindu–Muslim riots, 291
Hira Kaji, 158
Hiranya Garva Devi, 40, 42
Hiroshima and Nagasaki, 256
History of Nepal, 83–84
Hitler, Adolf, 193
Hodgson, Brian, 17–18
House of Lords, 115
Hukumi Sashan, nomenclature of,
   114
Humanitarian measures, 87
Hunting expedition, 42, 247
Husband, Colonel Francis Young, 63
Husn Pari (angel of beauty), 51

Idolatry, abolition of, 77

Indian Air Force, 268
Indian National Congress (INC), 59,
   143, 154, 235
Indian railway line to Jogbani
   extension, 202
Indian uprising of 1857, 36–38
Indo-Burman origin, 4
Indo-Gangetic plains, 3–4
Indo-Nepal affairs, 367
Indo-Nepal Treaty of Peace and
   Friendship, 312
Indo-Tibet trade route, 47
Indra Jatra festival, 11, 147
Industrial Act, 111
Industrial Council, 249
Industrial policy, 111–114
Industrial revolution, 108, 121
Industrial township, 199
Infrastructural development, 64–67
Interest-free loans, 113
International Communist
   Movement, 235
International diplomacy, 63
International Olympic Committee,
   248
Iron Curtain, 174
Ishk Pari (angel of love), 51

Jagir or Birtas, 10, 20, 188
Jagirdars, 46, 187
Jalan, Radha Krishna, 329
Jallianwallah Bagh, massacre at, 211
Jana Mukti Sena, 182, 187, 253,
   257–259, 312, 320, 327, 334,
   337, 340, 345, 360, 367–369,
   373–374, 376, 385
Jana Mukti Sena, 182, 253–259, 312,
   327, 334, 337, 340, 345, 367,
   369, 373–374, 385
Janmabhoomi, 145, 211, 213
Jayatu Sanskritam, 173, 291–296,
   326

Jinnah, Mohammad Ali, 228–229
Jit Jang, 49
Joshi, Madhav Raj, 77, 79, 151
Joshi, Ram Hari, 228
Joshi, Ram Prasad, 127
Joshi, Satya Mohan, 159, 310
Juddha, 61, 79, 83, 89–113, 121,
    124–128, 130, 132–133,
    147–159, 180, 182, 193, 195,
    247, 249–251, 263–264, 269,
    276, 300, 309, 358, 385
    Final Phase of, 152–153
Jung Bahadur, Death of, 45
Jung, Jagat, 40, 43–45, 49
Jungs vs. Shumshers, 44

Kabir, 208
Kalidas, Dittha Saheb, 199
Kalwar, Raja Lal, 130
Kamal Raj, 376, 378–379
Kansakar, Prem Bahadur, 156286
Kantabati, 14
Karmacharya, Raja Ram, 156
Karnat rulers, 7
Kasi, 88, 208, 209–210, 212, 218,
    295
Kathmandu Radio, 381
Kaur, Rani Chand, 39
Kedarnath, 34
Khadga Man, 93, 96
Khan, Bismillah, 208
Khan, Dhundi, 51
Khan, Wastaj Taj, 51
Khanal, Yadu Nath, 127
Khas kingdom, disintegration of, 10
Khas language, 121–122
Kidwai, Rafi Ahmad, 346, 367
Kidwai, Rafi Mohammad, 246
Kilburn, Robert, 315
Kilnox, Captain, 16
King George V, 63, 74, 227
Kishanjee (Krishna Prasad

Bhattarai), 232
Kitchener, Lord, 63
Koirala family, joined the non-
    cooperation movement, 212
Koirala, B.P., 60, 80, 185, 196,
    198, 215, 203, 218, 240, 253,
    269, 271, 295, 320–322, 344,
    350–352
    Bharat's letter to, 299
    call for united action, 271–274
    and Democratic Socialism,
        218–222
    dynamic leadership of, 260
    enters Kathmandu in disguise,
        320
    juxtaposition of psyche, 219
    and the Socialists, 269–270
Koirala, Dharani Dhar, 128, 203,
    211, 223
Koirala, Divya, 204
Koirala, G.P., 204, 232, 276–280
Koirala, Kalidas, 198
Koirala, K.P., 80, 155, 195–197, 199–
    206, 209–213, 215–217, 219,
    221–222, 224, 232, 269–270,
    274, 333, 363
    committed to the principle of
        non-violence, 212
    leadership and Gandhi's political
        guidance, 216
Koirala, M.P., 329, 336, 362–363,
    367
Koirala, Manisha, 205
Koirala, Matrika, 193, 280, 282, 289,
    303, 331, 330, 333, 344, 375,
    386
Koirala, Nandikeshwar, 196
Kosi River, 198
Kshatriyas or Chhetriyas (Chhetri or
    Khas), 3–4
Kul devata (family deity), 61
Kumari, Dibya, 196

Kunwar, Bal Narsingh, 21

Labour force, 4, 46, 154
Labour strike, 276–280
Lal Mohur (royal seal), 31, 35–36, 40–41, 43, 45, 55, 336
Lal, C.K., 189
Lale Joker, *see* Chitrakar, Lal Prasad
Lall, Bihari, 236
Lama, D.B., 230
Lama, Nirmal, 259
Lamahood, status of, 76
Land tax (Malpot), 107, 167
Land tax, 167
Lapierre, Dominique, 225
Law and Order, 114–115
Law Commission, 114
Law Courts, 141
Laxmi Rajya, 93
Laxmi, Queen, 23
Le Opinion Publique, 28
Legal tenets, 32
Liberal and reformist awakening, 78
Liberal political order, 264
Liberal political reforms, 81, 264, 312
Liberal reforms, 71, 92, 249, 309
Liberation Army, 362, 373, 387, 389
Licchavis, 6
Life of Mahatma Lenin, 296
Linkage, institutionalized system of, 137
Lion of Punjab *see* Ranjit Singh
Lissanevitch, Boris, 241, 252
Literary symposium, 299–300
Lockhart, Sir Allen, 242
Lohia, Ram Manohar, 155, 220, 269, 273, 307
Lohini, Kul Nath, 127
Lok Bhakta Laxmi (Bada maharani), 40, 204
Lucknow Loot, 36–38, 49

Macdonald, Lt Col, 109
Machine-made goods from England, 47
Madan Puraskar Pustakalaya, 298
Madhesis, 17, 121, 188–190, 194
 influx of, 188–194
Magar, Sarbajeet, 13
Magnanimity, 10
Mahabharata, 4, 18, 165, 185, 187, 298, 371
Mahakali river, 13, 30
Mahal, Baber, 138
Maharajdhiraj, Paanch, 187, 333, 373
Mahavir Institute, 126
Mahila Baje, 234
Mahila Gurujyu, 103, 150, 294
Mahila Sangh, 296–297
Mahipalas or Gopalas, 6
Majithia, Surjit Singh, 316, 321, 324, 346
Makaiko Kheti (Corn Farming), 80
Malaviya, Madan Mohan, 222
Malik, Deepak, 224
Malla rulers, 8
Malla, Jayasthiti, 7
Mangala Devi, 297, 357
Manu Smriti, 149
Marriage alliances, 40
Marshall Plan, 315
Marx and Democratic Socialism, 218–222
Marxism, authoritarian, 220
Marxism Study Circle, 235
Matrimonial alliance, 21, 40, 61
Mechanism and modalities, 332
Military Code, 33, 35
Military precision, 257, 331
Mill-made merchandise, flow of, 154
Misrule and uncertainty, 19
Mixed club, 242
Model states, 110
Moneylenders, 169

Mongoloid characteristics, 4
Montz, Laura, 28
Mool Bato, 66
Morang Cotton Mills, 278
Morang of Nepal, 192
Morley, Lord, 60
Mountbatten, Lord, 289
Movement of goods, Duty on, 8
Mugali Thapas, 188
Mujib-ur Rehman, 234
Mukherjee, Hiren, 234–235, 237, 242
Muktinath, 5
Mukunda Indira, 126
Mulmi, Rudra Lall, 302
Muluki Ain, 8, 30–32, 149
   codified legal principles of a common law, 31
   comprehensive and uniform legal code, 30
   public and private law, 32
   rule of law under, 109
   sanction to bodies of religious practices, 31
Muralidhar, Pandit, 131, 133
Muslim League, 229
Muslim, concept of, 229

Nagar, Hanuman, 155 156
Nagarik Adhikar Samiti, 130
Naibedya, 128, 203, 211
Naina Bahadur, 96
Nakkhu jail, 342
Nana Sahib Peshwa, 39
Napoleon, 16
Narayan Hiti Palace, 45, 50, 54
Narayan Nidhi, Mahendra, 232
Narayan, J.P., 155, 220–221, 269, 273, 327, 334–335, 351
Narendra Dev, Acharya, 273
Narsing, Badri, 29
National Economic Planning

Commission, 314
National growth, 107–111
Natural justice, 117
Naulakha haar, 39
Nava Yuvak Sangathan, 181
Naxalbari, 366
Nehru family, 246
Nehru, Jawaharlal, 92, 212, 221, 246, 250, 256, 261, 273, 301, 312, 324, 326–327, 345–346, 349, 355–356, 363, 365, 367, 381–384, 387–388
Nehruvian model, 314
Neo-classical Rana, 140
Nepal Bureau of Mines, 112
Nepal Democratic Congress, 257–260, 385
Nepal Democratic Radio station, 352
Nepal Mahila Sangh (NMS), 297
Nepal National Congress (NNC), 163, 224, 236, 253, 270, 274–276, 283, 388, 390, 376
   division in, 303–304
   armed insurgency of the, 228
Nepal Praja Panchayat (NPP), 318
Nepal Praja Parishad (NPP), 105, 140–152
Nepala Rashtra Sashtra, 8
Nepalese Court, volatile history of, 29
Nepali Students Union, 222–224
Nepal–Tibet Treaty of 1856, 63
Neville Chamberlain, 104
Newari cultural, 8
Newari language, recognition of the, 157
Newari people, lifestyle of the, 156
Nirvana, 4
Non-aligned movement, 381
Non-conformist trait, 196
Non-violence, practice of, 301, 223

Palpa Gaunda, Governor of, 166
Palpa governor, 165
Palpa Sahayak Mandal, 180
Palpa, fall of, 380
Pande, Bir Keshar, 23
Pande, Damodar, 13–14
Pandes vs. Thapas, 14
Pandey, Hem Raj, 69, 150, 292
Pandey, Rudra Raj, 125, 127
Parbate Bhasa (language of the hill people), 5
Parcel episode, 206
Pariyar, D.B., 270, 274
Pariyar, D.N., 230
Parliament, supremacy of, 129
Pashupatinath, 7, 77, 89, 210
Patel, Sardar Vallabhbhai, 355
Pazani system, 46, 118–120
Peaceful revolution of Palpa, 379
Peasants' revolt, 59
Peissel, Michel, 134
People's Republic of China, 312
People's Revolution of 1990, 136
Peoples Liberation Army, see Jana Mukti Sena
Phohra Durbar (fountain palace), 50
Pindaris, gangs of, 16
Plantation and conservation of trees, 175
Political authority, devoid of, 21
Political climate, 343
Political learning school, 269
Political prisoners, 282–283, 288, 289–290, 342, 379, 384, 389
Political reforms, 81, 132, 200, 249–250, 264, 267, 312, 326, 385
Political upheaval, 345
Political, Social and Religious Resistance Groups, 156–157
Postal Route, 66
Prachanda Gorkha, 92–96, 389
    claim of, 95

Prachanda, Pushpa Kamal Dahal, 279
Pradhan, Bhuwan Lal, 106, 267, 322, 385
Pradhan, D.N., 274
Pradhan, Sahana, 285
Pradhananga, Sarbhagya Man, 172
Praja Panchayat, 303, 317–320, 322, 334, 357
Praja Parishad, 105–106, 125–126, 131, 133–134, 140, 144, 146, 149, 151, 163, 247, 274, 321, 389–390
    episode of October 1940, 247
Prasad, Rajendra, 269
Pratap Shah, 12
Pravasi Nepali, 75, 129
Premchand, Munshi, 208
Princely States, 109–110
Principal departments, 30
Prisoners' Trek, 280–282
Prithvi Bir Bikram, King, 55, 45
Prithvi Narayan Shah, Gorkha invasion of, 185
Private resources (Ghar-gharana), 107
Progressive Study Circle, 235, 237
Promotion of Education, 265–267
    drive for expansion, 266
    Gandhian model of basic education, 265–266
    medium of education, 266
    Vedic culture, 266
Public Limited Companies, concept and institution, 111
Public Service Commission, 304
Punishing campaign, 10
Putali, 40, 42

Quasi-judicial powers, 107
Quit India Movement, 155, 221
    involvement of Nepalese, 224

Radhakrishnan, Sarvapalli, 223
Rai, Bal Bahadur, 185–186, 372
Rai, Indra Bahadur, 138
Raj Dharma, 18
Raj Kulos (royal canal system), 50
Raja of Gorkha, 9
Raja, Laxman, 95
Rajendra Bikram Shah, King, 18–19,
    22–24, 209
Rajendra Laxmi, 13
Rajeshwari, Queen, 14
Rajya Laxmi, Queen, 19, 22, 40, 45,
    209
Raktapat Mandali, 105–106, 148, 247
Ram Raja, 142
Ram, Jagjivan, 269
Ramanand, 208
Ramayana, 4, 121
Ran, Nir Jung, 374
Rana Bahadur, King, 14
Rana hierarchy, 126, 288
    liberal faction in, 287
Rana Jung Pande, 18–19
Rana oligarchy, 38, 59, 62, 92, 95,
    143, 154, 163–164, 187–188
    awareness against, 212
    consolidation of, 38–42
    fate, 224
    pillars of the, 187–188
    public rebellion against, 106
    revolution against, 207, 227
    suppression and injustice of, 81
    yoke of the, 247
Rana regime
    arms against, 255
    assault against, 253
    atrocities committed by, 146
    fall of, 79
    fortunes of the, 385
    indignation against the, 150
    movement against the, 230, 236

    protest of the, 351
Rana, Abhiman Singh, 22–23
Rana, Dimon Shumsher, 136
Rana, Jung Bahadur, 20–26, 32, 35,
    41, 49, 65, 174, 208
Rana, Kishore Narsingh, 179
Rana, Mintu Jung, 374
Rana–Congress coalition
    government, 385
Rana–Nepali Congress coalition
    government, 388
Ranga Nath Pandit, 24
Rani Mahal, 166
Ranjit Singh, 22
Ranodip, Cold-blooded murder of,
    48
Rapid Revolution, 267–269
Rashtrabadi Gorkha Parishad, 389
Rashtriya Sabha, 305, 317
Ratna Lal Brahman, 233
Rato Durbar (red palace), 50
Ravi Shankar, Pandit, 208
Ravidas, 208
Raya, Indra Bahadur, 281
Rayamajhi, Keshar Jung, 233
Reforms, 32, 54, 64, 67–68, 71, 75,
    78, 87, 92, 110–114, 119, 127,
    132, 148, 181, 203, 249–250,
    254, 264, 267, 287, 289–290,
    304–305, 307, 309, 317, 326,
    332, 383, 385
Reforms Committee, 304
Regency Council, 383
Regmi, D.R., 223, 237, 271, 274
Regmi, Kamal Raj, 172, 181, 295,
    376
Rehabilitation and reconstruction,
    99
Reins of governance (1802), 15
Religious
    riots, 235
    tolerance, 8

Retired Gorkhas, 154
Revolution of 1951, 376–380
Revolutionary ideas, 80
Revolutionay Communist Party, 246
Right fundamentalists, 235
Rimal, Gopal Prasad, 318
Rishikesh Shah, 127, 246
Roll of Succession, 41, 43, 48, 53,
    65, 82, 136, 182
Roll of Succession
    C-class Ranas into, 84, 91
    families expelled from, 182
    new twist in, 90–91
    Prachanda, 380
    pressing issue, 98
    removal of illegitimate members,
        82
    restructured, 90
    through a Lal Mohur, 41
Rowdy mischief-makers, 287
Roy, Avnesh Chandra, 137
Roy, B.C., 246
Roy, Raja Ram Mohun, 68, 77
Royal Calcutta Turf Club, 244
Royal Hotel, 252
Royal proclamation, 19
Rudra Giri, 363
Rule of law, 31, 109, 114, 129, 319
Rule of Law, principle of, 117
Russian dominance, 63
Russian Revolution (1917), 241
Ryots, 46

Samrajya Laxmi, Queen, 19
Sanatana Dharma, 4
Sapkota, Devi Prasad, 211, 270
Saraswati, Swami Dayanand, 77
Sati, 15, 32, 42, 68, 77
    legal abolition of, 68
Saturday Club, 241
Satyagraha, 92, 131, 143, 211, 253,
    282–287, 290, 292, 296–297,

303, 321, 326, 333–334, 345
Security Council, 355
Self-reliant economy, 75
Semi-autonomy in local governance,
    11
Separate hookah, 186
Sepoy Mutiny (Mutiny of 1857), 36,
    226
Seto Durbar (white palace), 50
Shah, Dravya, 10
Shah, Laxman Bikram, 94
Shah, Mohan Bikram, 142
Shah, Prithvi Bir Bikram, 44
Shah, Prithvi Narayan, 9–10, 46
    expansion of the Kingdom, 12–14
    meltdown of the monarchy, 12–14
Shahi, D.K., 231, 270
Sharma, Bal Chandra, 270
Sharma, Bhola Nath, 379–380
Sharma, Jeev Raj, 144
Sharma, Ramhari, 125, 140, 144,
    150, 389–390
Sharma, Shribhadra, 291, 327
Shatabdi Purush, see Joshi, Satya
    Mohan
Sheikh Mujib-ur, 234
Short History of Development of
    Education in Nepal, 125
Shree Paanch Maharajdhiraj, 94,
    187, 333, 356, 373
Shree Teen Maharaj, 35–36, 43, 68,
    159, 187, 386
Shreshta, Pushpa Lall, 152, 156, 210,
    236–238, 275, 284–286, 296,
    303, 325, 376
Shreshta, Siddhicharan, 128
Shreshta, Tulsi Mehr, 113, 136, 301
Shri Ram library, 179
Shukra Raj, 79, 132–133, 147, 149,
    151
Shumsher, Baber (General), 72, 144,
    287, 294

Shumsher, Bahadur, 289
Shumsher, Bharat, 298
Shumsher, Bhim, 61, 195, 219
Shumsher, Bhim, 86–96
Shumsher, Bir, 48, 67, 100
Shumsher, Chandra, 45, 53, 55, 59–
    85, 72, 78, 85–86, 88, 117, 122,
    143, 176, 179–180, 194–195,
    200, 204–206, 209, 211, 213,
    219, 276, 298
Shumsher, Daman (General), 381
Shumsher, Dev, 52–55, 67, 122, 136,
    150–151, 200
Shumsher, Dhir (General), 27, 35,
    37, 43–44, 60, 166
  powerful intervention of, 43
Shumsher, Gehendra, 54
Shumsher, Gopal, 183, 374
Shumsher, Hari, 323
Shumsher, Hiranya, 90
Shumsher, Jagat, 27
Shumsher, Juddha, 83, 97, 148–149,
    193, 195, 263, 269, 300
Shumsher, Kiran, 250
Shumsher, Mahavir, 238–239,
    333–334
Shumsher, Mohan, 137, 150–151,
    182, 260, 263, 287, 294, 310–
    314, 317, 322, 341, 346, 351,
    370, 374, 385–386, 389, 391
  proclamation of, 389
Shumsher, Mrigendra, 137
Shumsher, Nara, 147, 151
Shumsher, Padma, 70–71, 104, 156,
    181, 249, 263, 270, 286, 289
  reforms of, 289–291
Shumsher, Prachanda (General), 379
Shumsher, Pratap, 180
Shumsher, Ram, 90, 238
Shumsher, Rudra (Field Marshall),
    82, 143, 259, 379
  presence of, 182

Shumsher, Subarna, 183, 245–246,
    256–257, 275, 290, 303–304,
    323, 331, 333, 338, 361–362, 366
Siddhartha, Prince, 4
Siddhi Lal, 135, 302
Sindure Jatra, 54, 310, 317
Singh, C.P.N., 315, 341, 346–347,
    350, 356, 381, 387–388
Singh, Ganesh Man, 106, 133, 141,
    150, 157–158, 342, 273, 283,
    320, 328, 342–343, 390, 392
Singh, Jaya Prithvi Bahadur, 53
Singh, K.I., 344, 374–375, 389
Singh, Khadga Man, 92–93, 95–96,
    389–390
Singh, Marich Man, 64, 103, 328
Singh, Mathbar, 19
Singh, Mohan, 243, 256
Singh, Purna (Major), 256–258, 367
Singh, Raja Prithvi Bahadur, 187
Singh, Ranodip, 32, 43
Single stone diamond ring, 39, see
    also Taylor, Elizabeth
Sinha, Krishna, 367
Sinha, S.K., 347, 357
Sinha, Satya Narayan, 269
Sitara Devi, 208
Skanda Purana, 208
Skill heritage, 113
Slavery, 4, 32, 53, 173
Slaves, 4, 53, 67, 358
  treatment of, 67
Smallpox, 14, 172
Social democratic movement, 156
Social discrimination, state of, 173
Social reforms, 111–114
  commitment to, 67–70
Socio-economic issues, 254, 264
Socio-political
  awareness, 126
  defiance, 82
  ferment in Benares, 211–217

reforms, 200
strata, 21
Socio-religious hierarchy, 21
Sovereign country, 27
Sovereign nation-state, goal of, 71
State revenue, 8, 107, 110, 167, 176, 314
Stock market, 239
Subba Adibhakta, 201
Subba, Ranadhir, 255
Subsidiary trekking routes, 176
Subsistence economy, 174
Substantial contribution to state revenue, 110
Suhrawardy, H.S., 229
Sundari, Lalit Tripura, 15
Supreme Command Council, 333, 366
Supreme War Council, 375
Surendra, King, 29, 35–36, 40–41, 43–44, 394
Surendra, Prince, 19–20, 22–25
Swadeshi movement, 113
Swayambhu Stupa, 146
Sycophants, 330

Tagore, Rabindranath, 241
Tale of Two Cities and War and Peace, 129
Tandon, Krishna Gopal, 176
Tanka Bilas, 288
Tanka Prasad, 141–146, 150, 274, 303, 389–390
spirit of rebellion, 142
Tata, J.R.D., 241–242
Taylor, Elizabeth, 39
Tea garden, 29, 129, 178, 227, 255, 258, 363
Teen Maharaj, 35–36, 43, 68, 159, 187, 386
Terai plains, 3, 38, 66, 165, 173, 188, 371

Thamouti (retention), 94, 118
Thapa, Amar Singh, 16
Thapa, Badri Bikram, 258
Thapa, Bhimsen, 14–16, 18–19, 21, 194
authority of, 18
Thapa, Bishwa Bandhu, 214, 366
Thapa, Chandra Bahadur, 284, 293
Thapa, Padma Jung, 194–195
Thapa, Ram Chandra, 188
Thapa, Ram Lakhan, 42
Thapalia, Nutan, 156, 266, 310
Thapathali Durbar, 21, 48, 53
Tharu community, 184
Tharus, 17
Theory of gradual erosion of the mountains, 6
Thir Bam Malla, 331
Three Musketeers of Calcutta, 244
Tibet war, 14
Tiger Cinema, 331–332, 344
Tight Control of Education, 70–71
Tika Prasad, 141–143
Tika Ram Gahat Raj, 168
Trailokya, Crown Prince, 40, 43
Trans-Himalayan trade, 9
Treaty of Friendship, 71, 74, 312
Treaty of Sugauli, 12, 15–20, 17, 37, 74, 140
Tremors, 352–360
Tri Chandra College, 71, 91, 122, 125, 152, 144, 152, 233, 266, 286, 298–299, 359
Tribhuwan, King, 93, 95, 100, 105, 145, 149–150, 186, 240, 248, 250–252, 259–260, 273, 275, 296, 310, 330, 335, 336, 339, 345–347, 349, 351, 353–354, 358–359, 374, 379–381, 383, 386–388, 391–394
letter of support from, 260–262

secret movements in The 300
   Club, 252
triumphant return of, 392–394
Tripura Sundari, Queen, 15, 18
Trisuli river, 22
Tropical forests, 3, 105
Tucker, Sir Francis, 16, 37, 60
Tulsi Mehr, 78–79, 113, 136, 266,
   301
Umesh Bikram Shah, 94

UNESCO World Heritage list, 8
Unification, first formal approach
   for, 327–328
United Marxist-Leninist (UML), 286
United Nations, 313, 355
Unity of the Democratic Forces,
   325–327
Universal primary education, 53, 70
Untouchability, evil of, 168
Upadhyaya, Ragini, 205
Upadhyaya, Surya Prasad, 223, 246,
   258, 275, 329, 333, 346
Updhyaya, Shailendra, 236

Vaidya, Siddhi Gopal, 302
Valley of Kathmandu, 6
   devastating earthquake, 7
   harmony and prosperity, 8
   idyllic location, 6
   legends and myths, 6
   people of, 6
   prosperity

rich cultural heritage, 7
trade route between Tibet and
   Hindustan, 6
Vasudhaiba Kutumbakam, 216
Viceroy Lord Dufferin, 49
Victoria, Queen, 27–28
Vidya Parishad, 125
Vijay Shumsher, 353, 383, 388
Vijayalakshmi Pandit, 273
Vyasa, 208

War in Europe, 73, 148
Watershed management programme,
   112
Waziristan War, 89
Welfare measures, 32, *see also*
   Reforms
Wellesley, Lord, 26
Women's Committee, 204
World War I, 64, 72, 71–75, 108,
   129, 167, 176, 201, 244, 254
   advent of the, 108
World War II, 153, 158, 176, 221,
   229, 235, 239, 253, 255, 271,
   276–277, 315, 335
   dividend of, 153–155
Wright, Daniel, 122
Wylie, Colonel, 48, 62

Yadav, Chitralekha, 190
Yadav, Sriram, 190
Yakthumba, G.B., 367
Young Turks, 192